I0199856

God as Father in Paul

God as Father in Paul

Kinship Language and Identity Formation in Early Christianity

Abera M. Mengestu

PICKWICK *Publications* • Eugene, Oregon

GOD AS FATHER IN PAUL
Kinship Language and Identity Formation in Early Christianity

Pickwick Publications
An Imprint of Wipf and Stock Publishers
199 W. 8th Ave., Suite 3
Eugene, OR 97401

www.wipfandstock.com

ISBN 13: 978-1-4982-6392-4

Cataloguing-in-Publication data:

Mengestu, Abera M.

God as father in Paul : kinship language and identity formation in early Christianity / Abera M. Mengestu.

xx + 236 pp. ; 23 cm. Includes bibliographical references.

ISBN 13: 978-1-4982-6392-4

1. Bible. Epistles of Paul—Criticism, interpretation, etc. 2. Bible. Epistles of Paul—Socio-rhetorical criticism. 3. God—Fatherhood—Biblical teaching. 4. Kinship in the Bible. I. Title.

BS2655 F3 M35 2013

Manufactured in the U.S.A.

To Aster

and our daughters: Madu & Omega

Contents

Acknowledgments

THIS STUDY IS A revised version of my doctoral dissertation which I defended at Brite Divinity School, Texas Christian University in April 2011. The task of writing a dissertation is both an arduous and fulfilling undertaking that builds on the contributions of others and flourishes through support and encouragement from many sides. I am very grateful to Carolyn Osiek, in whose class of Social Scientific Approach to the New Testament, my interest to approach the self-understanding of early Christians through the analytical category of kinship language took shape. I express my deep gratitude to Dr. Osiek for graciously agreeing to supervise this study in her retirement. Dr. Osiek's tranquil supervision of this work, with important insights and direction from her rich knowledge in early Christianity, has been invaluable for the completion of this research. I am thankful for my readers, Warren Carter and Leo G. Perdue. Dr. Carter introduced me to the importance of recognizing the Roman Empire as forming a foreground in the study of early Christianity. He has also opened up for me the venture of "mixing up" approaches to probe the issue at hand from several perspectives in view of moving towards a fuller understanding. His incisive comments have clarified my thoughts and always pushed me a step further in terms of engaging the issue in depth. Dr. Perdue introduced me to postcolonial biblical interpretation. It was in that class, through rigorous discussion of the benefit of postcolonial theories to biblical interpretation, that, ironically, I began to seek for approaches that go beyond oppositional categories. It is a testimony for what kind of scholar he is in allowing his students to pursue truth wherever it leads.

I owe many thanks to Brad and Betty Lapsley, Martha Johnston of the Lamb Foundation, Sherrie Ross and Fred Sharpe, and Pastor Dr. Bedilu Yirga and the Ethiopian Evangelical Church in Dallas for believing in my ability to pursue doctoral study and for their continued support and encouragement. I would like also to thank Pastor John Messemann of St. Paul Lutheran Church of Fort Worth, and Rev. Ron Heimsoth of Trinity

Lutheran Church of Fort Worth (who has gone to his eternal home in 2009) for their generosity when the going was rough.

Words could not express my gratitude to my wife, Aster Temesgen Gebresilssie, who is my dearest friend and faithful companion, who graciously made my multifaceted journey enjoyable for the past seventeen years. Her unwavering support has been an anchor in the journey that at times has been windy and turbulent. I also thank my daughters, Madu and Omega, who have been always willing to rearrange their wants and needs to see their daddy finish "his writing," as they have come to call it. I owe also the deepest gratitude to my mother, Abaynesh Demissie, and my father, Mitiku Mengestu, who did not only initiate me to become the follower of Christ, but also set me on the course of pursuing higher education early on. Finally, I express the greatest of my gratitude to God, the originator and founder of the community of Christ-followers, by whose grace I have become a contributing member of this community.

Abbreviations

AB	Anchor Bible
ABD	*Anchor Bible Dictionary*. Edited by D. N. Freedman. 6 vols. New York, 1992.
AE	*American Ethnologist*
AnBib	*Analecta Biblica*
ANRW	*Aufstieg und Niedergang der römischen Welt: Geschichte und Kultur Roms im Spiegel der neueren Forschung. Edited by H. Temporini and W. Hasse. Berline, 1972–*
ANTC	Abingdon New Testament Commentaries
ARS	*Annual Review of Sociology*
BASOR	*Bulletin of the American Schools of Oriental Research*
BEC	Baker Exegetical Commentary
BibInt	*Biblical Interpretation*
BRev	*Biblical Review*
BNTC	Black's New Testament Commentaries
BT	*The Bible Translator*
BTB	*Biblical Theological Bulletin*
CBR	*Currents in Biblical Research*
CBQ	*Catholic Biblical Quarterly*
CJPS	*Canadian Journal of Political Science*
CQ	*Classical Quarterly*
EDNT	*Exegetical Dictionary of the New Testament*. Edited by H. Balz, G. Schneider. Grand Rapids, 1990–1993.
ExpTim	*Expository Times*

HALOT	*The Hebrew and Aramaic Lexicon of the Old Testament*. Edited by L. Koehler, W. Baumgartner , and J. J. Stamm. 2 vols. Leiden: Brill, 2001.
HSM	Harvard Semitic Monographs
HTR	*Harvard Theological Review*
HTS	*Harvard Theological Studies*
HUCA	*Hebrew Union College Annual*
HUT	Hermeneutische Untersuchungen zur Theologie
JAAR	*Journal of the American Academy of Religion*
JBL	*Journal of Biblical Literature*
JCSI	*Journal of Current Social Issues*
JETS	*Journal of the Evangelical Theological Society*
JSAH	*Journal of the Society of Architectural Historians*
JSJ	*Journal for the Study of Judaism*
JSNT	*Journal for the Study of the New Testament*
JSNTS	Journal for the Study of the New Testament Supplement
JSNTSup	Journal for the Study of the New Testament: Supplement Series
JSOT	*Journal for the Study of the Old Testament*
JSOTSup	Journal for the Study of the Old Testament: Supplement Series
JSPSup	Journal for the Study of the Pseudepigrapha: Supplement Series
JTS	Journal of Theological Studies
LCL	Loeb Classical Library
NAC	New American Commentary
NCBC	New Century Bible Commentary
NET	*New English Translation. Novum Testamentum Graece. New Testament*. Edited by Michael H. Burer, W. Hall Harris III, and Daniel Wallace. Deutsche Bibelgesellschaft: NET Bible Press, 2004.
NIGTC	New International Greek Testament Commentary
NICNT	New International Commentary on the New Testament

NRSV	New Revised Standard Version
NTS	*New Testament Studies*
RBL	*Review of Biblical Literature*
RQ	*Römische Quartalschrift für christliche Altertumskunde und Kirchengeschichte*
SBLDS	Society of Biblical Literature Dissertation Series
SBLEJL	Society of Biblical Literature Early Judaism and Its Literature
SBLSP	*Society of Biblical Literature Seminar Papers*
SNTSMS	Society for New Testament Studies Monograph Series
SNTIW	Studies of the New Testament and Its World
TAPA	*Transactions of the American Philological Association*
TDNT	*Theological Dictionary of the New Testament*. Edited by G. Kittel and G. Friedrich. Translated by G. W. Bromiley. 10 vols. Grand Rapids, 1964–1976.
TDOT	*Theological Dictionary of the Old Testament*. Edited by G. Johannes Botterweck and Helmer Ringgren. Translated by John T. Willis. Grand Rapids, 1974–1986.
TJT	*Toronto Journal of Theology*
TynBul	*Tyndale Bulletin*
TZT	*Tübinger Zeitschrift für Theologie*
VT	*Vetus Testamentum*
WBC	Word Biblical Commentary
WUNT	Wissenschaftliche Untersuchungen zum Neuen Testament
WW	*Word and World*

Introduction

Kinship language, a discourse of belonging, permeates the New Testament writings. From Matthew and Luke's use of genealogical discourse to present the identity of Jesus in relation to the founding and noteworthy ancestors, kinship language such as addressing God as Father, Jesus as the Son, followers of Jesus as children of God, brothers and sisters, and language of inheritance are used by the New Testament writers to depict their relationship to God, to Jesus, and to each other.[1] A large part of such use is found in Pauline writings: God is referred to as "*Abba*, Father," "Father," and "our Father" twenty seven times, believers are referred to as brothers and sisters 114 times, and they are also referred to as "children of God," and "heirs of God" and "heirs of Christ" repeatedly.

In ancient Mediterranean societies, kinship was the primary social institution which virtually touched almost every social relationship, institution, and values.[2] Greco-Roman as well as wide-ranging Jewish writings attest that

1. See Hanson and Oakman, *Palestine*, 20; Hanson, "Kinship," 62–79; Malina, *The New Testament World*, 82–83, 134–60; deSilva, *Honor, Patronage, Kinship and Purity*; and Hellerman, *The Ancient Church as Family*. Banks, *Paul's Idea of Community*, 53–54, describes family language as a "key image," and the "most significant metaphorical usage" that compares the Christian community with a "family"; Minear, *Images of the Church*, 165–72; 253–52, explains the family "image cluster" as depicting the "fellowship in faith"; Meeks, *The First Urban Christians*, compares the use of the language of belonging in Paul with similar contemporary entities such as households, voluntary association, synagogue, and philosophical and rhetorical schools. See also Petersen, *Rediscovering Paul*; Osiek and Balch, *Families in the New Testament World*; Moxnes, *Constructing Early Christian Families*; Brady, "Brotherly Love"; Fiorenza, *In Memory of Her*, 107–10.

2. See Saller, "Roman Kinship"; Bettini, *Anthropology and Roman Culture*; Dixon, *The Roman Family*, chapter 1; Nathan, *The Family in Late Antiquity*; Hall, *Ethnic Identity in Greek Antiquity*; and idem, *Hellenicity*, who argues for the centrality of the concept of kinship in defining and establishing what he calls "intrahellenic" and Hellenic identities; for the importance of kinship to create diplomatic relationship see Jones, *Kinship Diplomacy*; for kinship in Bible and biblical times see Hanson and Oakman, *Palestine*, 20; Hanson, "Kinship," 62–79; Malina, *The New Testament World*, 82–83,

kinship discourse is used to produce a shared understanding that reflects shared identity.[3] As a central organizing principle that defines a person's identity in ancient Mediterranean society, the use of kinship language serves as evidence of both self-understanding and understanding of others.

On the importance of looking for identity signifiers and representation in studying identity in the Roman world, Janet Huskinson explains that "representation and self-representation are important sources for studying identity in the Roman world."[4] This is because representations "deal with perceptions of self and others," "show the values claimed by a particular cultural identity," and "show how an identity is (sometimes literally) constructed from a selection of particular features."[5] Self-representation as well as representation of others played a central role both in the process of Romanization, the process by which Roman culture spread and diverse people "either incorporated or aligned themselves with the Roman empire," and in the process of local cultures presenting themselves and others.[6] Such a process of creating, disseminating, maintaining, and contesting culture and identity is carried out through written, visual, and oral communication.[7]

One of the key features used in this process of self-representation and representation of others in the Greco-Roman world is kinship language. As such, the use of family language by early Christians, which constitutes part of "common modes of formulating and communicating identity or belonging" in ancient Mediterranean society, serves to signal the self-understanding of early Christians and their understanding of others.[8]

134–60; see also Joubert, "Managing the Household," 75–95; Osiek and Balch, *Families in the New Testament World,* 36, 41; for family in ancient Israel and early Judaism see Perdue, *Families in Ancient Israel.*

3. For Greco-Roman writings see n1 above. For the significance of kinship in biblical covenants see Kalluveettil, *Declaration and Covenant*; idem, "Covenant and Community," 94–104; McCarthy, *Treaty and Covenant*, 254–73; Cross, "Kinship and Covenant;" idem, *From Epic to Canon*, 3–21; Steinmetz, *From Father to Son*; Wright, *God's People in God's Land*; Miller, *Biblical Faith and Fathering*; Oden, "Jacob as Father, Husband, and Nephew," 189–205; Donaldson, "Kinship Theory in the Patriarchal Narratives," 77–87; Boer, *Fatherhood and Motherhood*; Andersen, "Israelite Kinship," 29–39; Hahn, *Kinship by Covenant*; van Henten and Brenner, *Families and Family Relations*.

4. Huskinson, "Looking for Culture, Identity and Power," 16–17.

5. Ibid.

6. Ibid., 20; Woolf, "Becoming Roman, Staying Greek," 116–43.

7. Miles, "Communicating Culture, Identity and Power," 29–62.

8. Harland, *Dynamics of Identity*, 61; see also Jones, *Kinship Diplomacy*, 132, who compares the role of kinship in the rise of the Roman Empire and Christianity as follows: "Diplomatic appeals to kinship . . . existed through most antiquity, and the permutations of such kinship diplomacy can serve as a platform from which to view political changes in the Greco-Roman world. Of these the most salient is the rise of

In biblical studies, it is noted that repetitive use of kinship language in reference to groups and their members "plays a role in the process of re-socialization by which an individual's identity is revised and knit together with the identity of the group . . ."[9] Sandnes writes, "The social matrix of early Christianity was *oikos* and kinship. From the very beginning the movement was marked by kinship logic and precepts."[10] However, while the use of kinship language serves as evidence of self-understanding, it began to be used as analytical category in studying the development of the self-understanding of early Christians only recently. As recently as the last decade, J. H. Neyrey lamented that issues of "family and (fictive) kinship remain underdeveloped in [biblical] scholarship."[11] In a similar tone Trevor J. Burke writes, "This neglect not only relates to the gospels but to the Pauline letters as well, which is surprising, given the fact that Paul's theology was inextricably related to social reality."[12]

This neglect is true in regard to studying the use of God as Father as well as in approaching the formation of early Christianity. While "father" is a kinship term which was also employed to refer to the Greco-Roman god(s) and to refer to the Roman Empire and emperor, only the contribution of "philosophical theologies and the development of Christology have received some recognition" in its interpretation.[13] The study into the formation of early Christianity for its part was predominantly pursued in terms

Rome to the status of a world power. Second only in importance is perhaps the rise of Christianity, with its competing vision of kinship within the church."

9. Meeks, *The First Urban Christians*, 86; see also Stegemann, "The Emergence of God's New People," 23–40, 37, who writes, "Unlike the many other ancient peoples, the *Christianoi* as God's people shared no common genealogical descent from a common ancestor. Instead, they were connected through fictive kinship, which means that they belonged to the household of God (*familia dei*) and ultimately traced their birth to and from God (baptism as symbolic (re-) birth)"; Stark, *The Rise of Christianity*, who, applying his findings on modern new religious movements, argues that social ties played as significant a role as ideology in the rise of Christianity; and White, *Social Networks*, 34, who writes "perhaps the most readily discernible network structures from the Roman world are the familial organization of the extended household and the operation of patronage. Indeed, patronage may be seen both as a kind of 'friendship' structure, as Aristotle conceived it, or as a kind of quasi-kinship structure."

10. Sandnes, "Equality within Patriarchal Structures,"153.

11. Neyrey, "Loss of Wealth, Loss of Family and Loss of Honor," 139–58, 57.

12. Burke, *Family Matters*, 3.

13. D'Angelo, "*Abba* and 'Father,'" 623, further notes that in the Roman Empire that "loomed largest on the horizons of ancient Christianity and Judaism," while the use of the kinship term "father" was "a major step in the emergence and solidification of the new world order," it received no attention. Balla, *The Child-Parent Relationship*, 190, points out that a monograph can be written on the use of God as the Father in the NT.

of crisis-focused oppositional hermeneutics that centers on controversy and stereotypes a multifaceted reality into two opposite types leaving aside a range of interaction and negotiation.[14] As the history of research chapter of this study will show, early Christianity is predominantly prejudged as emerging in opposition to external world and in conflict and crisis in terms of its internal makeup.[15] Not only is early Christianity seen as standing against Judaism and Hellenism, but Judaism and Hellenism are also portrayed as existing independent of each other. It is becoming, however, evident that such presuppositions are not only inaccurate reflections of the process of the formation of early Christianity but also are impediments to understanding its multifaceted and dynamic nature.

This book will focus on the use of one specific kinship language, God as Father in Paul, and its relation to familial expressions that Paul uses to depict Christ-followers (children of God, brothers and sisters). I will examine how Paul's use of this kinship term to refer to God and its relation to other familial language shaped the self-understanding of the emergent community. Since such use of kinship is not unique to Paul but it is a shared/common way of constructing identity in Jewish as well as the larger Greco-Roman socio-religious contexts, this study will not focus on particular controversies within the emerging community or polarities with the outside world, thereby limiting self-understanding to crisis and oppositional situation. Instead, this study will locate the use of the kinship term "Father" to refer to God and the related familial terms that are applied to Christ-followers in Pauline writings within the broader socio-religious context and examine how such use shaped the self-understanding of early Christians both in crisis as well as stable situations.[16] In so doing, it puts the study of God as Father in Paul in relation to the study of identity formation in early Christianity, and it also relates the study of kinship in the Bible with the study of identity formation in the Bible. The thesis of this study is that by using kinship language that categorizes and identifies (i.e., creates social identity) through a network of relationships, Paul constructs a self-understanding by developing a narra-

14. Gerdmar, *Rethinking the Judaism–Hellenism Dichotomy*, 19.

15. Ibid. For studies that address approaches that dichotomize Judaism and Hellenism in Pauline studies see articles in Engberg-Pedersen, *Paul Beyond the Judaism/Hellenism Divide*; for argument against limiting the formation of early Christianity to crisis and conflict situation see Harland, *Dynamics of Identity*, 1–22, 25–26, 63–66; for more discussion see chapter 2 of this book.

16. For similar approach see Riches, *Conflicting Mythologies*, 8, who, instead of focusing on particular debate within the church to study identity, focuses on kinship and geography. For the argument that early Christianity's self-understanding should not be studied only in terms of crisis situation but also in terms of stable situation see Meyer, *Early Christians*, 30.

tive that images the community of Christ-followers as a family that belongs to God, who, together with "the Lord Jesus Christ," bestows on them "grace and peace" and inheritance. The narrative so constructed forms the foundation for the members to be referred to as children of God as well as brothers and sisters. The self-understanding ensuing from such a narrative aims at shaping the whole life of the community of the followers of Christ.

To expound this thesis, I will use what I will call Kinship-Identity Approach (KIA) which begins with a recognition that in ancient Mediterranean society kinship played a significant role in constructing self-understanding and understanding of others. As will be explained below, the approach combines theoretical foundations on kinship construction and identity formation with narrative and imperial critical approaches to Paul.

Chapter one will focus on the history of research on God as Father as well as on identity formation in early Christianity. The discussion will show what has been done, what is lacking, and the contribution of this study. Chapter two will focus on the Kinship-Identity Approach, outlining its various aspects and how these are combined to pursue the study of God as Father in Paul and its role in the identity formation of early Christians. The kinship aspect of the Kinship-Identity Approach will be located within the anthropological theory of kinship as well as within the use of kinship in ancient Mediterranean society.

Chapters three, four, and five will focus on the contexts of Paul in which his use of "Father" to refer to God and related familial expressions are understood by his audiences. In chapter three, I will examine the use of "father" to portray the Greco-Roman god(s), the Roman Empire and emperor, and the contribution of such use for constructing identities.

In chapter four, the depiction of God as Father and related familial expressions in the Hebrew Bible will be studied within the framework of the role kinship plays in the process of being and becoming. Sources from the Hebrew Bible are examined in relation to the overall objective of identifying the identity formation contribution of the use of the kinship language "Father" to refer to God and related familial language. Similarly, chapter five will focus on the use of God as Father and its related familial language. I will examine how such use contributed to the self-understanding of the Jewish people.

In chapter six, Paul's use of the term "Father" to refer to God and its relation to the familial terms to refer to Christ-followers are studied within the framework of the role kinship plays in the process of identity creation. The findings from the preceding chapters will form multiple contexts in relation to which Paul's use of God as Father and its relation to associated familial language are analyzed in view of understanding its contribution for the self-understanding of early Christianity. My argument is that Paul uses the kinship term "father" to refer to God and related familial expressions to refer to the Christ-followers to image the emerging community as a family that belongs to God.

Finally, in chapter seven, I will draw conclusions regarding the importance of Paul's use of "Father" to refer to God and related familial expressions for the self-understanding of the early Christians in terms of their relation to God, to each other, and to the outside world. I will also reflect on the importance of using kinship as an analytical concept to study the formation of early Christianity and on the importance of not limiting studying early Christians to a crisis situation and oppositional hermeneutics.

1

History of Research

THIS STUDY SEEKS TO situate the study of God as Father in Paul and its relation to Paul's depiction of the Christ-followers as children of God and as brothers and sisters within the study of God as Father in the NT and the study of identity formation in early Christianity. The discussion on the history of research below will include the study of identity formation in early Christianity, the study of God as Father in the NT, the study of the use of God as Father in Paul, the study of Christ-followers as children of God, and the study of the use of sibling language in Paul. In each case, an attempt will be made to show what has been done, what is lacking, and what contribution this research will make. Since the study of the identity formation of early Christianity is as old as Christianity itself, this history of research focuses on modern studies and only those pertaining to the study at hand.

Study of Identity Formation in Early Christianity

The inquiry into the process of the formation of early Christianity has been undertaken predominantly in terms of controversy within the early church, and in terms of placing Christianity in opposition to Hellenistic and Jewish contexts, setting in motion a primarily oppositional and crisis-focused hermeneutics.[1] Ferdinand Christian Baur's synthesis of the Petrine and Pauline conflict as shaping the formation of early Christianity,[2] the history-of-religions school (*religionsgeschichtliche Schule*)[3] and Walter Bauer's orthodoxy and heresy are some of the early major examples of approaching

1. Riches, *Conflicting Mythologies*, 7.
2. Baur, "Die Christuspartei in Der Korinthischen Gemeinde," 61–206.
3. See Bousset, *Kyrios Christos*.

the formation of early Christianity.[4] The history-of-religions school with its emphasis on Christianity as a phenomenon in the history of religions gave impetus for the study of the nature of early Christianity in relation to contemporary religions.[5] While the focus to understand early Christianity in relation to contemporary religions was a way forward, the continued oppositional presentation of Judaism and Hellenism was one of the lingering problems.[6] As W. E. Nunnally's research shows, debate about the context of the Fatherhood of God in the NT was one of the issues in this chain of approaches using oppositional hermeneutics.[7] It was placed within the study of the relationship between Judaism and early Christianity, which are framed in opposition to each other.[8]

Studies of early Christianity in the latter part of the twentieth century also primarily follow this route, a route that predominantly focuses on the chasm between Judaism and Hellenism, between Judaism and Christianity, and Christianity and Roman Empire. James Dunn's explicit statement that the Jewish/Gentile "issue or tension" has been "a constant stimulus" in his study of early Christianity and Crossan and Reed's subtitle, "How Jesus' Apostle Opposed Rome's Empire with God's Kingdom," reflect the predominant oppositional approach in the study of early Christianity.[9]

Such oppositional approach was even evident in the studies on the self-definition of Judaism and Christianity sponsored by McMaster University that are published in three volumes under the major title *Jewish and Christian Self-Definition*. The task was set for these studies from the outset as examining the "two-fold movement" in "the process of achieving normative self-definition."[10] This "two-fold movement" is the movement by both

4. Bauer, *Orthodoxy and Heresy*.

5. Rudolph, "Early Christianity," 10.

6. Engberg-Pedersen, *Paul Beyond the Judaism/Hellenism Divide*, 4, explaining the shortcomings of the *religionsgeschichtliche Schule* writes, "The problem is that the stand point from which comparisons are made is often frightfully skewed, as if *either* the Jewish *or* the Hellenistic material is in the end the really important one"; Meeks, "Judaism, Hellenism and the Birth of Christianity," 21, describes the commonality between the history of religions school and the Tübingen school as the "evolutionary perspective" that tended to see phases in the development of early Christianity "beginning with the purely Jewish circle of the earliest Jesus movement and ending with the wide world of syncretistic Hellenism."

7. Nunnally, "The Fatherhood of God."

8. Ibid., 1–32; for further discussion on this see below under "Studies of God as Father in the NT."

9. Dunn, *Unity and Diversity*, xvi; see also idem, *The Partings of the Ways;* Crossan and Reed, *In Search of Paul*.

10. Sanders, *Jewish and Christian Self-Definition*, ix–x.

Judaism and Christianity "towards excluding some view of what it means to be either Jewish or Christian" and taking "measures to assure that the favored options became normative."[11] In one of the essays written in honor of E. P. Sanders, the series editor, Jouette M. Bassler, looking back to what these symposia achieved, points out that in this two-fold movement self-definition is approached "as a process of separation and boundary drawing over against internal and external opponents" focusing "on the thoughts and deeds of group leaders as they hammered out in polarized situations . . . a vision of their group's distinctive self-definition."[12] With few exceptions "exclusionary process" was the prevailing model by which the Jewish and Christian self-definition was approached.[13] Furthermore, not a few of those who study early Christianity in terms of its social world assess the place of Jews and Christians within Greco-Roman society in terms of conflict, tension, and separation from society "to the neglect of other aspects of group-society relations."[14]

This approach has not been without critics. Since 1966, Hengel challenged the sharp dichotomy between Judaism and Hellenism, stressing that by the time of Jesus and early Christians Palestine had been under Hellenistic influence for more than three centuries.[15] Several essays in the book, *Paul Beyond the Judaism/Hellenism Divide*, edited by Troels Engberg-Pedersen, call for "a new research program" that shies away from playing out Christianity, Judaism, and Hellenism against one another and instead looks "open mindedly at the facts" to examine the ways in which these are interrelated.[16]

11. Ibid.

12. Bassler, "The Problem of Self-Definition," 43.

13. Ibid.; for exceptions cited by Bassler see Charlesworth, "Christian and Jewish Self-Definition," 186–200.

14. For the discussion see Harland, *Associations, Synagogues, and Congregations*, 11; for socio-cultural approaches that focus on conflict and separation see Wilson, *Religious Sects*; Elliott, "1 Peter," 61–78; idem, *A Home for the Homeless*; for opposing view see Balch, "Hellenization/Acculturation in 1 Peter," 79–101.

15. Hengel, *Judaism and Hellenism*. See also recent studies by Borgen, *Early Christianity and Hellenistic Judaism*, 2; Gruen, *Heritage and Hellenism*, xv; Rajak, *The Jewish Dialogue with Greece and Rome*, 3–10, all of which point to the obsoleteness of such dichotomy.

16. Engberg-Pedersen, *Paul Beyond the Judaism/Hellenism Divide* , 1–16; see also essays in this book that question the ideological basis of such approach, Meeks, "Judaism, Hellenism, and the Birth of Christianity," 17–28; Martin, "Paul and the Judaism/Hellenism Dichotomy," 29–62; and Alexander, "Hellenism and Hellenization as Problematic Historical Category," 63–80; also see Malherbe, "Graeco-Roman Religion and Philosophy and the New Testament," 11, who writes, "The whole range of possible ways in which religions react when they meet, extending from opposition or rejection through amelioration to assimilation, conscious and unconscious, should be taken into

In a monograph published the same year, Anders Gerdmar also challenges the dichotomist approach among other things on the ground that it "stereotypes a complex reality into two main types" leaving "other phenomena outside."[17] In a similar way, a few decades back, Ben F. Meyer rightly notes that studying early Christianity's self-understanding in terms of opposition alone is limiting: it limits the development of self-understanding to a crisis situation only, neglecting the process of identity formation in stable situation.[18] This applies not only to studying the self-understanding of early Christians in terms of its internal dynamics but also to studying its self-definition in relation to the larger milieu.

In this regard, Judith Lieu's contention that early Christianity should be seen as both "implicated in" as well as "contributing to" the world in which it was situated not only states succinctly the dynamic situation early Christianity was in but also lays a ground for a more balanced approach that depicts a way forward. She forcefully states:

> . . . the Christian rhetoric of identity, even when making universalist claims, is articulated in the terms also used in Greco-Roman ethnography and identity formation. In this, as in many other areas, early Christianity needs to be seen as implicated in, as well as contributing to, the dynamics of the world in which it was situated. We should look for continuities as well as for discontinuities between Greek, Roman, Jewish, and Christian efforts to construct and to maintain an identity for themselves, in interaction with their past as well as with each other.[19]

Her argument takes into consideration seriously the fact that Christianity emerged from its own surroundings and also lived, not in isolation as an island by itself, but in relation to the same surroundings, though ever enlarging, within which it emerged. As such it is inevitable that it did not only share the terms of identity formation and articulation but also contributed to such terms. The situation is further perceptively summarized by Vernon K. Robbins and David B. Gowler in the following rather long citation which, however, provides a methodological underpinning for this study:

> [D]iscourse is a social phenomenon . . . No narrative is created in a literary, cultural, social, or historical vacuum, and no discourse is created *ex nihilo*. New Testament narratives . . . were created

consideration. This will require the type of empirical investigation that is uncongenial to generalization, should be pursued despite the bogeyman of 'positivism.'"

17. Gerdmar, *Rethinking the Judaism-Hellenism Dichotomy*, 19.

18. Meyer, *Early Christians*, 15.

19. Lieu, *Christian Identity*, 20–21.

> and preserved in conversations with their cultural environments, and they partake, vigorously at times, in that dialogical social discourse. Speakers do not utilize pristine words—"untainted" and straight out of a dictionary—but rather those words have already existed in the mouths of others and thus already partially belong to others—each word "tastes" therefore of the contexts in which it has lived its socially-charged life in the previous speaker's personal, cultural, social, and ideological contexts. It is from those places that one must take the words and attempt to make them one's own. What therefore may first appear to be "original" utterances are actually rejoinders in a greater dialogue, incorporating, in different ways, the words of others.[20]

They situate NT studies within a study of discourse as a social phenomenon. In stating that discourse is "created and preserved in conversations" with cultural contexts, which "partake(s), vigorously at times," in "dialogical social discourse," they foreground what has been simply considered as forming a "background." It is not a one-time, one-way linear relationship; it involves ongoing multidimensional dialogue.

This critical assessment is being heeded by scholars of early Christianity and fruitfully applied to the NT studies. In this regard, in their recent works, John K. Riches and Philip Harland consciously avoid employing a primarily oppositional, crisis-focused hermeneutics in the study of the nature of early Christianity.[21] John K. Riches examines the identity formation in the Gospel of Mark and Matthew not by focusing on "particular debates within the church," but by using topics of kinship and geography.[22] Harland observes that crisis-focused hermeneutics diminishes "a range of perspective and practices" among Jews, Christians, and others "with regard to separation and involvement in various aspects of society."[23] In his book, *Dynamics of Identity in the World of the Early Christians: Associations,*

20. Robbins and Gowler, "Introduction," 12; they explain, "language is never a neutral medium that passes freely and easily into a new conceptual system; it is a difficult, complex, and often conflictual process . . . differing groups partake in the heteroglossia of the ancient Mediterranean world and actively orient themselves amidst that heteroglossia. They move in and occupy a position for themselves within, against, and in concert with other groups and their social languages . . . Such is the nature of groups; such is the nature of societies; such is the nature of language."

21. For similar work on approaching early Christianity in relation to the Roman Imperial ideology from the perspective of "wide-ranging negotiation," see Oakes, "Remapping the Universe," 301–22; Carter, *The Roman Empire*, 1–5, and the discussion on imperial critical approaches in chapter 2 of this study.

22. Riches, *Conflicting Mythologies*, 2, 8.

23. Harland, *Associations, Synagogues, and Congregations*, 8.

Judeans, and Cultural Minorities, Harland highlights the dynamic nature of identity formation in the life of Jews, Christians, and contemporary associations. He writes,

> An individual member's place within a group and that group's identity in relation to surrounding society is an ongoing, shifting process of negotiation . . . processes of negotiation entail both differentiating and assimilating forces. On the one hand, the self-understanding of a member or the group as a whole can be expressed in terms of distinction from common cultural categories in the majority culture . . . On the other hand, that majority culture can supply a primary means by which identity is expressed. Specific concepts and categories from the majority culture or local manifestations of that culture can be central to the expression of identities in a majority group. Both of these forces are often at work at the same time.[24]

Several important features emerge from Harland's argument. The formation of one's identity in relation to his/her surrounding is a negotiation which: (1) is ongoing and shifting, (2) entails both differentiation and assimilation, and (3) will result in expressing identity not just in terms of distinction but also in terms of assimilation.

Aspects of the development away from crisis-focused oppositional hermeneutics in the study of the self-understanding of early Christians is helped by the growing use of the concept of identity as an analytical category[25] as well as the increasing awareness of the importance of the socio-anthropological elements in early Christianity.[26] In regard to the former, Lieu observes that although the concept of identity as an analytical category only "entered scholarly discourse in the 1950s," it has now become ubiquitous in the study of early Christianity.[27] Among other things such use highlighted both the fluidity and flexibility in identity construction as well as the recognition that identity construction emerges not just in contrast and opposition but also in wide-ranging interaction within early Christianity as well as with the outside society.[28]

24. Harland, *Dynamics of Identity*, 47; for importance of language in identity construction and communication see Howard, "Social Psychology of Identities," 369–91.

25. Lieu, *Christian Identity*, 11; See also Horrell, "Becoming Christian," 309–35, 311, who writes, "Identity has become something of a buzzword in recent social science and in studies of early Christianity." See also Holmberg, *Exploring Early Christian Identity*.

26. For various articles on social science approaches see Blasi, et al, *Hand Book of Early Christianity*.

27. Lieu, *Christian Identity*, 11.

28. Holmberg, *Exploring Early Christian Identity*, 1–32.

Writing about early Christians, Horrell convincingly argues that early Christian identity can be adequately studied and understood only "as part of an ongoing process. Like all social institutions and structures they are continually in the process of production, reproduction, and transformation, in the process of becoming, and never 'arrive' or reach a point where one can say that development 'stops.'"[29] Ben F. Meyer describes the self-understanding of the early Christians as a learning process, by which, as they encountered different people, situations, and events, they were compelled to have repeated reflection and reassessment which affected their self-understanding as a whole.[30] The ongoing reflection both clarifies the understanding of the original experience and continues to shape the self-understanding as can be seen in the Cornelius episode (Acts 10–11) and in the apostolic meeting in Jerusalem (Acts 15, Gal 2).[31] This ongoing reflection, however, is not free floating. At its center it has something given from the start which Ben F. Meyer describes as "the risen Christ and the Spirit he received and poured out . . . to vitalize the new race gathered around him . . ."[32] The self-understanding that comes from this center must be "manifested, clarified, and reconfigured continuously as part of the 'self-definition' of the group."[33]

Furthermore, the increasing awareness of the importance of the socio-anthropological elements in early Christianity brought multifaceted forms of interaction to the fore in the identity formation of early Christianity. The distinctive feature of kinship construction and norms in the cultures of early Christianity is recognized and began to be used for examining biblical texts. Scholars such as K.C. Hanson, Bruce Malina, Raphael Patai, and Robert R. Wilson have made use of kinship in conjunction with social scientific method to analyze kinship terminologies in the Bible.[34] While Hanson's studies focus on the Herodians and Mediterranean kinship in terms of genealogy and descent, marriage and divorce, and economics, Malina's study provides an introductory kinship analysis along with its importance for biblical studies. In recent years studies by David deSilva and Hellerman make a more detailed use of kinship in biblical studies. DeSilva gives a relatively detailed

29. Horrell, "Becoming Christian," 331.

30. See Meyer, *Early Christians*; see also the two collections of Meyer's essays in *Critical Realism and the New Testament*; Holmberg, *Exploring Early Christian Identity*, 25.

31. Holmberg, *Exploring Early Christian Identity*, 25.

32. Meyer, *Early Christians*, 20; see also Dunn, *Unity and Diversity*, who argues that although early Christianity was diverse, it had unity in the fundamental parts of faith.

33. Holmberg, *Exploring Early Christian Identity*, 27.

34. Hanson, "Kinship;" idem, "The Herodians and Mediterranean Kinship. Part I," 75–84; idem, "The Herodians and Mediterranean Kinship. Part II," 10–21; Patai, *Sex and Family*; Wilson, *Genealogy and History*, 7; Malina, *The New Testament World*.

treatment of kinship and its relation to "the household of God" in the NT.[35] Hellerman's study, using kinship extensively, depicts the church as family.[36]

Going a step further, Harland relates the use of family language to identity formation and argues that Judeans and early Christians' discourses that employ family language reflect "common modes of formulating and communicating identity or belonging within certain groups in the ancient Mediterranean."[37] Such use reflects one of the overlaps in the way early Christians use familial language just like others in their surroundings.[38] He also rightly notes that early Christians "could express their identity in a variety of ways, and this included the use of family language to express belonging."[39]

The use of the concept of identity as an analytical tool as well as the application of kinship to biblical studies proves to be a way forward in the study of identity formation in early Christianity. Yet studies that combine the two are noticeably rare. The importance of kinship that is noted by social anthropologists as a category that shapes social organization and self-understanding has not been fruitfully utilized in biblical studies, particularly in Pauline studies. The very few exceptions that relate kinship and identity formation in a limited way in Pauline studies are works by Lloyd Alexander Lewis, Mary Katherine Birge, Caroline Johnson Hodge, Reidar Aasgaard, and Trevor J. Burke who utilize kinship as an analytical category in a detailed form.[40] Lewis, in his 1985 dissertation, approaches the function of the family language in Paul from the perspective of what he calls "pseudo-family in anthropological literature."[41] A recent study by Hodge effectively uses kinship and ethnicity to examine the construction of identities and argues that Paul constructs kinship and ethnic ties as effective means of arguing for "a new arrangement and a new status for a people."[42] Likewise using a rhetorical analysis of kinship language, Birge examines Paul's argument in 1 Corinthians and argues that Paul used the same kinship images and language in different pastoral situations to address the division in the Corinthian church.[43] Similarly, Reidar Aasgaard examines

35. deSilva, *Honor, Patronage, Kinship and Purity.*

36. Hellerman, *The Ancient Church as Family*, 92–126.

37. Harland, *Dynamics of Identity*, 63.

38. Ibid.

39. Ibid.

40. Hodge, *If Sons, Then Heirs;* Aasgaard, '*My Beloved Brothers and Sisters!*'; Birge, *The Language of Belonging*; Burke, *Family Matters.*

41. Lewis, "As a Beloved Brother."

42. Hodge, *If Sons, Then Heirs*, 151.

43. Birge, *The Language of Belonging*, 1–6.

Paul's use of sibling language using a combination of methods from cultural anthropology, sociology, socio-linguistics, rhetoric, and metaphor theory.[44] Aasgaard identifies the family life in antiquity as the principal context for Paul's use of sibling language and argues that by means of it Paul sought to stimulate a sense of identity that is based on a sense of harmony and belonging and honor. He explains, "Christian relations . . . were understood and experienced in terms of natural family and siblingship" and as such carry characteristic features related to rights and obligations. Trevor J Burke has published books and articles on familial language in the New Testament.[45] He examines kinship terms in 1 Thessalonians using a socio-historical approach and the language of adoption and inheritance in Galatians and Romans. As we shall see below, in this development the application of kinship and identity concept to the study of God as Father both in Paul and the rest of the NT is noticeably absent. What is also missing is a study that relates the use of God as Father to the self-understanding of early Christians.

Studies in God as Father in the NT

In general, for the longer part of its history, the approach to God as Father in the NT has been dominated by two extremes followed by recent developments that are too general or too narrow in scope. On the one hand, there is a tendency that is evident in critical commentaries which takes the use of "Father" to refer to God for granted and moves over it with only a passing remark. On the other hand, there is an approach that dominated the history of the study of God as Father in the NT for a long time that is characterized by an oppositional hermeneutics which is rightly referred to as "no-Fatherhood-of-God-in-early-Judaism" school.[46] Regarding the former, Gail R. O'Day observes that "Father" is "most frequently accepted as a straight forward descriptive noun that requires no comment" and hence commentaries do not stop to examine it.[47] The latter is evident in the studies that took place towards the end of nineteenth century and the first half of the twentieth century which placed it within the study of the relationship between Judaism and early Christianity.[48] Evident in works from Wilhelm Bousset

44. Aasgaard, *'My Beloved Brothers and Sisters!'*, 8.

45. Burke, *Family Matters*; idem, *Adopted into God's Family;* idem, "Adopted as Sons;" idem, "Paul's Role as 'Father.'"

46. Nunnally, "The Fatherhood of God," 1–32.

47. O'Day, "Show Us the Father," 392–93.

48. See Bousset, *Jesu Predigt*; Moore, "Christian Writers," 197–254; Bultmann, *Theology of the New Testament*; Jeremias, *The Prayers of Jesus*, 53–54; idem, *New Testament*

to Joachim Jeremias, the "no-Fatherhood-of-God-in-early-Judaism" school argued for the uniqueness of Jesus' address to God as Father, and by extension Jesus' followers' relation to God.[49] Such an approach to the Fatherhood of God reached its peak in the study of Jeremias, which then loomed over most of the studies in the second half of the twentieth century.[50]

Jeremias' study emphasized the unique relationship of Jesus to the Father. He focused on the designation of God as Father in the sayings of Jesus and on Jesus' address of God as Father with particular emphasis on Jesus' use of "*Abba*, Father" in Mark 14:36. His writings on this issue appeared in most of his books.[51] He sees Jesus' use of the Aramaic word "*Abba*" in addressing God as Father as being behind the rest of the usages in the Gospels.[52] In his comparison, he used texts that come from Palestinian Judaism, texts that represent an individual rather than a collective body of people speaking of God as Father, and texts that do not just speak about God as Father but address God as Father. He rejected texts from Diaspora Judaism such as Sir 23:1, 4; 3 Macc 6:3; and Wis 14:3 as being influenced by the Greek example of calling God "Father." Based on such comparison, Jeremias concludes, "there is no *analogy at all* in the whole literature of Jewish prayer for God being addressed as *Abba*. This assertion applies not only to fixed liturgical prayer, but also to free prayer . . ."[53] Support for Jeremias' position is seen in the studies of Robert Hamerton-Kelly. He asserts: "[A]lthough not without critics, the thesis that the Abba experience of Jesus is the starting point of

Theology, 67; idem, *The Central Message of the New Testament*, 20–27.

49. Nunnally, "The Fatherhood of God."

50. Thompson, *The Promise of the Father*, 21–33; for the influence of Jeremias' study on Jesus' use of *abba* in addressing God see Dunn, *The Evidence for Jesus*, 48, who writes, "'*Abba*' was a surprising word to use in addressing God. In its natural usage it was a family word and usually confined to the family circle . . . It was a word resonant with family intimacy . . . The point is that to address God in such a colloquial way, with such intimacy, is hardly known in the Judaism of Jesus' time . . . What others thought too intimate in praying to God Jesus used because of its intimacy"; Caird, *New Testament Theology*, 400–401, writes, "The further back we go, the more we discover the intense conviction of Jesus that God is his Father and he is His son. This is supported by the word *abba*, an address used at times by children to their father, indicating an intimacy and directness not contained in the more formal *abinu*. Certainly other Jews believed in the fatherhood of God, but this was a creedal affirmation . . . The synoptic passages speak of an intimacy of filial relationship . . . For Jesus the fatherhood of God has become a profoundly personal religious experience, long before it became a doctrine to be communicated to others."

51. Jeremias, *Abba*; idem, *The Prayers of Jesus*; idem, *The Central Message of the New Testament*, 9–30; idem, *Jesus and the Message of the New Testament*, 63–110.

52. Jeremias, *The Prayers of Jesus*, 55.

53. Ibid., 57.

Christology; and the key to Jesus' eschatology, commands widespread support . . . It has become one of the assured results of modern scholarship."[54] Jeremias' claim, however, has been questioned by several scholars on several grounds and the texts from Qumran subsequently made his argument untenable, opening the way for studies that explore other dimensions such as it relation to similar construction in different Jewish and Greco-Roman writings.[55] Most of these studies, however, rarely approach it from its kinship characteristics and community formation role in the emerging community.[56]A relatively thorough study of the Fatherhood of God at Qumran is undertaken by Nunnally in his unpublished dissertation.[57] Due to the dismissal of Jewish liturgy, Rabbinic, apocryphal, pseudepigraphical, and non-Palestinian texts as evidence by the "no-Fatherhood-of-God-in-early-Judaism," Nunnally limits his work to materials from Qumran.[58] He situates the study of the Fatherhood of God at Qumran squarely within a long chain of scholarly debate concerning the relationship of Jews and Christians.[59] He traces Jeremias' argument of the uniqueness of Jesus' relation to God on the basis of the Fatherhood of God back to Wilhelm Bousset, showing a successive scholarly chain that uses the term "Father" to refer to God as a mark that distinguishes Christianity from Judaism.[60] Contrary to such a view, Nunnally concludes that "the sectarian literature indicates pre-Christian, Palestinian evidence for the existence of a concept of the Fatherhood of

54. Hamerton-Kelly, "God the Father," 101; also see idem, *God the Father*.

55. Barr, "*Abba* Isn't Daddy," 28–47; idem, "*Abba* and the Familiarity of Jesus' Speech," 173–79; D'Angelo, "*Abba* and 'Father,' 616; idem, "Theology in Mark and Q," 149–74; Fiorenza, *In Memory of Her*, 145–51; Boucher, "Scriptural Readings," 28–32; Thompson, *The Promise of the Father*, 28–29; Mawhinney, "God as Father," 181–89; VanGemeren, "*Abba* in the Old Testament?" 385–98; for Qumran texts see Schuller, "4Q372 1: A Text about Joseph," 343–70; idem, "The Psalm of 4Q372 1," 67–79.

56. Chen, *God as Father*, 2. For similar assessment see Bovon, "Studies in Luke-Acts," 175–96; for general studies on the fatherhood of God see Hofius, "Father," 614–21; Witherington and Ice, *The Shadow of the Almighty*, 1–65; Turek, *Towards a Theology of God the Father*; Wright, *Knowing God the Father*; Tasker, *Ancient Near Eastern Literature and the Hebrew Scriptures*; Miller, "*God as father*," 347–54; for the discussion on God as Father in the Church Fathers see Widdicombe, *The Fatherhood of God from Origen to Athanasius*; Schinder, "Gott als Vater in Theologie und Liturgie des christlichen Antike."

57. Nunnally, "The Fatherhood of God," x–xiii.

58. Ibid.

59. Ibid., 1–33.

60. Ibid.; also see Bousset, *Jesu Predigt*; Moore, "Christian Writers on Judaism," 197–254; Bultmann, *Theology of the New Testament*; Jeremias, *The Prayers of Jesus*, 53–54; idem, *New Testament Theology*, 67; idem, *The Central Message of the New Testament*, 20–27.

God in the Qumran community" and that this concept is derived from the Hebrew Scriptures.[61]

In addition to her critical assessment of Jeremias' position, M. M. Thompson surveys the idea of God as Father in the Hebrew Bible, in Second Temple Judaism, and in the New Testament, and identifies three main elements in the image of Father: (1) "the source or origin of a family or clan, who as a founding father protects and provides an inheritance to his children," (2) protector and provider for his children, and (3) requiring obedience and honor from his children.[62] She traces how the understanding of God as Father in the Hebrew Bible and early Judaism stressed not God's role as creator but God's election and providence. For Thompson the confession of God as Father "both presses back to the Old Testament and strains forward to the eschatological fulfillment of God's promises to be a Father to all his people."[63] While Thompson emphasizes continuity between the understanding of God as Father in the Hebrew Bible, in early Judaism and the NT, Witherington and Ice argue for a major discontinuity between the NT, particularly Jesus' use of the term "Father" to refer to God, and the Hebrew Bible and early Judaism.[64] They see a shift in relationship between God and his people following the unique sonship of Jesus.[65] As will be shown in this study, there are features of the use of God as Father in the Hebrew Bible and ancient Judaism that are continued in the NT (e.g., God's Fatherhood is exclusively related to God's people), and there are features that are discontinued (e.g., God's Fatherhood extends to non-Jewish people of God).

In the midst of all these studies, feminist voices also made contributions to the discussion of the Fatherhood of God. On the use of the gendered term "Father" to refer to God, feminist voices range from "rejectionist" to "loyalist."[66] One of the contributions out of these conversations is

61. Nunnally, "The Fatherhood of God," 236.

62. Thompson, *The Promise of the Father*, 39.

63. Ibid., 157.

64. Witherington and Ice, *The Shadow of the Almighty*, 1–65.

65. They write, "It is primarily the discontinuity with the past situation of the relationship between God and human beings, rather than the continuity, which Jesus and this language [addressing God using intimate terms] are emphasizing. Paul's placing of the discussion of *abba* in the context of a discussion of the final salvific work of Christ and the Spirit reflects the impact of Jesus' usage of *abba*," Witherington and Ice, *The Shadow of the Almighty*, 25.

66. Osiek, "The Feminist and the Bible," 93–106, classifies hermeneutical alternatives followed by feminist biblical interpreters as "rejectionist, loyalist, revisionist, sublimationist, and liberationist"; for a range of feminist approaches to biblical interpretation see also Sakenfeld, "Feminist Uses of Biblical Materials," 55–64; Tolbert, "Defining the Problem," 113–26; idem, "Protestant Feminist and the Bible," 5–23; for

that, unlike almost all of the other studies, some feminists try to relate their discussion of the use of God as Father to the idea of kinship.[67] Although the application of the idea of kinship is very brief and undeveloped, such an attempt employs a neglected way of approaching the discussion of the Fatherhood of God.

In terms of studying the use of God as Father in specific books, compared to the epistles, studies in the Gospels are abundant.[68] In the Synoptic Gospels studies of God as Father in Matthew and Luke are relatively high compared to similar studies in Mark.[69] The reason for this variation probably could be explained by the number of times "Father" is used to refer to God: 42 in Matthew, 4 in Mark, 22, in Luke and 121 in John. In Matthew, studies by Robert L. Mowery focus on examining the successive emphasis on "Lord," "God," and "Father." He points out the portrayal of the Father as "an authoritative figure who knows what people need before they ask, expects people to do the divine will, promises forgiveness to those who forgive, and will reward righteousness."[70] In his recent study, Warren Carter approaches the use of "Father" in Matthew in relation to the use of the term "father" to refer to Augustus.[71] Burnett observes that Father as a term for God occurs in Matthew only in the speech of Jesus, only in contexts which relate to his disciples, and only "in semantic connection with the will of God

---

feminist interpretation of the use of "Father" to refer to God see Daly, *Beyond the Father*; Fiorenza, *In Memory of Her*, 145–53; D'Angelo, "Theology in Mark and Q," 149–74; Ruther, *Sexism and God-Talk*, 64–68.

67. Fiorenza, *In Memory of Her*, 150, reads the Fatherhood of God in relation to Jesus' teaching of "call no one father for you have one father . . ." (Matt 23:8–11), and takes it as a ground for the "new kinship of the discipleship of equals"; D'Angelo, "Theology in Mark and Q," 172, argues that the function of "Father" as divine title in Mark as well as in earlier and contemporary Judaism is "to invoke kinship with God as protection in persecution, as an assurance of mercy and forgiveness, and as a claim to upon divine providence, " and she explains that in the experience of the community the term "Father" as applied to God functions "in the self-knowledge by which they know their divine sonship and their kinship with a divine father and in the practice which they ground in that knowledge."

68. For early studies see Sparks, "The Doctrine of the Divine Fatherhood in the Gospels," 241–62; Montefiore, "God as Father in the Synoptic Gospels," 31–46; Bennett, "The Sons of the Father," 12–23; and Argyle, *God in the New Testament*, 57–90.

69. Bennett, "The Sons of the Father," 12–23; Montefiore, "God as Father in the Synoptic Gospels," 31–46; Sparks, "The Doctrine of the Divine Fatherhood in the Gospels," 241–62; Zeller, "God as Father in the Proclamation and in the Prayer of Jesus," 117–29.

70. Mowery, "From Lord to Father in Matthew 1–7," 654; idem, "God, Lord, and Father," 24–36; idem, "The Activity of God in the Gospel of Matthew," 400–411. See also Burnett, "Exposing the Anti-Jewish Ideology," 155–91; Gunilka, "Zum Gottesgedanken in der Jesusüberlieferung," 144–62; Douglas, "Family, Power, Religion."

71. Carter, "God as 'Father' in Matthew," 81–102.

the father."[72] He describes Matthew's characterization of God as Father as "the basic norm which guides one's reading of Matthew."[73]

The study of God as Father in Mark is less common compared to Matthew and Luke and focuses largely on the significance of Jesus' use of "Abba, Father."[74] This emphasis limited most of the studies in Mark to the interaction with Jeremias' argument. After comparing the use of the term "father" in Mark with its use in early Judaism, D'Angelo concludes that its use in Mark "evokes the imperial (or anti-imperial) context, as well as the traditional uses of father for God as the refuge of the persecuted and the giver of forgiveness."[75]

Studies of God as Father in Luke are sometimes pursued in the larger context of Luke-Acts and sometimes are limited to the Gospel of Luke.[76] Chen's work, *God as Father in Luke-Acts*, is entirely devoted to examining the role of God as Father in Lukan narrative in relation to various contemporary religious and cultural contexts.[77] Earlier works by Mowery examine the use of "Father" for God both in the broader context of Luke-Acts and in Luke alone arguing, based largely on the frequency of usage, that divine titles "Lord" and "God" are emphasized more than the term "Father" in Luke-Acts.[78] Chen rightly criticizes Mowery's conclusion on the ground that "the significance of the concept cannot be determined solely on the basis of how often a term is used in a text."[79] However, Mowery's studies in Luke-Acts highlight a very significant point of the disappearance of the reference to God as Father in the book of Acts. Given Luke's depiction of Jesus' preference to address God as "Father" and the fact that he taught his disciples to pray to the Father addressing God as Father, one would have expected that Luke would have depicted Jesus' followers addressing God as Father in Acts. However, Luke only portrays them addressing God as Lord.[80]

72. Burnett, "Exposing the Anti-Jewish Ideology," 165.

73. Ibid., 156.

74. Fitzmyer, "*Abba* and Jesus' Relation to God," 14–38; D'Angelo, "Theology in Mark and Q," 149–74.

75. D'Angelo, "Theology in Mark and Q," 161.

76. Chen, *God as Father*, 2. Mowery, "The Disappearance of the Father," 353–58; idem, "God the Father in Luke-Acts," 124–32; idem, "Lord, God and Father," 82–101; Doohan, "Images of God in Luke-Acts,"17–35.

77. Chen, *God as Father*, 3.

78. Mowery, "God the Father in Luke-Acts," 124–32.

79. Chen, *God as Father*, 9, explains that "God is explicitly called "Savior" only once in the whole of Luke-Acts (Luke 1:47), yet it is an important image for God by virtue of the centrality of the theme of salvation."

80. Mowery, "The Disappearance of the Father," 354.

Studies of God as Father in the Gospel of John are numerous, probably due to the high frequency of such identification which is considered to be "one of the distinctive features of John's Gospel."[81] Semeia volume 85 (1999) is fully devoted to essays that examine God as Father in the Gospel of John.[82] The focus ranges from the original meaning of the usage in its contemporary context to its importance in self-understanding in the twenty-first century.[83] Carter helpfully summarizes the perspectives from which the identification of God as Father is examined as: (1) the possible origin studied in relation to the Hebrew Bible, the historical Jesus, or Greco-Roman influence,[84] (2) the implication of "such a gendered image of God" for John's readers,[85] (3) examining the distinctive nature of John's reference to God as "Father" in line with its implication for Father-Son relationship,[86] and (4) examining John's language in relation to the language "Father" that is used to refer to the Roman emperor.[87]

Thus, while the study of God as Father in the Gospels is rightly moving away from oppositional hermeneutics and is abundant compared to the study of God as Father in Paul, the need for detailed study of Paul's use in terms of kinship construction in ancient Mediterranean society and its contribution for identity formation in early Christianity still remains.

The Study of God as Father in Paul

Apart from the cursory reference in commentaries and passing remarks in other Pauline studies, detailed study of God as Father in Paul is remarkably rare. I have come across only one unpublished study with a relatively detailed treatment of the Pauline use of God as Father, and even this one is a comparative study of God as Father in synoptic Gospels and Paul.[88] It focuses on examining the grammatical construction and the literary forms

81. A collection of studies in *Semeia* 85 (1999) explores the use of God as Father in the Gospel of John; Carter, "John's Father and the Emperor as Father," 235–55.

82. Reinhartz, "Introduction," 1–10; for the rest of the essays see *Semeia* 85 (1999).

83. Reinhartz, "Introduction," 2.

84. D'Angelo, "Abba and 'Father,'" 611–30; O'Day, "Show Us the Father," 11–18; Lacey, "Patria Potestas," 121–44; Stevenson, "The Ideal Benefactor," 421–36.

85. See Soskice, "Can a Feminist Call God 'Father'?," 15–29; Lee, "Beyond Suspicion?," 140–54; Reinhartz, "And the Word Was Begotten," 83–105.

86. Barrett, "The Father is Greater than I," 19–36; Thompson, *The Promise of the Father*, 133–54; Reinhartz, "And the Word Was Begotten;" Anderson, "The Having-Sent-Me Father," 33–57.

87. Carter, "John's Father and the Emperor as Father," 235–55.

88. Koop, "God as Father."

in which the expression is used and makes broad generalization that the fatherhood of God in Pauline literature refers to "the paternal relationship" God has with the believers and with Jesus.[89] Studies that examine God as Father in Paul in relation to the use of kinship language are noticeably absent. What is also clearly absent is any attempt to study the contribution of such use for the identity formation of early Christians, for the building of sibling relationship among Christ-believers and for the imaging of Christ-believers as children of God. This absence is even more striking, as will be shown below, when seen in light of the distinctive features of the Pauline usage of "Father" to refer to God.

Paul makes use of family terms such as "mother," "father," "brother" "sister," "slave," and "servant" abundantly.[90] There are twenty seven instances in which Paul uses the term "Father" to refer to God in his undisputed letters.[91] Out of these, nine are in the form of "God our Father," two are in the form of "our God and Father," seven in the form of "the Father," two in the form of "Abba, Father," one in the form of "your Father" in the quotation from 1 Sam 7, and three in the form of "the Father of the Lord Jesus Christ." Out of twenty three uses that refer to God as the Father of the followers of Christ, ten are in the salutation, eight in thanksgiving and prayer context, two in status/inheritance related contexts, one in a dyadic formula (1 Cor 8:6), and two are used in context of Jesus' exaltation (Phil 2 and 1 Cor 15). The following table (see next page) compares the use of God as Father in undisputed letters of Paul with similar uses in the Gospels, in the disputed letters of Paul, in the General Epistles and Hebrews, and in the book of Revelation. As can be seen from the table, the use of the term "Father" to refer to God is exceedingly frequent in Johannine writings, and Matthew comes second. The frequency of the Lukan use is comparable to Paul. In the case of the disputed Pauline writings, the use of God as Father continues. However,

89. Ibid., 229.

90. Banks, *Paul's Idea of Community*, 54–61; Sandnes, "Equality within Patriarchal Structures," 150–165; Aasgaard, "Brotherhood in Plutarch and Paul," 166–82; idem, '*My Beloved Brothers and Sisters!*'

91. By undisputed letters of Paul I refer to Romans, 1 and 2 Corinthians, Galatians, Philippians, 1 and 2 Thessalonians, and Philemon. However, it needs to be noted that Pauline authorship of 2 Thessalonians is highly debated. Even so, there are still prominent New Testament scholars who argue for Pauline authorship. For a survey of arguments for non-Pauline character of 2 Thessalonians see Wanamaker, *1 and 2 Thessalonians*, 17–28. For arguments supporting Pauline authorship see Malherbe, *Thessalonians*, 349–76; Donfried, *Paul, Thessalonica, and Early Christianity*, 49–66; Still, *Conflict at Thessalonica*, 58; Witherington, *1 and 2 Thessalonians*, 9–16.

as one goes from Ephesians to Titus, the frequency decreases, as there is only one usage in each of the Pastoral Epistles.

NT Writings	Number of times God is referred as Father	Remarks
Synoptic Gospels	68	42 in Matt, 4 in Mark, and 22 in Luke
Johannine Writings	140	121 in John, 12 in 1 John, 3 in 2 John, and 4 in Rev
Undisputed Pauline Writings	27	4 in Rom, 3 in 1 Cor, 5 in 2 Cor, 4 in Gal, 3 in Phil, 4 in 1 Thess, 3 in 2 Thess, 1 Phlm
Disputed Pauline Writings	15	8 in Eph, 4 in Col, 3 in the Pastorals
General Epistles & Hebrews	10	3 in Heb, 3 in 1 Pet, 1 in 2 Pet, 2 in Jas, and 1 in Jude

Table 1: God as Father in the NT

At first sight, the use of "Father" in reference to God in Paul appears to be insignificant compared with the frequency of its usage in the Matthean and Johannine writings. The Pauline use, however, is significant for several reasons: (1) it reflects the earliest Christian use of the term "Father" to refer to God in writing;[92] (2) the nature of the Pauline use is different from the Gospels—while the use of "Father" in the Gospels is found almost entirely on the lips of Jesus and Jesus only once used the expression "our Father" in his instruction to the disciples, never joining himself with them, Paul uses the plural pronoun "our" to refer to God as "our God and Father/ "God our Father" thirteen times.[93] (3) The context in which Paul uses "Father" to refer to God exhibits a deliberate consistency that is markedly different from the Gospels— more than half of Paul's usage is found in the opening formulas where both the sender's and the receivers' identity is laid out. The remaining instances are used in the context of thanksgiving, prayer/benediction, and inheritance. (4) The vocabulary/language associated with the use of "Father" to refer to God in Paul constitutes a further feature: the words "grace,"

92. It is curious that while Luke uses "Father" to refer to God about twenty two times in the Gospel, he has only three such uses in the book of Acts. See Mowery, "The Disappearance of the Father," 353–58, for a brief discussion.

93. Unlike in Matthew 6:9, Paul's reference to God with plural possessive pronoun never stands alone simply as "our Father." It is invariably coupled with "God" either in the form of "our God and Father," or "God our Father."

"peace," and "our Lord Jesus Christ" are used in conjunction with the expression "God our Father." (5) Out of the three uses of "Abba, Father!" in the NT, two are found in Paul (Gal 4:6 and Rom 8:15).[94] (6) Paul uses sibling terminologies such as brothers and sisters quite often (about 114 times in his seven undisputed letters) to refer to the followers of Jesus, raising the question as to how such use is related to his calling God, "Father."[95]

While the use of the kinship term "Father" to refer to God in Paul is significant both in terms of its frequency and in terms of its distinct features, and while kinship construction is a primary vehicle to shape social relationship, institutions, and values in the ancient Mediterranean world, a study that explores the identity formation significance of the use of God as Father and the related kinship terms in Paul is missing. Scholars have noted the importance of studying Paul by using the Greco-Roman milieu as context instead of a background, yet in the case of Paul's use of God as Father this is not the case.[96]

Christ-Followers as Children of God in Paul

The image of Christ-followers as children of God, although not as frequent as in the Gospels, is present in Paul. Paul refers to Christ-followers as children of God in four passages (Gal 3:26—4:7; Rom 8:14–17; Phil 2:15–16; 2 Cor 6:14—7:1). He uses υἱοὶ (Gal 3:26; 4:6, 7; Rom 8:14), τέκνα (Rom 8:16; Phil 2:15), and υἱοὺς καὶ θυγατέρας (2 Cor 6:18) to identify Christ-followers as children of God. He uses these terms interchangeably in Rom 8:14, 16, 19, indicating that they are synonymous in his use.[97] Another term Paul uses to describe Christ-followers' identity as children of God is υἱοθεσία. In the New Testament this term occurs only in Paul (Gal 4:5; Rom 8:15, 23; 9:4), and in Ephesians 1:5. The term does not occur in the LXX nor does it occur in other Jewish writings.

Studies on Paul's identification of Christ-believers as children of God are pursued primarily by focusing on the term υἱοθεσία.[98] The discussion on Paul's use of υἱοθεσία focuses on two aspects: the background that primarily informs Paul's use, and whether it is to be translated as "sonship" or

94. Jeremias, *The Central Message of the New Testament*, 9–30; idem, *Jesus and the Message of the New Testament*, 63–110.

95. See Table 2 below.

96. Engberg-Pedersen, *Paul in His Hellenistic Context*; see also Engberg-Pedersen, *Paul Beyond the Judaism/Hellenism Divide*.

97. Schneider, "τέκνον," 341–42.

98. Scott, *Adoption as Sons of God*.

"adoption." In dealing with these issues, as usual, an "either-or" approach is dominant. Some scholars argue that even though the term is not found in the LXX or other ancient Jewish writings, the concept is known as reflected in 2 Sam 7:14, which they see as reflecting divine adoption of the Israelite king.[99] These scholars also support their argument by referring to Paul's use of the term in Rom 9:4 to refer to Israel's privileges. A slightly different view from this is advanced by Brendan Byrne. While Byrne agrees with Scott that the Jewish writings form the primary context for the Pauline use of υἱοθεσία, he sees the use of sons/children to refer to the people of Israel as God's children as forming the basis for Pauline usage instead of the dubious adoption language in 2 Sam 7.[100] He argues that since "adoption in the strict sense was not a Jewish custom . . . it may be best not to tie *huiothesia* too narrowly to this meaning [adoption], but rather to see behind the term . . . principally the long-standing biblical tradition of Israel (Israelites) as 'son (sons) of God.'"[101]

Other scholars, pointing to the absence of the term in the LXX and ancient Jewish writings, argue that Paul's use of υἱοθεσία comes from Greco-Roman background.[102] Objecting to the "either-or" approach, Burke rightly argues that the context of υἱοθεσία is as complex as Paul's own background, "which is a rich tapestry of Jewish, Roman and Greek cultures."[103] He explains that "[t]o try to separate these in the quest . . . is difficult and should not be simplistically reduced to an 'either or' conclusion."[104] Burke states his position as in-between the Greco-Roman—Jewish dichotomy. While he sees Greco-Roman "adoption" as providing the vocabulary and idea for Paul, he also sees the Hebrew Bible and ancient Jewish depiction of God's people as sons/children of God as informing the Pauline use of υἱοθεσία.[105]

Noticeably absent here too is relating the depiction of Christ-followers as children of God with the identity formation of early Christianity as well as with the depiction of God as Father and Christ-followers as siblings. Focusing excessively on Paul's use of υἱοθεσία and its possible background as the sole locus of deciphering his depiction of Christ-followers as children of God, scholars have neglected how Paul's use of terms such as υἱοὶ, τέκνα,

99. Ibid.; Malul, "Foundlings and their Adoption," 97–126.

100. Byrne, *'Sons of God,'–'Seed of Abraham'*, 79–196.

101. Byrne, "Sons of God," 157–58.

102. Lyall, *Slaves, Citizens, and Sons*; idem, "Roman Law," 456–68; Mawhinney, "Huiothesia."

103. Burke, *Adopted into God's Family*, 30.

104. Ibid.

105. Ibid., 29, and chap 3.

θυγατέρας, and υἱοθεσία work together with other familial terms Paul uses. The self-understanding such construction would shape and express and what such self-understanding entails is not explored. This study places Paul's use of terms such as υἱοὶ, τέκνα, θυγατέρας, and υἱοθεσία to depict Christ-followers as children of God in relation to Paul's use of God as Father and Christ-followers as siblings. I will explore the nature of networks of relationships this combined use constructs and the orienting framework such use shapes and advances.

Sibling Language in Paul

Among familial language used in the NT, sibling language is by far the most frequent. As the table below shows, there are 190 occurrences of addressing believers as brothers and sisters.[106] Out of 190 occurrences in the NT epistles, we have 114 in undisputed letters of Paul. The high frequency in Romans and 1 Corinthians may at first sight suggest that the frequency goes with the length of the letter. However as we find 19 in 1 Thessalonians and 10 in Galatians, the frequency does not appear to correspond to the length of the letter. This observation is not limited to Pauline writings. For instance, we have 20 in James and 13 in 1 John but only 8 in Hebrews.

NT Letters	Direct Address	Design-ation	*Total*	Remarks
Undisputed Letters	64	50	*114*	20 in Rom, 39 in 1 Cor, 12 in 2 Cor, 10 in Gal, 9 in Phil, 19 in 1 Thess, 5 Philm
Disputed Letters	11	18	*29*	5 in Col, 2 in Eph, 4 in 1 inTim, 1 2 Tim, 9 in 2 Thess
Hebrews & General Epistles	21	26	*47*	8 in Hebrews, 20 in James, 1 in 1 Pet, 2 in 2 Pet, 13 in 1 John, 3 in 3 John
Total	*96*	*94*	*190*	

Table 2: Sibling Language in the NT

While the high frequency of sibling language has been noticed for a long time, studies on its meaning and function in Paul have been too general. Although Hellerman and deSilva discuss the use of the sibling language in the NT within the context of kinship, their treatment is very sketchy. The

106. The list is adopted from Aasgaard, *'My Bleloved Brothers and Sisters!'* Appendix I and II; see also Horrell, "From ἀδελφόι to οἶκος θεοῦ," 293–311.

only detailed study is the one by Reidar Aasgaard, "My Beloved Brothers and Sisters!" Studies prior to Aasgaard approached sibling language in NT in a general way without addressing individual texts.[107] Some who approach specific texts usually deal with sibling language broadly under some other topic such as a discussion of the image of the church as family,[108] or the nature of relationship between early Christians, particularly focusing on the question of egalitarian or hierarchical structure.[109]

The concern of this book is how sibling language in Paul is related to his use of God as Father. Here too, there is no detailed treatment of this issue. However, from those who do address it in general terms, most see Paul's use of sibling language as a derivation of having God as Father.[110] For instance Petersen sees the idea of being brothers and sisters as being derived from the idea of believers being children of God.[111] On the other hand, Aasgaard argues that assertions such as Petersen's are unfounded. He writes, "the claims which several scholars have made of a notion of Christians as a 'family of God' in Paul, in which God is Father and Christ and the Christians are his children and each other's siblings, are not sufficiently supported . . ."[112] He argues that Paul's "notions of Christian siblingship are derived from a socio-historical context . . ."[113] But what he writes next tends to contradict his assertion: "Still, Paul in some cases makes use of specific theological justifications in connection with sibling language: occasionally, a Christological, a soteriological, or an eschatological explanation is at hand

107. Banks, *Paul's Idea of Community*, 49–56; Meeks, *The First Urban Christians*, 74–110.

108. Hellerman, *The Ancient Church as Family*, 26–28; Sandnes, *A New Family*, 34–37; deSilva, *Honor, Patronage, Kinship, and Purity*, 199–228.

109. Those who argue from sibling language for relationship of equals include scholars such as Fiorenza, *In Memory of Her*, 147–51; Petersen, *Rediscovering Paul*, 23–25, 101, 289; Hellerman, *The Ancient Church as Family*, 221; those who question such interpretation include Sandnes, *A New Family*; idem, "Equality within Patriarchal Structures," 150–65; Bartchy, "Undermining Ancient Patriarchy."

110. Those who see sibling language in Paul as derived from God's Fatherhood include the following: Petersen, *Rediscovering Paul*, 23, 266–67; Sandnes, *A New Family*, 78–80; Hellerman, *The Ancient Church as Family*, 26–28; Allmen, *La famille de Dieu*; Scott, *Adoption as Sons of God*; Lewis, "As a Beloved Brother"; Meeks, *The First Urban Christians*; Esler, "Keeping It in the Family," 168; from those who question the connection are Aasgaard, *'My Beloved Brothers and Sisters!'* 309.

111. Petersen, *Rediscovering Paul*, 266.

112. Aasgaard, *'My Beloved Brothers and Sisters!'* 309.

113. Ibid.

. . . However, Paul does not explicitly link them to siblingship per se . . . he neither elaborates on them, nor utilizes them actively in the letters."[114]

This book will argue that the use of kinship language to refer to God as Father of the followers of Christ and the family image it creates employs kinship logic to ground Paul's use of "brothers" and "sisters" to refer to believers as connected to sharing one Father, God. As Paul is writing to the horizon of his audiences' understanding of kinship, he did not have to present a detailed logical explanation each time he uses a kinship term for he expects his audience to make such a connection.

Contribution of this Book

In order to show the contribution of this book, I will first summarize the gaps observed in the preceding assessment of the history of research in the study of identity formation in early Christianity, in the study of God as Father in the NT, and in the study of God as Father in Paul, proceeding from the latter to the former.

1. Apart from one study on grammatical construction and the literary form of the use of God as Father in Paul in comparison to the Gospels, there is no full study in the use of God as Father in Paul which deals with the unique features observed above. There is no detailed study that relates it to Paul's use of sibling language. There is no study that examines its contribution to the self-understanding of the Pauline community. And there is no study that approaches it from the perspective of the use of kinship language in ancient Mediterranean society.
2. While studies of God as Father in the Gospels are abundant, I have not come across a study that approaches it in relation to the use of kinship language in ancient Mediterranean society and expounds its contribution to the identity formation for their respective communities.
3. While studies of identity formation in early Christianity are rightly moving away from crisis-based oppositional hermeneutics to employ the concept of identity and kinship as analytical category, studies that combine the two in the study of identity formation are rare. More importantly, what is also missing is a study that examines the contribution of the use of God as Father for the identity formation of early Christians in Pauline communities which would have given a further insight into their self-understanding.

114. Ibid.

By studying the use of God as Father in Paul and its contribution for the self-understanding of early Christians in terms of the use of kinship language in ancient Mediterranean society, this study attempts:

1. to provide a fuller study of Paul's use of God as Father and its relation to his depiction of Christ-believers as children of God and to his use of sibling language,
2. to show how the Pauline use of God as Father and its relation to his depiction of Christ-believers as children of God and to his use of sibling language contribute to the identity formation of the Pauline community,
3. to give additional methodological insight for the study of God as Father in the NT that would flesh out its contribution to the identity formation of early Christianity,
4. to bring to fore the utilization of the concept of kinship and identity together as analytical tools in the study of identity formation in early Christianity, and the contribution that the use of God as Father in the NT makes for the inquiry into the self-understanding of early Christians. This study will take the use of kinship as analytical tool in biblical studies further (a) *by grounding it* in the anthropological insight on how kinship is related to identity formation, and in the use of kinship in identity formation in ancient Mediterranean society; (b) *by combining* it with other approaches—social identity theory, imperial critical approach, and narrative approach—that make possible the probing of the use of kinship in identity formation from different perspective.

2

Kinship-Identity Approach

The choice of Kinship-Identity Approach (KIA) to frame this study with its theoretical foundations and specific approaches, emanates from several grounds. To begin with, since the term "Father" that is used to refer to God is a kinship term which is part of the common mode of expression of belongingness in ancient Mediterranean society, Paul's use of the image is studied more profitably in terms of the utilization of kinship in that society. This would bring to the foreground the use of "Father" to refer to God in the Hebrew Bible and Jewish writings, its use in contemporary Greco-Roman society, and the use of "father" to refer to the Roman emperor. Furthermore, as will be shown below, since kinship language through categorization and identification creates a narrative that provides an orienting framework that shapes self-understanding and understanding of others, the use of God as Father should also be probed from this angle to grasp its function in the life of the emerging Pauline communities. A study such as this is fruitfully approached by enlisting theoretical as well as interpretative approaches that would together enable the discussion of the term from these different perspectives.

The approach that will be used to this end, KIA, will bring together theoretical (kinship and social identity theory) as well as interpretative approaches (imperial critical approach and narrative approach to Paul). The theoretical foundations and interpretative approaches are interrelated; they will be used together in a complementary way to examine thoroughly the use of God as Father in Paul. They will be used in such a way that several aspects of the use of God as Father in Paul will be brought out and in ways that show how these aspects have contributed in the identity formation of the Pauline community. Before laying out what features constitute KIA and how it will be applied in this study, the relevance of each aspect of the KIA to the study at hand and how the different approaches cohere to form the KIA will be discussed below. I will begin with a discussion of the role of kinship in identity formation from an anthropological perspective. This will be followed by an analysis of kinship in ancient Mediterranean society and its use in biblical interpretation.

Kinship and Identity Formation in Anthropology

Since the pioneering work of Lewis Henry Morgan in the 1870s,[1] kinship relationships have been predominantly understood as emanating from biogenetic relationships, biological connections created through sex and birth or conception and parturition,[2] which are reflected in the sharing of blood, bone, semen, or some other substance transmitted in the process of procreation.[3] In other words, for a long period of time, anthropologists defined kinship as a relationship based on consanguinity and affinity, relationship based on blood or biogenetic substance, and relationship based on marriage respectively. Following this understanding, the different ways in which people in different societies define who is related to whom and organize kinship relationships were "explained by falling back on the notion that this diversity nevertheless must have a referent in the natural facts of life, the natural process of human sexual reproduction."[4]

Contrary to such understanding, however, further studies revealed not only that the notion of procreation is understood differently in different societies but that kinship relationships are also constructed on non-procreation bases in different societies and are as equally valid and real as kinship constructed on the basis of biogenetics.[5] Such findings led anthropologists to see

1. Morgan, *Systems of Consanguinity and Affinity*; idem, *Ancient Society*; Parkin and Stone, *Kinship and Family*, 2. See also Schneider, "What is Kinship All About?" 258, who explains that kinship for Morgan (and also those who followed his theory which is a predominant theory up until 1970s), was about "the way in which a people grouped and classified themselves as compared with the real, true, biological facts of consanguinity and affinity."

2. Emphasizing this situation, Fox, *Kinship and Marriage*, 10, writes, "Kinship is to anthropology what logic is to philosophy or nude is to art; it is the basic discipline of the subject." Holy, *Anthropological Perspectives*, 1, points to a huge body of literature on kinship that accumulated between the pioneering works of Maine, McLennan, and Morgan in the second half of the 19th century and the time Fox expresses the centrality of kinship in anthropology as probably accounting for "more than half of the total literature of anthropology" during this time.

3. Holy, *Anthropological Perspectives*, 10.

4. Gross, "Kinship," 5182.

5. For instance, Shimizu, "On the Notion of Kinship," 388 explains that a theory of

the foundation of any kinship system in a folk-cultural theory that is designed to account for how women become pregnant and give birth to children.[6] Such a shift from conceptualizing kinship solely as biological bonds arising out of procreation to socio-cultural aspects led to an emphasis on genealogical relations instead of biological relations in kinship studies. Kinship theories differentiate genealogical relations from biological or genetic relations by describing them as "relations deriving from the engendering and bearing of children *as this process of human reproduction is known or understood in any given society and not as it may be known by biologists or geneticists*."[7]

However, even genealogy limits kinship to the notion of procreation as understood in a given society, leaving out kinship relationships conceptualized on other non-biogenetic grounds such as on sharing food, having common residence, and common rituals.[8] Kinship ties that are not genealogical (that are not built on the notion of procreation) have been referred to as "fictive," "pseudo," "ritual," "artificial," "play," and "as if" relationships, giving a wrong impression that they are less real than the biogenetic or genealogical kinship.[9] In this regard, a number of social anthropologists argued that since what constitutes kinship is different from one ethnographic setting to another, and since viewed from a culture's own perspective, all kinship relationships make sense and hence "the natives do not have to resort to tags like "artificial" to describe their own system,"[10] using terms such as "fictive" has no "analytical utility."[11]

What is common to kinship in all societies is sharing.[12] In general, people's explanations as to why some of them are more closely related than others are based on what Pitt-Rivers calls "a notion of consubstantiality" —a sense of sharing common substance. In some cultures, the common substance is considered to be blood, bone, semen, or some other substance transmitted in the process of procreation. In other cultures, it is consid-

---

human reproduction, how women become pregnant, the child's relation to its father and mother differ from society to society. For instance, the Yap has a monosexual theory of procreation whereby a spirit called *maan* enters into the belly of a woman and perform the task of impregnating her. The husband is only indirectly related to the process of procreation through the blessing of the elders and the dead relatives.

6. Scheffler, "Kinship, Descent, and Alliance," 749.

7. Holy, *Anthropological Perspectives*, 15, emphasis added.

8. Strathern, "Kinship, Descent and Locality," points out some New Guinea groups who construct kinship based on residence on common place (land) and sharing food.

9. Marshall, "The Nature of Nurture," 643.

10. Ibid., 656.

11. Kelly, *Constructing Inequality*, 522.

12. Marshall, "The Nature of Nurture," 656; Pitt-Rivers, "The Kith and the Kin," 92.

ered to be suckling of the same milk, eating the same food, living on the same land, sharing produce of the same land, etc.[13] Watson describes the first notion of mutual relatedness as "nature kinship" and the second one as "nurture kinship."[14] These two notions of conceptualizing kinship, however, should not be seen as unrelated categories of kinship in the life of an individual or kinship group. Rather, both these notions of kinship as well as the construction of kinship itself should be seen as a process. Anthropological studies of kinship since the 1990s have shown that in many societies "kinship statuses or ties are not set once and for all by acts of birth, but rather emerge, strengthen, or fade through the process of human interactions."[15]

A representation that comes closer to depicting the process of how nature and nurture kinship could be related is probably Akitoshi Shimizu's "working model for the cultural construction of kinship."[16] By conceptualizing the construction of kinship as "constitutive of personhood and social human being," he approaches kinship construction as consisting of three phases: kinship-by-procreation, constructed kinship, and ideological kinship.[17] From the very beginning, Shimizu rightly notes that these phases of kinship should not be taken as linear. Rather, he likens "the multiple construction of kinship in a society" to "a series of circles partially overlapping with one another" making 'non-kin' in one context a kin in another and a kin in one context a non-kin in another.[18] The first stage, kinship-by-procreation, which he takes as minimal basis for discerning kinship, is related to

13. Pitt-Rivers, "The Kith and the Kin," 92; Holy, *Anthropological Perspective,* 9; Marshall, "The Nature of Nurture," 655, his study of the Truk District of Micronesia points out that the distinction between those who share biological substance and those who share land, food, labor, or residence is blurred and various people who do not share substance acknowledge each other as kin. Based on this observation, he suggests that what was common to kinship is not limited to physical substance but the concept of sharing that is "expressed through a variety of culturally specific symbolic and interactive media"; in similar vein Strathern, "Kinship, Descent and Locality," 29, writes, "Food builds their bodies and gives them substance just as their father's semen and mother's blood and milk give them substance in the womb and as small children. Hence it is through food that the identification of the sons of immigrants with their host group is strengthened. Food creates substance, just as procreation does, and forms an excellent symbol both for the creation of identity out of residence . . ."

14. Watson, *Tairora Culture.*

15. Stone, "Kinship," 273. The understanding of kinship as a process instead of a once-and-for-all set fact is championed predominantly by feminist anthropologists such as Janet Carsten, Sarah Franklin, and Susan Mckinnon. See Carsten, *Culture of Relatedness*; Franklin and Mckinnon, *Relative Values.*

16. Shimizu, "On the Notion of Kinship," 377–403.

17. Ibid.

18. Ibid., 397.

defining a person at the initial stage of social existence in terms of "folk categories" that indicate the notion of physical procreation.[19] The second stage, constructed kinship,[20] refers to "all states of kinship thus transformed out of kinship-by-procreation," forming a person through a series of life-cycles by constructing further a person's identity through the process of growth. These cycles of identity construction through kinship construction involve forming a spiritual and substantial bond, legitimization through legal regulation of "relations other than ones of kinship-by-procreation in the same terms as those of the procreators and their children."[21] This transformation process of kinship may involve recruiting outsiders who were perceived as non-kin at different transformative stages into the category of constructed kinship. Certain aspects of kinship that are constructed may contradict each other, calling for redefinition and adjustment by selectively emphasizing the dominant features leading to a construction of ideological kinship. Shimizu explains ideological kinship as "[a] symbolic apparatus" that selectively highlights what have become salient aspects of kinship in order to resolve the contradictions and "provide a structural device to meet the functional requirements of broader social circumstances."[22] Such a process in the construction of kinship shows that the nature of kinship is context bound and that "when a social condition sustaining a certain state of constructed kinship is no longer what is used to be, then that state of kinship will cease to be marked out as before."[23]

While there is no single agreed-upon definition of kinship, a comprehensive definition that comes closer to reflecting the processual conceptualization of kinship as well as several features of kinship raised above is the definition of Raymond C. Kelly. Since this study will follow major components of this definition, it is quoted below at length. According to Kelly, kinship refers to:

> social relations predicated upon cultural conceptions that specify the processes by which an individual comes into being and develops into a complete (i.e. mature) social person. These processes encompass the acquisition and transformation of both spiritual and corporeal components of being. Sexual

19. Ibid., 395–96; the notion of physical procreation may not be necessarily biological.

20. I keep the term "constructed" for the lack of a better word since all "kinship-by-procreation," "constructed kinship," and "ideological kinship" are constructed kinship.

21. Shimizu, "On the Notion of Kinship," 396.

22. Ibid., 396–97.

23. Ibid., 397.

> reproduction and the formulation of paternal and maternal contributions are an important component of, but are not coextensive with, the relevant processes. This is due to the ethnographic fact that a full complement of spiritual components is never derived exclusively from the parents. Moreover, the sexually transmitted ingredients of corporeal substance are frequently transmitted in other ways as well . . . Foods may also constitute essential ingredients in the spiritual or corporeal completion of personhood . . . Finally, maturation frequently entails purging, replacing, adding, and/or supplementing spiritual and corporeal components of personhood. There is no analytic utility in artificially restricting the category of kin relations to relations predicated on some but not all of the constitutive processes of personhood because these processes are culturally formulated as components of an integrated system and the social relations they predicate are all of the same logical type, i.e. relations of shared substance or shared spirit.[24]

This definition highlights the process of modifying substances and spiritual components involved in forging kin relations. By distinguishing kinship from biology and by broadening it to the "process of how persons come into being," this definition shifts the investigative focus "to ways in which kinship is embedded in the social life of people and to its connection to aspects of culture such as religion."[25]

Thus, kinship refers to relationships among individuals and groups that are based on descent and marriage in some cultures and on sharing food, land, worship, common residence, and common rituals in other cultures.[26] Although societies vary in how they conceptualize relationship, they use such relationships to form important groups linking individuals and groups together into larger kinship units. These units of relationships apply not only to contemporaries but also to ancestors and mythical figures.[27] Kinship is "one of the universals in human society" and plays an important role in "the formation of social groups," "in the regulation of behavior," "in maintaining group cohesion and solidarity," and "in orienting the individual members to the social maze."[28]

Kinship language, as a set of relationship terms, "defines the status of an individual in terms of relationship and contributes to the notion of

24. Kelly, *Constructing Inequality, 521–22.*
25. *Encyclopedia of Religion*, 5183.
26. Stone, "Kinship," 271; see also Parkin and Stone, *Kinship and Family*, 2.
27. Gross, "Kinship," 5182.
28. Eggan, "Kinship: Introduction," 390.

personhood."[29] It designates relationship categories that connect some individuals as more closely related to each other than they are to other people, and serves as "a means of identifying and ordering social relations,"[30] providing legitimization and rationalization for varied interactions that accord differential rights, roles, and statuses.[31] As such, kinship provides an "orienting framework for the content and ideology" of social relations as well as "hegemonic idioms" in terms of which "all-encompassing relationships are cast."[32] It has social as well as cultural significance.[33] As to the former, it shapes patterns of relationships, networks, strategies, and behavior; as to the latter it helps conceptualize ideas of symbols, beliefs, rules, roles, and plans.[34]

To sum up, the features of kinship that emerge from the above discussions can be summarized for application in this study in terms of what kinship is, how it is constructed, and what it does. Seen in terms of what it is, kinship is a process of being and becoming through networks of relationships that apply both to the contemporaries and the ancients, to spiritual as well as corporal relationships. Its construction varies from culture to culture but the common features in all construction of kinship are (1) a sense of sharing something—substance and/or spirit, nature and/or nurture, (2) the dynamic, versatile, and elastic nature that exhibits "purging, replacing, adding, and/or supplementing spiritual and corporeal components," that enables it to make a non-kin in one point in time into kin in another time and situation, and kin in one situation into non-kin in another situation. As to its function, it has social (it shapes patterns of relationships, networks, strategies and behavior) as well as cultural (it helps conceptualize ideas of symbols, beliefs, rules, roles, and plans) significance.[35] It creates a narrative that identifies and sets a framework to understand self and others, to define relationship categories and to form and transform groups.

As will be seen below, the Greco-Roman and Jewish kinship structures under which early Christianity emerged and which Paul evoked in using the kin term "Father" to refer to God exhibit, in one way or another, these features of kinship, laying a solid ground for using the kinship concept in the analysis of the identity formation of early Christians in general, and in

29. Geertz, *The Interpretation of Culture*, 363.

30. Beattie, *Other Cultures*, 94.

31. Holy, *Anthropological Perspectives*, 142–43.

32. Peletz, "Ambivalence in Kinship," 416.

33. Keesing, *Kin Groups and Social Structures*, 121–22.

34. Ibid. For the significance of kinship in social relationships see Goodenough, *Property, Kin and Community*; for the significance of kinship in conceptualizing cultural ideas, symbols, etc., see Schneider, *American Kinship*; idem, "What is Kinship All About?"

35. Keesing, *Kin Groups and Social Structures*, 121–22.

examining how Paul's reference to God as Father is related to this identity formation in particular.

Kinship in Ancient Mediterranean Society

Classical historians as well as anthropologists underscore the significance of kinship in the fabrics of the Greco-Roman as well as Jewish society.[36] Kinship was constructed in terms of sharing common god(s), ancestors, common philosophy, language, food, and land, revealing the prominence of sharing something in kinship construction. Such sharing was invoked between people, cities, leagues, kings, and among members of voluntary associations and intellectual/philosophical associations for a variety of purposes.[37] Terms such as ἔθνη, οἶκος, *domus,* and *familia* reflect kinship patterns and frameworks.[38] The versatility of the nature of kinship construction is fruitfully exploited to shape varying aspects of the Greco-Roman as well as Jewish society. In one situation it might take an ethnic framework, in another situation an ideological framework, to constitute group identity within the same ethnic group. Depending on what is perceived to be shared at a given point in time, kinship discourse is created.

Kinship was used to forge the identity of the Roman Empire and Roman emperors. Concerning Rome, Virgil's *Aeneid* traces the mythologized ancient history of Rome to Augustus himself.[39] Zanker explains that Virgil "imbued the myth of Venus, the fall of Troy, and the wanderings of Aeneas with a new meaning, in which not only the future rule of the Julian house,

36. Bettini, *Anthropology and Roman Culture*; Saller, "Roman Kinship"; Jones, *Kinship Diplomacy*; Elwyn, "Interstate Kinship," 261–86; Gruen, "The Jewish-Spartan Affiliation," 254–70; Wiseman, "Legendary Genealogies," 153–64; Zanker, *The Power of Images*, 36, 44; Quint, *Epic and Empire*; Hall, *Ethnic Identity in Greek Antiquity;* Dixon, *The Roman Family*, Chapter 1; idem, "Conflict in the Roman Family,"149–67; Nathan, *The Family in Late Antiquity*, 1–15.

37. For the discussion of the use of kinship diplomacy in Greek as well as Roman period, see Jones, *Kinship Diplomacy*; also Hall, *Ethnic Identity in Greek Antiquity*, 36-37, who points out that "*[s]yngeneia* is the regular word for family kinship, though it is important to note that it does not signify an *externally defined* system of cognative relationships between siblings and cousins, but rather the kin relationships that a particular individual might recognise at any one time *by reference to shared ancestors in the lineage*. In other words, a *syngenes* is one who is recognised as belonging to the same *genos* as ego, whether or not this is biologically the case. But, just as *genos* can be extended beyond the scope of the family to refer to larger collectivities, so *syngeneia* can refer to the wider kinship that individuals might share with one another by virtue of their belief in shared descent."

38. Wilhite, *Tertullian the African* 81.

39. Quint, *Epic and Empire*, 7–11, 21–31, 45–46; see also Zanker, *The Power of Images.*

but the whole history of Rome was portrayed as one of predestined triumph and salvation."[40] Dionysius of Halicarnassus, a Greek writer with a stated purpose of proving that the founders of the city of Rome "were Greeks and came together from nations not the smallest nor the least considerable" configures the history of Rome so as to relate the ancestors and geographic origin of Rome to Greece.[41] Through such configuration Dionysius "creates a bond of kinship between Greeks and Romans from which he can derive power . . . (and) confers upon the Romans all the honor, history, and prestige of a Greek heritage."[42]

Julius Caesar's genealogical kinship is traced to kings and an immortal goddess, Venus.[43] In this genealogical kinship construction, Julius Caesar presents himself and his family as descendants of Venus, and in another genealogy as descendants of Aeneas. He publicized it by minting coins with Venus on one side and on the other side Aeneas and the building of a temple to Venus.[44] Augustus took this further by promoting Julius Caesar's cult as a god, thereby creating a situation to present himself as "Emperor Caesar, son of God."[45] This way of building genealogical kinship enables a person or an ethnic group to define its present identity in terms of the past, the new in terms of the old, the unfamiliar in terms of the familiar.[46]

Kinship construction between cities is seen in the alleged correspondence between the Spartans and Jews according to 1 and 2 Maccabees (1 Mac 12.7.19–23; 2 Macc 5.9, 12:6, 14:20) which constructs kinship that identifies Abraham as common ancestor of the two people.[47]Although the importance of kinship diplomacy between cities and kings for protection against enemies and for recognition of immunity became nonessential

40. Zanker, *The Power of Images*, 193.

41. Dionysius of Halicarnassus, *The Roman Antiquities*, 1.5.1, 1:9–70.

42. Hodge, *If Sons, Then Heirs*, 36.

43. Suetonius, *Divus Julius* 6.1.

44. Wiseman, "Legendary Genealogies," 153; Zanker, *The Power of Images*, 36, 44.

45. Zanker, *The Power of Images*, 35.

46. Hodge, *If Sons, Then Heirs*, 36.

47. Josephus, *Jewish Antiquities*, 12:226–27, reads, "Areus, king of the Lacedemonians, to Onias, sends greetings. We have met with a certain writing, whereby we have discovered that both the Jews and the Lacedemonians are of the same family, and are derived from the kindred of Abraham. It is but just, therefore, that you, who are our brethren, should send to us about any of your concerns as you please. We will also do the same thing, and esteem your concerns as our own, and will look upon our concerns as in common with yours. Demotoles, who brings you this letter, will bring your answer back to us. This letter is four square; and the seal is an eagle, with a dragon in his claws."

during the Roman Empire, kinship remained a powerful tool for cities in their dealings with Rome for "privileges and titles."[48]

Kinship construction played an important role in the identity construction within associations and organizations of various kinds (ethnic, occupational, gymnastic, civic, cultic, and other groups).[49] From a wealth of inscriptions from Greece, Asia Minor, and Greek cities of the Danube and Bosporus, Harland shows how kinship language such as "brothers," and less often "sisters," "mother," and "father" was at work within small group settings to address each other and their leaders, respectively.[50] Compared to the frequency of usage in Christian writings, the evidence from inscriptions shows a relatively less frequent use. The difference probably lies in the nature of the evidence. While the evidence for early Christian use of kinship language comes from written correspondence, the evidence from small groups comes predominantly from inscriptions. Explaining this Harland writes, "(t)he happenstance of the nature of evidence from epigraphy would suggest that these are momentary snap-shots of what was likely common usage within some other associations about which we happen to know less."[51] It, however, still provides an opportunity to see the "common ground among some associations, synagogues, and congregations in the expression of belonging and group identity."[52]

Greco-Roman philosophers also reconstruct family based on moral and religious values. The following text from Epictetus indicates who the cynic would consider children, and how the cynic relates to them and why.

> . . . the cynic has made all [humankind] his children; the men among them he has as sons, the women as daughters; in that spirit he approaches them all and cares for them all . . . It is as

48. Jones, *Kinship Diplomacy*, 107.

49. Harland, *Dynamics of Identity*, 80.

50. Ibid., 61–96; for a list of the use of kinship terms such as "father" and "mother" among association members see Harland, *Associations, Synagogues, and Congregations*; 30–33.

51. Harland, *Dynamics of Identity*, 80.

52. Ibid. Scholars differ in their view of the importance of the use of kinship language in associations for understanding similar use in Christian writings. Among scholars who emphasize differences are Meeks, *The First Urban Christians*; Fox, *Pagans and Christians*; Burkert, *Ancient Mystery Cults*; and Hellerman, *The Ancient Church as Family*. Among scholars who emphasize similarity and the importance of kinship language in associations for the study of Christian material are: Nock, "The Historical Importance of Cult-Associations," 105–9; Barton and Horsley, "A Hellenistic Cult Group and the New Testament Churches," 7–41. See also Ascough, "Voluntary Association and Community Formation;" idem, "The Thessalonian Christian Community," 311–28.

> father he does it, as a brother and as a servant of Zeus, who is Father of us all. (Epictetus, *Discourses*, 3.22.81–82; *LCL*)

The cynic "inhabits" the world that is constructed through kinship based on the belief that Zeus is "Father of us all." The cynic is "a brother and a servant of Zeus," who is the father of "all humankind." The cynic considers men as sons and women as daughters and relates to them and cares for them in that spirit. Similarly Philo constructs kinship based on similarity of character rather than relationship merely by blood.

> For we should acknowledge only one relationship, and one bond of friendship, namely, a mutual zeal for the service of God, and a desire to say and do everything that is consistent with piety. And these bonds which are called relationships of blood, being derived from one's ancestors, and those connections which are derived from intermarriages and from other similar causes, must all be renounced, if they do not all hasten to the same end, namely, the honor of God which is the one unbreakable bond of all united good will. For such men will lay claim to a more venerable and sacred kind of relationship. (Philo, *Spec. Leg.* 1.316–17)

This text from Philo shows that for him relationship and a "bond of friendship" that count are not based on blood and marriage ties. He renounces kinship by blood ("relationships of blood, being derived from one's ancestors . . . from marriage and similar causes") in favor of kinship that has common religion and shared devotion and piety to it. He particularly considers a common devotion to Torah as sufficient basis to make people kin. In so doing, he relativizes the importance of kinship based on blood and marriage. He constructs a kinship that is based on "mutual zeal for the service of God, a desire to say and do everything that is consistent with piety."

From this, the features of kinship that emerged from the anthropological discussion above, which see kinship as a process of being and becoming through networks of relationships that apply both to the contemporaries and the ancients, to spiritual as well as corporal, are evident in the Greco-Roman world. Both the sense of sharing as well as the dynamic and versatile nature, the "purging, replacing, adding, and/or supplementing spiritual and corporal components" that enable it to make a non-kin in one situation into kin in another situation, and kin in one situation into non-kin in another situation, are all at work in various levels. In terms of function the constructed kinships created narratives that function as orienting frameworks that help to understand self and others.

Social Identity Theory (SIT)

The identifying and categorizing function of the use of kinship in ancient Mediterranean society in general and Paul's use of God as Father in particular can be examined by employing features of social identity theory (SIT). The notion of identity is central to understanding self as well as others. Richard Jenkins describes identity as "a process of 'being' or 'becoming'"[53] that entails "the human capacity—rooted in language—to know 'who's who' . . ."[54] It involves "knowing who we are, knowing who others are, them knowing who we are, us knowing who they think we are . . ."[55] It is "a multidimensional classification or mapping of the human world and our places in it, as individuals and as members of collectivities."[56] Jenkins further points out that "all human identities are . . . *social* identities" as identifying oneself or others "is a matter of meaning, and meaning always involves interaction: agreement and disagreement, convention and innovation, communication and negotiation."[57]

Social identity theory was developed in the 1970s and 1980s by Henri Tajfel and his colleagues at Bristol University.[58] Tajfel defines social identity as "that *part* of the individuals' self-concept which derives from their knowledge of their membership of a social group (or groups) together with the value and emotional significance attached to that membership."[59] This knowledge of membership is formed through the process of social identification and categorization, which play a significant role in the formation of social identity. Tajfel explains social categorizations as "discontinuous divisions of the social world into distinct classes or categories."[60] Social categorizations "define a person by systematically including them within some, and excluding them from other, related categories. They state at the same time what a person is and is not."[61] According to John C. Turner, social identification can refer to "the process of locating oneself, or another person, within a system of social categorizations or, as a noun, to any social categorization

53. Jenkins, *Social Identity*, 17.

54. Ibid., 5.

55. Ibid.

56. Ibid.

57. Ibid., 17.

58. Tajfel, *Differentiation between Social Groups*; Turner, "Social Categorization and the Self-Concept."

59. Tajfel, *Social Identity and Intergroup Relations*, 2.

60. Ibid., 17, 40.

61. Turner, "Towards a Cognitive Redefinition," 21.

used by a person to define him- or herself and others."[62] It is the putting together of these social identifications which are "used by a person to define him- or herself" that forms one's social identity.[63] This putting together of social identifications to form social identity is an ongoing, dynamic process. In this regard Rubin writes, "it is something that is presented and represented, constructed and reconstructed in interaction (including in written communication)."[64]

In terms of its formation, social identity is "self-appropriated as well as other-ascribed."[65] To some degree it is imposed by others and to some degree it is embraced by the self.[66] One's attraction "to the idea of the group, the consensual prototypical image" increases the extent of social cohesion.[67] In terms of impact, it is observed in many cases that acquired social identities have "a greater impact on a person's behavior than ascribed ones" as people "who adopt new religious, ethnic, or national identities show greater devotion to ingroup beliefs, values, and norms than people with ascribed identities.[68] Karina V. Korostelina explains that "[a]quired identity can completely change the structure of the social identity system: it can become the most salient identity, replacing other core identities and modifying their meaning."[69] Identity does not develop following the principle of "superposition," where new identities are added to other identities "as new layers or strata."[70] Rather, changes in the existing identity "lead to the differentiation of previously connected subsystems and integration of new, distinctly recognizable identities into the overarching system."[71] SIT distinguishes two basic processes through which identity development advances: (1) assimilation and accommodation which involves "the restructuring of new components of the identity system" and (2) estimation which involves "evaluation of the significance and value of new and old identities."[72] The result might be

62. Ibid.

63. Ibid.

64. Rubin, *Composing Social Identity in Written Language*, 9.

65 Ibid., 10.

66. Ibid.

67. Brown, *Group Processes*, 46.

68. Korostelina, *Social Identity and Conflict*, 82.

69. Ibid.

70. Ibid., 115.

71. Ibid.

72. Korostelina, *Social Identity and Conflict*, 115 explains that "the characteristic features of an identity system is the existence of mechanisms of competition between identities, which ends in the selection of the most stable identities, the rise of new identities, and the breaking of established pattern of behavior. The development mechanism

that newly developed identities replace several elements of previous identity without changing the core identity, or newly developed identity may stand in contradiction with previous core identity leading to changing some of the salient aspects of the core identity.[73] The following are some of the strategies used to form social identity which will be relevant for the purpose at hand: (1) revitalizing the group's past history and traditions, (2) redefining the value and meaning attached to a given tradition, (3) adding new dimensions to the group's past history and traditions, and (4) selecting new out-groups.[74]

The group may use polemical discourse as well as non-polemical discourse in group identity formation, emphasizing aspects of "affinity and estrangement."[75] While in polemical discourse the "other" is clearly identified mostly in negative terms, in non-polemical discourse the group simply proceeds to describe what it is and to cultivate what constitutes the "we/us."[76] The process of social identity formation is fostered among other things through written language.[77] Kelber points out that the ancient media of orality and scribality were tools that were used both by the elite and by the marginalized groups "as instruments of identity formation, control, and domination."[78] He explains that "scribality, literacy, identity formation, and cultural memory constituted a syndrome" that is used to create and legitimate social, religious, and political identity.[79]

Relating social identity to kinship, Jenkins explains that no matter when or where one lives, "kinship is the most important element in individual identification, by self and others."[80] Membership in kin-group "epitomizes the collectivity of identity, locating individuals within a field that is independent of and beyond individually embodied points of view" establishing relations in terms of "collective antecedents and contemporary affiliations."[81]

In recent years, social identity approaches have been used in Pauline studies. Pioneering the use of one aspect of social identity approach, social

of the identity system ensures the greatest possible initial variety of identities; within this context, important and insignificant elements are revaluated and irrelevant identities are discarded."

73. Ibid., 113–14.

74. Hogg and Abrams, *Social Identifications*, 55–59; for the application of this to the study of Qumran MSS see Jokiranta, "Social Identity Approach," 85–110.

75. Lincoln, *Discourse and the Construction of Society*, 9–10.

76. See Newsom, "Constructing 'We, You, and the Others,'" 13–22.

77. Gumperz, *Language and Social Identity*, 17.

78. Kelber, "Roman Imperialism and Early Christian Scribality," 97.

79. Ibid., 96.

80. Jenkins, *Social Identity*, 86.

81. Ibid.

categorization, in his book, *Conflict and Identity in Romans*, Philip Esler reads Paul as building new common ingroup identity in view of solving tensions among the Christians in Rome.[82] He made use of aspects of social identity approach in his studies of Galatians and the Gospel of John.[83] In his comparative study of 2 Corinthians, Epictetus and Valerius Maximus, V. Henry T. Nguyen uses social identity approach to examine the social aspects of early Christianity in line with "the primary sources that reveal the dynamics of social relations in the ancient Greco-Roman world."[84] As far as using kinship concept in conjunction with SIT in biblical studies, Esler brings the two together to examine the concept of family in 1 Thessalonians and Galatians, describing kinship as a "noteworthy feature of the group orientation."[85] This study will use SIT in conjunction with the concept of kinship to highlight and examine the identity constructing elements of the use of the kin term "father" to refer to god(s) and to emperors in the Greco-Roman world as well as in Paul. In what ways does such use relativize the addressees' past history and traditions? How does it redefine the value and meaning attached to a given tradition? What new dimensions does it add to the addressees' past history and traditions? What new out-group does it forge?

Imperial Critical Approach (ICA)

The emerging Roman Empire was increasingly portrayed as *Patria* and the Roman emperor as *Pater Patriae*. This raises an interpretive question regarding how portraying God as the Father of the emerging Christian community relate to such imaging of the empire and the emperor. At the beginning of the twentieth century, Adolf Deissmann noted that "the New Testament is the book of the Imperial age."[86] Based on his studies of parallel discourses, he reminded NT students that Paul and early Christians must not be seen as going through their world "blindfolded, unaffected by what was then moving the minds of men in great cities."[87] Until very recent time, however, NT studies approached Paul and early Christians as going through their world, particularly the Roman Empire, precisely as "blindfolded" and

82. Esler, *Conflict and Identity in Romans.*

83. Esler, *Galatians*; idem, *Lazarus, Mary and Martha.*

84. Nguyen, *Christian Identity*, 1–2. For detailed discussion on the use of SIT in the NT see also Baker, *Identity, Memory, and Narrative in Early Christianity*, 1–30; Tucker, *You Belong to Christ*, 36–60.

85. Esler, "Keeping It in the Family," 147.

86. Deissmann, *Light from the Ancient East*, 341.

87. Ibid., 340.

"unaffected" by it.[88] A recent example is Seyoon Kim's book, *Christ and Caesar: The Gospel and the Roman Empire in the Writings of Paul and Luke*, which continues to argue against any imperial reading of Paul or Luke.[89]

On the contrary, in recent years NT studies has begun to see seriously the NT as "the book of the Imperial age."[90] In this recent development, the Roman Empire is understood not as forming "the NT background" but as forming "the foreground."[91] Carter writes, "The Roman Empire provides the ever-present political, economic, societal, and religious framework and context for the New Testament's claims, language, structures, personnel, and scenes. The New Testament texts guide first-century followers of Jesus in negotiating Rome's power that crucified Jesus."[92]As such "the New Testament texts assume and engage Rome's world in every chapter. Even when the New Testament texts seem to *us* to be silent about Rome's empire, it is, nevertheless, ever present. It has not gone away."[93]

While in general, imperial-critical approaches recognize that the Roman Empire forms the foreground for the NT, there are, however, differences regarding the nature of the relation that the NT texts in general and the Pauline texts in particular have to the Roman Empire. For the purpose of this study, they can be broadly classified into two: (1) protest and (2) a range of negotiations. Richard Horsley and Crossan and Reed tend to see Paul more in opposition to the Roman Empire than in negotiation. Horsley writes, "Paul set his gospel of Christ and the new communities he catalyzed in opposition to the Roman imperial order."[94] He even goes further to read Paul "[i]nstead of being opposed to Judaism," as being "opposed to the Roman Empire."[95] Like the sub-title of their book, "How Jesus's Apostle Opposed Rome's Empire with God's Kingdom," Crossan and Reed also

88. See Stendahl, "The Apostle Paul and the Introspective Conscience," 199–215; also introductions in Horsley, *Jesus and Empire*; idem, *Paul and Empire*; idem, *Paul and Politics*; idem, *Paul and the Roman Imperial Order*.

89. Kim, *Christ and Caesar*, 68, writes, "there is no anti-imperial intent to be ascertained in the Pauline Epistles. All attempts to interpret them as containing such an intent, as shown above, are imposing an anti-imperial reading on the epistles based merely on superficial parallelism of terms between Paul's gospel preaching and the Roman imperial ideology, while the texts themselves clearly use those terms to express other concerns"; for an incisive review see Carter, Review of *Christ and Caesar*.

90. See Carter, "Proclaiming (in/against) Empire," 149–58; idem, "Lecture Imperialiste," 273–305.

91 See Carter, *The Roman Empire*, 1–5.

92. Ibid., 1.

93. Ibid.

94. Horsley, *Paul and the Roman Imperial Order*, 3.

95. Ibid.

emphasize Paul's opposition to the Roman Empire.[96] They write, "What is *newest* about this book is our insistence that Paul opposed Rome with Christ against Caesar. . ."[97] On the other hand, Oakes and Carter see the NT texts as exhibiting a wide range of interactions and negotiations with the Roman Empire. Carter writes,

> Because of their commitment to Jesus' teaching and actions, *they frequently* dissent from Rome's way of organizing society. *Often, though not always,* they seek to shape alternative ways of being human and participating in human community that reflect God's purposes. *Often, though not always,* they offer practices and ways of living that often differ significantly from the domination and submission patterns of Rome's world. *Often, though not always,* they provide different ways of understanding the world, of speaking about it, of living and relating — all the while rejecting options of total escape from or total compromise with Rome's empire [emphasis added].[98]

Peter Oakes' work on Paul in general proceeds with this realization. Oakes writes, "There is inevitably some interaction between first-century Christianity and Roman imperial ideology. Such interaction presumably consists of some combination of four broad possibilities: Rome and Christianity follow common models; Christianity follows Rome; Rome conflicts with Christianity; Christianity conflicts with Rome."[99] While practically it is difficult, as he himself admits, to maintain these categories as distinct from each other, his point that the interaction is multifaceted is heuristically helpful. Keeping these options separate as interpretive alternatives is important to examine the modes in which one discourse picks up elements of another.[100] This is because the modes can vary sharply "from admiring imitation to violent conflict."[101] When parallel elements are noticed between Paul's use of God as Father and that of Rome these four options suggested by Oakes can be used profitably to examine the nature of the link.

96. Crossan and Reed, *In Search of Paul*, x.

97. Ibid.

98. Carter, *The Roman Empire*, 13.

99. Oakes, "Re-mapping the Universe," 302.

100. For instance Oakes, "Re-mapping the Universe," 303, writes, "The reality is that certainty about independence of influence, as discussed in option (1), can rarely be achieved."

101. Ibid., 304.

Narrative Approach to Paul (NAP)

Due to the epistolary nature of Pauline writings, in general the idea of narrative does not come to mind as one approaches to study his writing.[102] The assertion made by J. C. Beker that "Paul is a man of the proposition, the argument and the dialogue, not a man of the parable or story"[103] is the predominant perception that has directed Pauline scholarship until the last three decades. Within this predominant perception, however, there have been NT scholars who recognized narrative theme(s) which Paul develops but mostly they reduced it to one or two central theme(s).[104] Commenting on these scholars Richard Hays points out that although they "offered readings of Paul which stress various aspects of what I am calling the narrative substructure of Paul's theology, none of them carries through an interpretation of Paul's theology as being rooted in story."[105] As a result, "their treatment of narrative aspects of Paul remains, although essential, implicit."[106] Continuing his assessment, Hays also mentions scholars such as Wilder, Crites, Sanders, and Beardslee as those who explicitly mentioned that "Paul's thought as grounded in some sort of narrative paradigm."[107] Their thoughts, however, are "expressed in 'throwaway' comments" and "brief provocative

102. After observing this perception, Witherington, *Paul's Narrative Thought World*, 2, points out that in Paul's letters there are not only narratives about Christ, about Paul himself, about Israel, about the origins of the Christian community but also that Paul alludes "to larger narratives by means of brief phrases or quotations of narratives . . ."

103. Beker, *Paul the Apostle*.

104. For critical survey see Hays, *The Faith of Jesus Christ*, 33–72, who presents on the one hand scholars like Bousset, Schweitzer, and Bultmann as those who recognized that "Paul drew upon narratives patterns (whether Gnostic or apocalyptic)," but who nonetheless "believe that the gospel is capable of being restated in ways which minimize its narrative elements and thus make its real meaning more apparent. These critics see the narrative *Vorstellungen* in Paul's thought world as imperfect gropings towards articulating a nonmytholigical, non-narrative *kerygma*." On the other extreme, Hays presents scholars such as Cullmann, Dodd, and Via as those who "think that a narrative pattern is integral to the gospel message, though each of them defines this narrative pattern in a different way" (70); see Bousset, *Kyrios Christos*; Schweitzer, *Mysticism of Paul*; Bultmann, *Theology of the New Testament*, 293–300; Cullman, *Salvation in History*; idem, *Christ and Time*; Dodd, *The Apostolic Preaching*; idem, *According to the Scriptures*; idem, "The Framework of the Gospel Narrative," 396–400; Via, *Kerygma and Comedy*; idem, "Narrative World and Ethical Response," 123–44.

105. Hays, *The Faith of Jesus Christ*, 9.

106. Ibid.

107. Ibid. See also Wilder, *Early Christian Rhetoric*; Crites, "The Narrative Quality of Experience," 291–311; idem, "Angels We Have Heard"; Sander, "Torah and Christ," 372; Beardslee, "Narrative Form in the NT," 301–15.

remarks" and hence they are not developed "into a more comprehensive interpretation of Pauline theology."[108]

Since the 1970s, however, following the works of literary critics,[109] narrative gained increasing significance as an analytical category in biblical studies, particularly in what has become known as Narrative Theology.[110] Shortly after, in the 1980s, through the pioneering work of Richard Hays that argues for a narrative substructure in the writings of Paul, narrative as a methodological framework gained importance in Pauline studies. Based on aspects of the works of Northrop Frye, Paul Ricoeur, and Robert Funk, Hays develops three methodologically helpful assumptions:[111]

1. There can be an organic relationship between stories and reflective discourse because stories have an inherent configurational dimension (*dianoia*) which not only permits but also demands restatement and interpretation in non-narrative language.
2. The reflective restatement does not simply repeat the plot (*mythos*) of the story; nonetheless, the story shapes and constrains the reflective process because the *dianoia* can never be entirely abstracted from the story in which it is manifested and apprehended.
3. Hence, when we encounter this type of reflective discourse, it is legitimate and possible to inquire about the story in which it is rooted.

Based on these assumptions he proceeds to identify "allusions to the story" within the discourse and to inquire "how this story shapes the logic of argumentation in the discourse."[112] While recognizing that the reflective discourse does not simply repeat the story, Hays heavily emphasizes the

108. Hays, *The Faith of Jesus Christ*, 9.

109. See Turner, *The Literary Mind* who argues that stories are building blocks of human thought; for literary studies that are believed to have given impetus for increasing use of narrative as analytical category see Auerbach, *Mimesis*; Scholes and Kellogg, *The Nature of Narrative*; Kermode, *The Sense of an Ending*; Mink, "History and Fiction."

110. Barclay, "Paul's Story," 133; Longenecker, "Narrative Interest," 4; for works on narrative theology see Hauerwas and Jones, *Why Narrative*; Crites, "The Narrative Quality of Experience;" Fasching, *Narrative Theology after Auschwitz*; Goldberg, *Theology and Narrative*.

111. Hays, *The Faith of Jesus Christ*, 28; Frye, *Anatomy of Criticism*, 77–79; idem, *Fables of Identity*; Ricoeur, "The Narrative Function," 37–56, 183–84; idem, "Biblical Hermeneutics," 29–148; Funk, *Language, Hermeneutic, and Word of God*.

112. Hays, *The Faith of Jesus Christ*, 28.

constraining and shaping force of the story to the extent that ignores the narrative-creating potential of the reflective discourse.

Several years after the publication of Hays' study, following a similar path, but with a sociological twist,[113] N. R. Petersen in his book, *Rediscovering Paul: Philemon and the Sociology of Paul's Narrative World*, argued for a narrative reading of Pauline writings.[114] He begins with the most pertinent assertion to our purpose, "Letters have stories, and it is from these stories that we [readers] construct the narrative worlds of both the letters and their stories."[115] Petersen rightly highlights that letters have stories not just as a background but in themselves, in what they tell.[116] He explains the notion of narrative world(s) as "that reality which the narrator bestows upon his actors and upon their actions, a reality into which he authoritatively invites his audience . . ."[117] In an attempt to understand, the audience moves "from letters to their stories," and "also back to the letters from stories."[118] In other words the "readers unconsciously transform non-narrative texts like letters into narrative texts in order to comprehend them."[119] They do this by projecting narrative frameworks within which these non-narrative texts are understood. When these narrative frames are reconstructed, one can come to see how "a letter persuades the reader to take up certain perspectives and adopt certain values."[120] Compared to Hays, Petersen takes the narrative approach to Paul a step further. He emphasizes the narrative that the text creates and the narrative which the reader constructs to understand the text.

In the early 1990s, in his major work, *The New Testament and the People of God*, N. T. Wright, among other things argued for approaching Pauline writings "in terms of stories he tells."[121] He writes,

> Within all his letters . . . we discover a larger implicit narrative . . . Like his own story, this larger narrative is the Jewish story, but with a subversive twist at almost every point. Paul presupposes this story even when he does not expound it directly, and

113. Longenecker, "Narrative Interest," 7.

114. Petersen, *Rediscovering Paul*.

115. Ibid., 43.

116. Ibid., ix, 2, 43.

117. Ibid., 7.

118. Ibid., 43.

119. Ibid., 118–21.

120. Ibid.

121. Wright, *The New Testament*, 403; see also p. 141 where he explains that he sees the biblical story as consisting five acts: (1) creation, (2) fall, (3) Israel, (4) Jesus, (5) from the early Christians onwards, the writings of the NT forming "the first scene in the fifth act."

> it is arguable that we can only understand the more limited narrative worlds of the different letters if we locate them at their appropriate points within this overall story-world, and indeed within the symbolic universe that accompanies it.[122]

While here he tends to limit the narrative world of Paul to the "Jewish story," in his subsequent work he appropriately enlarged it to include the interplay between several stories. He rightly points out that Paul's world "could profitably be described in terms of its multiple overlapping and sometimes competing *narratives*"[123] which constitute:

> the story of God and Israel from the Jewish side; the pagan stories about their gods and the world, and the implicit narratives around which individual pagans constructed their identities, from the Greco-Roman sides; and particularly the great narratives of empire both the large-scale ones . . . and the smaller ones of local culture.[124]

Stephen E. Fowl's study approaches the narrative aspect of Pauline writings by focusing on the ethical significance of the hymnic materials in Paul.[125] As the title of his book, *The Story of Christ in the Ethics of Paul*, suggests, his concern is to examine how the story of Christ that is narrated in the hymnic material undergirds Paul's ethical teachings and to show how ethical discourse is carried by constructing a narrative of the way the world is and how the community fits into this world.[126] Ben Witherington in *Paul's Narrative Thought World: The Tapestry of Tragedy and Triumph* argues that "*all* Paul's ideas, all his arguments, all his practical advice,

122. Ibid., 405.

123. Wright, *Paul in Fresh Perspective*, 6–7.

124. Ibid.

125. Fowl, *The Story of Christ*.

126. Ibid., 199; explaining the relationship between moral discourse and narrative he writes, "several ethicists have come to see that moral discourse does not draw its coherence from its relationship to a historical, universally recognized concepts such as goodness and justice. Rather, these concepts and the moral discourse which they sustain, are themselves sustained by the narrative employed by any given community to render an account of the way the world is and how the community fits into that world. The intelligibility of any community's moral discourse will, then, depend on the power of its narratives to provide a truthful account of the community's existence and identity, and on the community's faithfulness in ordering its own practice in a manner appropriate to such narrative" (200). Applying this to Paul, Fowl further observes that "in deploying the hymnic passages as he does, Paul makes a critical correlation between an interpretation of the traditions to which he and his audience are heirs, cast in the form of a narrative about Christ, and the specific situation faced by each audience" (201).

all his social arrangements are ultimately grounded in a story, a great deal of which" comes from Jewish sources (Hebrew scriptures and oral tradition).[127] Witherington formulates "four interrelated stories comprising one larger drama" and through them reads Paul.[128] Depending heavily on insight from previous narrative studies on Paul, Witherington did not advance the discussion on methodology.[129]

In recent years it is being increasingly discussed among Pauline scholars that Pauline writings carry narrative features that are an integral part of his thought.[130] Even when it is not used as analytical category, aspects of narrative features appear in the discussions and writings on Pauline studies.[131] Pauline scholars began to see Paul's theological discourse as "the product of a storied perception of reality."[132] However, the old hermeneutical question which Adams and Dunn bring back in recent projects that discuss narrative dynamics in Paul, still remains to be addressed in order to make use of a narrative approach in Paul.[133] They ask, "Where is the narrative?" Dunn poses the question in "either-or" format:

> Is the narrative to be found (1) *within* the text—to be read off the page, perhaps with some slight assemblage here and there, but nonetheless integral to the text? Or is it (2) *behind* the text, informing, enriching, and constraining the logic within the text's discourse? Or is it (3) *in front* of the text constructed by the reader from discursive elements in the text . . . ?[134]

127. Witherington, *Paul's Narrative*, 2.

128. The four stories which Witherington, *Paul's Narrative*, 5, sees underlying Paul's thought are "(1) the story of the world gone wrong; (2) the story of Israel in that world; (3) the story of Christ . . . (4) the story of Christians . . ."

129. Ibid., 7n11, credits the studies of Hays, Petersen, N. T. Wright, and Fowl for helping him to crystallize his reflections about "Paul's narrative thought world"; also see Matlock, "The Arrow and the Web," 47, who points out that Witherington bypasses questions of method; Fisk, review of Witherington, *Paul's Narrative*, 552–54, writes, "The book cries out for a theoretical discussion of method."

130. For recent assessment of the merits and demerits of narrative approach to Paul see the articles and responses published in Longenecker, *Narrative Dynamics*, 3; see also Longenecker, "Narrative Interest in the Study of Paul, 3. Also see Hays, *Echoes of Scripture*; idem, *The Faith of Jesus Christ*; Petersen, *Rediscovering Paul*; Wright, *The New Testament*; Witherington, *Paul's Narrative*.

131. Horrell, *An Introduction to the Study of Paul*, 55–56; Dunn, *The Theology of Paul*, 17–18.

132. Longenecker, "Narrative Interest," 5.

133. Adams, "Paul's Story of God and Creation," 19–43; Dunn, "The Narrative Approach to Paul," 217–32.

134. Dunn, "The Narrative Approach," 219; Adams, "Paul's Story of God and Creation," 41.

Such a way of posing the question gives the wrong impression that one has to choose only one of these options. The answer Adams gives to the similar question he raises, however, rightly goes beyond the "either-or" limitation: "narrative presence may be three-dimensional: narrative components may exist on all three levels": in the text, behind the text and in front of the text.[135] There are pre-textual components of the narrative to which the text refers or alludes, there are textual components of the narrative which the writer develops, and there are the "in front of" textual component which the readers construct based on the text, pre-textual components, and his/her own background and perception.

Assessed in light of this, narrative approaches to Paul, with the exception of Petersen, predominantly focus on "pre-textual" ingredients that factored into and influenced Paul's reflections at any given point."[136] This is evidenced by the language used—"Echoes of Scripture in the Letters of Paul,"[137] "Narrative Substructure,"[138] "Paul's Narrative Thought World"[139]—to characterize the nature of narrative in Paul.

While such an aspect of a narrative approach to Paul helps to situate what Paul is doing within the multiple, overlapping, and sometimes competing narrative thought world(s) that inform and shape his argument, it gives the impression that Paul is simply putting them together in his writings. It does not focus on the narrative thought, the discourse, which Paul himself is *creating* through his writings. It tends to imagine Paul as being "armed with the story waiting to be told" instead of being armed with "a story that lives in the telling."[140] Furthermore, the themes that are considered to form a narrative substructure for Pauline writings are very broad, bordering themes of biblical theology. From the outset there is a tendency to limit the interpretation of the text to these broad themes, thereby minimizing the possibility of other narrative themes within a given text.[141] Dunn notes that "[t]he danger in all these cases is of postulating an established form and deducing *from the*

135. Adams, "Paul's Story of God and Creation," 41.

136. Longenecker, "Narrative Interest," 4.

137. Hays, *Echoes of Scripture.*

138. Hays, *The Faith of Jesus Christ.*

139. Witherington, *Paul's Narrative.*

140. Matlock, "The Arrow and the Web," 53.

141. For instance see, Longenecker, "Narrative Interest," 12–13, for the themes chosen by a recent project that studies narrative approach(s) to Paul: God and creation, Israel, Jesus, and Paul; also see John Barclay, "Paul's Story," 134–35, who, commenting on N. T. Wright's use of "Jewish story" as "a grid within which the Pauline letters are read," writes, "[t]here are multiple echoes here of the emphasis in an earlier generation" on themes such as 'salvation history' as a grid within which to read Paul.

postulated form the function and significance of various particulars within the letter, sometimes even despite the internal logic of the letter itself."[142]

Responding to such concern Edward Adams writes, "Paul is not . . . just *mediating* a prior narrative. He is consciously *working* with it—reshaping, amplifying, and advancing the story" originating stories in his "*narratological* intentions" (emphasis original).[143] Admittedly, Hays and Petersen's methodological approach also signals the multi-location of narrative components. But they tend to emphasize one locale heavily to the extent that others are ignored. For instance Hays in his three foundational assumptions states that the inherent configurational dimension of stories "not only permits but also demands restatement and interpretation in non-narrative language," and that such "reflective restatement [and interpretation] does not simply repeat the plot (mythos) of the story."[144] In so doing he acknowledges that the reflective discourse develops the narrative that undergirds it. But he quickly emphasizes more the constraining power of the narrative that undergirds the text rather than how the text develops that narrative. Petersen, on the other hand, tends to emphasize the narrative that develops in the interaction between the text and the reader. He begins with the assertion that letters have stories and from these stories readers construct "the narrative worlds of both the letters and their stories."[145]

The readers' part has also to be brought into the mix of studying Paul's narrative construction. It is the assumption that Paul has about his audiences' familiarity with the narrative elements that allows him "to make allusive comments," being confident that "the audience will pick them up . . . and fill out the ellipses and shorthand references."[146] He writes to his mixed audiences' "horizon of expectation," expecting that they would fill in "the gaps of signification."[147] Dunn explains, "Just as we can assume that he did not have to spell out every point he wanted his audience to take from his letter; he could also confidently expect that key members of his churches would fill in the 'gaps of signification' that he no doubt deliberately left."[148]

142. Dunn, "The Narrative Approach," 221.

143. Adams, "Paul's Story of God and Creation," 34.

144. Hays, *The Faith of Jesus Christ*, 9.

145. Petersen, *Rediscovering Paul*, 43.

146. Dunn, "The Narrative Approach," 222.

147. For "horizon of expectation," see Jauss, *Toward an Aesthetic of Reception*; for "gaps of signification" see Iser, *The Implied Reader*; idem, *The Range of Interpretation*. For oral tradition and reception theory formulated in terms of "metonymic referencing-the part evoking the whole" see Foley, *Immanent Art*; for a discussion relating these to narrative approach in Paul see Dunn, "Narrative Approach," 222.

148. Dunn, "Narrative Approach," 223.

In the audiences' oral performance various allusive phrases and formulae trigger off associations in the hearers.[149]

As such, when Paul converses with his audience through his letters, he is not engaging them only at the level of theological reflection but also at the level of their narrative thought, sometimes to affirm and sometimes to change. He creates a narrative world in which he intends his readers to find their identity, a discourse that creates a sense of community, constructing identity for its community. Emphasizing the importance of the various aspects of the written discourse of early Christians for identity construction, Averil Cameron cogently states, "if ever there was a case of the construction of reality through text, such a case is provided by early Christianity."[150] She rightly argues that the early Christians "built themselves a new world" out of "the framework of Judaism, and living as they did in the Roman Empire and in the context of Greek philosophy, pagan practice, and contemporary social ideas."[151] They did this using both their practice ("a mode of living and a communal discipline") as well as their discourse.

This study proceeds to make use of narrative approaches to Paul by focusing on three levels: the prior multiple, overlapping, and competing narratives that form the context for the Pauline use of God as Father; the narrative(s) he constructs using the Fatherhood of God; and the possible self-understanding that emerges in his readers' interaction with the text. First, narrative element(s) within the texts in which Paul refers to God as Father is determined on the basis of allusions and intertextuality. Second, the identified element(s) is examined to determine to what specific "behind the text" category (Jewish, Roman, Greek, all, or some) it relates. Third, the similarity and difference between Pauline use and other previous as well as contemporary uses will be examined to determine how Paul configures the narrative element(s) compared to its original "behind the text" nature, and in so doing what narrative elements he sets in motion.

Kinship-Identity Approach (KIA)

The use of kinship-identity approach (KIA) is grounded on the recognition of the importance of kinship in the process of self-understanding and understanding of others in the ancient Mediterranean context and on the recognition that Paul's use of kinship signals identity-constructing features which can be examined within the larger contemporary context. It allows

149. Ibid., 222.

150. Cameron, *Christianity and the Rhetoric of Empire*, 21.

151. Ibid.

studying self-understanding and understanding of others as an ongoing dynamic process of negotiation and learning about self and others. It allows studying identity apart from particular debates and crisis situations in the early church, opening doors to examine a range of negotiations and perspectives in the process of understanding self and others.

To this end, KIA combines relevant features from anthropological insights of kinship, SIT, imperial critical approach, and from narrative approaches to Paul. From anthropological insights it focuses on (1) the realization that kinship is a process of being and becoming through networks of relationships that apply both to the contemporaries and the ancients, to spiritual as well as corporal, (2) the realization that the common features in its construction include a sense of sharing something—substance and/or spirit, nature and/or nurture, (3) its dynamic, versatile, and elastic nature that exhibits "purging, replacing, adding, and/or supplementing spiritual and corporeal components" that enables it to make a non-kin in one situation into kin in another, and kin in one situation into non-kin in another situation, (4) the awareness that it has social (it shapes patterns of relationships, networks, strategies, and behavior) as well as cultural (it helps conceptualize ideas of symbols, beliefs, rules, roles, and plans) significance, and (5) that it creates a narrative that identifies and sets an orienting framework in order to understand self and others, to define relationship categories, and to form and transform groups.

From elements of SIT, KIA looks for how the use of the kin term "Father" to refer to God creates identity. How does the use of the kinship term "Father" to address God advance the process of identity? Is it by assimilation and accommodation? Does it involve the process of estimation by which the significance of the new and old identities is evaluated? Does it relativise the group's past history and traditions? Does it redefine the value and meaning attached to a given tradition? Does it add new dimensions to the group's past history and traditions? Is there a group (in-group/out-group) identification element? Does it use polemical or non-polemical discourse?

To this, imperial critical approach adds the sensitivity to look for how the language Paul uses and the claims he makes in relation to his use of "Father" to refer to God negotiate with the overarching presence of Roman Empire. Does Paul's construction follow or mimic the Empire's construction of identity? Is there an element of dissension or conflict? Is there an element of difference in understanding the world, self, and others? In terms of narrative approach, attention will be given to examine what "pre-textual" ingredients factored into and influenced Paul's imaging of God as Father. Are these "pre-textual" ingredients overlapping or competing narratives? What is the place of the story of God and Israel from the Jewish side? What is the place of other Greco-Roman stories about themselves, their gods, and their world? How is it related to the narratives of the empire? In what ways has Paul reshaped, amplified, and/or advanced the "pre-textual" stories? What new dimension does he add? How would his mixed readers understand the narrative he creates? How does this contribute to their self-understanding?

In each of the following chapters, relevant aspects of these features of KIA will be used in examining texts which use the kin term "father" to refer to God/gods and emperors in order to examine God as Father in Paul within the kinship dynamics of the ancient Mediterranean world. Such assessment of Paul's use of God as Father holds considerable weight in deciphering the development of the self-understanding of early Christians. When Paul uses the term "Father" to refer to God he is doing so "within a range of shared understandings and values that condition any intended meaning"[152] of kinship relationship but at the same time "with a twist."[153] In order to bring out both the former and the latter sense, this study compares Paul's use of "Father" to refer to God with the use of father in the Greco-Roman world, the Hebrew Bible, and in ancient Judaism. Examining other texts using the same theoretical as well as interpretive approaches to survey the identity formation effect of the use of the kin term "father" will establish a solid ground for comparison and contrast.

152. Bossman, "Paul's Fictive Kinship Movement," 164.

153. Balch and Osiek, *Early Christian Families in Context*, xvi.

3

God(s), Empire, and Emperors as Fathers in the Early Roman Empire

Kinship and Identity Formation in the Early Roman Empire

In concluding his study on kinship diplomacy in the ancient world, Christopher P. Jones underlines the importance of kinship in the study of the rise of Rome to power and its comparable importance in study of the rise of Christianity. He writes,

> Diplomatic appeals to kinship between states, whether as small as the average *polis* or as large as the Roman Empire, existed through most of antiquity, and the permutations of such kinship diplomacy can serve as a platform from which to view political changes in the Graeco-Roman world. Of these the most salient is the rise of Rome to the status of the world power. Second only in importance is perhaps the rise of Christianity, with its competing vision of kinship within the church.[1]

The comparison shows not only the wide ranging-significance of kinship in the fabric of the Greco-Roman world but also the use of a common mode of identity expression between Christianity and the larger Greco-Roman world, laying a foundation for comparative study. Early Christians shared both the need for identity formation and features of identity formation with the emerging Empire (and those within it such as Jews, Roman

1. Jones, *Kinship Diplomacy*, 132.

philosophers, poets), which needed to define itself in a way that shaped the self-understandings of the people of the Empire.

Both the Empire and those within it, including the early Christians, were in the making. The Roman Empire with approximately sixty million people spanning from Gaul and Spain in the west to Judea and Syria in the east, from Britain in the north to North Africa in the south[2] was "unprecedented in geographical scale, filled with many ethnicities and languages, dominated by large cities and webbed by a well worn network of trade and military activity, and governed from the city of Rome."[3] A new self-perception of the Roman Empire with a common horizon began to be established during the reign of Augustus through identifiers of the Empire and the emperors using different media such as images, rituals, and writings.[4] Constructing identities involved shaping a particular culture in which "Greek" no longer meant what it used to mean and "Roman" no longer meant what it once meant.[5] The reason is that it is not only Rome, but also the rest of the world that is taken by Rome, that now has itself become "a zone in which quests for origin and myths of origin prospered as rarely before or since," creating "a shared high culture under one Empire."[6] Consequently, writings that create and sustain representations and memories in the form of stories that depict relationships and alleged benefits were widely used. Commenting on the success of Rome, Thomas N. Habinek writes, "one reason the Roman Empire succeeded as well as it did . . . is that it created, in large part through its literary system, a Roman nation that served as a unifying focus for an otherwise disparate and far flung Empire."[7]

2. Carter, *John and Empire*, 11.

3. Connolly, "Being Greek/Being Roman," 30.

4. Krasser, "Shifting Identities," 45, writes, "It was during Augustus' reign that the Roman Empire began to be established as a common horizon of self-perception. It is referred to on different levels and in different media," see also Dilke, *Greek and Roman Maps*, 41–53 for Agrippa's map of the Augustan Empire which is placed in the *Porticus Vipsania* in Rome; Rüpke, "Kalender und Öõffentlichkeit," 165–88, for the reformation and spreading of the Roman calendar; Katherine, "Universal Perspective on Historiography," 249–79, for the increasing number of universal histories and geographic works; Carter, *Matthew and Empire*, 29, who writes, "Decorated gates, arches, columns, statutes, buildings, coins, images, and various inscriptions spread the message. Likewise, temples and altars, liturgical practices such as prayers, vows, and sacrifices, celebrated with different intensity and levels of significance in different parts of the Empire, solicit submission and consent."

5. Hinds and Schmitz, "Constructing Identities," 3.

6. Ibid., 3.

7. Habinek, *The Politics of Latin Literature*, 6–7.

Just as Rome needed to define and understand itself as it moved from republic to Empire, from one location to multi-locations, early Christianity (and others within the Empire such as philosophers, poets, and historians) needed to define and understand itself as it moved from national Jewish faith to transnational Jew-Gentile faith with the event of Christ. Just as the imperial ideology that was disseminated through different media aimed at shaping the self-understandings of the people of the Empire, the earliest Christian writings had as the primary aim the "shaping of the life of the Christian communities."[8] While the Empire creates a common need and forms a common ground for early Christians and the Roman philosophers, historians, and poets' self-understanding, the early Christians had additional dimensions to their quest for identity, and these additional dimensions include things such as the event of Christ, the Jewish context, and the inclusion of gentiles, and all these within the reality of the Roman Empire.

As stated above, one of the modes of self-understanding and understanding of others commonly employed by the Roman Empire and those within it is the use of kinship language, an aspect of which is the use of the kin term "father" to refer to the Empire, the Roman emperors and god(s). While Paul refers to God as "our Father," and "Father," the Roman Empire was referred as *patria*, and the emperor as *pater patriae*, and the Roman philosophers, particularly the Stoic philosophers, referred to Zeus/Jupiter as "father."[9] Thus, forming the context for Paul's use of God as Father is both the use of the kin term "father" to refer to the Empire, the emperors, and to god(s) as well as the common social, political, and religious context that necessitated the need for the understanding/definition of self and others. In the first section of this chapter I will explore the use of "father" in reference to the Roman Empire and the Roman emperors, and in the second section, I will examine the use of the term "father" to refer to god(s) in Roman Stoic philosophers, with emphasis on Epictetus.

The Roman Empire as *Patria*

In the imaging of the emerging Roman Empire, the image of the nation as *patria* and the Roman emperors as *pater patriae* acquired increasing

8. Meeks, *The Moral World of Early Christians*, 12.

9. While god(s) are referred to as "father" in various Greco-Roman writings, from the early period of the Empire to the end of first century A.D., it is used extensively by the Stoic philosophers and particularly by Epictetus. This study will focus primarily on the detailed use of the term "father" to refer to Zeus in Epictetus and compare it with the use of the terms to refer to the Roman emperors.

significance. The narrative development that images the Empire as *patria* went hand in hand with similar discourse that presents the Roman emperors as "father." Using the kin term "father," the Roman Empire and its emperors created a network of relationships both with the ancients (such as Romulus) and the contemporaries throughout the Empire, presenting the Empire as "a big household presided over by the emperor."[10] Such a network of relationship constructs an orienting framework on how the diverse population of the Empire sees itself in relation to the Empire: the Empire as *patria*, the emperor as *pater patriae*, and the people of the Empire as children.

The use of the kinship concept of *patria* to refer to one's country was not new. In the Greco-Roman world, states are described as "fatherlands" symbolizing "the state as parent with the citizens as its children."[11] Stevenson explains that the description likely refers to the state in a physical as well as political sense based on the "fundamental perceptions of a benefactor-beneficiary relationship."[12] The benefactor-beneficiary relationship is conceived in such terms as "the produce of the land sustains life, the state brings people together as in a family, it affords protection, it is owed loyalty as to a parent, its laws regulate the lives of citizens and guard against civil discord, and so on."[13] Such connection with the land and state is extended to the leader "who might be thought to embody the state or to carry out its functions," and, "by extension referred to as a 'father.'"[14] However, the use of the kinship language, *patria*, to refer to the Roman Empire, is not limited to reflecting the benefactor-beneficiary relationship. It evokes the image of family and the concept of sharing, communality, and belongingness, which are the characteristic features of kinship. The patronage social relationship is presented with kinship construct and is given positive image.[15] Here we see what Osiek characterizes as "the

10. Carter, *John and Empire*, 12.

11. Stevenson, "Ideal Benefactor," 429; for examples see Liddell and Scott, "πάτρα," 1348.

12. Stevenson, "Ideal Benefactor," 430.

13. Ibid.

14. Ibid.; also see Kirk, "Peasant Wisdom," 35, who explains, "The Emperor was the ultimate patron (*pater patriae*), and he governed by granting favorable hearings and benefits (*beneficium principis*)—including tax relief and food distributions—to his network of clients bound to him by some form of personalized relationship (kinship or friendship), and through them as brokers of their networks of clients"; see also Alföōldy, *The Social History of Rome*, 101, who writes, "[t]he relationship of the subject masses to the emperor approximated to that of clientes to a powerful patronus. When Augustus took the title *pater patriae* in 2 BC the whole Empire became almost clients under his 'fatherly' protection."

15. For a good summary of characteristics of benefactor-beneficiary relationship see Neyrey, "God, Benefactor and Patron," 465–92, who explains that a "Kinship glaze"

meetings of ways" of the politics of patronage and politics of kinship.[16] Alan Kirk explains that kinship language provides the "paradigmatic trust relationships" for unequal patron-client relations.[17] Behind this merging of kinship and patronage stands an effort to create inward unity in terms of familial understanding that would promote communality and a sense of belongingness.[18] Such narrative through which the Empire aims at transforming aggregate ethnic groups into "a *communis patriae*" is predicated upon the emperors as "these were the men who provided and participated in the symbolic representation of *Romanitas*, who wrote and featured in the *res gestae populi Romani*, and who defined and defended the *orbis Romanus*."[19] *Pater patriae* referring to the Roman emperors in turn builds on the understanding of the Empire as a great *familia*.[20]

While Rome was referred to as *patria* long before the Empire, the tradition was taken and transferred to the republic and then to the Empire, acquiring increasing significance in the portrayal of the Empire. G. D. Williams describes well the growing significance the *patria* concept had for the construction of the sense of identity:

> Central to the literary creation of a Roman national consciousness and sense of identity in (and before) the Augustan age is the emotional draw of *patria*, whether in the positive Virgilian representation of Italy as the object of longing and as a near perfect utopia . . . or as the focus of Ovid's exilic nostalgia and lament . . . Through this deeply ingrained sense of attachment to Rome and *patria*, the Augustan writers contributed much to the consolidation of central power and to the intimidating capacity of the institutions which safeguard res Italas . . .[21]

---

by presenting a patron in familial terms "reduces the crassness of the exchange"; for further discussions see Eisenstadt and Komgtr, *Patrons, Clients and Friends*, 43–64; Malina, "Patron and Client," 143–45; Moxnes, *The Economy of the Kingdom*, 40–47; Wallace-Hadrill, *Patronage in Ancient Society*, 1–8.

16. Osiek, "The Politics of Patronage and the Politics of Kinship," 143–52.

17. Kirk, "Karl Polanyi, Marshall Sahlins, and the Study of Ancient Social Relations," 189, explains that the use of kinship language in portraying patron-client relationship presents the situation as "sharing, generosity," and friendship.

18. Eder, "Augustus and the Power of Tradition," 118.

19. Ando, *Imperial Ideology*, 19.

20. Severy, *Augustus and the Family*, 153–86; D'Angelo, "Abba and 'Father,'" 623; also see Hannestad, *Roman Art and Imperial Policy*, 44–55; Lacey, "Patria Potestas," 139.

21. Williams, *De Otio; De Brevitate Vitae*, 11; for Virgil's description of Italy as a an object of longing see *Aeneid*, 1.380, 7.122; Ovid in *Tristia*, 3.3.53 compares losing his country because of exile to an early death: "When I lost my native land, then must you think I perished; that was my earlier and harder death;" same translation will be followed unless otherwise noted.

As the Empire emerges, so does the comparably high significance of *patria* in association with it. In emerging years of the Empire, long before Augustus' acceptance of *pater patriae*, Cicero makes a distinction between a reference to *patria* as a local birth place and as the larger republic in the following text:

> Atticus: this place . . . Arpinum, is your own fatherland? Have you then two fatherlands? Or is our common fatherland (*patria communis*) the only one? Perhaps you think that Cato's fatherland was not Rome but Tusculum? Marcus: Surely I think that he and all natives of Italian towns have two fatherlands, one by nature and the other by citizenship . . . so we consider both the place where we were born our fatherland, and also the city into which we have been adopted. But that fatherland must stand first in our affection in which the name republic signifies the common citizenship of all of us. For her it is our duty to die, to her to give ourselves entirely, to place on her altar, and as it were, to dedicate to her service, all that we possess.[22]

Recognizing that there are two *patriae* for everyone, he attaches "pre-eminent" affection and significance to the "res publica," which he identifies as "the common citizenship of all of us" and the one that must "stand first" in their affection, to which they give their whole being and "dedicate to her service" all that they possess.

This sense is reflected as Ovid introduces his plea of forgiveness to the emperor by describing the Empire as "our father land, which is safe and secure with you as its parent."[23] Assessing Ovid's longing for *patria* Williams observes, "exiled by Augustus, himself of course *pater patriae* . . . Ovid for one paid for his non-conformity at Rome by his exclusion not just from the literal *patria* but from *patria* as the emotional center of his Roman 'belonging.'"[24] Ovid pleads mercy stating his longing even to be closer to the *patria* in which he has a share, though he is away.[25]

W. Eder points out that Augustus "identifies the *res publica* and *patria* as early as the first sentence of the *Res Gestae*, making each in its turn identical

22. Cicero, *De re publica; De Legibus*, 2.5.

23. Ovid, *Tristia* 2.157 and 181.

24. Williams, *De Otio; De Brevitate Vitae*, 11.

25. Ovid, *Tristia*, 2.181, "Spare me, father of our country! Do not, forgetful of this name, take from the hope that sometime I may appease thee! I pray not for return, even though we may believe that more than the prayer has oft been granted by the mighty gods. Grant me a milder and nearer place of exile, and large part of my punishment will be lightened"; see also *Tristia* 2.574; 3.1.49; 4.4.13.

with Rome."[26] Augustus' conclusion of the *Res Gestae* with his acclamation as *pater patriae* appears to show his emphasis on the transformation from *res publica* to *patria* on the basis of the broadest consensus.[27] It marks "the terminus of the road to the common fatherland" through his leadership.[28] Continuing the tradition, Valerius Maximus addresses Tiberius as the "surest salvation of the fatherland."[29] The extent to which this discourse had developed subsequently is seen in the writing of Pliny after a century. Describing Rome's mission as being the creation of a single *patria* "of all the races," Pliny highlights that it is "chosen by the providence of the gods to make heaven itself more glorious," with the purpose of uniting "scattered Empires," drawing "together in converse by community of language the jarring and uncouth tongues of so many nations, to give mankind civilization."[30]

Thus, the image of the Empire as *patria* is constructed in such a way that it provides an orienting framework that shapes and expresses "national consciousness and sense of identity," which is charged with a familial emotional draw that calls its children to give preeminent affection and significance to the *patria*, its ways and its leader.[31] As the following section will show, this familial depiction of the Empire is strengthened further with the imaging of the emperor as *pater patriae*.

The Roman Emperor as *Pater Patriae*

Pater Patriae: Pre-Augustan Use

The use of *pater patriae* to refer to the Roman emperors reached its peak in its Augustan use establishing a conceptual framework that solidly images the Empire as family that is characterized as *patria*, the emperor as *the head of the family*, and the people as children.[32] While Augustus' *pater patriae*

26. Eder, "Augustus and the Power of Tradition," 118.

27. Ibid., 17; for discussion on the transformation from res *republica* to *patria* see ibid., 111–22.

28. Eder, "Augustus and the Power of Tradition," 111–22.

29. Maximus, *Memorable Doings*, Preface to Book 1, p. 13.

30. Pliny, *Natural History*, 3.39–40.

31. Williams, *De Otio*, 11; Cicero, *De re publica*, 2.5.

32. For a standard discussion see A. Alföldi, *Der Vater des Vaterlandes im römischen Denken*; *Pater patriae* referring to the Roman emperors associating them with peace, victory, fertility, gods, and war is found on coins and inscriptions: for coins see Mattingly, *Coins of the Roman Empire in the British Museum*; for inscriptions see Sherk, *The Roman Empire*; for a discussion on the relationship between *Parnes Patriae* and *Pater patriae* see Chen, *God as Father*, 44, who notes that while *Parnes Patriae* is an older

is modeled in line with *the founders and saviors*,[33] linking Augustus to the father of the Roman clan, Aeneas,[34] and to the founding and saving fathers of Rome through mythology and achievement, its Augustan use went beyond anything known before. To aid our grasp of the extent to which the Augustan use of *pater patriae* is a peak towards which all the previous uses developed and in terms of which the subsequent uses were measured, I will begin with a discussion of the pre-Augustan uses of *pater patriae*. This will be followed by a discussion of developments in the Augustan and subsequent uses of *pater patriae*.

According to Virgil, Aeneas is the father of the entire Roman clan, in particular the father of the clan of Julii, who descended from Venus, the ancestor of Julius Caesar.[35] Virgil connects Augustus with Aeneas both in terms of kinship and in terms of achievement using the prediction of Jupiter, "the Father of men and gods." In response to the plea of Venus, Jupiter divinely predicts the founding and saving works of Aeneas, Romulus, and Caesar culminating in the coming of "Julius Augustus," through whom "wars shall cease and savage ages soften . . . The gates of war, grim with iron and close-fitting bars, shall be closed."[36] With such an account, Virgil por-

---

form, both *Parens Patriae* and *Pater patriae* are used in reference to the same person and hence probably are interchangeable designations, compare Suetonius, *Jul.* 76.1 and 85; regarding its background, based on Cicero's statements in *Cat.* 3.2. and *Rep* 1.64, 2.17 that saviors as well as benefactors of the community were called κτίστης; Weinstock, *Divus Julius*, 177, points out that the use of *Pater patriae* in the Roman Empire probably has its precedents in the experience of the Greeks calling "a benefactor or a savior a new κτίστης of their city"; Stevenson, "*Parens Patriae* and Livy's Camillus," 27, characterizes it as a polyvalent title which is "capable of evoking the traditional Greek antithesis between the good king (who behaves as a gentle father to his people) and the tyrant" and "was intended as positive characterization."

33. Severy, *Augustus and the Family*, 175; see also Stevenson, "Parens Patriae and Livy's Camillus," 27–46, who argues that Livy's portrayal of Camillus (Book 5) deliberately draws parallel between Camillus (who is called "Father" and the second founder of Rome sometime at the midpoint between Romulus, the founding father of Rome, and Augustus) and Augustus.

34. Ibid., 172–73, Severy writes, "Aeneas embodied both the familial tie to all Romans and the specialness of the Julians within that larger clan," and this is depicted in the forum.

35. Virgil, *Aeneid*, 1.257–96, 6.755–853.

36. Ibid., 1.95–96; for the divine lineage of Julius Caesar see Suetonius, *Divus Julius*, 6.1, where in the eulogy of his aunt Julia, Julius Caesar traces his ancestry: "My aunt Julia is descended on her mother's side from the Kings, and on her father's side is akin to the immortal Gods; for the Marcii Reges, from whom comes the name of her mother's family, are derived from Ancus Marcius, and the Julii, the family of which ours is a branch, from Venus. Our stock therefore has at once the sanctity of Kings, who among men are most powerful, and the claim to reverence which attaches to the Gods, to whom Kings themselves are subject."

trays Augustus as someone towards whom the divinely decreed Roman history was moving. As will be seen below, accepting this portrayal of himself, in the Augustan forum, one of the places where the *Res Gestae* inscription had to be posted, Augustus places himself in the midst of Aeneas and other founding fathers.

The kin term "father" is used as title of honor for Romans who were believed to be founders and saviors of their country and people by preserving and/or renewing its life.[37] Romulus is referred as "father" who founded the city of Rome and the whole community in about 716 B.C.[38] According to Ennius, Romulus "acted at the same time as guardian of the fatherland and as father and god, whereas others presented themselves as masters, lords, and kings.[39] Mourning for Romulus, the people talked among themselves, characterizing him: "O Romulus, godly Romulus, what a guardian of your country did the gods beget you! O father, O begetter, O blood sprung from the gods! . . . You it was who brought us forth into the world of light."[40] As such he is portrayed as having kinship with gods ("blood sprung from the gods"), he is considered as "*o pater, o genitor*," "father and founder of the community, the source and origin of its existence."[41] After his death he was "hailed as a god, son of god, and father of the city of Rome."[42]

As the founder of Rome, Romulus gained "a political topicality at Rome," whereby "whoever saved it from ruin and rebuilt it became a 'new founder', another Romulus."[43] Romulus' prototypicality is evident in Livy's comparative description of Camillus, who overcame the Gauls and upon

37. Quintilian, *The Institutio Oratoria*, 3.7.26 writes, "Cities are praised after the same fashion as men. The founder takes the place of the parent, and antiquity carries great authority, as for instance in the case of those whose inhabitants are said to be sprung from the soil. The virtues and vices revealed by their deeds are the same as in private individuals. The advantages arising from site or fortifications are however peculiar to cities. Their citizens enhance their fame just as children bring honour to their parents"; also see Chen, *God as Father*, 44–45, who explains, "A founding father is likened to a parent, and the citizens his children, because the community owes its very existence to its founder," the latter enhancing "the fame of their founding father" in a similar way "good children bring glory to their father's reputation"; Weinstock, *Divus Julius*, 201; see also Carter, *John and Empire*, 236.

38. Ennius, *Ann.* 113V; Cicero, *Div.* 1.3, and Livy 1.16.

39. Ennius, *Ann.* 117–21V; Cicero, *Rep.* 1.64; *Div* 1.3; Tacitus, *History*, 1.84 refers to him as "the Father and Founder of the city," who instituted "this order . . . which has lasted without interruption and without decay from the Kings down to the Emperors," which "we will bequeath to our descendants, as we have inherited it from our ancestors."

40. Ennius, *Ann.* 117–21V.

41. Carter, *John and Empire*, 236.

42. Livy, 1.16.3.

43. Weinstock, *Divus Julius*, 177.

his return was received "with sincere praise as a Romulus and as father of his country and second founder of his city."[44] Cicero was also honored as "the savior and founder of his country" and given the title of "father of his country" after defeating the Catalines. However, there was not a consensus in honoring Cicero with such designation, for some accused him of massacre against the Catalines. Such action was perceived as contrary to the expectation of a saving father who should exercise judgment and *clementia* in his saving activity.[45]

Following similar practice, Julius Caesar was also given the title of "father of his country" and was referred as "savior and refounder of Rome" in literary texts, on coins, and inscriptions, with the title *PP*.[46] To his achievement of bringing the civil war to an end, his clemency towards his enemies and political opponents tended to give a more balanced image to his title of *pater patriae* compared to Cicero who was accused of lacking such balance.[47] With the title *pater patriae*, he combined the virtue of *clementia*.[48] The extent to which this last aspect of *pater patriae* was accentuated is seen from the dedication of a temple to *Clementia Caesaris*, the personified goddess of *Clementia*.[49] In Caesar's oration, Anthony states that the title "Father of his country" was given to him as "a testimonial of his clemency."[50]

44. Livy, 5.49.7; 7.1.10.

45. Cicero, *Sest.* 109; Chen, *God as Father*, 47; this situation would form a crucial background to read Augustus' emphasis in the *Res Gestae* on how he was given the title emphasizing the consensus, he writes, "the senate and the equestrian order and the entire Roman people gave me the title Father of my Country," *Res Gestae*, 35; also see Chen, *God as Father*, 47; who observes that "[b]ecause of the controversy, the title *Parens Patriae* at best place him (Cicero) in the company of past savior-fathers, but unlike Augustus there was not much more Cicero could do to further benefit from it."

46. Appian, *Civil Wars*, 2.106, 2.144; Suetonius, *Julius Caesar*, 76.1; 85; Dio, *Roman History*, 44.4.4, says, "In addition to these remarkable privileges they named him father of his country, stamped this title on the coinage, voted to celebrate his birthday by public sacrifice, ordered that he should have a statue in the cities and in all the temples of Rome, and they set up two also on the *rostra*, one representing him as the saviour of the citizens and the other as the deliverer of the city from siege, and wearing the crowns customary for such achievements. They also resolved to build a temple of Concordia Nova, on the ground that it was through his efforts that they enjoyed peace, and to celebrate an annual festival in her honour"; see also Weinstock, *Divus Julius*, 180–84; 200–203; Chen, *God as Father*, 48.

47. Chen, *God as Father*, 48–49; Dio, *Roman History*, 43.5.2.

48. Weinstock, *Divus Julius*, 203; Chen, *God as Father*, 50, explains, "when coins were minted with the lettering "*Patri Patriae*" stamped inside an oak wreath, the implication was that the Father of the country was not merely a savior, but a *merciful* savior."

49. Chen, *God as Father*, 50; Dio, *Roman History*, 44.6.4.

50. Appian, *Civil Wars*, 2.144.

The title *pater patriae* came to mean more than glory as it is used to reinterpret and define Caesar's political power and his relationship to his subjects and his subjects to him.[51] This can be seen in Caesar's victory speech where he urges the senate and the Roman people to relate to him as father.[52] In his intention to create unity, he urges the senate and the Roman people to unite their interests "by forgetting all past events," by "beginning to love each other without suspicion" as if they were "new citizens." To this end he constructs kinship relationship, a sense of new community, whereby they relate to him and he to them as "father." As father he promises "forethought and solitude" and treatment of his subjects as his own children. Dio also explains this situation as a development.[53] While bestowing the title "father" used to signify a "betokened honor," it came to carry authority, "the authority which fathers once had over their children," portraying the emperors as loving fathers to their subjects and exhorting the subjects to "revere them as they would their fathers."[54] Explaining the change in relationship between Caesar and the Roman people, Weinstock writes, "they were now bound to him, like the son to his father, by pietas, they began to pray for his welfare and to swear by it, to worship his Genius as if it were their own."[55] Breaking such a bond came to result in the exclusion from the community, in the form of exile, where those who broke the bond "were not allowed to show themselves in his presence, just as a banished son was not allowed to return to the house of his father."[56]

51. Weinstock, *Divus Julius*, 204, writes, "Caesar was the first for whom the title meant more than glory."

52. His victory speech as given by Dio, *Roman History* , 43.17.2 reads, "Let us, therefore, Conscript Fathers, confidently unite our interests, forgetting all past events as if they had been brought to pass by some supernatural force, and beginning to love each other without suspicion as if we were in some sort new citizens. In this way you will conduct yourselves toward me as toward a father, enjoying the forethought and solicitude which I shall give you and fearing nothing unpleasant, and I will take thought for you as for my children, praying that only the noblest deeds may ever be accomplished by your exertions, and yet enduring perforce the limitations of human nature, exalting the good citizens by fitting honors and correcting the rest so far as that is possible."

53. Dio, *Roman History*, 53.18.3, "The term 'Father' perhaps gives them a certain authority over us all — the authority which fathers once had over their children; yet it did not signify this at first, but betokened honour, and served as an admonition both to them, that they should love their subjects as they would their children, and to their subjects, that they should revere them as they would their fathers."

54. In so doing it carries the long-standing characterization of good and bad king as father and tyrant. See Cicero, *Rep*. 1.64; Weinstock, *Divus Julius*, 200–201

55. Weinstock, *Divus Julius*, 204.

56. Ibid.

Thus, while in the use before Julius Caesar *pater patriae* emphasizes the "official gratitude on past achievements," in its use by Julius Caesar and in its Augustan use it constructs an ongoing present role.[57] As Chen rightly observes, however, Caesar did not live long enough "to fully exploit the propagandist potential of the title *Parens Patriae*."[58]

Pater Patriae: Augustan Use

While being modeled in accordance with the founding and saving fathers and mythological figures, the full-fledged utilization has come with Augustus, "the *Pater patriae* of the golden age, who had the opportunity and the administrative savvy to rid this prestigious title of controversy and impregnate it with further significance."[59] Chen is right in stating further that there was none before or after Augustus "who demonstrated what it means to be *Pater Patriae* in a more comprehensive way."[60] He imbued *pater patriae* not only with the concept of saving, founding, protecting, and providing for the community of the Roman Empire, hence a paterfamilias of a big household, but also with virtues of *auctoritas, clementia, liberalitas, pietas*, and *modestia*, becoming an "exemplary model for subsequent emperors to emulate."[61]

Consequently, in addition to the concepts of saving, founding, protecting, and providing that generally depict a paterfamilias of a big household, the use of *pater patriae* added features of virtue such as *auctoritas, clementia, liberalitas, pietas*, and *modestia*, which coalesce to form an orienting framework on how the people of the Empire should view the emperor.

Augustus moved scrupulously towards imaging himself as *pater patriae*. While the discourse of *patria* was being increasingly created, Augustus considered the title Romulus before taking Augustus, and then after continuous refusal in 2 B.C. accepted the title *pater patriae* in tears.[62] However,

57. Ando, *Imperial Ideology*, 400.

58. Chen, *God as Father*, 50.

59. Ibid., 51.

60. Ibid., 56.

61. Ibid., 56.

62. Suetonius, *Augustus*, 58, shows Augustus was given the title on three occasions: first by a deputation of the plebs to Augustus at Antium, which he declined; and then the acclamation in the theatre at Rome; and finally by the motion of Valerius Mesalla in the senate. The text reads, "The whole body of citizens with a sudden unanimous impulse proffered him the title of Father of his Country: first the Commons, by a deputation sent to Antium, and then because he declined it, again at Rome as he entered the theater, which they attended in throngs, all wearing laurel wreaths; the

he had been referred to as *pater patriae* long before he accepted the title from the senate in 2 B.C.[63] The significance of the image of *pater patriae* for Augustus can be seen from his acceptance speech, the place he gave it in the *Res Gestae*, the content leading to it, the form it is given (inscription), and the places it was to be inscribed (the entrance of Augustus house, the senate-house, and Forum Augustum), all of which together indicate the extent to which Augustus wanted, more than any other image, to portray the Empire as *patria*, himself as *pater patriae*, and the whole Roman people as children.[64] In his acceptance speech Augustus states that in this he has attained his "highest hopes," and that his further longing is only to "retain this same unanimous approval . . . to the very end of my life."[65]

In his list of achievements in *Res Gestae*, Augustus portrayed *pater patriae* as his crowning achievement, a culmination of his duty, which was conferred on him by the consensus of the senate, the equestrian order and "the entire Roman people," decreeing to make it visible and imposing as a climactic representation of the Empire and the emperor.[66] According to *Res Gestae*, leading to this honor are his selfless caring for the Empire in the form of protection, providence, and mercy on the one hand and unassuming at-

Senate afterwards in the House, not by a decree or by acclamation, but through Valerius Messala. He, speaking for the whole body, said: "Good fortune and divine favor attend thee and thy house, Caesar Augustus; for thus we feel that we are praying for lasting prosperity for our country and happiness for our city. The senate in accord with the people of Rome hails you Father of your Country"; all the remaining quotations from Suetonius are from same translation.

63. Weinstock, *Divus Julius*, 204; explains that Augustus was referred to as father of his country in literature, on inscriptions, and on coins long before he accepted the title officially in 2 B.C. after long reluctance; see also Dio, *Roman History*, 55.10.10; Horace, *Carm.* 1.2.50; 3.24.25; Ovid, *Fast.* 2.127–30.

64. Elsner, "Inventing Imperium," 52, describes the *Res Gestae* as "the signature of Empire, a written contract for the relations of center and periphery and an articulation of the place of the individual citizens within a new world system defined by the imperial 'I' which governs the verbs of the document;" Judge, *Social Pattern*, 32, describes the *Res Gestae* as "a manifesto addressed to the public, putting on permanent record the long list of benefits they had received, and the honours they had returned him, and culminating in the act that expressed the essential character of their relation to him, the formal and universal acknowledgment of him as *Pater patriae*."

65. Ibid.

66. "While I was administering my thirteenth consulship the senate and the equestrian order and the entire Roman people gave me the title of Father of my Country, and decreed that this title should be inscribed upon the vestibule of my house and in the senate-house and in the Forum Augustum beneath the quadriga erected in my honour by the decree of the senate. At the time of writing this I was in my seventy-sixth year," *Res Gestae Divi Augusti*, 35; the quotations in the following page from *Res Gestae* are from the same translation.

titude towards authority positions on the other. The *Res Gestae* depicts that Augustus found the Republic in chaos and restored it to peace and prosperity as he "restored liberty to the republic."[67] In terms of military protection, he raised an army by his own initiative and expense and not only brought to an end the era of "the tyranny of a faction" but also extended borders.[68] He brought peace on land and sea as it has never been before.[69] According to *Res Gestae* 12, the altar was built "to Pax Augusta" memorializing the peace he brought through his "successful operations." In order to promote this image, annual sacrifices were ordered to be made by "the magistrates and priests and Vestal virgins." To this, *Res Gestae* 13 adds that his achievement of peace is exceedingly superior. There is no consensus about the nature and extent of peace that was claimed to have been brought.[70] Hardwick presents the Augustan peace as having two main aspects: "civic accord at home," and "victory abroad."[71] The victory aspect presents Augustus in a more positive light as a deliverer and restorer.[72] This shows that peace is also intimately linked to the emperor and seen as a benefit brought by the emperor. This idea of Augustan peace was invoked later on by Vespasian who celebrated it in coins and by erecting the Temple of Peace.[73] This indicates that the notion of the emperor as the bringer of peace was not limited to Augustus as it was carried on later.

Augustus' multifaceted munificence is seen in the form of monetary gifts to the public and towns; financial assistance for the government; assistance in the form of distribution of grain; rebuilding the capital, the senate-house, several temples, aqueducts, and theaters; and organizing games and

67. Ibid., 1.

68. Ibid., 1 and 26.

69. In *Res Gestae*, 13, Augustus writes, "Janus Quirinus, which our ancestors ordered to be closed whenever there was peace, secured by victory, throughout the whole domain of the Roman people on land and sea, and which before my birth recorded to have been closed but twice in all since the foundation of the city, the senate ordered to be closed but twice in all since the foundation of the city, the senate ordered to be closed thrice while I was princeps"; also see *Res Gestae*, 25, 26; Ovid, *Tr.* 2.574, calls him "O Father, O protector and salvation of thy native land"; idem, Chen, *God as Father*, writes, "Having put an end to fourteen years of power struggle and civil wars after Caesar's death, Augustus was the savior of the Roman people and the founder of the *Pax Romana*."

70. See Hardwick, "Concepts of Peace," 335–68; Carter, *Matthew and Empire*, 30–33.

71 Hardwick, "Concepts of Peace," 338.

72. Ibid.

73. Josephus, *Jewish War*, 7.158–61.

restoring tradition.[74] He showed mercy to conquered foes.[75] He describes himself as doing all these with an unassuming attitude towards power as he did not accept the dictatorship, the position of the overseer of laws and morals, and the priesthood in the place of the living high priest, and as he "transferred the republic from [his] control to the will of the senate and the Roman people."[76] He concludes with a sense of satisfaction that while he "took precedence of all in rank," he did not possess any more power than those who were colleagues.[77]

The nuanced discourse of *pater patriae* is developed further through carefully chosen media of communication, namely, inscription and forum.[78] Suna Güven observes that inscriptions have an "active aspect . . . as interpretive instruments in *forming* history."[79] This is because as cultural products, depending on the context in which they are put, inscriptions have the capacity of forming "continuous and multiple narratives."[80] The reading of any inscription is influenced by the circumstances in which

74. He reformed the city of Rome through urban projects. Suetonius, *Aug.* 28, writes, "Since the city was not adorned as the dignity of the Empire demanded, and was exposed to flood and fire, he so beautified it that he could justly boast that he had found it built of brick and left it in marble. He made it safe too for the future, so far as human foresight could provide for this"; for his distribution of grain and money see *Res Gestae*, 15–18; through these actions as Chen, *God as Father*, 53, 55, observes, he transformed the concept of father "from private to the public sphere" as Rome was "transformed into a characteristically Augustan city to symbolize the *domus* of the *Pater patriae*."

75. *Res Gestae*, 3, "Wars, both civil and foreign, I undertook throughout the world, on sea and land, and when victorious I spared all citizens who sued for pardon. The foreign nations which could with safety be pardoned I preferred to save rather than to destroy"; in educating Nero, Seneca, *De Clementia* 1.10.3 presents Augustus as an example of *Clementia*: "Augustus was a good prince . . . he well deserved the name father, this we confess for no other reason than because he did not avenge with cruelty even the personal insults which usually sting a prince more than wrongs"; among the examples of Augustus' mercy which Seneca mentions are Augustus' mercy to his daughter Julia for committing adultery (*Clem*, 1.10.3–4), and to Cinna, the grandson of Pompey (*Clem*. 1.9.2–12).

76. See *Res Gestae*, 5, 6, 10, 34.

77. Ibid., 34.

78. Luce, "Livy, Augustus, and the Forum Augustum," 127–28, explains that while the Res Gestae "is a great comparative document," the Forum Augustum is "a great comparative monument," both of which carried a "continuous emphasis by statement and suggestion on those matters in which Augustus was the first to do this or that or did more than others or had done so with greater glory and greater effect"; also see Miles, "Communicating Culture, Identity and Power," 41, who points out that the *Res Gestae* was not only inscribed to the front of the tomb, but also "exported, translated and inscribed on the walls of temples dedicated to the imperial cult in the provinces."

79. Güven, "The Res Gestae," 30.

80. Ibid., 30.

it was raised, "the framing devices which were placed around it and the associations with the place of reading."[81] The *Res Gestae* inscription was placed in different places and was not limited to the Forum of Augustus. In fact, our main source of the *Res Gestae* inscription comes from the Roman province of Galatia in Asia Minor. While the tablets of *Res Gestae* have not been found, the text form of the *Res Gestae* in Greek and Latin was found in the sixteenth century at Ancyra in Galatia; since then Latin fragments have been found in Pisidian Antioch and a Greek fragment at Apollonia in Pisidia.[82] As such it was not "a static record chiseled in stone to serve recollection"; rather by its "architectonic design, which gave the narrative persuasive direction," it touches the senses and operates to generate the desired narrative.[83] By purporting to represent the contemporary history which is presented in a way that appeals to the minds and hearts of the Roman people, the *Res Gestae* was also meant to ensure "the continuity of Empire spawned and nurtured by Augustus."[84] Güven observes that the "culturally heterogeneous and geographically distant audiences were deftly guided to become related through the common bond of an imperial vision personified by the quintessential emperor, Augustus, and his lofty ideals, a vision (made) universal through the *Res Gestae*."[85]

In addition to the *Res Gestae* inscriptions, there are several inscriptions that identify Augustus as "Father of his country." In an inscription from Narbo, Gaul, that celebrates the dedication of the imperial cult with an altar to Augustus in A.D. 11, Augustus is again referred to as "Father of his country" three times (lines A7, B6, and B25).[86] In an inscription that honors the dead Gaius Caesar from Pisae in Etruria, Augustus is referred as "Father of his country" three times (lines 8, 47, 52).[87] Showing wide range of recognition of Augustus as father of the Empire, there is also an inscription from the city of Lepcis from the province of Africa where Augustus is referred to as "Father of his country" (line 2) celebrating its liberation from the Gaetulian War.[88]

81. Barrett, "Chronologies of Remembrance," 237.

82. See Sherk, *The Roman Empire*, 50; Güven, "The Res Gestae," 32.

83. Güven, "The Res Gestae," 30, 40; for studies on the role of inscription to produce different perceptions see Barrett, "Chronologies of Remembrance," 236–47; Holiday, "Roman Triumphal Paintings," 130–47.

84. Güven, "The Res Gestae," 30.

85. Ibid., 40.

86. Sherk, *The Roman Empire*, 12–13.

87. Ibid., 34–36.

88. Ibid., 37.

Furthermore, the *Res Gestae* was configured with the Forum of Augustus and all things associated with it.[89] Not only was the title *pater patriae* officially conferred on Augustus at the dedication of the Forum of Augustus in 2 B. C.,[90] but the forum also brings together what Zanker calls a "gallery of worthies" with the Julian family.[91] Augustus is placed in the midst of the greatest luminaries of Rome such as Aeneas and Romulus.[92] By including Aeneas and the Alban kings, "the legendary ancestors of the Julian gens," Augustus asserts kinship ties with all the Romans.[93] By being "a public tribute for Roman achievements," and a place where Augustus took over "both the role of *pater* and of guarantor of victory," the forum also depicts Augustus and his family as the culmination of Romulus' legacy as well as the Romans' history.[94] It was from this place that young men were enlisted in the military; provincial governors departed on campaign; the victorious would wear a victory emblem; the senate proclaimed war, peace, and triumphs; and it was a place where men of Augustus' family celebrated triumphs carrying the impression that they have a "unique responsibility for the military and for victory."[95] Enacting "the glory of the present" against "the background of the past,"[96] the forum became a "carefully constructed ideological space" which subsumed all of "Rome's past and future heroes . . . into the family of state of which Augustus was not just *imperator* but *pater*."[97] Such activities, symbolism, and imagery not only "changed the Roman experience of traditionally public and private spaces" but also "combined them to present a new conception of the state" in which a *pater* headed the *patria*.[98] This is how Augustus wanted "his countrymen to view the sweep of Roman history and his place in it."[99]

89. Luce, "Livy, Augustus, and the Forum Augustum," 127–28.

90. Zanker, *The Power of Images*, 129.

91. Ibid., 210.

92. Ibid.

93. Chaplin, *Livy's Exemplary History*, 177.

94. Severy, *Augustus and the Family*, 174; Chaplin, *Livy's Exemplary History*, 177.

95. Dio, *Roman History*, 55.10.2–3.

96. Ibid.; Suetonius, *Augustus*, 31.5; Pliny, *Natural History*, 22.13; Zanker, *The Power of Images*, 214.

97. Zanker, *The Power of Images*, 175.

98. Severy, *Augustus and the Family*, 180.

99. Luce, "Livy, Augustus, and the Forum Augustum," 123.

Pater Patriae: Increasing Role as Reflected in Roman Writers

The continuous development of the *pater patriae* narrative went hand in hand with a contemporaneous development of the conception of the role that is expected of the emperor as *pater patriae* as can be gleaned from the contemporary writers. Although Augustus accepted the *pater patriae* in 2 B.C., Horace who died in 8 B.C. depicts Augustus as father both by comparing him to Jupiter as well as by explaining the role of being a father to a city. Comparing Augustus' rule with Jupiter, Horace writes, "We believe thunderous Jupiter rules the sky" while "Augustus is considered a god on earth," through his accomplishment of expanding the Empire.[100] Horace asserts that Caesar rules with justice the earth, whether it is "the conquered Persians, menacing Latium, that he leads, in well-earned triumph, or the Seres and the Indians who lie beneath Eastern skies," under Jupiter, whom he describes as "Father, and guardian of the human race" to whom "the care of mighty Caesar was given."[101] Ando points out that Horace in addressing Jupiter as "father and guardian of the human race," "with Caesar next in power," not only honored Augustus but also "assigned him a heavy burden."[102] As a requirement for being referred to as "City Father," Horace attaches winning "fame among posterity" by reining in "unbridled license" that manifests itself in the form of lawlessness.[103] Addressing Caesar as "our prince and father," Horace urges Caesar to lead by providing continuous protection.[104] As such, for Horace, being a father of a city carries the responsibility of the "task of creating a people or community in which the civic order is secure and morality renewed."[105]

100. Horace, *Odes*, 3.5.1–5.

101. Ibid., 1.12.49–57: "Father and Protector of the human race, o son of Saturn, you have been entrusted by fate with the care of mighty Caesar; may you have Caesar as vice regent of your kingdom. Whether it be the Parthians . . . that he conquers and leads in a justified triumph, or the Chinese and Indians who live close to the region of the rising sun, he will rule in fairness over a happy world."

102. Ando, *Imperial Ideology*, 400; see Ovid, *Metamorphoses* 15.858–60; *Trist.* 2.215–18.

103. "O whoever would end impious killing, and civil disorder, and would desire to have 'City Father' inscribed on their statues, let them be braver, and rein in unbridled license, and win fame among posterity: since we, alas, for shame, filled with envy, hate chaste virtue, and only seek it when it's hidden from our eyes," Horace, *Carm.* 3.24.25–29.

104. Horace, *Odes* 1.2.50.

105. Carter, *John and Empire*, 241.

Ovid, who outlived Augustus and had the opportunity to witness the development of the *pater patriae* narrative past 2 B.C., repeatedly uses the narrative to his advantage in his plea for mercy from Augustus. He writes,

> Holy Father of thy Country, this title hath been conferred on thee,
> by the people, by the senate, and by us, the knights.
> But history had already conferred it; yet didst thou also receive;
> though late, thy title true; long time hadst thou been the Father
> of the World.
> Thou bearest on earth the name Jupiter bears in high heaven: of
> men thou art the father, he of gods.[106]

Ovid extols Augustus as the "Father of the Country" and "the Father of the World," by the consensus of the senate, the people, and the knights and all the events leading to the granting of the title. He compares the role of Augustus as a father with Jupiter's fatherhood in heaven, the latter as father of gods, the former as father of people. He calls Romulus to give way for an exceeding accomplishment of Caesar Augustus that made Rome mighty:

> Romulus, thou must yield pride of place. Caesar by his guardian care makes great thy city walls; the walls thou gavest the city were such as Remus could o'erleap. Thy power was felt by Tatius, the little Cures, and Caenina; under Caesar's leadership whate'er the sun beholds on either side is Roman.[107]

Celebrating Augustus, Ovid not only compares Augustus' exceedingly superior task to Caesar but also compares him to Jupiter:

> Jupiter controls the heights of heaven,
> and the kingdoms of the triformed universe;
> but the earth is under Augustus' sway.
> Each is both sire and ruler.[108]

Indicating Augustus' ongoing fatherly role, Ovid uses expressions such as the world "depends on you," "the weight of Rome's name is not so light, pressing its burden on your shoulders," "the city and the guardianship of

106. Ovid, *Fasti*, 2.127–32; same translation for *Fasti* will be followed below unless otherwise noted.

107. Ibid., 2.133–36; continuing the comparison, Ovid in *Fasti* 2.137–44 writes, "You owned a little patch of conquered land: Caesar possesses all beneath Jupiter's heavens. You raped married women: under Caesar they are ordered to be chaste: you permitted the guilty your grove: he forbids them. Force was acceptable to you: under Caesar the laws flourish. You had the title Master: he bears the name of Prince. Remus accused you, while he pardons his enemies. Your father deified you: he deified his father."

108. Ovid, *Metamorphoses*, 15.857–61.

your laws," the "morality you desire to be yours," the peace "that you grant the nations" by waging "restless wars," and all "wearies you."[109] In his plea for mercy, admitting his failures, Ovid entreats Augustus to act in the likeness of Jupiter who does not hurl "his lightning, every time men sinned" for that would have made him weaponless long ago, but who when through thunder he "scared the world with noise, he scatters the rain-clouds and clears the air."[110] Such character makes it right "to call him the father and ruler of the gods" and "it is right the wide world owns nothing greater than Jove."[111] Applying this to Augustus, Ovid writes, "You also, since you're called father and ruler of the land, should follow the ways of the god with the same title" indicating that "fatherhood is now a role rather than a title."[112]

According to Suetonius, Augustus himself in his acceptance speech of *pater patriae* highlights this ongoing aspect of the title: "Having realized the object of my prayers, Conscript Fathers, for what am I now to pray to the immortal gods, other than that it be permitted to me to retain this your consensus until the end of my life."[113] After mentioning the titles given to Augustus, "Great," "Blessed," and "August," Seneca writes that "we have given the name *pater patriae* [to our princeps] so that he should know that a father's power has been given to him, constraining him to think of his children's interests and placing his after theirs."[114] Assessing the past and the present of the Roman Empire's administrative success, Strabo in his *Geography* states that it was "by turning it (the administration) over to one man, as to a father" that "Romans and their allies thrived in such peace and plenty as that which was afforded them by Augustus Caesar, from the time he assumed the absolute authority."[115]

109 Ovid., *Tristia* 2.215–36, expressing the ongoing demand, Ovid writes, "so whilst thou dost gaze about upon the world that depends upon thee . . . Shouldst you, forsooth, the prince of the world, abandon thy post and read songs of mine set to unequal measure. That weight of the Roman name does not lay so light a burden upon your shoulders . . . Now Pannonia, now the Illyrian coast's to be subdued by thee, now the wars in Raetia or Thrace bring thee anxiety; now the Armenian seeks peace, now the Parthian Horseman extends to thee with timorous hand his bow and the standards once he seized . . ."; see also *Tristia*, 2.225–30.

110. Ibid., 2.36, 38–39.

111. Ibid., 2.40–41.

112. Ibid., 2.42–43; Ando, *Imperial Ideology*, 401; Ovid, *Tristia*, 2.157, 181.

113. Suetonius, *Augustus*, 58.1–2.

114. Seneca, *Clemency*, 1.14.2.

115. The full quotation reads: "But it were a difficult thing to administer so great a dominion otherwise than by turning it over to one man, as to a father; at all events, never have the Romans and their allies thrived in such peace and plenty as that which was afforded them by Augustus Caesar, from the time he assumed the absolute authority,

Pater Patriae: Post-Augustan Use

Although it was with Augustus that its multifaceted image reached a peak, *pater patriae* continued to shape self-portrayal of the Empire and its emperor. Although, according to Suetonius, Tiberius declined the title of "father of his country," the attributes of *pater patriae* were used to describe him. Valerius Maximus describes him as the "surest salvation of the fatherland, in whose charge the unanimous will of gods and men has placed the governance of land and sea, by whose celestial providence" virtues are fostered and "the vices most sternly punished."[116] He depicts him as "our leader and parent" (5.5.3), "our leader and savior," (8.13), "our leader and father" who holds "in his saving hand" "the reins of Roman Empire," (9.11.4). An inscription on a stone stele from Gytheion in Laconia which enumerates a law for a festival of the imperial cult refers to Tiberius as "Father of his country" (line 3).[117]

Gaius Caligula is referred to as *pater patriae* on coins from Gaul, Rome, and Caesarea.[118] Claudius is referred to as "father of his country" on coins from Rome, Asia Minor, Caesarea, and Gaul,[119] and on inscriptions.[120] He is identified as "Father of his country" on an inscription from Rusellae in Etruria in 45–46 A.D. that celebrates Claudius' victory in Britain (line 7), an inscription from Tridentum in Italy that has Claudius granting Roman citizenship in 46 A.D. (line 8), and a milestone from Feltria in northern Italy referring to Claudius' repairs of road in 47 A.D. (line 7). A letter of Claudius on a marble block in Miletus in 48–49 A.D. (line 3), an inscription from Stabiae in Italy in 52 A.D. containing a letter from Claudius that discharges a sailor, and an inscription in Rome at Porta Praenestina in 52–53 A.D. that refers to the building of the Aqua Claudia all identify him as "Father of his country."[121] Nero is referred as "Father of his country" in an inscription from Charput in Aremenia Minor (line 3), from Philippopolis in Thrace (line 10), and an inscription containing a decree of Akraiphia in Boetia celebrating

and is now being afforded them by his son and successor, Tiberius, who is making Augustus the model of his administration and decrees, as are his children, Germanicus and Drusus, who are assisting their father," Strabo, *Geography*, 6.4.2; See also Dio, *Roman History*, 53.18.3.

116. Maximus, *Memorable Doings* Preface to Book I.

117. Sherk, *The Roman Empire*, 53.

118. Mattingly, *Coins*, vol. 1, 150, 152, 157, 158.

119. Ibid., 170, 172–74, 190–92.

120. Sherk, *The Roman Empire*, 94–96, 99.

121. Ibid., 94, 95, 96, 99 and 100 respectively.

an exemption from taxation granted by Nero.[122] He is also referred to as PP on coins from Rome and Gaul.[123] Vespasian, Titus, and Domitian were also referred as "Father of the Fatherland."[124]

In summary, the above growing role expectations, the continued use of *pater patriae* for Roman emperors, as well as the portrayal of the Empire as *patria* spanning at least a century, to the extent that Pliny claims it as Rome's greatest mission and achievement, shows how the kinship narrative based on the kin term "father" developed to provide an orienting framework to the people of the Roman Empire.

The concept of *patria* which was used to symbolize Rome as parent and its citizens as children was transferred to the Empire which came to be depicted as a single *patria*. It is portrayed as divinely chosen with an expectation of bigger mission ("the purpose of uniting scattered Empires . . . to give mankind civilization,") which it superbly achieved in terms of uniting, providing (land, produce, justice, peace), and regulating and protecting its citizens. It soundly images the Empire as family, a big household. While carrying aspects of relationship that go with the concept of benefactor-beneficiary, it evokes the image of family (communality, belongingness) and the concept of sharing which are characteristic features of kinship. As such it generates a sense of community, transforming aggregate people into "a *communis patria*," creating the feeling of attachment that calls for unsurpassed affection and devotion. Linking with the missions of the past founders and saviors of Rome to establish and lead a community, *patria* as applied to the Empire boasts the culmination of that dream in the generation of the Roman Empire.

The concept of *Pater Patria* as applied to Augustus is packed with a narrative that promotes the image of Empire as *patria* and its emperors as the ones who not only made it possible (begetters, source, and origin who brought it forth) but also as the ones who sustain it. The discourse is imbued with the concept of founding, saving, protecting, and providing for the community of the Empire.[125]

122. Ibid., 106–7, and 110–12 respectively. For inscription referring to Vespasian and Titus as "Father of the country," see pp. 126–30, 134–35 respectively.

123. Mattingly, *Coins*, 200–284, coin numbers 9, 10, 12–51, 79–80, 114–21, 122–30, 130–224, 251–60.

124. For Vespasian, see Sherk, *The Roman Empire*, 126–30; for Titus, ibid., 134–35; for Domition, see Mattingly, *Coins*, vol. 2, 297–420, nos. 7–35, 37–50A, 70–129A, 139–40, 145–70, 176–98, 200–207, 214–26, 230–37, 248, 260–86, 323–67, 371–452, 458–80, 512–20; and Sherk, *The Roman Empire*, 137; also see Pliny the Younger, *Letters, and Panegyricus*, 2.3, 10.6, 42.3, 57.5, 57.1; cf. Carter, *John and Empire*, 254.

125. Chen, *God as Father*, 56.

Such discourse that depicts the duty and beneficence of *pater patriae* in comparable terms only to gods was disseminated through strategic media. It gave the Empire a kinship identity that highlights communality, belongingness, and sharing. The dynamic and versatile nature of kinship is exploited to make "non-kins" kin. As the Empire expanded and ethnic groups with different traditions and backgrounds are added, the discourse of the new family provides new dimension to their previous background to aid them to develop their self-understanding in relation to the new phenomenon called the Roman Empire.

The extent to which this kinship narrative relativizes and redefines the previous self-understanding of each people that was brought together under the Empire is difficult to assess and may vary from place to place and from social status to social status. However, its presence was felt abundantly in the form of texts, inscriptions, coins, and emperor cults with the intent of providing an orienting framework to an ongoing self-understanding, promoting trust and making exhortation to suspend suspicions.[126] It undeniably creates a family/community image which "presents a complex and idealized relationship" between the *patria* and *pater patriae* on one hand, and the children on the other. It aims to shape the life in the Empire in such a way that while the children are "expected to render obedience and duty," the *patria* and *pater patriae* are expected to "lovingly seek their well-being, reward their efforts . . . punish the non-compliant, and inherit the task of preserving, whether by government or military action, the life of the city and its Empire."[127]

While the growing family image based on the kin term "father" brings together the idea of benefactor-beneficiary (patronage) with kinship, the question still remains as to what extent the kinship concept succeeded in embellishing the patronage with communal image. Addressing such question Ando rightly notes, "[t]he provincial population of the Empire was probably never unanimous in its appreciation of Rome, nor would all residents of the Empire have agreed on every detail of their shared culture."[128] Then he expresses the inherent ambivalence stating that "[t]he existence of the *communis Patria* relied not on any genuine identity between the patriotic sentiments of its members, but on their faith in the existence of such an identity," which is partly "predicated upon the universality of Rome and her emperors."[129] They believe that such identity as *communis patria* (as well as

126. Carter, *John and Empire*, 237–38.

127. Ibid.

128. Ando, *Imperial Ideology*, 19.

129. Ibid.

the idea of the *pater patriae*) exists, but they do not necessarily share in the "patriotic sentiments" that it promotes. As J. H. Elliot observes, the reality of "the principate was anything but the harmonious interaction of benevolent father with household servants and subjects."[130] But still "the idea of a common family . . . apparently served the interests and aims of *patres* and *patria* alike"[131] as "the established notion of an emperor as father" is used "to secure and insure the perpetual memory of a benevolent ruler (however despotic), the filial loyalty and subservience of subjects (however exploited)."[132]

Commenting on the use of "father" to refer to the Roman emperor, Stevenson explains that such characterizations "both reflect and perpetuate the inherent ambivalence" between the ideal image the term generates and the daily reality of life under the emperor/Empire. There is a gap between the expectation that "an ideal benefactor is totally unselfish, and an ideal beneficiary is genuinely grateful" as "neither was the emperor completely selfless, nor the subjects consistently loyal."[133] This ambivalent situation compels "the two sides to negotiate the power differential between them."[134]

As will be seen in the next section, this ambivalence is exploited by the Stoics, particularly Epictetus, who compares the fatherhood of Caesar with Zeus, and Rome's universality with the universality of humanity and depicts Zeus' fatherhood and the universality of humanity as being by far superior to the *pater patriae* of Roman emperors and the *patria* of the Roman Empire. A similar trend can be observed in Paul in his depiction of God as Father who together with the Lord Jesus Christ bestows grace and peace on the followers of Jesus.

God(s) as Father in Roman Stoics

While the Roman Empire and emperors construct a narrative based on kinship language that images the Empire as a big household with the emperor as the father, the Stoics construct a discourse of an even a bigger household of humanity, namely cosmopolitan universalism. It maps out the world and

130. Elliot, *A Home for the Homeless*, 178; Chen, *God as Father*, 59, Chen, following a similar conclusion, writes, "Indeed, the image of father is a powerful one with which to view the emperor, because it is based on the time-honored ideals of kinship, loyalty, and paternal authority. On the surface, the idea of *Pater patriae* allows Augustus to promote patriotism and make claim to a benign authority. Behind that façade, his manipulation of paternal power might have yielded a more ambivalent picture."

131. Elliot, *A Home for the Homeless*, 178.

132. Ibid.

133. Chen, *God as Father*, 58.

134. Ibid.

humanity's place in it in terms of divine-human kinship which is expressed in terms of the fatherhood of god(s). By locating humanity's place within cosmopolitan universalism, it relativizes one's previous identity with respect to one's birth place as well as with respect to kinship to Caesar. In order to examine the identity formation role of the use of the term "father" to refer to god(s) in relation to similar use of kinship language, I will explore the narrative created, the image constructed, the kinship features used, and how such uses were meant to shape life.

The concept of kinship, both between humanity and god(s) and among humanity itself, is central to the philosophical discourse of Stoicism, which was one of the three leading philosophical movements of the Hellenistic and Roman period, the others being Epicureanism and Skepticism.[135] Stoicism is conventionally classified into three phases: early Stoicism, middle Stoicism, and Roman Stoicism.[136] The major tenets of Stoicism which follow the three recognized divisions of philosophy (physics/cosmology, logic, and ethics)[137] and the theme of the unity of humankind[138] remained the same while the emphasis and teaching about each varied from period to period and from one teacher to another. Roman Stoicism focused more on ethics

135. Stoicism began through the teaching of Zeno of Citium in Cyprus (334–262 B.C.) on a *stoa* (porch). He was then succeeded by Cleanthes (331–231 B.C.), and Chrysippus (280–206 B.C.). While Cleanthes is widely known for his short "Hymn to Zeus," Chrysippus is known for systematically laying down the tenets of the Stoic teachings, the basic structure of which, physics, logic, and ethics remained the fundamental frame for the subsequent Stoic teachings. The second phase of Stoicism, middle Stoicism, was largely carried by Panaetius (185–10 B.C.) and Posidonius (135–50 B.C.) and formed the basis of Cicero's philosophical treatises on Stoicism. The third phase, Roman Stoicism, extends from second century B.C. to second century A.D. and has Seneca (A.D. 1–65), Musonius Rufus (A.D. 30–100), Epictetus (A.D. 55–135) and Marcus Aurelius (A.D. 121–80) as its leading figures; see Inwood, *The Cambridge Companion to the Stoics*; idem, "Stoicism," 222–51; Belliotti, *Roman Philosophy and the Good Life*, 61–96, 181–221; Morford, *The Roman Philosophers*; Long and Sedley, *The Hellenistic Philosophers*; Algra et al., *The Cambridge History of Hellenistic Philosophy*; Audi, *The Cambridge Dictionary of Philosophy*, 768.

136. *The Cambridge Dictionary of Philosophy*, 768; Colish, *The Stoic Tradition*, 7.

137. Laertius, *Lives of Eminent Philosophers*, 7.39, writes, "The Stoics divide reason according to philosophy, into three parts; and say that one part relates to natural philosophy, one to ethics, and one to logic. And Zenon, the Citiaean, was the first who made this division, in his treatise on Reason; and he was followed in it by Chrysippus . . .;" however, see Inwood, "Stoicism," 225 and also White, "Stoic Natural Philosophy (Physics and Cosmology)," 124, who explain that Xenocrates, Plato's follower, was the first to divide philosophy formally into three parts, the Stoics from Zeno on adopting this division.

138. Plutarch, *Moralia*, 329; also see Baldry, *The Unity of Mankind*, 151–66, 177–94, who traces the theme of the universal unity of humanity from early Stoics through the middle Stoics; Shaw, "The Divine Economy," 28; Connolly, "Being Greek/Being Roman," 36.

than on physics and logic. As Colish noted, however, all the three phases of Stoicism agree that "ethics is the most important part of philosophy, and that physics and logic should be studied not merely for their own intrinsic interest but for the light which they shed on ethics."[139] Ethics is "integrally and organically related to physics."[140]

With such an emphasis, the Stoics in general and the Roman Stoics in particular created discourse that sets an orienting framework that has bearing on the process of being and becoming. Scholars have noted broadly that through various means philosophers not only conveyed "their own understanding of the goal (*telos*) of human life and how to achieve it" but, in a similar way to early Christianity, they were engaged in creating an understanding of self and others.[141] Philosophers commonly thought that they could effect change in their listeners through their teaching by turning them to the rational life or by converting them to philosophy (i.e., to educate them morally)."[142] The philosophers' words are considered to be like "arrows aimed at the soul" that focus on "purifying and curing listeners by bringing them to their senses."[143] They speak and teach with the expectation that the person who listens changes, responding both emotionally and rationally.[144]

In the need to define identity during the Roman Empire, Roman Stoicism brought together the long standing view of cosmopolitan universalism that is based on divine–human kinship, divine–human fatherhood, and the ensuing human–human kinship. The Stoic language of cosmopolitan universalism "suited itself to Roman (Empire) needs and purposes" that seek to integrate the different population into one big household, and as such "Hellenistic Stoicism becomes the enabler and justifier of the Roman Empire."[145] At the same time, however, as Schofield notes, in the discussions

139. Colish, *The Stoic Tradition*, 23.

140. Ibid.; on the relationship between these parts of Stoic philosophy, Diogenes Laertius, *Lives of Eminent Philosophers*, 7.40, writes, "No single part, some Stoics declare, is independent of any other part, but all blend together. Nor was it unusual to teach them separately."

141. Ascough, *What Are They Saying About The Formation of Pauline Churches?* 32; for comparative assessment of the relationship between early Christianity and Hellenistic philosophy see Nock, *Conversion*; Conzelmann, "Paulus und die Weisheit," 231–44; idem "Luke's Place in the Development of Early Christianity," 298–316; Judge, *The Social Pattern*, chap. 4; Wilken, "Collegia, Philosophical Schools and Theology," Malherbe, *Paul and the Thessalonians*; Engberg-Pedersen, *Paul and the Stoics*.

142. Malherbe, *Paul and the Thessalonians*, 21.

143. Ibid., 23.

144. Ibid., 24–25; Musonius Rufus, *Fragment*, 49.

145. Connolly, "Being Greek/Being Roman," 37; see Gill, "The School in the Roman Empire," 35.

of the Roman Stoics "the claims of citizenship of the universe come to dwarf those of the existing societies . . . (as) the cosmic perspective increasingly overshadows the vantage point of ordinary life."[146] The Stoic teaching of cosmopolitan universalism as such cuts both ways.

Connolly writes, "a central tenet of Stoicism was that all men (humankind) are, in some sense, universal brothers (and sisters); the corollary to this was that the traditional identity framework of city-state or kingdom cannot hold."[147] This universalistic bent was not new to the Roman Stoics. The Hellenistic kingdoms brought changes in political values and actions within cities creating "a new political framework . . . for the old *poleis*."[148] A change from city-state to imperial state "created critical problems of identification, not just (perhaps least) for the subjects, but also for the ruling orders that found themselves cast into a political realm in which there were few reliable signposts provided by the world of the city-state."[149] The Stoics' concept that "the ultimate frame of reference for individual men was not the *polis* or any of its moral or political ideas . . . but rather the universe . . ."[150] began to serve as an orienting framework. Shaw points out that such a conception would lead people to "identify with a social and political framework larger than the *polis* in the process of being subjects" under the new Empire.[151] The following assessment of Zeno's universalism by Plutarch noticeably reflects this situation:

> The much-admired Republic of Zeno, the founder of the Stoic sect, may be summed up in this one main principle: that all the inhabitants of this world of ours should not live differentiated by their respective rules of justice into separate cities and communities, but that we should consider all [humanity] to be of one community and one polity, and that we should have a common life and an order common to us all, even as a herd that feeds together and shares the pasturage of a common field. This Zeno wrote, giving shape to a dream or, as it were, shadowy picture of a well-ordered and philosophic commonwealth; but it was Alexander who gave effect to the idea.[152]

146. Schofield, "Social and Political Thought," 770.
147. Connolly, "Being Greek/Being Roman," 36.
148. Shaw, "The Divine Economy," 24.
149. Ibid., 25–26.
150. Ibid., 16–54, 35; Connolly, "Being Greek/Being Roman," 36.
151. Shaw, "The Divine Economy," 28–29.
152. Plutarch, *Moralia*, 329.

Consideration such as this images the Stoic universalism in terms of "all inhabitants of this world" becoming "one community and one polity" who have "a common life and an order common" to all as evidenced by Alexander's Empire. This lends itself well for the Roman Empire's portrayal of itself as a big household with one community, one polity, order, and a common life. What the application of this aspect of Stoic universalism—the idea that all humanity are "members of a notional community or 'city'"—actually seems to have done is that it relieved the Empire from the limitation exerted on one's self-understanding by being a member of a *polis*.[153]

However, this is only a limited application of the Stoic universalism. As will be seen below, in Seneca as well as in Epictetus, the same idea of Stoic universalism undercuts the Roman Empire's portrayal of itself as the ideal *patria*. What is seen in Seneca and Epictetus is the application of the broader sense of Stoic universalism. Schofield explains, "(a)s developed by Chrysippus, the ideal city of Zeno's Republic is indeed in a sense a universal community, whose citizens are . . . *kosmopolitia*. However, it is universal not in that it includes all mankind (humanity), but because it is made up of gods and sages wherever they may be."[154] Accordingly, Stoic universal community is not simply "a wider community, but a wholly different sort of 'community'"[155] the membership of which is limited to the wise.[156] Lisa Hill writing on Roman Stoics' universalism explains that "membership of the universal state is limited to those who exercise *humanitas*, those who apprehended and comply with the laws of reason and of nature, rather than the contingent and variable mores of a single locality."[157] In a similar vein, in her comparative study of the

153. Ibid., Shaw, "The Divine Economy," 28–29; Baldry, *The Unity of Mankind*, 151–66, 177–94.

154. Schofield, "Social and Political Thought," 768.

155. Ibid.

156. Baldry, *The Unity of Mankind*, 155, 157, 165.

157. Hill, "The Two Republicae of the Roman Stoics," 68; see also Pangle, " Socratic Cosmopolitanism," 241–42, who explains well in writing, "the life of the wise, because it is a life centered on devotion to moral virtue as the end in itself, is a life spent chiefly in performance of the "perfect duties." By thus living in obedience to the law of nature or reason, the wise man becomes the true friend of the gods, and their only true priest, the knower of the proper sacrifices, to whom the gods communicate divinations of the future through dreams and scientific auguries, and whose soul they may preserve after death, at least until the next cosmic conflagration. The wise philosopher becomes a citizen in a cosmic city or world-state ruled by the gods; he thereby transcends in an important measure the tawdry demi-monde of the many parochial cities with their ethnic divisions and prejudices, wars, slavery, traditional families, and conventional private property. From this trans-national, sublime, spiritual height the wise man looks down in con-tempt, though he sees it his duty to participate in politics and family life in his own pure and sententious manner."

concept of body in Stoics and Paul, Michelle Lee writes, "while Stoic humanity is indeed universal, it is 'exclusive' in its own particular way, in that it excludes those who do not participate in reason . . ."[158] Thus, the Stoic universalism is on one hand broader than the Roman Empire as it includes humanity and god(s), but on the other hand it is narrower than the Roman Empire as it is limited to the wise. This ambivalent nature of Stoic universalism might have allowed the Roman Stoics to have a range of relationship with the Roman emperors. On one hand Roman Stoic philosophers worked closely with the Roman emperors—Augustus had two Stoic philosophers (Athenodorus of Tarsus and Arius Didymus) as moral advisors and teachers of philosophy, Nero had Seneca as a tutor and then as adviser, Musonius Rufus was a Roman "knight," which is the second highest social order, and was engaged in politics. On the other hand, Seneca was suspected of conspiring against Nero and was exiled, and Musonius Rufus was exiled twice both under Vespasian and Nero, and Epictetus was exiled by Domitian.[159]

The Stoics' teaching of the unity of humankind and their ensuing ethical teaching is based on divine–human kinship, the fatherhood of god, and the ensuing human–human kinship.[160] As Dobbin comments, while "[t]he kinship of god and man was an axiom of Graeco-Roman religion," the Stoics identify this kinship in terms of having a portion of the divine, which is identified as "reason," as something common between humanity and god.[161] To ascend and assimilate "to god or to the divine half" is meant for

158. Lee, *Paul, the Stoics, and the Body of Christ*, 13–14; she further notes, "this provides a striking similarity with Paul's method of defining the community because both are composed of those who partake of reason, although for the Christians it is a specific type of reason, the νοῦς Χριστοῦ. Paul's and Seneca's notions of fellowship are more similar than may appear at first glance"; for the opposite view see Sevenster, *Paul and Seneca*, 1, who argues that Paul's view of fellowship and the church is radically different from Seneca's universal community as Paul's is limited to believers and writes, "For Paul continually, or at all events primarily, has in mind the Church, while Seneca is thinking of that vast organic whole in which men are united not as believers but as human beings. Is not fellowship in Paul restricted in a way that is alien to Seneca's broad cosmopolitanism?" For more moderate studies see Engberg-Pedeersen, *Paul and the Stoics*; deSilva, "Paul and the Stoa," 549–64; Sterling, "Hellenistic Philosophy and the New Testament," 313–58; Malherbe, *Paul and the Popular Philosophers*; idem, "Hellenistic Moralists and the New Testament," 267–33.

159. Gill, "The School in the Roman Empire," 35.

160. The idea of the kinship of god(s) and humankind is found long before the teachings of Roman Stoics. Homer in *Iliad* 1.544 designates Zeus as "father of both gods and men" and the address "Father Zeus" is found repeatedly in *Iliad* (e.g., 1.587; 3.365; 4.288; 5.762; 6.259) and in *Odyssey* (e.g., Od. 4.341; 7.311; 8.305; 12.371; 14.441). However, such use in the Stoics became closely tied with their teaching on ethics and the unity of humanity.

161. Dobbin, *Epictetus: Discourses Book I*, 86.

humanity to result both in the life of reason/contemplation and in the exercise of virtues.[162] In his well-known Hymn to Zeus, Cleanthes, the second head of Stoicism, describing Zeus as "Most majestic of immortals, many-titled, ever omnipotent Zeus, prime mover of nature," asserts that "alone of all mortal creatures which are alive and tread the earth we bear a likeness to god."[163] Humanity's likeness derives from being the "offspring" of Zeus, a ground to address him "Father" and to share in his "everlasting reason" that would lead to "a good life in partnership with intelligence."[164]

This thread of thought continued among the leading figures of Roman Stoicism, Seneca, Rufus, and Epictetus, though it is in Epictetus that we have the most frequent and detailed argument of divine-human kinship, fatherhood of god, and human-human kinship that is meant to advance universal self-understanding of humanity. He is also the one who compares divine-human kinship with kinship with Caesar and finds the latter wanting. For this reason, after briefly discussing the use of divine kinship and the kin term "father" to refer to Zeus/Jupiter in Seneca and Rufus, this study will primarily focus on Epictetus.

Lucius Annaeus Seneca (4 B.C.–A.D. 65), who was close to the Roman emperors Caligula and Nero, evokes in his teachings divine kinship, particularly the fatherhood of Zeus/Jupiter, as a foundation for his argument

162. Ibid., 88; see also Long and Sedley, *The Hellenistic Philosophers*, 323–32; Long, *Epictetus*; Belliotti, *Roman Philosophy*.

163. Long and Sedley, *The Hellenistic Philosophers*, 326.

164. Ibid., 326–27, Long and Sedley explain that the Stoic use terms such as god, Zeus, reason, universe, and nature interchangeably and the specific meaning of each of such terms has to be figured out case by case. Diogenes Laertius' explanation in 7.134 and 7.137 is helpful in this regard: "They hold that there are two principles in the universe, the active principle and the passive. The passive principle, then, is a substance without quality, i.e., matter, whereas the active is the reason inherent in this substance, that is God. For he is everlasting and is the artificer of each several thing throughout the whole extent of matter"; and in 1.137 "The term universe or cosmos is used by them in three senses: (1) of God himself, the individual being whose quality is derived from the whole of substance; he is indestructible and ingenerable, being the artificer of this orderly arrangement, who at stated periods of time absorbs into himself the whole of substance and again creates it from himself, (2) they give the name cosmos to the orderly arrangement of the heavenly bodies . . . (3) . . . to that whole of which these two are parts." Furthermore, Long and Sedley, *The Hellenistic Philosophers*, 331 summarize the Stoic god as (1) "an immanent, providential, rational, active principle imbuing all matter . . . sometimes identified with nature or with fire," (2) "the whole world, or its constituent elemental masses," and (3) "the traditional gods of the Greek pantheon, interpreted allegorically as symbolizing the Stoic immanent deity in these various aspects," and the vacillation between singular 'god' and plural 'the gods' may "reflect the deity's multiplicity of guises, but is probably to a larger extent indiscriminate, as often in Greek usage."

regarding the need to obey "the universal will," and to understand the providence and benefits humanity received from the gods. Although compared to Epictetus the explicit mention of the concept of divine-human kinship is limited in Seneca, the concept is abundantly expressed in terms of the sharing of reason, the fatherhood of Zeus, and the universality of humankind.

In Epistle 41 Seneca states firmly how the divine is immanent in human beings.[165] He writes, "We do not have to uplift our hands towards heaven or to beg the keeper of a temple to let us approach his idols' ear, as if in this way our prayers were more likely to be heard. God is near you, he is with you, he is within you."[166] In Ep. 95 Seneca states the unity between the divine and human and also among humankind as follows: "all that you see, that which comprises both god and man, is one —we are the parts of one great body. Nature produced us related to one another, since she created us from the same source and to the same end. She engendered in us mutual affection, and made us prone to friendships."[167] Accordingly, not only gods and humanity "are the parts of one great body" and are created "from the same source and to the same end" but because of this they are also "prone to friendship" and "mutual affection." Following the early and middle Stoics' emphasis on the universality of humanity that is based on the kinship rooted in cosmic reason, Seneca explains the existence of what he calls "two republics":

> The first is large and truly 'public' and includes gods and human beings. In it we do not look at this or that corner, but we limit the boundaries of our republic with the sun. The second republic is that which the circumstances of our birth have enrolled us. This will be Athens or Carthage or some other city which belongs not to all human beings but to a definite group . . . This former, greater, republic we can serve even as private individuals—indeed, perhaps better in private so that we can enquire into the nature of virtue.[168]

Seneca indicates that each individual has two republics: local, definite, with many kinds of boundaries (ethnic, geographic) and also trans-local, indefinite, without boundary, which includes "gods and human beings." The latter one is superior to and greater than the former. He applies this broader perception of one's identity to the need for ongoing participation in virtuous life even after retirement from life in politics. He writes, "with a generous spirit we have not shut ourselves inside the walls of one city, but we have sent

165. Morford, *The Roman Philosophers*, 173.

166. Seneca, *Epistle*, 41.

167. Ibid. 95.

168. Seneca, *De Otio*, 4.1–2.

ourselves to interact with the whole world. We have declared that *the universe is our fatherland*, so as to give ourselves *a broader field for virtue*."[169] He makes a distinction between the localized identity and the universal identity and describes a Stoic as "a citizen of the universe for whom every place is a *patria*," the world is "his *patria*, his *domus*, his *urbs*."[170] Seneca writes, "The person you are matters more than the place to which you go; for that reason we should not make the mind a bondsman to any one place. Live in this belief: 'I am not born for any one corner of the universe; this whole world is my country.'"[171] As such, using terms that have evocative significance for the Roman Empire, he tends to relativize the imperial identity in terms of the universal identity.[172]

In Epistle 107 Seneca grounds his teaching against complaining about hardship in life on the fatherhood of Zeus and on the communality of humanity. He exhorts his students to approach Jupiter, whom he calls "the pilot of this world mass," in a way similar to how "great Cleanthes" addressed him in his hymn to Zeus:

> Lead me, O Master of the lofty heavens,
> My Father, whithersoever thou shalt wish
> I shall not falter, but obey with speed.
> And though I would not, I shall go, and suffer
> In sin and sorrow what I might have done
> In noble virtue. Aye, the willing soul
> Fate leads, but the unwilling drags along.[173]

While Zeus as father leads, Seneca and his students were to follow without complaining about hardship in life. He characterizes life as a long journey where one is bound "to slip, collide, fall, become weary" but in the midst of all these one has to travel it realizing that it is common to all humanity. Seneca stresses that this is common to all humanity, arguing that life is part of that "which is laid down for all" by Zeus and being part of the whole humanity one might experience even that which he/she has escaped. Thus, one has to be sure to understand well what he calls, "this sense of equity." Such contemplation and self-understanding should lead one to "endure and attend uncomplainingly upon the God under whose guidance everything progresses for it is a bad soldier who grumbles when following his commander." Realizing the nature of life, which is characterized by fate that is set by Jupiter, prepares one

169. Morford, *The Roman Philosophers*, 181.

170. Seneca, *De Otio*, 11.

171. Seneca, *Epistle* 28. 4.

172. Seneca, *De Otio*, 11.

173. Seneca, *Epistle*, 107.

to meet what the course of life brings. Based on such understanding Seneca exhorts, "Let us live thus, and speak thus; let Fate find us ready and alert." But on the other hand he characterizes one "who struggles and maligns the order of the universe," as a "weakling and a degenerate" person who "would rather reform the gods than reform himself."[174]

Musonius Rufus, Epictetus' teacher, who lived approximately from 30–100, spanning the Julio-Claudian era (from Augustus to Nero) and the Flavian emperors (from Vespasian to Domitian), was from an Etruscan family, a member of the equestrian order, and was at the height of his influence in the time of Nero,[175] when Paul's ministry was about to end. He did not leave his teachings in writings. His *discourses* come from the hand of his student named Lucius and were compiled from the notes of Rufus's lectures. There is also a collection of anecdotes and sayings gathered from the works of Stobaeus, Epictetus, and Aulus Gellius.[176] Musonius makes various uses of the kinship of humanity to gods in responding to specific questions addressed to him. In each case, understanding one's identity in relationship to god(s) is meant to be the basis of one's understanding of the issue at hand and how one should live in accordance with such understanding. Similar to his predecessors, Musonius taught that "of all creatures on earth"[177] humanity is "the nearest of kin to the gods"[178] and "alone resembles God."[179] Humanity has Zeus as "the common father of all men and gods"[180] to whom it must listen and follow more than anybody else. Even when the law of Zeus is in conflict, for instance, with what a human father demands, one has to follow the law of Zeus. He describes Zeus as "guardian of the race," "god of friendship," and "guardian of the family."[181] Being kin to Zeus, humanity should be "nourished in a manner most like the gods."[182] As "the image of Him,"[183] humanity, irrespective of social status, should live like Zeus exhibiting the "same virtue that He has."[184] Accordingly, Musonius describes the character

174. Ibid.

175. Tacitus, *Ann*, XIV, 59; Lutz, "*The Roman Socrates*," 14; Belliotti, *Roman Philosophy*; Morford, *The Roman Philosophers*.

176. Belliotti, *Roman Philosophy*, 157; Morford, *The Roman Philosophers*, 205.

177. Frag., 18, 17.

178. Ibid., 18.

179. Ibid., 17.

180. Ibid., 16.

181. Ibid., 15.

182. Ibid., 18.

183. Ibid., 17.

184. Ibid.

of a good king in terms of the king's likeness to Zeus: "it is of the greatest importance for the good king to be faultless and perfect in word and action, if, indeed, he is to be a 'living law' as he seemed to the ancients, effecting good government and harmony, suppressing lawlessness and dissension, a true imitator of Zeus and, like him, father of his people."[185]

The self-understanding of a king as the "true imitator of Zeus," as the "father of his people," is depicted as a ground to be "faultless and perfect in word and action." Musonius provides an orienting framework for a king to effect "good government and harmony."

It is in Epictetus' teaching, however, that we have a detailed and sustained argument on the use of divine-human kinship, the use of the term "father" to refer to god(s) and its implication. Epictetus (A.D. 55–A.D. 135) was born in Hierapolis in Phrygia and was a slave in Rome.[186] While still a slave, he studied under the Stoic teacher Musonius Rufus in Rome. He was manumitted later, and in about 89, he was banished from Rome by the emperor Domitian along with other philosophers. He went to Nicopolis in Epirus and opened his own school which attracted many students, one of whom was Flavius Arrian (A.D. 86–A.D. 160) who later composed the *Discourses* and the *Handbook.*

Explaining the theology of Epictetus A. A. Long writes, "the primary goal of Epictetus' theology is the light it can shed on *human self-understanding* and *moral orientation*."[187] Epictetus' use of the concept of kinship with Zeus and fatherhood of god repeatedly highlights the identity of his students as one that shares divine kinship and plays a significant role in the process of their becoming who they are because of their divine kinship. In so doing, he creates a narrative that identifies and sets an orienting framework for his students, himself, and others who would pursue what the divine kinship (fatherhood) dictates. Such understanding forms the foundation for his universal humanity as well as ethical teaching.

He characterizes Zeus as "the caring father of human beings" (1.3.1) whose fatherhood is by far superior compared to being adopted by the Roman emperor (1.3.2).[188] In a similar way to the role of kinship in identity formation that is noted by anthropologists, Epictetus' kinship concept creates a sense of sharing: between humanity and god, sharing among human beings, and sharing between humans and animals. He uses divine kinship

185. Ibid., 8.

186. Long, *Epictetus*, 10–17.

187. Ibid., 156; emphasis added.

188. Ibid., 144.

and the fatherhood of god in the context where he explains the universality of humanity, social relations, and "the true nature of good" (2.8).

Epictetus' detailed teaching on divine kinship in general and fatherhood in particular are found in *Discourses* 1.3, 1.9, 1.13; 2.8; 3.11, 3.22. For the purpose of this study, I will group these texts into two groups: texts that deal with humanity's kinship to the divine in general (1.9; 2.8) and texts that deal with the fatherhood of god in particular (1.3; 1.13; 3.11, 3.22). In the texts that deal with divine-human kinship (2.8), Epictetus begins by grounding the "true nature of good" in the "true nature of God" which he describes as "intelligence, knowledge, [and] right reason" (2.8.1). Human beings as "a fragment of God himself" have in themselves "a part of him"—intelligence, knowledge, right reason—which is "the true nature of good." As his discourse below shows, based on this sharing of "a fragment of God," "part of him," "the true nature of good," which he describes as intelligence, knowledge, and right reason, he urges his students to have the self-understanding that reflects their divine kinship and live accordingly:

> Why are you then ignorant of your own kinship? Why do you not know the source from which you have sprung? Will you not bear in mind, whenever you eat, who you are that eat, and whom you are nourishing? Whenever you indulge in intercourse with women, who are you that do this? Whenever you mix in society, whenever you take physical exercise, whenever you converse, do you not know that you are nourishing god, exercising god? You are bearing god about with you, poor wretch, and know it not! Do you think I speak of some external god of silver or gold? No, you bear him about within you and are unaware that your are defiling him with unclean thoughts and foul actions. If an image of God were present, you would not dare to do any of the things you do; yet when God himself is present within you and sees and hears all things, you are not ashamed of thinking and acting thus: O slow to understand your nature, and estranged from God.[189]

In this text, using expressions such as "your own kinship," "the source from which you have sprung." and "your nature" which repeatedly mark out one's identity, Epictetus urges his students, with repeated questions that are meant to sharpen his argument, to come to their divine–human kinship self-understanding. This self-understanding is meant to shape almost every area of the life of his students: eating, intercourse, mixing in society, physical exercise, and conversation.

189. Epictetus, *The Discourses*, 2.8.11–13, same translation is followed unless mentioned otherwise.

In 1.9, Epictetus fleshes out the implication of divine-human kinship in terms of the universality of humanity. He impresses upon his students the connotation of what it means to say, "we are akin to God" (συγγενεῖς ἧμᾶς εἶναι τῷ θεῷ). According to Epictetus, what one can learn from the philosophers' teaching (λεγόμενα υπὸ τῶν φιλοσόφων) about the implication of "the kinship of God and men" (τῆς συγγενείας τοῦ θεοῦ καί ἀνθρώπων) is the self-understanding that one is "a citizen of the universe" (1.9.1).[190] Drawing comparison between one's local habitation and one's citizenship in the universe, Epictetus argues for the superiority of the latter, and at the same time discourages "the impulse to abandon one for the other" and exhorts to persist wherever god has assigned.[191]

> For why do you say you are an Athenian, instead of mentioning merely that corner into which your paltry body was cast at birth? Or is it clear you take the place which has a higher degree of authority and comprehends not merely that corner of yours, but also your family and, in a word, the source from which your race has come, your ancestors down to yourself, and from some such entity call yourself "Athenian," or "Corinthian"? Well, then, anyone who has attentively studied the administration of the universe and has learned that "the greatest and most authoritative and most comprehensive of all governments is this one, which is composed of men and god; and that from Him have descended the seeds of being, not merely to my father or to my grandfather, but to all things that are begotten and that grow upon earth, and chiefly to rational beings, seeing that by nature it is theirs alone to have communion in the society of God, being intertwined with him through reason,"—why should not such a man call himself a citizen of the universe? Why should he not call himself a son of God?[192]

One's affiliation to one's own family in terms of location and race as well as one's kinship with Caesar or any other powerful ones in Rome (τὸν Καίσαρα η συγγένεια ἢ ἄλλον τινὰ τῶν μέγα δυναμένων ἐν Ρώμῃ) is compared to one's kinship to god (τῆς συγγενείας τοῦ θεοῦ καί ἀνθρώπων) and found to be inferior. The ensuing partaking in "the society of God" which is "composed of men and God" (τὸ σύστημα τό ἒξ ἀνθροώπων καὶ θεου), and which according to Epictetus represents "the greatest and most authoritative and most comprehensive government of all" (1.9.2–8) is universal and

190. See also Epictetus, *Discourses*, 2.10.3.

191. Dobbin, *Epictetus*, 123.

192. Epictetus, *Discourses*, 1.9.2–6.

by far superior even compared to having kinship with Caesar. One who "has attentively studied" (ὃ . . . παρηκολουθηκὼς) and "has learned" (μεμαθηκώς) the government of the universe (τῇ διοικήσει τοῦ κόσμου) should call himself "citizen of the universe" (κόσμιον), "son of God" (υἱὸν θεοῦ), and as the result should not "fear anything that happens among men" (1.9.6). The basis of this affiliation between "men and God" is because of "the seeds of being" (τὰ σπέρματα) which have "descended" (καταπέπτωκεν) "to all things that are begotten and that grow upon earth, and chiefly to rational beings" (1.9.4). This creates a situation where humanity is intertwined with god through reason laying the foundation for the self-understanding that it is humanity's alone "to have communion in the society of God" (κοινωεῖν . . . τῷ θεῷ τῆς συναναστροφῆς). Such self-understanding (kinship with god, belonging to the universe) and having "God as our maker, and father and guardian" is believed to lead beyond fear concerning "anything that happens among men" (1.9.6). It is sufficient to enable one "to live securely" far more than having kinship with Caesar or any other powerful person.

In *Discourses* 1.3; 1.13; 3.11, 3.22, the divine–human kinship is portrayed in terms of the fatherhood of Zeus, who is described as "father of men and gods." The fatherhood of god is tied to being "begotten of god" (γεγόναμεν υπο τοῦ θεοῦ). In 1.3 Epictetus argues that the understanding that "god is the father of human beings" (τὸν θεὸν πατέρα εἶναι τῶν ἀνθρώπων) should shape one's self-understanding. It should make possible for one to move away from having "ignoble and mean thoughts" about self and to become conscious of the far superior kinship one has with Zeus which is greater than kinship with Caesar. Accordingly, what one thinks in terms of kinship shapes not only one's self-understanding but also what one does with that self-understanding. The nature of self-understanding that Epictetus is trying to impress upon his students entails being able to feel affinity (συμπαθῆσαι κατα ἀξίαν δύναιτο), to what he calls "this doctrine" (τῷ δόγματι τούτῳ). He explains what he calls "this doctrine" as pertaining to the idea that "we are all primarily begotten of God and that God is the father of men as well as gods" (1.3.1).[193]

As he does most of the time, Epictetus compares kinship with Zeus to kinship with animals because of our body (τὸ σῶμα μὲν κοινὸν πρὸς τὰ ζῷα), as well as to kinship with Caesar (1.9.7; 1.14.15; 3.13.9–14). In the former case, he depicts humanity as having dual kinship: kinship with gods and kinship with animals. Kinship with gods exists in terms of our "reason and intelligence in common with gods," kinship with animals exists

193. In Stoic teaching there appears to be a hierarchy of gods and Zeus, the supreme god, is not only the father of human beings but he is also the father of gods as well as animals. For discussion of this subject see Long, *Epictetus*, 142–80.

in that we have a "body in common with the animals," which he describes as "miserable and mortal" aspect of our kinship. Assenting to the doctrine of our kinship with god is the basis for humanity not to have "ignoble or mean thoughts" about itself. Stressing that most of the time this is not the case, Epictetus locates the problem in most people's self-understanding and resultant attitude that gravitate more to humanity's kinship to animals than to humanity's kinship to god. While only few "incline" to divine kinship, many incline towards the aspect of kinship with animals and see themselves as "poor, miserable . . . wretched bit(s) of flesh," and become "like wolves, faithless and treacherous and mischievous," neglecting that they possess "something better." The way not to become "some of these miserable things," according to Epictetus, is by having a self-understanding that we have divine kinship. The answer one gives to the question, "what am I?" (τί . . . εἰμί), shapes one's self-understanding as well as one's actions. When one defines himself/herself more in terms of "kinship with the flesh," according to Epictetus, one will end up having "ignoble or mean" thoughts about oneself and behaving "like wolves, faithless and treacherous and hurtful" (1.3.7–9). On the other hand the divine kinship is something much better than kinship with flesh.

Comparing human-divine kinship and kinship with Caesar, Epictetus shows to what extent the latter is deficient. For instance in 3.13.9–13 he recounts Caesar's claim to provide "profound peace" which is central to Augustus' portrayal of himself in *Res Gestae*. He admits that Caesar is able to provide peace as "there are no wars any longer, nor battles, no brigandage on a large scale, nor piracy, but at any hour we may travel by land, or sail from the rising of the sun to its setting." However, he describes this as only a limited sense of peace. Pointing out that Caesar cannot provide peace from physical, natural and emotional problems such as fever, shipwreck, fire, earthquake, lightening, love, sorrow, or envy, Epictetus exhorts his students to heed "the doctrine of the philosophers' promises" in order to have superior peace. He explains this "doctrine of the philosophers' promises" as the doctrine that proclaims peace from "God through reason." In 1.9.7 Epictetus compares the self-pride that comes from being adopted by Caesar to what knowing that one is a "a son of Zeus" should entail—"elation" (ἐπαρθήσῃ) that shapes how one sees himself/herself.

Epictetus sees this divine-human kinship as shaping social relations between slave and master, father and son, and between brothers. Based on humanity's common relationship to Zeus, Epictetus asserts kinship between slave and master and claims it as a foundation for social intercourse. In 1.13, the discourse entitled, "How Each Thing may be Done in a Manner Pleasing to the Gods," Epictetus deals with respectful and considerate relationship between master and slave on the basis of shared divine kinship. Epictetus writes,

> Slave, won't you put up with your own brother, who has Zeus as his ancestor and is a son born of the same seed as yourself, and has the same noble descent? But if you have been placed in a position above others, will you straightway set yourself up as a tyrant? Don't you remember who you are and who you command, that they are kinsmen, brothers by nature, offspring of Zeus? But you have a bill of sale for them, and they have none for me?' Don't you see that it is to the earth, to the pit, to these wretched laws of the dead, that you are looking, and not to the laws of the gods?[194]

The slave and master have Zeus as their common ancestor and are of the same seed, with same descent, and hence "are kinsmen, brothers by nature, and offspring of Zeus." Irrespective of their social differences, having kinship that originates from being kin with Zeus, forms an unshakable basis for respectful and considerate relationship. Epictetus rejects ownership of a slave as a basis of how masters should relate to and treat their slaves, instructing that one should look to the laws of gods instead of the "wretched laws of the dead," which to him are distorted and narrow.

Accordingly, where one looks as a guide determines how one relates with others. Using the law of human society as a sole basis instead of the divine law has a very blinding and limiting effect. It limits one to behaving according to the custom of the society whatever that may be in a given time. According to Epictetus, the divine law would guide one to realize who he/she is (*who you are*) and to whom he/she is relating (*whom you command*), both of which deal with one's self-understanding and understanding others.

Finally, following the same line of argument, in *Discourse* 3.11, Epictetus presents the fatherhood of Zeus as the basis for children-father, brother-brother, and any other social relationships. Children should not dishonor their fathers as all fathers, whether bad or good, are from Zeus, who is "the God of the Fathers." He uses similar logic as a basis to shape brother to brother relationship as well as all other relationships. While fathers are the representations of Zeus who is the father of all, brothers are representations of Zeus who is "the God of kindred," and Zeus oversees all "other social relations."

194. Epictetus, *Discoures*, 1.3.

Summary Conclusion

In summary, the teachings of the Roman Stoics develop a narrative that depict human beings as kin to gods due to sharing "a fragment of god," "a part of god," "the true nature of good" which is described as "intelligence, knowledge, and right reason." This discourse images humanity as "citizens of the universe" forming the basis for a universal society that has gods and human beings as their members. The universal community, which is portrayed in terms of the fatherhood of Zeus, who is depicted as the source, originator, and sustainer, guardian of this universal community, is a fatherland, "a broader field for virtue," and is superior to any other community. While it is open to all human beings, only those who live by "the fragment of god" that is in them could assent to it. The Roman Stoics call their students to have such a self-understanding and to have it shaping their living. This discourse and the image created through it relativizes any local, specific, and previous kinship ties and the self-understanding and commitment pertaining to them.

Regarding loyalty to the Empire, on the one hand, through the notion of universal cosmopolitanism, the Stoics aided the Roman Empire in developing the idea of trans-local *patria*. On the other hand, by giving far more importance to the universal citizenship compared to the Roman, and also by giving more significance to having Zeus as father than Caesar, the Stoics undercut the Empire's self-portrayal. Furthermore, the fact that the aforementioned Roman Stoics worked closely with the Roman Emperors or leaders (in the case of Epictetus) at some point suggests that they had positive relationship and have made some contribution to the emerging Empire. However, the fact that, at one point or another, all of them were exiled suggests that their relationship was ambivalent.

In conclusion, in this chapter I have examined the identity formation role of kinship in general and the use of the kinship term "father" to refer to the Roman Empire, emperors, and gods in particular in order to lay a context for the study of the role of the use of "father" to refer to God in Paul for the self-understanding of the emerging Christian community. We have seen that while kinship in general and the language of "father" in particular is used by the Roman Empire to image the Empire as a big household that is characterized as *patria* with the emperor as the father and the people as the children, kinship with god(s) and the fatherhood of Zeus is used by the Roman Stoics to construct a bigger household of humanity which presents itself as superior to all. In the next chapter, I will explore the identity formation role of kinship in general and the use of the term "father" to refer to God in particular in the Hebrew Bible and in the ancient Jewish literature.

4

God as Father in the Hebrew Bible[1]

The Hebrew Bible forms one of the multiple narrative frameworks for Paul.[2] In the previous chapter we have seen one of these multiple narrative frameworks that comes from the image of god(s), emperors, and empire as fathers in the early Roman Empire. Another framework derives from ancient Jewish writings that will be discussed in chapter 5. In this chapter, I will examine the use of God as Father in the Hebrew Bible to lay the ground for the study of the use of God as Father in Paul. I will discuss how kinship language in general and familial language associated with the Fatherhood of God in particular[3] is used to shape and express Israel's self-understandings in the Hebrew Bible. The result will inform the study of the use of God as Father in Paul and its role in shaping and expressing the self-understandings of the early Christians. I will begin with a discussion of the role of kinship language for identity formation in the Hebrew Bible. This will be followed by the use of God as Father and its role for identity formation in the Hebrew Bible.

1. I use the term "Hebrew Bible" in the sense of the term "Old Testament" but not in contradistinction to the Septuagint to refer to the text written in the Hebrew language.

2. Wright, *Paul in Fresh Perspective*, 6.

3. By familial language related to the Fatherhood of God I am referring to the use of kinship language such as "son(s) and children of God" and sibling language to refer to Israel, and the use of "son" to refer to the Israelite king. While son(s) and children, when they refer to the people of Israel, include all the community irrespective of gender or status, I retain the language of "son(s)" in order to reflect the aspect of inheritance that it carries.

Kinship and Identity Formation in the Hebrew Bible

The role of kinship in identity formation in the Hebrew Bible constitutes one of the milieus to understand Paul's use of Father and kinship language. Following the Hebrew Bible at many levels, Paul uses kinship with Abraham (Gal 3–4; Rom 8), God as Father (e.g., Rom 1:7; Gal 1:1–4), God's people as children (e.g., Gal 3:26; Rom 8:14–16), and God's people as brothers and sisters (e.g., 1 Cor 8:10–13) to construct networks of relationships that shape and express identity. Just as kinship language helps to locate Pauline community ties within the broader context of humanity, in the Hebrew Bible it plays a significant role to locate the people of Israel within humanity. Explaining the importance of familial narrative in locating Israel within humanity as the people of God from the composition of the book of Genesis, James Muilenburg writes,

> The traditions of the *Urgeschichte* (Gen. 1–11) from the first man to Abraham are drawn from many sources. Yet all these materials, utterly diverse . . . have been fashioned into *a family narrative*, from first man to first Hebrew, from first Hebrew . . . *to Israel the people of God*. It is a work for which we vainly seek any parallel in the history of world literature.[4]

In similar vein Leo G. Perdue further points out how the concept of familial relationship provided images that help to conceptualize "God, Israel, the land, and the nations" as follows:

> Throughout its history, ancient Israel's major understandings of God, creation, the nation, the nations and morality were forged in large part by the social character and experience of *the family household. Many of the key metaphors for imaging God, Israel, the land, and the nations originated in the household.*[5]

The concept of family in the Hebrew Bible is not simply defined by blood and marriage, but it is also "a social world constructed by tradition, ethos, law, customs, and religion."[6] It projects "a reality of . . . people bound

4. Muilenburg, "Father and Son," 177; the latter two emphasis added.

5. Perdue, "The Household, Old Testament Theology, and Contemporary Hermeneutics," 225, emphasis added; also see Brueggemann, "The Covenanted Family," 18–23, who writes, "in the world of Biblical faith, the family is the primary unit of meaning which shapes and defines reality"; Meyers, "The Family in Early Israel," 2, who points out that understanding Israelite society in large measure rests on understanding of the Israelite family. She explains, "when examining the period of Israelite beginnings, the study of early [premonarchic] Israel is nearly equivalent to the study of the family."

6. Perdue, "The Israelite and Early Jewish Family," 178–79.

together in solidarity by the common effort to promote the well-being of the whole."[7] Perdue explains further that Israel's familial narrative is

> grounded in the order of creation (Gen 1:26–28; 2:21–24). It . . . defined social and economic roles for human interaction, with the common goal of group survival and continuation; received religious legitimation through divine actions in history, rehearsed in story and ritual; and responded to divine imperatives that shaped socio-religious life and moral behavior.[8]

Similarly, commenting on the self-understanding of Israel, Frank Crüsemann writes, "at the entrance of the Torah, Israel has written itself into the world of peoples and has defined its location within the framework of the entire humanity created by God."[9] Humanity as a whole is "represented as a family" from which "an increasing concentration on Israel as the mainline of descent" is depicted.[10] Tracing back to the primordial couple, humanity is portrayed as family which then unfolds itself, narrowing down to Abraham who received "a mediating role for God's blessing on the whole human race, consisting of many peoples."[11] Israel "emerges in history, twenty generations after the creation of the human species in the image of God . . . It is neither descended from the gods nor divine itself."[12] Reinhard Feldmeier points out as a remarkable feature of Israel that its ancestors "are not stylized as heroes of former times. One's origins lie not in demi-gods but, on the contrary, in a 'wandering Aramaean, near to death.'"[13] He explains, "To reassure oneself one does not here tell of '*the fame of the deeds of the dead,' as is customary among other nations, but of God's action*, which created his people from miserable 'outcasts.'"[14] Explaining the implication Jon D. Levenson writes, "[t]he placement of the story of cosmic creation by God (*'elohim*) at the beginning of the entire Bible . . . establishes a universal horizon for the particular story of Israel, which occupies most of the rest of that sacred book."[15] While the origin of Israel is portrayed with an increas-

7. Ibid.

8. Ibid.

9. Crüsemann, "Human Solidarity and Ethnic Identity," 58.

10. Ibid., 66.

11. Ibid., 66, 73.

12. Levenson, "The Universal Horizon of Biblical Particularism," 147, further notes, "The creation stories in Genesis serve as a powerful warrant for a Jewish doctrine of human solidarity and as a formidable obstacle to any attempt to mix Judaism with racism."

13. Feldmeier, "The 'Nation' of Strangers," 244.

14. Ibid.

15. Levenson, "The Universal Horizon of Biblical Particularism,"146, contrasting

ing particularization, the identity of Israel is depicted as something that "can only be grasped within the framework of the whole" as part of "the entire coherence of humanity."[16] Israel's portrayal of itself links "humanity and the peoples into a unity" as "all of humanity and the kinships of Israel are grasped in one single system" though there exists between them "an abundance of intermediate stages and a continuous scale of linkages."[17]

In chapter 2 we have seen that kinship is a *process of being and becoming through networks of relationships* that apply *both to the contemporaries* and *the ancients, to spiritual connection as well as corporal descent.* As a common feature, kinship has a sense of sharing something (substance and/or spirit, nature/nurture) that provides an orienting framework that helps to conceptualize self-understanding and the understanding of others. In this self-understanding endeavor that categorizes and identifies Israel as people of God, kinship features play a significant role. Using kinship language the Hebrew Bible creates a discourse of identity and narrates God's people being and becoming. It is used to create shared belief in the common story that includes common ancestry with a promise from the ancestral God, the Exodus from Egypt, the revelation at Sinai, the wanderings in the wilderness, and the journey to the promised land, becoming "a symbolic shaper of community, joining people together around common ethnic, cultural, and religious identity."[18] The formative discourse recounts God's election of the founding ancestors with a promise of descendants to shape their present and future.[19] This formative discourse was integrated by historians, prophets, and priests with the larger national epic.[20]

---

the Hebrew Bible creation story with a Babylonian, he writes, "Marduk's creation of the world culminates in the construction of Babylon, his city and his palace. Like *'elohim*, Marduk is also a cosmic creator-god; his power is not limited to Babylon. But, as emphatically not the case in Gen. 1:1—2:3, his special relationship to a particular community is embedded in the very structure of cosmic order." He observes that in the Genesis account (Gen. 1:1—2:3) there is "no landmarks, no countries . . . Instead, men and women, created together, exist on undifferentiated dry land. No spot on earth can claim the prestigious status of primordiality. . ."

16. Crüsemann, "Human Solidarity and Ethnic Identity," 66.

17. Ibid., 65–66.

18. Hendel, *Remembering Abraham*, 8; see also Renan, "What is a Nation?" Anderson, *Imagined Communities*, 187–206; Smith, *Myths and Memories of the Nation*; Hallbwachs, *The Collective Memory*; for works in biblical studies see Yerushalmi, *Zakhor*, 14; Greenstein, "Mixing Memory and Design," 197–218; Blenkinsopp, "Memory, Tradition, and the Construction of Past in Ancient Israel," 76–82; Brettler, "Memory in Ancient Israel," 1–17; Smith, "Remembering God," 631–51.

19. Perdue, "The Israelite and Early Jewish Family," 167.

20. Ibid.

Israel as a nation is referred to in a variety of ways that recalls the tradition of the putative ancestors: Jacob, Israel, sons of Israel, the house of Israel.[21] Such familial construction of peoplehood is expressed by employing different kinship features which I will divide into three: (1) kinship features that are related to the expression "sons of Israel," (2) kinship ties constructed through genealogy, and (3) kinship features related to covenants. These features are interrelated and work together from different angles to image Israel as a people, a community, that belongs to God. The kinship phrase "sons of Israel" refers to the most inclusive group level, peoplehood, which is also described by terms such as "house of Israel," *'am* ("people") and *sibte-Israel* ("tribes of Israel").[22] It occurs 638 times in the Hebrew Bible and out of these 359 come out of the narrator's hand, 225 from the mouth of Yahweh, forty six from the Israelites themselves and eight from foreigners.[23] This indicates how the Hebrew Bible portrays Israel from the narrator's as well as from Yahweh's perspective. Both the narrator and Yahweh's perspectives coalesce to image Israel as God's people. While it is found in each major segment of the Hebrew Bible, "the Exodus traditions account for well over 50 per cent of the total" indicating that it is significantly a formative narrative.[24] Apart from a few instances, it is used "quite consistently, in a collective sense, referring to the people belonging to the nation. In most instances the entire nation [as constituted by God] is in mind."[25] Its latter use looks back to the earlier formative uses. For instance, Block points out that it is used to appeal to the "sons of Israel" to return to the God of Abraham, Isaac, and Jacob,[26] to

21. Block, "Israel's House," 257.

22. Stager, "The Archaeology of the Family in Ancient Israel," 20, 22.

23. Block, "'Israel'—'Sons of Israel,'" 301–2, Block also points out that the use of the phrase by the foreigners derives from the earlier formative texts: "Ex 1:9, Pharaoh is concerned about 'the people of the sons of Israel,' becoming mightier than his own people; 12:31, he commands Moses and the 'sons of Israel' to leave; Josh 2.2, the king of Jericho receives the report of the spies from the 'sons of the Israel"; 10:4, Adonizedeck complains that Gibeon has made peace with the "sons of Israel."

24. Block, "'Israel'—'Sons of Israel,'" 320.

25. In few instances it is used in reference to the literal sons of Jacob (Gen 45:21; 46:5, 8; 50:25; Ex 1:1; 13:19), to males as opposed to females (Deut 23:28; Josh 5:2, 3; 1 Sam 9:2), and to antithetical counterparts (Lev 25:39–55; Jug 19:10; 2 Sam 21:2; 1 Kings 9:20–22; 11:1–2).

26. 2 Chron 30:6.

recall the exodus from Egypt and the wilderness wandering,[27] and to recall God's covenant with Israel[28] and the conquest.[29]

The related expression, "the house of Israel," occurs 146 times in the Hebrew Bible, the majority in the prophetic books particularly in Ezekiel (83x), Jeremiah (20x), and Amos (8x).[30] In the narrative context, which is the majority of its use, it appears to be a stylistic variant of sons of Israel.[31] Block suggests that the difference between the two usages when they refer to the nation is that while sons of Israel "stresses the plurality of individuals of whom the whole consists," the phrase "'house of Israel' places the emphasis on the nation as a unified body."[32] Both reflect the self-perception of peoplehood.

Associated with the expression "sons of Israel" and "the house of Israel" are three levels of kinships, *Bayit* or *bet 'ab* ("Father's house"), *mispaha* ("clan") and *sebet* or *matteh* ("tribe"), which are used to express different levels of kinship organizations.[33] The three levels of kinship are reflected in passages such as Josh 7:16—18; 1 Sam 10:20; Judges 6:15.[34] It was with such kinship units, particularly with smaller ones, that a person found his or her identity "as a member of the covenant people of Israel, and learned his or her obligation to the society and to the God of Israel."[35]

Bayit or *bet 'ab* ("house of one's father") is the central kinship unit that identifies an individual Israelite.[36] Father's house (household) comprises "the dead ancestors of the past, those living in the present, and those yet to be born" hence strengthening the solidarity of the Israelite and early Jewish family by "the wide sweep of the generations of its existence."[37] "Beyond

27. 1 Sam 10:18; 15:6; 2 Sam 7:6, 7; 1 Kings 6:1; 11:2; 2 Kings 17:7; 18:4; Neh 8:14, 17; 1 Chron 6:49; 2 Chron 5:10.

28. 1 Kings 8:9; 19:10, 14; Neh 1:6; 2 Chron 6:11.

29. 2 Sam 21:2; 1 Kings 9:20, 21, 22; 14:24; 21:26; 2 Kings 16:3; 17:8, 9; 21:2, 9; 2 Chron 8:8, 9; 28:3; 33:2, 9.

30. Block, "Israel's House," 258.

31. Ibid., 259.

32. Ibid., 259.

33. Stager, "The Archaeology of the Family in Ancient Israel," 20, 22; Wright, "Family," 61–62.

34. For instance Joshua 7:16–18 reads, "So Joshua rose early in the morning, and brought Israel near tribe by tribe, and the tribe of Judah was taken. He brought near the clans of Judah, and the clan of the Zerahites was taken; and he brought near the clan of the Zerahites, family by family, and Zabdi was taken. And he brought near his household one by one, and Achan son of Carmi son of Zabdi son of Zerah, of the tribe of Judah, was taken" (NRSV).

35. Wright, "Family," 763.

36. Ibid.; Perdue, "The Israelite and Early Jewish Family," 176.

37. Perdue, "The Israelite and Early Jewish Family," 176.

the household," Stager explains, "a villager's identity and social status are enmeshed in larger kinship net-works. Residential propinquity frequently expresses the kinship ties linking several households."[38]

Clans refer to the next higher level of grouping from the father's house and were held together by ancestral stories and by economic and defense solidarity.[39] The tribe refers to "a large social unit that provided the major geographical and kinship organization (real and fictional) for ancient Israel."[40]

Explaining the need for such kinship construction, Mendenhall writes, "as social units become larger, kinship ties [based on blood and marriage] become increasingly dysfunctional as the basis for the larger group; but kinship terminology seems to become more used to express the new bond that ties the larger group together."[41] He explains further, "(o)nce the true lineage band of primitive society gives way to larger . . . forms of social organization, relationships of individuals likewise become more complex and multilateral."[42] The location of the individual is "virtually always that of center of a series of overlapping and concentric circles. If he (she) is a member of a family, he is also a member of a larger group which may or may not actually be held together by traced lineage bonds."[43] In a similar vein Perdue explains:

> The community of the tribes *formed the people*, or nation, of Israel (Josh 24:1, 31) . . . It is important to note that even this larger federation understood itself as the *extended, multigenerational household of Israel* (Jacob). This self-understanding, largely fictional, provided the ethos of solidarity and the corporate identity for the entire nation. Israel was both *a people and a community* . . .[44]

38. Stager, "The Archaeology of the Family in Ancient Israel," 20.

39. Perdue, "The Israelite and Early Jewish Family," 167.

40. Ibid., 178; Perdue also explains that broadly speaking, Israel was comprised of twelve tribes named after one household—the sons of Israel (Jacob), which included two grandsons, Ephraim and Manasseh (Joseph's two sons).

41. Mendenhall, *The Tenth Generation*, 176; see also idem, "Social Organization in Early Israel," 132–51; Geus, *The Tribes of Israel*, 120–64; Gottwald, *The Tribes of Yahweh*, 129–344; Wilson, "The Mechanisms of Judicial Authority in Early Israel," 59–75; Stager, "The Archaeology of the Family in Ancient Israel," 1–35; Brichto, "Kin, Cult, Land, and Afterlife–A Biblical Complex," 1–54.

42. Mendenhall, *The Tenth Generation*, 176–77.

43. Ibid.

44. Perdue, "The Israelite and Early Jewish Family," 178.

Another aspect of kinship that is used to shape Israel's self-understanding is genealogy.[45] It is used widely in the texts that deal with Israel's early history (Genesis, Exodus) and in the literature from the post exilic period (Chronicles, Ezra, Nehemiah). It uses "the idiom of kinship" and expresses "all sorts of social, political, and religious relationships."[46] Crüsemann explains, "The place of each individual in society—and beyond that, in part, the entire creation— is grasped by them (genealogies), i.e., rank and status, claims and expectations of all kinds. The kinship connections remain, wherever a state is young or weak, the basic framework of order. The world is experienced and described as family."[47] This is seen at important junctures in the life of the people of Israel in formative texts, pre-exilic, exilic, and post-exilic as well. This indicates that "the family and family-oriented thinking played . . . an astonishingly important role (even) after the breakdown of the state."[48] Crüsemann observes, "The cohesiveness of the people, as well as their relationships with other peoples, could be described and grasped by genealogical thinking, independently of institutions like the kingship."[49]

Finally, the covenants, which are another predominant feature in the Hebrew Bible, are also expressions of familial relationship. Grounding the concept and institution of covenant in the kinship-based social organization of West Semitic tribal groups, Cross explains covenant and oath as "a wide spread legal means by which the duties and privileges of kinship may be extended to another individual or group, including aliens."[50] Cross rightly argues that although familial language such as brotherhood, fatherhood, love, and loyalty are asserted to be covenant terminologies, this turns "things upside down."[51] The reason is that "the language of covenant, kinship-in-law, is taken from the language of kinship, kinship-in-flesh" not

45. Johnson, *Biblical Genealogies*; Wilson, "Between 'Azel' and 'Azel,'" 10–22; idem, "The Old Testament Genealogies," 169–89; idem, *Genealogy and History*.

46. Wilson, "Genealogy," 930.

47. Crüsemann, "Human Solidarity and Ethnic Identity," 62–63; he further explains the depth of genealogies in Genesis writing, "Persons are 'naturalized' into the kinship system who, in a strict sense, are not biologically related but are nevertheless socially integrated. However, none of the parallels known from ethnology, or from the ancient Near East, has a structure such as the system of Genesis. Genesis encompasses single families and entire ethnic groups, including connections with an ancestor from primordial time. Indeed, a system with the propensity to encompass all of humanity, all neighboring peoples as well as the whole internal structure of one's own people that is something extraordinary."

48. Ibid., 64.

49. Ibid.

50. Cross, "Kinship and Covenant," 8.

51. Ibid., 11.

vice versa.[52] In similar vein, Hahn argues that covenant is "an extension of familial relationship."[53] Explaining the significance of family in the fabric of the Israelite society in relation to covenants, Perdue suggests that "another, and perhaps even more formative, location for shaping the formal character and conceptual understanding of the covenant and its binding obligation is the household in ancient Israel and early Judaism."[54]

Thus, Israel's peoplehood is narrated predominantly using these kinship features. The use of God as Father in the Hebrew Bible belongs within this common mode of construction of the identity of the people of Israel. All the three major kinship features are also reflected in one way or another in the contexts where the use of God as Father is found. The use of God as Father in the Hebrew Bible will be studied as part of this larger practice of Israel to portray its being and becoming using different kinship features. Through categorization and identification, this image of God defines Israel's being and becoming by creating membership in the peoplehood that images itself in the form of a kin-group.

God as Father in the Hebrew Bible

In the Hebrew Bible the term "father" is applied to God in two ways: (1) to depict God as Father of the people of Israel, and (2) to depict God as Father of Israel's king. There are sixteen occurrences, and eleven refer to God as Father of Israel[55] and five to Father of Israel's king.[56] There are, however, passages that describe Israel as son and children of God (e.g., Exod 4:22–23), and passages that depict Israel in sibling language (e.g., Exod 2:11; 4:18; Lev 25:35, 46; Deut 3:18) in relation to God where God is not explicitly identified as Father. These passages need to be considered together with passages that depict God as Father in order to get a fuller understanding of the use of the kinship term "father" to refer to God in the Hebrew Bible.

52. Ibid.

53. Hahn, "Covenant in the Old and New Testaments," 263–92; furthermore, commenting on the benefit of grounding covenant studies on kinship, Hahn explains that "it provides a paradigm for the integration of legitimate insights on the nature of covenant in earlier scholarship which, unfortunately and unintentionally, tended to be reductionist, focusing on single aspects of the covenant institution: the legal/ethical, cultic, political . . . The covenant bears all these aspects."

54. Perdue, "The Household, Old Testament Theology, and Contemporary Hermeneutics," 240.

55. Deut 32:6; Ps 68:5; 103:13; Isa 63:16 (twice); 64:8; Jer 3:4; 19; 31:9; Mal 1:6; 2:10.

56. 2 Sam 7:14; 1 Chr 17:13; 22:10; 28:6; Ps 89:26.

At first sight the frequency of the use of God as Father in the Hebrew Bible might tend to suggest that its use is not a major kinship feature through which Israel understood itself. However, when it is studied in conjunction with the portrayal of the people of Israel as the son/children of God and as siblings, it emerges as a significant part of the picture of Israel's self-understanding. In all these, the theme of formation (of peoplehood, community), restoration and covenant which is also related to formation and restoration of Israel is central to the textual contexts in which God is referred to as Father in the Hebrew Bible. As such, the portrayal of God as Father, Israel as son/children of God and as siblings, and God as Father of Israel's king and the king as the son of God creates a narrative that identifies and sets an orienting framework for how Israel understands itself in relation to God, in relation to each other, and in relation to the surrounding nations. A non-polemical and non-crisis centered self-understanding emerges. For the purpose of this study we divide these texts into four: passages that refer to God as the Father of Israel, passages that refer to Israel as son(s) and children, texts that portray Israel in sibling language, and texts that refer to God as Father of Israel's king and Israel's king as the son of God. In the following section, I will begin with passages that depict God as Father of Israel.

God as Father of the People of Israel

The portrayal of God as Father of Israel, although not frequent, is found in wide cross-section of the Hebrew Bible—Deuteronomy, Psalms, and prophets. Its use also exhibits a consistent cluster of relational emphasis: formation, protection, guidance, provision, covenant, inheritance, and restoration. The use asserts and then subsequently reminds that Israel owes its existence to God who formed, protected, guided, restored, and gave covenant and inheritance to it. The writers revitalize these traditions of Israel in line with God's Fatherhood evoking a family image that conjures up the privileges and responsibilities on both sides. Since Deuteronomy in general and Deut 32 in particular is believed to form a thematic foundation for subsequent prophetic literature (Isaiah, Jeremiah, Ezekiel),[57] I will start by discussing in some depth the importance of the portrayal of God as Father in Deuteronomy 32. This will lead directly to the discussion of God as Father in the prophets, and then in Psalms.

God is referred to as Father only once in the entire Pentateuch and that is in Deuteronomy 32 which is commonly known as the "Song of

57. Kaiser, "The Song of Moses," 486–500; Bergey, "The Song of Moses and Isaianic Prophecies," 33–54.

Moses," and also referred to as *Shirat Ha'azinu* in Jewish tradition following the opening Hebrew word (הַאֲזִינוּ).[58] It probably has the earliest written reference to God as Father.[59] Regarding the significance of Deuteronomy 32, Christensen writes, "No text within Deuteronomy has received more attention through the years than the Song of Moses (32:1–43), from ancient scribes who copied it to modern critical scholars who ponder its structure and meaning."[60] It "touches on familiar themes found elsewhere throughout the whole Hebrew Bible."[61] Its significance in the narrative of Deuteronomy is also reflected in the phraseology used to describe it: "compendium of Deuteronomic ideology,"[62] a song that "contains all of Torah's principles,"[63] a song that "provides a hermeneutical key by which to understand the Mosaic law in an age of disobedience,"[64] "a summary of Deuteronomic themes in memorable form,"[65] and the "*grande finale* of Moses' charges."[66] Allen argues that Deuteronomy 32 "opens a window onto other parts of Deuteronomy, setting forth a succinct summary of much of the book's ethos and message."[67] Countering those who see Deut 31–34 as appendix, E. Talstra argues that Deut 31–34 "seek to give a final interpretation to the entire book."[68] In similar vein Allen explains that these chapters are "a culmination or summary of prior material," and "they signal the climax of Moses' handover, stating the law's central import for life in the land; they look forward where Deut 1–11 looks backwards . . ."[69]

58. Christensen, *Deuteronomy 21:10—34:12*, 784 explains that In Jewish tradition, it forms "the tenth of the eleven weekly portions in the lectionary cycle of Torah readings from Deuteronomy"; Based on Rabbinic sources (RH 31a; TJ Meg. 3:7, 74b) Tigay, *Deuteronomy*, 513, writes, "the Levites read parts of the poem in the Temple while the Additional Offering (*musaf*) was being made on Sabbaths. They completed it over a six-week cycle and then began again."

59. For earlier date of Deuteronomy 32 see Eissfeldt, *The Old Testament*, 227; Wright, "The Law Suit of God, 26–67; idem, "Some Remarks on the Song of Moses," 339–46; Tigay, *Deuteronomy*, 513, argues that it is considerably older than the rest of Deuteronomy.

60. Christensen, *Deuteronomy 21:10—34:12*, 784.

61. Ibid.

62. Carlson, *David*, 237.

63. Falaqera's "Book of the Seekers" quoted in James L. Kugel, *Biblical Poetry*, 186.

64. Childs, *The Old Testament as Scripture*, 220.

65. Watts, *Psalm and Story*, 80.

66. Labuschagne, "The Song of Moses," 92.

67. Allen, "Deuteronomic Re-presentation," 21.

68. Talstra, "Deuteronomy 31," 102.

69. Allen, "Deuteronomic Re-presentation," 21.

Within the narrative context of Deut 31–34, the song functions as part of "the testamentary discourse of Deut 31–34,"[70] and its content and purpose are specifically delineated in Deut 31:14–30, 32:44–47. Brueggemann writes, "The poem is framed by the narrative introduction of 31:30 that situates the song in the 'assembly," and by the conclusion of 32:44–47 that reiterates the theme of "witness against" from 31:19."[71] The song describes itself as a teaching (v. 2), but if it is seen in its narrative context, the teaching is part of the witness (31:19). Brian Britt argues that "the text's self-reference as 'witness' and the concept of memorial reflect the overall function of the narrative in Deuteronomy 31–32."[72] He explains that "Like a stone monument, the text ascribes itself didactic and memorial purposes for a community and its generations to come."[73] As a textual memorial it emphasizes writing and reciting.[74] While as a "teaching" the poem has "a didactic purpose beyond its forensic one,"[75] as a "witness" it has a memorializing purpose that involves reiteration reinforcing emphatic affirmation.[76] Employing wisdom terminology to describe Israel's behavior (Deut 32:6, 28), the teaching also exhorts Israel to understand (Deut 32:7).[77] This shows the prescriptive nature of the song.[78] Rather than responding to a specific calamity, it instructs

70. Ibid., 24; for a discussion on Deuteronomy's testamentary character, see Olson, *Deuteronomy and the Death of Moses*, 17–22.

71. Brueggemann, *Deuteronomy*, 277; for detailed survey of studies on the song see Sanders, *The Provenance of Deuteronomy 32*, 1–98; for genre-related discussions see Thiessen, "The Form and Function of the Song of Moses (Deuteronomy 32:1–43)," 401–24; Tigay, *Deuteronomy*, 509, who explains that the poem "displays features of several different genres. The introductory summons is paralleled in didactic psalms, prophecies, and proverbs; similar summonses to heaven and earth and other elements of nature appear in prophetic indictment speeches. Its didactic retrospective on Israel's history has counterparts in hymnic historical psalms and in prophecies . . . Various features of wisdom literature appear throughout the poem, such as its characterization as a "teaching" (v. 2), its attribution of sin to foolishness (vv., 6, 28–29), its appeal to elders (v. 7)"; Wright, "The Lawsuit of God," 26–67; Boston, "The Wisdom Influence upon the Song of Moses," 198–202; Driver, *Deuteronomy*, 345; von Rad, *Deuteronomy*, 196, 200; Weitzman, "Lessons from the Dying, 377–93. He points out that while it may still be true that the different strains of the Song may have been secondarily added to the song, "their present combination reflects the literary logic governing the composition of the preceding narrative and the role of the song within that narrative."

72. Britt, "Deuteronomy 31–32 as a Textual Memorial," 374–75

73. Ibid.

74. Ibid.

75. Tigay, *Deuteronomy*, 299.

76. Britt, "Deuteronomy 31–32 as a Textual Memorial," 370.

77. Weitzman, "Lessons from the Dying," 377–93.

78. Thiessen, "The Form and Function of the Song of Moses," 424.

the people, "guiding the community's thinking, worship and response to YHWH," by identifying who they are, who their God is, and how they ought to relate to him.[79]

It is in this passage that we find a reference to God as Father of the people of Israel which probably is the basis for latter uses in psalms and prophetic literature.[80] As will be shown below, its use as part of the formation narrative in the context that calls for recital and remembrance of God's great deeds and obedience to the Torah revitalizes the people's past tradition in a way that forms an ongoing narrative of self-understanding. In the first section of the passage that sets the topic of the chapter (32:5–6), both Israel and God are identified using kinship language, Israel as children and God as Father. The rest of the chapter fleshes out the experience of this relationship. In v. 6, God is referred to as the Father of Israel ("your Father"), who "created . . . made . . . and established" Israel. That it is put in the form of a rhetorical question, "Is not he your Father?" suggests that there was such tradition of referring to God as Father behind this use and hence the narrator is appealing to shared cultural knowledge. It could also be based on the depiction of Israel as "son" in a formative text such as Ex 4:22 which could evoke the Fatherhood of God based on kinship logic. Verses 10–13 especially explain how God's fatherhood is seen in the life of Israel. God is identified as the one who "sustained . . . shielded, cared (for) . . . guarded" Israel (v. 10), who "guided . . . set . . . fed . . . nursed" Israel (vv. 11–13), and who "gave birth" to Israel as people (v. 18). The verbs ילד (*yalad*) and חיל (*holel,*) suggest the image of a mother as well as father.[81] In passages such

79. Ibid.

80. Concerning its relationship to the subsequent use, in the past some argued that Deut 32 is dependent on the prophetic literature. See Driver, *Deuteronomy*, 346. However, recent scholars have argued that the prophets depended on the song but not vice versa. Mendenhall, "Samuel's Broken *Rîb*"," 169–80, 171. Mendenhall describes Deut 32 as a major source of the prophetic movement of 7th-6th century; Kaiser, "The Song of Moses," 497–99 argues for "a direct and conscious dependency" between Isaiah and Deut 32. He points out that both the Song of Moses and Isaiah present Israel as divinely chosen by Yahweh and the fact that they are his special possession (Deut 32: 8–9; Isa 41:8–9; 42: 6; 43:10, 21; 44: 1–2; 45: 4), both include the idea of witness (Deut 31:19, 21; Isa 43:10, 12; 44: 8, 23; 45:14) as well as deliverance through the wilderness (Deut 32: 10–14; Isa 41: 17–20; 43: 19–20). Furthermore, creation is a theme in both Deuteronomy and Isaiah and in both cases it is used to depict both Israel's formation and her deliverance; for the list of parallels between the Song and Jeremiah see Holladay, "Jeremiah and Moses," 17–27; for a recent discussion of two centuries of research, see Sanders, *Deuteronomy* 32, 1–98, particularly 58–64 on the Song's correspondence with prophetic writings.

81. Tigay, *Deuteronomy*, 307, notes that the first verb *yalad* is used more often to giving birth than for fathering (208 times vs. 22 according to BDB) and the second refers to the mother's labor pain. Some commentaries simply translate the first verb as "fathered" and the second one as "gave you birth." See Merrill, *Deuteronomy*, 416.

as Gen 3:16 and Job 39:1, ילד is used to refer to giving birth to children.[82] However, in passages such as Gen 4:18; 10:18, it is used to refer to begetting, and in Nu 11:12, it is used to refer to bringing forth the people of Israel.[83] The polal form of היל has the meaning of "to be brought forth through labor pains."[84] Here the paternal and maternal image is used together to describe God.[85] The LXX translates ילד into γεννάω which means "to bring forth, to create,"[86] and היל into τρέφω, which indicates feeding, nourishing, rearing. Here too the paternal and maternal tone is brought together.[87] Israel is portrayed as "his . . . children" (vv. 5, 45), "the LORD's own portion" (v. 8), "his people," (vv. 36, 43), and "his servants," (v. 36).

In verse 7 the reference to God as Father of Israel is followed by a call "to remember the days of old," which "recalls the period of Israel's formation in the exodus from Egypt, the making of the covenant with YHWH at Mount Sinai."[88] Then, these descriptions of Israel's relationship to God are put in relation to the whole of humanity in vv. 8–9 and Israel is identified as uniquely God's "allotted share," and his "own portion."[89] Such themes of election, establishing, and also sustaining which are associated with creation language are presented as the features of the Fatherhood of God.[90] God's fatherhood of Israel and Israel's being children of God are "embedded in the narrative of his making them his people . . ."[91] Similarly, Tigay observes, "The Bible is quite conscious of the fact that Israel had not existed from time immemorial but owed its national existence to God. The poem does not specify when God created Israel, but verse 8 suggests that it was when He divided the human race into separate nations (see Gen 10–11)."[92]

The Father-children language expresses kinship relationship which entails both privilege and responsibility for each party. As Father, God "creates" (v. 6), nurtures, guides, protects (vv. 10–12), delivers (vv. 36, 43) and gives inheritance to Israel (vv. 13–14). One of the major themes of Deuteronomy

82. Koehler and Baumgartner, *HALOT*, 411.

83. Ibid.

84. Ibid., 311.

85. Miller, *Deuteronomy*, 230.

86. Lust, et al., *Greek-English Lexicon of the Septuagint*, 118.

87. Ibid., 619.

88 Christensen, *Deuteronomy 21:10—34:12*, 796.

89. "When the Most High apportioned the nations, when he divided humankind, he fixed the boundaries of the peoples according to the number of the gods, the LORD's own portion was his people, Jacob his allotted share."

90. McConville, *Deuteronomy*, 34.

91. Ibid., 453.

92. Tigay, *Deuteronomy*, 302.

is "the land that the LORD your God is giving you as an inheritance," (Deut 19:10) which is part of Israel's privilege.[93] As children, Israel is expected to fulfill its filial loyalty in return (v. 20).[94] Elsewhere, standards are prescribed to Israel as children of God based on God's creation and protection (Deut 1:31; 8:5; 14:1). Deuteronomy 32 measures this Father–children relationship and states that God is "perfect . . . just . . . and faithful" in keeping the fatherly role. On the other hand, Israel is found to be unfaithful (v. 20), "degenerate . . . a perverse, and crooked generation" (v. 5) and hence behaves as "non-children," or "pseudo-children," thereby "undermining the parent-child relationship."[95] As shall be seen below, such comparison permeates the prophets who speak of Israel's failure to live up to its filial duties to God.[96]

Thus, in Deuteronomy 32, God as Father is described as electing, founding, establishing, and sustaining Israel. Israel is depicted as children, God's people, and God's portion. This is put in relation to the "days of old" that evokes God's deliverance, covenant, and the founding of Israel. It also highlights Israel's privilege as well as its responsibility. The fact that this portrayal of God's Fatherhood is put in a context that presents itself as a testimony, witness, and instruction that should be recited, memorialized, and lived by creates a narrative that shapes Israel's self-understanding. Israel's being and becoming narrated in relation to the Fatherhood of God is rehearsed time and again not only in terms of how Israel needed to behave but also in terms of why Israel needed to behave in that way. It also has a particularizing effect as the Fatherhood of God is also formulated in terms of God's choosing of Israel from among the nations (32:8–9). If, as suggested here, this is the first written use of God as Father, coupled with the particularizing reference to Israel as "my first born son" (Ex 4:22), it constructs God's Fatherhood of Israel as one of the distinctive and defining features of Israel's identity.

The same emphasis is found in the prophetic depictions of God as Father of the people Israel. There are eight references to God as "Father": Isa 63:16 (twice); 64:9; Jer 3:4–5, 19; 31:9; and Mal1:6 and 2:10. The references emphasize the theme of the creation of Israel, its deliverance, and restoration. As will be seen below, like Deuteronomy 32, in these passages God's Fatherhood is depicted in relation to Israel being children of God.

Due to the chapter divisions in the book of Isaiah the three references appear to come from different sections. However, since Isaiah 63:7—64:12

93. This theme is widespread in Deuteronomy, see Deut 4:21; 15:4; 19:14; 21:23; 24:4; 25:19; 26:1; other passages that identify the land as inheritance from God to Israel include Ex 23:30; Num 34:2; 2 Chr 6:27; Ps 135:12; Jer 12:14; Ezek 47:14.

94. Tigay, *Deuteronomy*, 301.

95. Nelson, *Deuteronomy*, 371.

96. Tigay, *Deuteronomy*, 301.

is taken by most commentaries as forming a unit, these references should be taken together.[97] The unit comprises a lament over God's dealing with his people.[98] The unit begins by recounting (ריכזא) God's covenant loyalty (הוהי ידסח) in 63:7. The recounting serves not only as a title to the passage, but also notes the nature of the unit as one that brings to remembrance and "memorializes" God's relationship with the people of Israel.[99] Achtemeier observes that the unit "opens with a recital of the saving deeds of Yahweh," and it recalls God's covenant with Israel and deeds that manifest God's love.[100] She further explains that at the heart of this historical remembrance is the covenant relationship in which God made Israel his people (Ex 6:7; Jer 31:33).[101] As indicated by "all that the LORD has done for us . . . to the house of Israel" (63:7), the text identifies both the speaker and the audience with the house of Israel and with the recipients of those gracious acts, although they were performed in an earlier age.[102] Watts notes that "The third-person references to God had been accompanied in vv 7–14a with first person plural identification of the worshiping community with the age of salvation."[103]

The unit as a whole is divided into two: 63:7–14 recounts the history of God's compassion and the failure of God's people; 63:15—64:12 comprise a confession and request for divine intervention.[104] All three references to God as Father of the people of Israel are found in this latter section that records a confession and request for divine intervention (63:16; 64:8). Unlike Deut 32:6 which *identifies* God as the Father of Israel through a rhetorical question ("Is he not your father?"), both texts in Isaiah *address* God as "our Father" in the context of prayer (63:16; 64:8). God is identified as Israel's savior (63:8), the redeemer who "lifted them up and carried them all the days of old" (63:9). The people of Israel are identified as "the house of Israel," (63:7), God's people and children (v. 8, 14, 18; 64:9), and God's heritage (67:17). In 63:16, the fatherhood of God to Israel is presented as the founda-

97. Smith, *Isaiah 40–66*, 665.

98. Ibid., 665; Watts, *Isaiah 34–66*, 329–30, compares the message in this unit to sermons and prayers in Deuteronomy and Chronicles, and similar passages that use Israelite history and prayers.

99 Watts, *Isaiah 34–66*, 331.

100. Achtemeier, *The Community and Message*, 113.

101. Ibid.,113; See Gileadi, *The Literary Message of Isaiah*, 67–68 who argues that הוהי ידסח is covenant language; and also see Weinfeld, *TDOT*, 2.258; Tasker, *Ancient Near Eastern Literature*, 148.

102 Watts, *Isaiah 34–66*, 331.

103 Ibid., 333.

104. Smith, *Isaiah 40–66*, 667; see also Webster, "The Rhetoric of Isaiah 63–65," 89–102.

tion, the basis for the request to God to "Look down from heaven" (63:15) and to "Turn back for the sake of your servants, for the sake of the tribes that are your heritage" (63:17), for "Your holy people" (63:18), that are "called by your name" (v. 19). It reminds God of the special relationship God has with God's people at the center of which is the formation of Israel through covenantal relationship.[105] Achtemeier explains, "The complaint is that their God of mercy, the God who has always been a Father to Israel, is no longer acting like their Father and Redeemer."[106]

While in 63:16, the use of Father is part of lament, in 64:8 it is part of prayer and serves as a basis for appeal. After a confession in 64:6–7, ("We have all become like one who is unclean, and all our righteous deeds are like a filthy cloth . . . There is no one who calls on your name"), in 64:8 the speaker with "Yet, O LORD," *addresses* God as "you are our Father." This is accompanied by expressions that evoke the formation of Israel as people: "we are clay, you are our potter; we are all the work of your hand" (64.8) and hence "we are all your people" (64:9). It is presented as a basis not only for the request "not (to) remember iniquity" (v. 9), but also to rescue his people. Smith points out that since as Father, God is the head of the family, and since as potter Israel is a clay that God formed (43:1,7, 21; 44:21), "he must value and show some love for what he made."[107] Isaiah appeals to the relationship God entered with his people as Father in creating them, "like a potter created an earthenware vessel."[108]

Seen in relation to the whole passage, in v.16 the assertion "For you are our father" picks up the kinship theme from v. 8 which has God speaking of ancient Israel as his "children." As Watts notes, here the speaker wants to claim that the relation to ancient Israel which is depicted in v. 8 identifying Israel as God's people and his children and God as their savior "should apply to them also across all the intervening centuries."[109] As 64:8 introduces a climax to the passage with "now" (ועתה), it relates what has been said so far with the fatherhood of God to the people of Israel. Just as 63:17 picks up the kinship theme from 63:8, this verse also picks up the kinship theme "from the sermon on the age of salvation . . . to claim identity with the chosen and saved people" of the previous generation.[110]

105. Achtemeier, *The Community and Message*, 113; Motyer, *Prophecy of Isaiah*, 512, 515

106. Ibid., 116.

107. Smith, *Isaiah 40–66*, 667, 693.

108. Achtemeier, *The Community and Message*, 120.

109. Watts, *Isaiah 34–66*, 333.

110 Ibid., 336

The use of God as Father in Jeremiah exhibits similar themes with Deuteronomy and Isaiah. The first two uses of God as Father in Jeremiah are in the first section of the book which focuses on Judah's apostasy (2:1—4:4) and particularly in section 3:1—4:4 where the theme of repentance and return is developed.[111] Holladay sees a symmetry shaped by the use of kinship language "father" and "sons" from verse 4 to verse 24.[112] The two references here are as such part of the same literary unit. When vv. 4–5 and 19–20 are seen together, the latter resumes what is started in vv. 4–5. While in vv. 4–5 Israel is depicted as referring to God as Father to ask mercy from God, in real life Israel did not give recognition to God as Father. Vv. 19–20 describe that it was God's intention and desire to relate to Israel as Father by treating Israel as God's children, and by giving to it "a pleasant land, the most beautiful heritage of all the nations." Here the Fatherhood of God for the people of Israel is explicitly connected to giving them inheritance. However, Israel did not honor that relationship. God is identified as "my Father" (3:4, 19) and "our God" (3:22, 23, 24). His formation of Israel, the Exodus (2:4–6), and giving the land as inheritance (2:7) are recalled and God's faithfulness asserted. On the other hand, Israel is identified with kinship features such as "house of Jacob" and "house of Israel" (2:4, 26; 3:20), "faithless children" (3:14, 22), and with the phrase "my people" (2:11, 13, 31, 32), which consistently appear in the context where kinship features are used to describe Israel. Evoking Israel's portrayal in the formative narratives, Israel is located within humanity as "the first fruits" of God's "harvest" (2:3). While God is measured and found faithful, Israel is measured and found to be "faithless children." As faithful Father, God is depicted as continuing to call Israel, the "faithless children" (3:14, 22), to return with a promise of restoration (3:15–18). Jeremiah "portrays for us a parent who has labored and dreamed for a glorious day when the child would be old enough, responsible enough to receive all that has been saved for the child from the beginning. The father wants to give the child . . . (but) the child neither knows nor cares."[113]

The third reference to God as Father in Jeremiah is found in chapter 31:9 which is part of the section referred to as the book of consolation (chaps 30–33) and which focuses on the restoration and the new covenant. The book is filled with the language of restoration and deliverance that is reminiscent of the exodus account: wandering in the desert (v. 2), leading the people "by

111. McConville, *Judgment and Promise*, 28; for the relationship between Jeremiah and Deuteronomy see Cazelles, "Jeremiah and Deuteronomy," 89–112; Hyatt, "Jeremiah and Deuteronomy," 113–28.

112. Holladay, *The Architecture of Jeremiah 1–20*, 49–52; Tasker, *Ancient Near Eastern Literature*, 155.

113. Brueggemann, *To Pluck Up, To Tear Down*, 44.

brooks of water" (v. 9), entering into a covenant (v. 32), and taking the people by hand and leading them away (v. 32). Israel is identified as "my people" (30:3, 22; 31:1, 7, 14, 33), as "my dear son" and "the child I delight in" (31:20), "firstborn" (31:9), "faithless daughter" (31:22), and "house of Israel and house of Judah" (31:27, 31). God is identified as "a Father to Israel" (31:9) who loved Israel "with an everlasting love" and continued faithfulness to Israel (31:3). As indicated with a conjunction "for," God's being "a father to Israel," and Israel being his "firstborn" is the reason for God's promise to lead Israel back and to "let them walk by brooks of water, in a straight path in which they shall not stumble" (31:9b).[114] Here, too Israel is also located within humanity as "the chief of the nations" (31:7).[115] Relating this section with the use of "father" to refer to God in Jeremiah 3, Jones explains that "this unqualified declaration of divine fatherhood is the answer to the doubts expressed in 3:4, 19."[116] McCarthy observes that the restoration of Israel promised here is "the restoration of the father-son relationship. This is the context governed by 31:1, that is, by the proclamation of a new and better union between Yahweh and Israel based on a new covenant."[117]

Although God is featured as Father in Malachi explicitly only twice (1:6; 2:10), the theme of God as Israel's Father "runs through Malachi's prophecy."[118] Taylor and Clendenen explain that God's fatherhood is "implied in the opening declaration of God's love for Jacob (1:2) then used in 1:6 . . . It is alluded to in 3:17 in a promise of God's future compassion on Israel . . . [and] in 2:10 God's fatherhood is recalled and used to rebuke unfaithfulness."[119] Following the reference to the foundational story to show God's love to Israel in the election story (1:1–5), in 1:6 the priests are asked, "If then I am a father, where is the honor due to me?" Taylor and Clendenen explain that this passage is based on the accepted norm that a father deserves honor from his son and that God as Israel's creator is Israel's Father.[120] This is evidenced by the assertion, "A son honors his father, servants their master" (1:6a).

114. Keown, *Jeremiah 26–52*, 114; also see Holladay, *Jeremiah Chapters 26–32*, 185, who sees Deut 32 as "immediate stimulus for the image of 'father/son'" here in Jeremiah 31:9.

115. While the Hebrew Bible depicts other nations also as belonging to God (e.g., Amos 9:7 and also Isaiah 19:19–25), it limits to Israel the familial relationship to God.

116. Jones, *Jeremiah*, 389.

117. McCarthy, "Love of God in Deuteronomy," 45–46.

118. Taylor and Clendenen, *Haggai, Malachi*, 324.

119. Ibid., 324.

120. Ibid., 262.

While the passage does not share the common language of formation and restoration observed in other passages, it shares "a common technique of comparing the faithfulness of God to the faithlessness of his children."[121]

In 2:10, however, God is referred to as both Father and creator which "while not synonymous, should be understood as complementary."[122] In similar way to Deuteronomy 32 and prophetic literature (e.g. Mal 2:10), the creation motif highlights the formation of peoplehood associated with Israel's relationship with God and depicts that "Israel owed its existence to God."[123] Although in other places God is presented as the creator of all, here following passages that depict God as the Father of the people of Israel, the creatorship of God is applied to Israel in conjunction with God as Israel's Father in a particularized sense.[124] While in 1:6 the call is for proper response to God as one's Father, here the message is related to the proper treatment of fellow community members as one's covenant siblings as indicated with the phrase "with one another" (2:10b).[125] What is translated as "one another" refers to the participants in the covenant of their ancestors (2:10b), to whom God is "Father," and "creator."[126] As such, the sibling relationship is derived from God's Fatherhood and formation of Israel. Malachi 2:10b states the charge against Judah with a rhetorical question: "Why then are we faithless to one another, profaning the covenant of our ancestors?" Then, vv. 10b–15 explicate the charge as being unfaithfulness against both God (vv. 11–12) and fellow covenant members (vv. 13–15).[127] The argument is that since all of Israel have one Father and one creator who gave covenant to the ancestors, Israelites should not be "faithless to one another." Judah's belonging to one Father and creator who gave it the covenant is a ground not to act unfaithfully towards one another.

In vv. 11–12 Judah is accused of marrying "the daughter of a foreign god," and "anyone who does this," is sought to be "cut off from the tents of Jacob." Marrying "the daughter of a foreign god" echoes a long standing tradition in

121. Tasker, *Ancient Near Eastern Literature*, 163.

122. Taylor and Clendenen, *Haggai, Malachi*, 322.

123. Ibid., 324.

124. Chen, *God as Father*, 84; also see Mason, *Old Testament Pictures of God*, 31–34; for passages that depict God as the creator of all see Gen 1:1—2:22; Ps 8:3–8; 18:1; 32:6–9; 94:4–5; 103:2–30; Isa 40:28; 42:5; 44:24; 45:18.

125. Taylor and Clendenen, *Haggai, Malachi*, 324–25.

126. Ibid., 325. Taylor and Clendenen point out that the phrase translated "with one another," in v. 10b is literally "a man with his brother."

127. Ibid., Taylor and Clendenen explain that "the covenant to our fathers" here a reference to God's covenant with the patriarchs; see also McKenzie and Wallace, "Covenant Themes in Malachi," 551–52.

the Hebrew Bible that rejects mixed marriage (Deut 7:3–4; Ex 34:11–16; Neh 13:26). Taylor and Clendenen explain that "[F]oreign god" refers to any god other than the God of Israel, who "delivered them from Egypt and entered into an exclusive covenant relationship with them, the God who 'Father[ed]' and 'create[d]' them."[128] The phrase "the daughter of a foreign god" refers "collectively to women outside the community of faith . . . who worshiped a god other than the Lord."[129] Just as the people of God are considered children of God, worshipers of other gods are referred to as children of their god (Num 21:29). Hence the unfaithfulness of Judah is indicated here as "marriage outside the community of faith," God's children marrying the daughters of other gods. The idea is that the identity of God's people is being undermined by the mixed marriages with non-Israelite women as the foreign women cling to their own religious heritage and let elements of their religions penetrate their husbands' families. The penalty for such behavior is to be "cut off" from "the tents of Jacob," that is, from the community.[130] The divorce condemned in vv. 13–15 is considered as resulting from Jewish men abandoning their Jewish wives for non-Jewish women.[131]

Thus, the intermarriage and its result addressed in Mal 2:10–11 are considered as a relation that undermined the unity and identity of Israel *as family that belongs to God* and "entailed a faithless treatment of the Judean wife of one's youth."[132] It constitutes a threat to the unity and identity of God's people. As the "offspring and creatures of the one God," with the realization that "God brought them into existence as a united whole," the people of Israel should have been faithful not only to him but also to one another.[133]

In summary, in prophetic writings God is addressed as "our Father" (Is 63:16; 64:8), creator, savior, and redeemer. Israel is identified as "the house of Israel," children, and God's people and his heritage. With an exhortation to recall "the days of old," this portrayal of God and Israel is set frequently in relation to God's loyalty in a way that recalls and memorializes Israel's unique identity in relation to God (Is 63:7). When measured in terms of Father-children relationship, while God is found faithful, Israel is portrayed as unfaithful. God's Fatherhood is then presented as the basis for the request to forgive, rescue, and restore God's people. God's special relationship with

128. Taylor and Clendenen, *Haggai, Malachi*, 334.

129. Ibid., 336.

130. For similar teachings see Gen 17:14; Ex 12:15, 19; 31:14; Lev 7:20, 21, 27; 17:10; 20:3, 6.

131. Zehnder, "A Fresh Look at Malachi 2:13–16," 227–28.

132. van der Woude, "Malachi's Struggle," 65–71, 66.

133. Taylor and Clendenen, *Haggai, Malachi*, 325.

Israel that emanates from God's Fatherhood to Israel is depicted as making Israel "the chief of the nations" (Jer 31:7). At the center of such depictions is the formation of Israel as a people through the Fatherhood of God. That God's Fatherhood is evoked time and again in the plea of restoration when even the covenant is broken indicates that the Father-children relationship goes beyond covenantal relationship. It is grounded on the formative discourse that depicts Israel in familial relationship before Israel entered into a covenant with Yahweh (e.g., Ex 4:22). The restoration sought and promised is "the restoration of the father-son relationship."[134]

Finally, God is also referred to as Father of the people of Israel in two Psalms (Ps 68:5; 103:13). Psalm 68 begins by identifying two groups of people: God's enemies (v. 1–2) and the righteous (v. 3). The Psalmist seeks the enemies to be "scattered," to "flee," "melt," and "perish" (vv. 1–2) and the righteous to be "joyful," to "exult before God" (v. 3), and to "sing praises to his name" (v. 4). The righteous are identified as God's people (v. 7), God's heritage (v. 9), and God's flock (v. 10). God is identified as "the God of Sinai" (v. 8), "the God of Israel" (vv. 8, 35), "God of salvation" (v. 20), "our salvation" (v. 19b), "Israel's fountain" (v. 26), the one who "daily bears (Israel) up" (v. 19), and who gives "power and strength to his people" (v. 35).

God is further introduced with language that echoes the Exodus, "who rides upon the clouds" (v. 5) and is identified as "Father of the orphans and protector of widows" (v. 5) who "gives the desolate a home to live in," and "leads out the prisoners to prosperity" (v. 6). With these characterizations, God is depicted as meeting people at Sinai, Bashan, and Zion, each mountain becoming "more significant than the previous one, showing him to be in control over ever-widening aspects of Creation, all described in Exodus redemption terms."[135] As Father, God leads the prisoner out, and guides the people through the desert.[136] As the father of the fatherless and deliverer of the homeless and the prisoners, God goes forth before the people and leads them through a wilderness experience.[137]

In Psalm 103:13, too, God is featured as the one who "forgives . . . heals . . . redeems . . . crowns" with "steadfast love" (v. 3–4), who is "merciful and gracious . . . abounding in steadfast love," (v. 8), who made his ways known "to the people of Israel" (v. 7), and who has compassion "for those who fear" him as "a father has compassion to his children" (v. 13). God's fatherly compassion is based on this knowledge and remembrance of how

134. McCarthy, "The Love of God in Deuteronomy," 45–46.

135. Tasker, *Ancient Near Eastern Literature*, 119.

136. Ibid.

137. Tate, *Psalms 51–100*, 176.

Israel was made (v. 14). Although the Psalm begins with the Psalmist blessing God, in vv. 6–10 the Psalmist encourages the people of Israel to join him in praise.[138] The call to praise recounts incidents from the Exodus elaborating God's dealing with his people (vv.11–19).[139] The steadfast love of God is mentioned four times in the Psalm evoking God's covenantal relationship with God's people.

Summing up the use of God as Father to the people of Israel in the Hebrew Bible, while God as the Father of the people of Israel is *identified* as "Father" in most of its occurrences, God is also *addressed* as "our Father." As Father, God is portrayed as electing, founding, establishing, sustaining, and restoring Israel. On the other hand, Israel is depicted as God's children, people, portion, and heritage in a way that highlights Israel's privilege as well as its responsibility. God's special relationship with Israel that emanates from God's Fatherhood to Israel is depicted as making Israel "the chief of the nations" (Jer 31:7; Deut 32:8–9), providing an orienting framework for Israel's self-understanding. At the center of such depiction is the formation of Israel as a people through the Fatherhood of God. When measured in terms of Father-children relationship, while God is found faithful, Israel is portrayed as unfaithful. God's Fatherhood is then presented as the basis for the request to forgive, rescue, and restore his people. This is put in relation to recalling the "days of old" that evoke God's deliverance, covenant and the founding of Israel in a way that recalls and memorializes God's unique relationship with Israel. That God's Fatherhood is evoked time and again in the plea of restoration when even the covenant is broken indicates that the Father-children relationship goes beyond covenantal relationship. The restoration sought and promised is "the restoration of the father-son relationship."[140] As such, Israel's being and becoming is narrated in relation to the Fatherhood of God and is rehearsed time and again not only in terms of how Israel needed to behave but also in terms of why Israel needed to behave in that way. It also has a particularizing effect as the Fatherhood of God is also formulated in terms of God's choosing of Israel from among the nations (Deut 32:8–9).

Israel as Son(s)/Children of God

In addition to the texts in which God is referred to as Father that are discussed above, Israel is also referred to as children/son(s) of God both in formative as

138. Tasker, *Ancient Near Eastern Literature*, 127.

139. Ibid.

140. McCarthy, "The Love of God in Deuteronomy," 45–46.

well as prophetic texts that look back to the formative narrative.[141] Although not frequent, the language of children of God is found "in a fairly wide cross-section of the Old Testament literature as an expression of the bond between Yahweh and his people."[142] For the sake of this study, I will categorize such use into three: texts that state Israel as son/children of God (Ex 4:22; Deut 14:1), texts that measure Israel as son/children and often find them wanting (Hos 11:1–3; Isa 1:2–4; 30:1, 9),[143] and texts that seek and declare Israel's hope of restoration based on Israel's status as children of God.[144]

Among the first types of texts are Ex 4:22 and Deut 14:1, both of which are found in formative contexts in the Hebrew Bible. In Ex 4:22 God referred to Israel, even before Israel entered into a covenant, as "my son." When Pharaoh would "not let the people go" (Ex. 4:21), God's instruction to Pharaoh was based on Israel's identity as the son of God and God's first born.[145] It is presented as a reason why Pharaoh had to release and why, if he refused, God would deliver them by killing Pharaoh's firstborn son. The subsequent outworking of this assertion in the narrative of the Exodus "has initiated and underscored in many different ways the image of Israel as . . . the son of God."[146] Relating it with other features in Exodus, Schmitt further explains that "[t]he call of Israel, the covenant with Israel, the failures of and the promises of Israel all bear the marks of a father-son relationship. The book of Exodus is a major witness to Israel's sonship."[147] C. J. H. Wright

141. By "formative texts/narrative" I refer to passages, particularly in the Pentateuch, that tell/describe the story of the formation of Israel as people.

142. Byrne, *Sons of God-Seed of Abraham*, 16.

143. For the texts that measure how Israel fulfilled its sonship/children status see Deut 32:5, 18–19; Isa 1:2; 30:1, 9; 43:6; 63:16; 64:8; Jer 3:4, 19; 4:22; 31:9, 20; Hos 11:1; Mal 1:6; 2:10; while such texts include texts where God is referred to as the Father of the people of Israel, since I have discussed these texts above, here I will focus mainly on texts that do not have God as Father.

144. Here, too, texts that refer to Israel as children and are found where God is referred to as Father are not included. In most instances these three aspects come together in one text. However, presenting the data in this way will help to show that kinship terms that show the nature of familial relationship are used sometimes together and sometimes separately with the expectation that using kinship terms that depict one aspect of familial relationship would evoke the rest. This approach stands in sharp contrast to the argument of Aasgaard that since Paul does not clearly relate his sibling language with the fatherhood of God, views that relate Pauline use of sibling language to his use of God as Father are untenable; see Aasgaard, *'My Beloved Brothers and Sisters!'*, 308–9.

145. "Thus says the LORD: Israel is my first born son. I said to you, "Let my son go that he may worship me. But you refused to let him go; now I will kill your firstborn son" (Ex 4:22–23).

146. Schmitt, "Israel as Son of God," 73.

147. Ibid.

observes, "Israel is the firstborn son of Yahweh for no other reason than that Yahweh brought them as a nation into existence, just as they are the people of Yahweh for no other reason than that he 'sets his love upon' them and chose them for himself (Deut. 7:6–7)."[148] Israel as people owed its existence to God as the one who "created them and called them into the stage of history" as portrayed in the Hebrew Bible.[149] C. J. H. Wright explains, "it was not the case that Israel was an already existing nation whom God then subsequently decided to choose and use. Rather, Israel was brought into existence for this chosen purpose."[150]

Deut 14:1 applies this Father-son relationship to daily living. Israel is instructed as children of God to handle themselves differently when they mourn. The text reads: "You are children of the LORD your God. You must not lacerate yourselves or shave your forelocks for the dead. For you are a people holy to the LORD your God; it is you the LORD has chosen out of all the peoples on earth to be his people, his treasured possession." Their identity as children of God is related to their formation as people— their being "chosen out of all the peoples on earth" with the purpose that they will be God's people, "his treasured possession," and "the people holy to the LORD." As such, with all its privileges, their status as children of God brings responsibilities that set them apart from other nations.[151] Byrne explains that while sonship is the unique privilege of Israel as the people chosen and created by God for himself, it involves "in several notable instances (cf. Is 1:2f; 63:16; Ex 4:22f; Hos 1:10; cf. 2:23) a demand for acknowledgement—mutual acknowledgement between Yahweh and his people."[152]

It is this privilege and responsibility on which the texts that measure Israel as son/children focus. The privilege and responsibility of Israel as the children of God are a constant theme in the Hebrew Bible. The privilege is depicted among other things in terms of inheritance, protection, providence, and hope in time of crisis. The responsibility is depicted in terms of Israel showing undivided loyalty to Yahweh. The theme of inheritance is associated with Israel's sonship and God's fatherhood of the people of Israel.[153] The term "firstborn" that is associated with Israel's sonship in Israel's forma-

148. Wright, *God's People in God's Land*, 18.

149. Wright, *Knowing God as Father*, 80.

150. Ibid.

151. Tigay, *Deuteronomy*, 136.

152. Byrne, *Sons of God-Seed of Abraham*, 16.

153. The language of inheritance in the Hebrew Bible has three major aspects: Israel as God's inheritance (Ps 33:12; 78:71; 1 Kgs 8:51ff;), the land as God's inheritance (Ex 15:7; Ps 68:7–10; 79:1; Jer 2:7; 12:7–9), the land as Israel's inheritance (Ps 105:11; 136:21–22). See Wright, *God's People in God's Land*, 19.

tive text is a language of inheritance. Thompson describes inheritance as the "(f)irst and foremost" among the features of God's fatherhood which carries "the notion of the father as the founder of a clan or head of a family who bestows an inheritance on his son and so also on subsequent generations."[154] Deut 4:37 identifies the inheritance with the land as follows:

> Because He loved your fathers, therefore He chose their descendants after them. And he personally brought you from Egypt by His great power, driving out from before nations greater and mightier than you to bring you in and to give you their land for an inheritance, as it is today.

In the context that recounts the deliverance from Egypt and the formation of Israel as people, Psalm136:21–22 states that God "gave their land as a heritage . . . Even a heritage to Israel His servant" (NAS).

The prophets use the picture of sonship both as an accusation and as grounds of hope. Israel's responsibility as children is assessed frequently and quite often the result is negative (Isa 30:1, 9; 57:4; 1:2; Deut 32; Hos 11:1; 1:10). As a ground of accusation, the prophets repeatedly measured to what extent Israel lived in accordance to what is expected of its sonship (Is 1:2–4; Jer 3:4–5, 19–20; Isa 30:1, 9, Mal 1:6). A well known passage in Hosea recalls God's love for Israel that is demonstrated in delivering Israel from Egypt. Israel is measured in terms of its identity as child and son and found wanting— "The more I called them, the more they went from me; they kept sacrificing to the Baals, and offering incense to idols" (11:1–3). According to Isa 1:2 God "reared children and brought them up," but they rebelled against God. As a result, they are described as a "sinful nation, people laden with iniquity, offspring who do evil, children who deal corruptly, who have forsaken the LORD, who have despised the Holy One of Israel, who are utterly estranged!"(Isa 1:4). And Isa 30:9 characterizes them as "rebellious people, faithless children, children who will not hear the instruction of the LORD. . ."[155] Commenting on the prophets' reflection of the Father-children relationship of God and Israel, Tigay writes, "God assigned Israel its land as a father assigns land to his children, and expected that Israel would acknowledge His fatherhood and remain loyal, and not "play false.' They often describe Israel's sins as the misbehavior of rebellious sons and daughters [Hos 11:1–3; Isa 1:2, 4]."[156]

154. Thompson, *The Promise of the Father*, 116.

155. See also Isa 30:1–2, "Oh, rebellious children, says the LORD, who carry out a plan, but not mine; who make an alliance, but against my will, adding sin to sin who set out to go down to Egypt without asking for my counsel, to take refuge in the protection of Pharaoh, and to seek shelter in the shadow of Egypt;" also 63:8; Jer 31:9; 38:9.

156. Tigay, *Deuteronomy*, 301.

When Israel's sonship is referred to in a negative sense, most of the time, the term "son" is used in the plural. C. J. H. Wright explains that "whereas the use of 'son' in the singular tends to express the indicative reality of Israel's status before God, the use of 'sons' in the plural tends to express the imperative expectation of obedience."[157] He further observes, "The Israelites are addressed as sons of Yahweh, but then rebuked for failing to fulfill the normal expectations of sons to fathers." Seen in relation to Deut 14:1 assertion, "You are children of the LORD your God," the plural use of Deut 14:1 sets the expectation which repeatedly went unfulfilled (Isa 1:2–4; Jer 3:4–5, 19–20; Isa 30:1, 9; Mal 1:6).[158]

The third type of texts declares Israel's restoration based on Israel's status as children of God. As a ground of hope, the prophets depend on God's unwillingness as father, "to cast off his errant son forever. The One who brought his firstborn out of Egypt would bring the same son back from exile."[159] As the one who "created," "formed," and "redeemed" Israel (Isa 43:1), God promises that God will gather them from the north and south. He declares, "Do not withhold; bring my sons from far away and my daughters from the end of the earth" (Isa 43:6) for they are "called by my name, whom I created for my glory, whom I formed and made" (Isa 43:7). In Hosea 1:10 at the center of the hope of Israel's gathering is the promise that "in the place where it was said to them, 'you are not my people,'" it shall be said to them "Children of the living God." As a Father-children relationship, "Israel's relationship to Yahweh can continue to be affirmed despite her alienation from her land."[160]

In similar way to the three types of texts discussed above, in texts that feature God as Father of the people of Israel, the identity of Israel as children is measured and depicted as lacking, rebuke is pronounced, and redemption promised. As such, the theme of fatherhood, sonship, and the privilege and responsibility thereof is brought together in these texts (Deut 32:5; Jer 31:9–10, 20). Thus, Israel's being and becoming is stated in terms of their identity as children of God and then their whole life is assessed accordingly. The use of the Father-children construct not only creates identity but also becomes an instrument of control, since Israel is constantly criticized for unfaithfulness. Most of the time, Israel is found wanting in not living up to its identity in relationship to God and to each other, they are accused and judged for it. The judgments under which they found themselves are

157. Wright, *Knowing God as the Father*, 81.

158. Ibid., 82–84.

159. Ibid., 85–86.

160. Forshey, "The Construct Chain nahalat YHWH / 'elōhîm," 53.

explained as happening because of their failure to live as children. The hope of restoration is also grounded precisely on their being the children of God.

Israelites as Siblings

The imaging of Israel as a family in the Hebrew Bible continues through the depiction of the people of Israel in sibling language, particularly in the formative texts.[161] Sibling kinship narrative is constructed so as to orient Israel on how to relate to each other. Although the use of sibling language in the Hebrew Bible is not as frequent as the Pauline usage, its use coupled with the teachings such as in Mal 2:10–15, is enough to show that Israel understood itself as a kin-group. In Exodus 2:11 and 4:18 Moses was depicted identifying himself with his "brothers" (אֶחָיו) instead of the Egyptians in whose palace he grew up. Early on, the Pentateuch narrative constructs the Israelites as a community of siblings.[162] In Exodus 2:11, after Moses grew up, "he went out to his brethren and looked at their hard labors and saw an Egyptian beating a Hebrew, one of his brethren" (NAS). In Exodus 4 after his encounter with God, Moses went to his father-in-law and asked permission to return to his "brothers who are in Egypt" (4:18). Durham explains that "Moses' identification with his people's plight is shown both by the repetition of the phrase "among his brethren."[163] While this identification probably is common to the surrounding culture, it is not incidental that it is introduced and repeated in a text that describes the formative story of Israel. Rather, from the very beginning it introduces the Israelites with a family image.

The same word "brothers" is used in Lev 25:35, 46 to describe how the people of Israel must help a fellow Israelite who is in need and must distinguish between fellow Israelite and a non-Israelite when charging interest and owning slaves. Under laws on the kinsman-redeemer in relationship to Jubilee (vv. 23–55), specific regulation is given on loans to fellow Israelites (35–38), on how to treat an Israelite enslaved due to debt (vv. 39–43), and on how to treat fellow Israelites who are slaves (44–46).[164] At the center of

161. It is widely noted that such use of sibling language to depict the relationship between the people of Israel is behind the extensive use of sibling language to describe the relationship between Christ-followers, see Horrell, "From ἀδελφοῖ to οἶκος θεοῦ," 293–311; von Soden, *TDNT* 1:145 writes, "There can be no doubt, however, that αδλφός is one of the titles of the people of Israel taken over by the Christian community."

162. The NRSV translates the term in the form of inclusive language as "his people," "member of the community," "neighbor." However, to maintain the sibling nature that is depicted, in this study I will maintain "brothers."

163. Durham, *Exodus*, 19.

164. Hartley, *Leviticus*, 422.

these regulations is Israel's sibling relationship, the foundation of which is the assertion, "I am the LORD your God, who brought you out of the land of Egypt, to give you the land of Canaan, to be your God" (vv. 38, 42). This assertion evokes the status of sonship that is central in the Exodus, which in turn conjures up the Fatherhood of God following a kinship logic.

The use of sibling image to depict Israel is more frequent in Deuteronomy than any other book in the Hebrew Bible.[165] In the first chapter of Deuteronomy, Moses recalls instructing the judges who were chosen from among the people to hear and judge the cases between their "fellow brothers and sisters" (Deut 1:16). In Deut 3:18, Transjordanian tribes are commanded to help their brothers by participating in the conquest: "Your men equipped for war shall pass over before your brothers, the children of Israel." They had to be a vanguard to their "brothers" until God would give rest to their "brothers" (v. 20).[166] The regulation regarding remission of debts every seven years (15:1–7), the exhortation to lend to the poor (15:7–11), and the regulation regarding manumission of indentured servants in the seventh year (15:12–18) all center on Israelites being siblings and in recalling that they were slaves in the land of Egypt and the LORD redeemed them (v. 15).[167] In vv. 3–18, the terms "his neighbor" (והער) "and his brother" (ויחאו) are used to refer to the same person.[168] The term "brothers" is the dominant structural feature in vv 7–11 and is used to emphasize the kinship relationship.[169]

In Deut 22:1–4 the expression "your brother," which appears five times in vv 1–4, emphasizes "kinship with the person in need in the broadest sense of being a fellow Israelite."[170] In Deut 23:19, similar to Leviticus, instruction is given not to charge interest from one's sibling. Deuteronomy 24:7 forbids stealing from one's Israelite siblings.[171] In 24:12 the term "your brother" (דיחא) refers to "Hebrew kinfolk—both male and female."[172] Christensen explains, "As the term חא, "brother," was paired with ער, "neighbor," in the הטמש-year law (vv 1–11), the term is paired with (ה)ירבע, "Hebrew," in the manumission law (vv 12–18)." The term "Hebrew" here calls attention to the

165. Birge, *The Language of Belonging*, 77, lists the following texts from Deut: 1:16, 28; 2:8; 3:18, 20; 10:9; 15:2, 3, 7, 8, 11, 12; 17:15, 20; 18:2, 7, 15, 18; 19:18, 19; 20:8; 22:1, 2, 3, 4; 23:7, 20, 21; 24:7, 14; 25:3, 11; 32:50.

166. Christensen, *Deuternonomy 1–21:9*, 61.

167 Ibid., 309.

168. Ibid., 312.

169. Ibid., 312.

170. Ibid., 494.

171. Ibid., 573.

172. Ibid., 320.

experience of slavery in Egypt when the Israelites were עבריםי , "Hebrews.[173] Furthermore, instruction is given that Israel's prophets (Deut 18:15) and kings (Deut 17:15) must be "brothers" and not foreigners. Although it is not as frequent as in Deuteronomy, the people of Israel are also described in sibling language in prophetic literature (Isa 66:5; Jer 22:18; Ezek 18:18) and in a well-known verse in Psalm 133:1.

These uses of sibling language image Israel as fellow members of God's family with a responsibility towards each other. Seen in relation to the use of God as Father of the people of Israel and Israel as children of God, the portrayal of Israel as siblings constructs a rounded image of a family with privileges and expectations. Together such multifaceted use of kinship language serves as a strong orienting force that helps the people of Israel understand itself in relation to God, to fellow Israelites, and to other nations.

God as Father of Israel's King

Although God's Fatherhood of Israel's king and Israel's king's sonship of God at first sight appears to be unrelated to imaging Israel as family, on several levels it is part of the process of describing Israel as a family of God. The reference to God as the Father of Israel's king and Israel's king as the son of God is an extension of God's Father-son relationship to the people of Israel. It is used as one of the foundations to construct hope and restoration in prophetic as well as ancient Jewish writings. Gerald Cooke rightly points out that "the figure of Israel's sonship appears to have offered the main content for the Davidic divine sonship."[174] Chen concurs that "the sonship of Israel's king cannot be understood apart from the sonship of Israel."[175] This is evidenced among other things by the textual indication that while Israel's king is not mentioned in the many passages that have God as the Father of the people of Israel, "Israel as a nation is repeatedly implicated in entirely different sets of texts that speak of God as the Father of the king."[176] Chen draws the implication as follows:

> It seems that the understanding of God as Father of Israel's king can be construed as a particular instance of what it means for God to be the Father of Israel. After all, the familial image of a father and his children is corporate by nature. God is first and

173. Ibid., 320.

174. Cooke, "The Israelite King as Son of God," 225.

175. Chen, *God as Father*, 104.

176. Ibid.

> foremost the Father of a people, among whom the king occupies a special position.[177]

Unlike the texts that have God as Father of the people of Israel and Israel as God's son and children, these texts draw together the fatherhood of God and the sonship of Israel's king. However, in a similar way to other texts, God's Father-son relationship with the Israelite king does involve rebuke and restoration. There is, however, a difference in that on an individual level it is only the king that is referred to as son of God in the Hebrew Bible.

The foundational text is Nathan's oracle to David (2 Sam 7:14).[178] From this text various expressions related to it appear in the Chronicler (1 Chr 17:13; 22:10, 28:6), in two royal psalms (Ps 2; 89), in the prophetic literatures and later Jewish writings.[179] On the importance of Nathan's oracle in relation to the rest of the Hebrew Bible and ancient Jewish writings, Heinz Kruse writes, "There is hardly any prophecy in the Old Testament that has had so many repercussions in biblical literature as the oracle given to King David by the prophet Nathan."[180] He notes that traces of different aspects of this prophecy are found ranging from detailed accounts to allusions in the latter prophets (Isaiah, Jeremiah, Ezekiel, Hosea) in the Hagiographa (Psalms, Chronicles), and in latter writings such as Ben Sira and 1 Macc, 2:57.[181]

In 2 Sam 7:14, God declares to David through Nathan that God will raise up David's offspring, promising to establish "his kingdom," and "the throne of his kingdom forever." The promise also states, "He shall build a house for my name, and I will be a father to him and he shall be a son to me" (vv. 13–14). The Father-son relationship between God and Israel's king would involve God building a kingdom for David and his offspring, and David's son building a house for God's name. As Hahn points out, while the opening statement, "the LORD will make you a house" (7:11), sets forth the center of the divine promise the "threefold meaning of the promise" is revealed by a wordplay on "house."[182] The word "house" refers to a dynasty to be established (7:12), to the temple to be built (7:13), and to "a *family* connotation that is linked to God's momentous declaration of divine sonship"[183]

177. Ibid.

178. Byrne, *Sons of God-Seed of Abraham*, 16–17.

179. Ibid.

180. Kruse, "David's Covenant," 139.

181. Ibid.

182. Hahn, *Kinship by Covenant*, 182.

183. "I will be his father, and he shall be my son" (7:14); Hahn, *Kinship by Covenant*, 182.

constituting "the heart of the covenant relationship."[184] Chen explains, "The juxtaposition of royal and familial language—kingdom, throne, house, and seed (or line)—combines royal succession with familial patrimony. Whereas Israelite families pass down land and property from one generation to the next, the royal family passes down throne and kingdom."[185] While the land is an inheritance for Israel as God's children, "the equivalent 'inheritance' for Israel's kings will be the Davidic kingdom which lasts forever."[186] However, as the family plot passed down as inheritance is ultimately understood as an inheritance from God the Father, when "each king assumes the throne, his kingdom is not merely an 'inheritance' from his earthly father, the previous king, but from YHWH, Israel's Father and King *par excellence*."[187]

The prayer of David following God's promise (2 Sam 7:23–24) locates the promise within God's relationship to Israel and also to humanity:

> Who is like your people, Israel? Is there another nation on earth whose god went to redeem it as a people, and to make a name for himself, doing great and awesome things for them, by dividing out before his people nations and their gods? And you established your people Israel for yourself to be your people forever; and you, O LORD, became their God.

With a comparative question, David's response situates the promise within the identity constituted for Israel as God's people. In vv. 23–34 alone, Israel is referred to as "people" five times: "your people" three times, "as a people" one time, and "his people" one time. This emphasis portrays that the promise given to David is also for the people of Israel. Based on Israel's relationship to God, with a further rhetorical question (v. 23), he compares the nature of the peoplehood of Israel with other nations on earth and portrays Israel as significantly unique. Israel is depicted "as a people" redeemed by its God with a purpose of making "a name" for God, and this was done "by driving out nations and their gods." A little further what is translated by NRSV as "May this be an instruction for the people, O LORD God" (7:19b) is taken by commentaries to refer to an instruction for humanity as a whole. W. C. Kaiser paraphrases v.19b as "This is the charter by which humanity will be directed."[188] Psalm 2 also echoes this wide ranging implication of the promise stating that "Ask of me, and I will make the nations your heritage, and the ends

184. Hahn, *Kinship by Covenant*, 182.

185. Chen, *God as Father*, 102.

186. Ibid.

187. Ibid.

188. Kaiser, "The Blessing of David," 311; see also Anderson, *2 Samuel*, 127; Beecher, *The Prophets and the Promise*, 238; Hann, *Kinship by Covenant*, 183.

of the earth your possession" (v. 8). This puts the Davidic promise both within the call of Israel and within God's purpose for humanity at large.

The narrative of the kinship relationship that God established with Israel's king to create a royal family line is taken up by the Chronicler(s), the Psalmists, and the prophets as major theme to advance the self-understanding of Israel as a community.[189] As mentioned above in Psalm 2, God's Father-son relation to the Israelite king is invoked and made part of God giving the nations to the Israelite king: "He said to me, 'You are my son; today I have begotten you. Ask of me, and I will make the nations your heritage and the ends of the earth your possession'" (vv. 7–8). Based on the Father-son relationship, this text promises heritage and possession which is not limited to the land but extends to the nations.

Nahum M. Sarna describes Psalm 89 as an "exegetical adaptation" of the promise to David.[190] It is a lamentation (vv. 39–52) "over the frustration of God's promises to the Davidic dynasty (vss. 20–38)."[191] The promise to David is depicted as "part of the celebration of Yahweh's creation of the world and of Israel."[192] The lament appeals "to the primordial action of Yahweh's still efficacious creation victory which included the establishment of the Davidide as the regent who exercises dominion over the nations."[193] Clifford sees the psalm making Davidic kingship an extension of God's kingship over all nations and hence the "defeat of Yahweh's lieutenant has thus raised in a most troubling way the validity of his promise never to reject his son."[194] In such crisis, God's creation and commission to David is used to instill hope that God would restore his king.[195] In vv 20–38, which is set forth with a divine speech, the Davidic king's relationship to God is depicted in terms of a Father-son relationship. Unlike 2 Sam 7 where it was God who states the Father-son relationship, this time it is the king who addresses God, "You are my Father, my God, and the Rock of my salvation" (v. 26). The similarity of this cry with the cry of the people of Israel to God in Isa 63:16, "you are our Father . . . you O Lord, are our Father; our Redeemer

189. See Hahn, *Kinship by Covenant*, 202–5; for specific texts see 1 Chr 17:3; 22:10; 28:6; Ps 89; 2; Isa 35:8–10; 51:9–11, 52:8–12; 63:10–18; Jer 23:5–8; Ezek 20:33–40; 34:23–28.

190. Sarna, "Psalm 89," 45; also see Fishbane, *Biblical Interpretation*, 466–67; Tate, *Psalms 51–100*, 417.

191. Ward, "The Literary Form and Liturgical Background of Psalm LXXXIX," 321; also see Clifford, "Psalm 89," 35–47.

192. Clifford, "Psalm 89," 44.

193. Ibid., 47.

194. Ibid.

195. Ibid.

from of old is your name" indicates "both Israel and its king have the same Father."[196] And God's response of promise starts with "I will make him the firstborn, the highest of the kings of the earth" (v. 27), echoing Israel's status declared in Exod 4:22–23.

The Chronicler retells the promise of David three times: one time in the words of Nathan (1 Chr 17:11–14) and twice in David's farewell address to Solomon (1 Chr 22:10–13), and then to the elders (1 Chr 28:4–10). In 1Chr 17:11–14 Nathan's oracle stating God's promise— "I will be a Father to him and he shall be a son to me"—comes following God's promise "to appoint a place" for God's people. The text reads: "I will appoint a place for my people Israel, and will plant them, so that they may live in their own place, and be disturbed no more and evildoers shall wear them down no more as they did formerly" (1 Chr 17:9). David's promise is put in terms of its implication for the people of Israel. Johnstone explains that "the pathos of these highly emotive terms used" for the people who are not yet in possession of the promise is significant.[197] The idea that God will give the people a place "is now set for realization through David."[198] The surety of its realization is set in terms of a familial bond, Father-son, that "transcends even that of covenant: it goes beyond the voluntary, contractual status of a mere agreement between two parties and has become the necessary and inescapable tie as between members of the same family."[199] The Chronicler further highlights this with David's prayer that relates the promise to the uniqueness of the people of Israel (v. 21). As in 2 Sam 7, Israel is described as "your people Israel" (2x), "one nation on the earth." It is redeemed to be "his people," making "a name" for God. It is described as God's people whom God "made" his people forever and became their God.

Prophetic literature, reflecting upon the tradition of the sonship of Israel's king, envisions "a king from the line of David, whom God will send to save his people."[200] Waschke writes, "It is hardly accidental that the texts are found primarily in prophetic books like Isaiah 1–39, Jeremiah, Amos, and Micah, which are understood to reflect the historical situation of the time of the Davidic monarchy."[201] As the texts themselves avoid any direct reference

196. Chen, *God as Father*, 103.

197. Johnstone, *1 and 2 Chronicles*, 204.

198. Ibid., 203.

199. Ibid., 206.

200. Chen, *God as Father*, 132; for texts see Isa 11:1–9; Jer 23:5–6; 33:14–16; Ezek 34:23–24; 37:24–25; Mic 5:2–5; Zech 6:11–12; 9:9–10.

201. Waschke, "The Significance of the David Tradition," 417; also see Hubbard, "Hope in the Old Testament," 40–43; Schniedewind, *Society and the Promise to David*; Pomykala, *The Davidic Dynasty Tradition*.

to a specific ruler, the promises remain open for an ongoing application as one of the central motifs with restorative force.[202] Such new interpretations and reinterpretations of the promise to David gain increasing importance in shaping the expectation of an "eschatological David" under "the kingly rule of God" as well as in "the transfer of the Davidic promise to the people of Israel (cf. Isa 55:3)."[203] Hence, "The progression that moves from the hope for a restoration of the monarchy to Israel's investiture as a royal people and then on to the universal and sole rule of God seems, therefore, to be a deliberate redactional choice."[204]

Therefore, as an extension of the Father-children relationship between God and the people of Israel, the Father-son relationship between God and the Israelite king highlights the uniqueness of Israel as the people of God to whom God promised to provide a Davidic dynasty forever. This is evidenced by the way David relates the promise to the unique relationship God has with Israel (2 Sam 7:23–24; 1 Chr 17:21). In this sense, just like the Fatherhood of God to the people of Israel, the Father-son relationship between God and the Israelite king has a particularizing image in Israel's self-understanding. However, associated with Father-son depiction of God and the Israelite king is also a depiction that relates the heritage of the Israelite king beyond the land to having the nations as the Israelite king's possession. This, on the other hand, presents the self-understanding of Israel in terms of its role to the nations.

Summary Conclusion

The use of kinship language in the Hebrew Bible locates the people of Israel within humanity as the people of God and provides images for Israel that help to conceptualize itself in relation to God, in relation to each other, and in relation to other nations. Through categorization and identification, it defines Israel's being and becoming by creating an understanding of membership in the peoplehood of Israel. It projects a "reality of . . . people bound together in solidarity by the common effort to promote the well-being of the whole."[205] It is connected using kinship features such as genealogy, covenantal terminologies, and kinship expressions such as "sons of Israel." Such use of kinship language constructs shared belief in a common narrative that

202. Waschke, "The Significance of the David Tradition," 417.

203. Ibid., 420.

204. Ibid.

205. Perdue, "The Israelite and Early Jewish Family," 178–79.

focuses on common ancestry with a promise from the ancestral God who is depicted as "Father."

The use of God as Father in the Hebrew Bible is part of this larger use of kinship to depict Israel's being and becoming. Used separately as well as together with the portrayal of Israel as children of God and as siblings, the use of God as Father evokes a family image that conjures up the privileges and responsibilities on both sides. While in the first part of Genesis, humanity as a whole is "represented as family," the Fatherhood of God is part of the "increasing concentration of Israel as the mainline of descent."[206] As Father, God is portrayed as electing, founding, establishing, sustaining, and restoring Israel. As a corollary to this, Israel is depicted as God's children, God's people, portion, and heritage in a way that highlights Israel's privilege as well as its responsibility. God's special relationship with Israel that emanates from God's Fatherhood to Israel is depicted as making Israel "the chief of the nations" (Jer 31:7; Deut 32:8–9). At the center of such depiction is the formation of Israel as a people through the Fatherhood of God.

Israel's being and becoming is also stated in terms of their status as children of God and then their whole life is assessed accordingly. When measured in terms of Father-children relationship, while God is found faithful, Israel is portrayed as unfaithful. The people of Israel are found lacking in terms of not measuring up to their identity in their relationship to God and to each other and are accused and judged for it. While the judgments under which they found themselves are explained as resulting from their failure to live as children, the hope of restoration is also grounded specifically on their being the children of God. God's Fatherhood is then presented as the basis for the request to forgive, rescue, and restore his people. This is frequently put in terms of recalling the "days of old" that evokes God's rescue, the giving of the covenant and the founding of Israel in a way that brings to fore and memorializes God's unique relationship with Israel. That the Father-children relationship is enduring is seen in the fact that even when the covenant is broken, the basis of the plea of restoration is grounded on the Father-children relationship of God and Israel.

The Father-son relationship between God and the Israelite king is depicted as an extension of the Father-children relationship between God and the people of Israel. It further highlights the uniqueness of Israel as the people of God to whom God promised to give a Davidic dynasty forever. In this sense, the Father-son relationship between God and the Israelite king has a particularizing image in Israel's self-understanding. However, as the nations are depicted as an inheritance to the Davidic king because of the Father-son

206. Crüsemann, "Human Solidarity and Ethnic Identity," 66.

relationship between God and the Israelite king, it has also an image that presents the self-understanding of Israel in terms of its role to the nations.

The use of sibling language images Israel as fellow members of God's family with a responsibility towards each other. Together with the use of God as Father of the people of Israel and Israel as children of God, the portrayal of Israel as siblings presents a full-fledged image of a family in the Hebrew Bible. Together, such multifaceted use of kinship language serves as an orienting framework that helps the people of Israel understand itself in relation to God, to fellow Israelites, and other nations.

Compared to the use of the kinship term "father" to refer to the Roman Empire and emperor, the use of God as Father in the Hebrew Bible shares the construction of a discourse that images their respective community as a family, a household. Similar to the discourse of Empire and emperor as father, in the Hebrew Bible the discourse of God's Fatherhood and Israel's sonship is imbued with the concept of founding, saving, protecting, and providing for the community. It also shares the formation of expectation that comes from being kin. In the Hebrew Bible this aspect even goes further in the sense that it is openly narrated time and again in a pronounced way, measuring both God as Father and Israel as children. As such the children of God share the construction of a narrative that sets an orienting framework that has bearing on the process of understanding their being and becoming a people. However, in the Hebrew Bible the imaging of family, household, is strengthened by consistently combining the Fatherhood of God with Israel's sonship and sibling relationship.

Compared to the Stoics use of Zeus as father, the use of God as Father in the Hebrew Bible shares the claim that the family, the household, that is constructed is depicted as being by far superior than any other family imagined. The cosmopolitan family is depicted as superior to Caesar's family. In the case of the Hebrew Bible, "the family of Israel" is portrayed as being uniquely superior to any other nation. However, it is different in at least two significant ways. First, while in the Stoics, the kinship relationship with Zeus has a universalizing effect, in the Hebrew Bible the use of God as Father has a particularizing effect. Zeus' fatherhood of all humanity is portrayed as a ground for cosmopolitan universalism, all humanity belonging to one family. On the other hand, the Fatherhood of God in the Hebrew Bible is related to the founding, establishing, providing, protecting, and restoring Israel as distinctively as possible from the rest of the nations. Second, while in the Stoics there is kinship between Zeus and humanity that comes from sharing reason, the Hebrew Bible does not portray the Israelites' kinship with God in terms of sharing but in terms of being created, established, sustained, and restored by God.

5

God as Father in Ancient Jewish Writings

THE LAST MATRIX THAT forms a narrative framework for Paul which I will consider in this study is the use of God as Father in ancient Jewish writings. By "ancient Jewish writings" I refer to Jewish writings that are not included in the Hebrew Bible and for which there is a general consensus that they were written before the end of the first century A.D.[1] The self-understanding of early Christians in one way or another was shaped by the world of ancient Judaism that was reflected in these writings. Nickelsburg characterizes the first-century Judaism that came out of the world of these writings as "the seedbed" and "roots" of early Christianity.[2] Relating it to Paul, N. T. Wright notes that "[t]his was the world from which Paul came, and in which he remained even though he said things which nobody within that world had thought of saying before."[3] Thus, the use of kinship language in general, and God as Father in particular in these writings could serve as one of the "seedbeds" to understand Paul's use of God as Father. Therefore, in this chapter, I will examine how kinship language in general and familial language associated with the Fatherhood of God in particular[4] is used

1. These are part of the Apocrypha and Old Testament Pseudepigrapha. See deSilva, *Introducing the Apocrypha*; Charles, *The Apocrypha and Pseudepigrapha of the Old Testament*; Charlesworth, *The Old Testament Pseudepigrapha*, vol. 1 and vol. 2; unless otherwise noted all English translations of the Pseudepigrapha texts are taken from idem, vol. 1 and 2; for Apocrypha texts unless otherwise noted all English translations are taken from *The New Oxford Annotated Bible*.

2. Nickelsburg, *Jewish Literature*, 2.

3. Wright, *Paul in Fresh Perspective*, 4.

4. As in chapter 4, by familial language related to the Fatherhood of God I am referring to the use of kinship language such as "son(s) and children of God" and sibling language to refer to Jewish people, the use of "son" to refer to the Davidic king/messianic figure. While son(s) and children when they refer to the people of Israel include all the community irrespective of gender or status, I retain the language of "son(s)" in

to shape the self-understandings in ancient Judaism(s). I will begin with a discussion of the role of kinship language for identity formation in ancient Jewish writings. This will be followed by the use of God as Father and its role for identity formation in the writings of early Judaism.

Kinship and Identity Formation in Ancient Jewish Writings

The role of kinship language in the identity formation of early Jewish writings, of which the use of God as Father is part, should be examined in terms of the overall matrix that generated the need for ongoing self-understandings that is reflected in ancient Jewish writings. For those in the Mediterranean world, the post-Persian period was a tumultuous time with a continuous flux in socio-political setting.[5] This was particularly challenging for Jewish people who were living both in and outside Palestine.[6] The spreading of Greek culture following Alexander's victory and the subsequent constant socio-political shifts thereof were marked by multifaceted transitions that quite often involved crises for the Jewish people. Among other things, these changing circumstances entailed for them the need to understand who they were in terms of what their tradition said about them and how that stood in the face of barrages of changes.[7]

One of the major ways of making sense of who they were as a people in the face of an incessantly changing milieu was remembering their past in terms of their present.[8] Commenting on making sense of one's identity, Lieu observes, "[w]ithout continuity there can be no identity, and it is continuity over time, with all its inherent ambiguities of change and sameness, that offers the greatest challenges and the greatest rewards."[9] John Gillis explains, "The core meaning of any individual or group identity, namely a sense of sameness over time and space, is sustained by remembering, and

---

order to reflect the aspect of inheritance that it carries.

5. Grabbe, *Judaism from Cyrus to Hadrian*, vols. 1 and 2; idem, *Judaic Religion in the Second Temple Period*; Hengel, *Judaism and Hellenism*; idem, *Jews, Greeks, Barbarians*.

6. Cromhout "A Clash of Symbolic Universes," 1091.

7. After Alexander, Palestine was dominated by the Ptolemies (301–197 B.C.), followed by the Seleucids (197–52 B.C.), the Hasmonaeans (152–63 B.C.), and the Romans after 63 B.C. For the need for Jewish self-understandings during these periods see Gruen, *Heritage and Hellenism*; Schmidt, *How the Temple Thinks*; Lieu, "Impregnable Ramparts and Walls of Iron," 297–313.

8. Lieu, *Christian Identity*, 62–86.

9. Ibid., 63.

what is remembered is defined by assumed identity."[10] Lieu concurs, "Thus, 'remembering' creates a history that provides a coherent continuity out of the discontinuities of all human experience; it not only explains the present but justifies it."[11] She further explains that "people in the process of searching for a new identity desire to be placed . . . within a well-defined historical and social setting. The best place for these would be at the very beginning of the nation's history."[12]

As one moves from the Hebrew Bible to ancient Jewish literature, one observes both continuity and change that are generated in the process of the self-understanding of the Jewish people.[13] The self-narratives that came out of such remembering were characterized by retelling and reinterpretation of Israel's traditions that are found in the Hebrew Bible.[14] This retelling and reinterpretation focused on issues such as the notion of election, the Torah, the land, the temple, the covenant and praxis associated with it (such as circumcision, food laws and ritual purity, the pilgrimage festivals), and the ancestral traditions.[15] Part of this retelling and reinterpretation involved using kinship narrative mostly to depict the uniqueness of the Jews and at times to claim a place in the larger Greco-Roman world.

Using kinship framework, "the Jews both connected themselves with a Hellenic cultural legacy and simultaneously defined a distinctive cultural identity of their own."[16] Ties to the founding father, Abraham, were used to show the unique identity as well as to connect Jews with the larger society. In terms of showing the unique identity, ancient Jewish writings such as *Jubilees*, *Psalms of Solomon*, and *1Enoch* articulated Jewish special identity using the familial link with the founding father Abraham.[17] Other texts relate Abraham widely with the nations. In *Sirach* Abraham is depicted as "the great father of a multitude of nations, and no one has been found like

10. Gillis, *Commemorations*, 3.

11. Lieu, *Christian Identity*, 63.

12. Ibid.,70.

13. For a summary discussion on the continuity and change between pre-exilic Israel and Second Temple Judaism and for unity and diversity within the later see Cohen, *From the Maccabees to the Mishnah*, 20–27.

14. This retelling and reinterpretation of their ancient tradition is variously described as "Rewriting the Bible," "Reinvention", etc. See Vermes, *Scripture and Tradition in Judaism*; idem, "Biblical Interpretation at Qumran," 184–91; Halpern-Amaru, *Rewriting the Bible*; Crawford, *Rewriting Scripture*; Gruen, *Heritage and Hellenism.*

15. Cromhout, "A Clash of Symbolic Universes,"1091.

16. Gruen, "Fact and Fiction," 72–74.

17. See Kamudzandu, "Abraham as a Spiritual Ancestor;" see *Jubilees*, 11, 12, 22; *1 Enoch* 3:15; *Psalms of Solomon* 9:8–9.

him in glory" (Sirach 44:19). The promise given to Abraham is portrayed as having two fronts. On the one hand "the nations would be blessed through his offspring" and that he would be made "as numerous as the dust of the earth." On the other hand, God will "exalt his offering like the stars, and give them an inheritance from sea to sea and from the Euphrates to the ends of the earth." (44:21).[18]

On the other hand, ancient Jewish writings such as *1 Maccaabees* and those of Josephus, used the figure of Abraham to create a link with the larger culture and claim a place for the Jewish people. Josephus creates ties between Abraham, Arabia, and Africa.[19] He also describes a marital tie between the descendants of Abraham and Heracles.[20] The copy of an alleged letter that was sent by Arius of the Spartans to the high priest Onias claims kinship ties through Abraham:

> This is the copy of the letter that they sent to Onias: 'King Arius of the Spartans, to the high priest Onias, greetings. It has been found in writing concerning the Spartans and the Jews that they are brothers and are of the family of Abraham. And now that we have learned this please write to us concerning your welfare; we on our part write to you that your livestock and your property belongs to us, and ours belong to you. We therefore command that our envoys report to you accordingly.[21]

Josephus similarly refers to the alleged letter that states "the Jews and the Lacedemonians are of one stock, and are derived from the kindred of Abraham. It is just, therefore, that you, who are our brethren, should send to us about any of your concerns as you please" (*Ant.*12.225–26). Based on such ties the Lacedemonians promised that they would regard the concerns of the Jews as their own and their concern "as in common" with the Jews (*Ant.* 12.227). A decree to Pergamum recalls the ancient ancestral ties between the Pergamenes and the Jews which alludes to "the days of Abraham, who was the father of all the Hebrews" (Ant. 14.247–55). Based on these alleged kinship ties, Jonathan writes a letter to the Spartans addressed as "the Jewish people to their brothers the Spartans" (1 Macc 12:6). The text addresses the Spartans as "our brothers" (vv. 7, 11) and intends to renew "family ties and friendship" (12:9). Explaining such construction of kinship

18. Siebeneck, "May Their Bones Return to Life," 411–28; see *Sirach* 44:21.

19. Josephus, *A. J.* 1. 214, 221, 239; 2.32.

20. Josephus, *A. J.* 1.241.

21. *1 Maccaabees* 12:19–23; see also Josephus, *Ant.* 13.164–70; for the concern regarding the authenticity of such letter and the related debate see Gruen, "Fact and Fiction," 75.

ties using Abraham, Van der Lans writes, "Abraham, as the progenitor of various peoples, has an appeal beyond the nation of the Jews . . . genealogical appeals to Abraham could be made to construe a relationship with another *ethnos* and contribute to Abraham's own renown and that of the Jews."[22] Although it is not mentioned in these texts, Genesis 12:3 which states that through Abraham "all the families of the earth shall be blessed" probably lies behind these claims.

In addition to the versatile use of kinship ties with Abraham, kinship narrative was also built based on shared belief and common devotion. The text from Philo mentioned earlier in chapter 2 rejects kinship by blood that does not rise up to common piety and devotion. Philo constructs kinship based on similarity of character rather than relationship merely by blood.

> For we should acknowledge only one relationship, and one bond of friendship, namely, a mutual zeal for the service of God, and a desire to say and do everything that is consistent with piety. And these bonds which are called relationships of blood, being derived from one's ancestors, and those connections which are derived from intermarriages and from other similar causes, must all be renounced, if they do not all hasten to the same end, namely, the honor of God which is the one unbreakable bond of all united good will. For such men will lay claim to a more venerable and sacred kind of relationship. (Philo, *Spec. Leg.* 1.316–17)

This text from Philo shows that relationship and "bond of friendship" are not based on blood and marriage ties. He renounces kinship by blood ("relationships of blood, being derived from one's ancestors . . . from marriage and similar causes") in favor of kinship that compares common religion and shared devotion and piety. He particularly considers a common devotion to Torah as sufficient basis to make people kin. In so doing, he diminishes the importance of kinship based on blood and marriage. He constructs a kinship that is based on "mutual zeal for the service of God, a desire to say and do everything that is consistent with piety."

The use of God as Father and the associated familial language with it in ancient Jewish literature is part of this mode of constructing kinship ties to make sense of one's identity in an increasingly changing socio-political matrix. It defines one's self-understanding in relation to God, in relation to fellow Jews irrespective of where they were, and also in relation to all humanity. In the following section I will examine the use of God as Father

22. Van der Lans, "Belonging to Abraham's Kin," 309.

and the familial language associated with it in ancient Jewish writings and its contribution for the self-understanding of the Jewish people.

God as Father in Ancient Jewish Writings

The term "father" is applied to God in ancient Jewish writings in a similar way to that of the Hebrew Bible. The frequency is also comparable to that of the Hebrew Bible. God is referred to as the Father of the Jewish people, God's people are referred to as God's children and as siblings, and the Davidic king/messiah is referred to as the son of God. While the idea of God as Father in these ancient Jewish writings exhibits continuity with the Hebrew Bible in this regard, there are also new trends. The new developments include limiting God's Fatherhood to the elect/righteous children of God, individuals addressing God as Father, portraying inheritance beyond the promised land, applying God's Fatherhood to an awaited messianic figure, and portraying God as a universal Father.[23] In the following sections, I will discuss each of these aspects following the same categories used in studying God as Father in the Hebrew Bible: God as the Father of the Jewish people, God's people as God's children, God's people as siblings, and God as the Father of the king/messiah figure. To these are added the following features from what is observed above: individuals addressing God as Father, and the depiction of God as universal Father. I will begin with the portrayal of God as the Father of his people.

God as the Father of the Jewish People

God is referred to as the Father of the Jewish people in Jubilees, Tobit, 3 Maccabees, and in the Wisdom of Solomon. Just as in the Hebrew Bible, themes of election, restoration, and protection are associated with the depiction of God as the Father of people. Israel's formative and restorative traditions are also recalled and applied to the present situation, forming an orienting framework together with the Fatherhood of God.

The book of Jubilees uses kinship language to image the people of Israel as the family that belongs to God. Right at the beginning of the book, in the first chapter that sets a framework for the rest of the account, the book of Jubilees identifies God as Father and Israel as God's "sons" (1:25).[24] Jubilees

23. Chen, *God as Father*, 126–37.

24. For studies on the Book of Jubilees see VanderKam, *The Book of Jubilees*; idem, "Studies on the Prologue and Jubilees 1," 266–79.

claims to record an account of the revelation given to Moses on Mount Sinai during his forty days' stay (Jub 1:25, 28). Israel's election is depicted as having occurred right at the time of creation.[25] Accordingly, on the Sabbath of the creation, "the special relationship between God and Israel is given a particular form."[26] In this account of the origination of Israel, in response to God's disclosure that Israel will forsake the Lord in the land of the promise (Jub 1:7–11), Moses intercedes to God not to abandon them by reminding him that they are God's people (Jub 1:19–21). In these short verses, Israel is repeatedly identified as God's people (1:19, 20, 21), and inheritance (1:19, 21) whom God saved from the Egyptians. These identifications highlight from the very beginning that Israel's identity is in relation to God. On the other hand, the Gentiles are identified as "their enemy," hence a sharp line is drawn between Israel and the Gentiles at the introduction of the book.[27] In response to Moses' intercession, in the promise of eschatological restoration, God describes himself as "Father" and Israel as "sons" (1:25). The text reads:

> After this they will return to me in all uprighteousness and with all of (their) heart and soul. And I shall cut off the foreskin of their heart and the foreskin of the heart of their descendants. And I shall create for them a holy spirit, and I shall purify them so that they will not turn away from following me from that day and forever. And their souls will cleave to me and to all my commandments . . . And I shall be a *father to them*, and *they will be sons to me*. And *they will all be called 'sons of the living God.'* And every angel and spirit will know and acknowledge that they are my sons and I am their father in uprightness and righteousness. (Jub 1:23–25)

The section predicts restoration of God's people. God promises that upon their repentant return, God "shall be a father to them" and that "they will be sons." It is also promised that they will be recognized as the "sons of the living God" by "every angel and spirit" and they "will all be called 'sons of the living' God'" (Jub 1:25). In many ways, the passage echoes the exhortation in Deuteronomy 10 to Israel to "circumcise . . . the foreskin" of their heart and also the restorative promise of God recorded in Jeremiah 31, both of which are filled with language reminiscent of Israel's formation. In Deut

25. Wintermute, "Jubilees," 35–142.

26. Van Ruiten, *Primaeval History Interpreted*, 57.

27. In his intercession Moses includes the following: "do not deliver them into the hand of their enemy, the Gentiles, lest they rule over them and cause them to sin against you" (Jub 1:19).

10:16 the following exhortation was made to Israel: "Circumcise, then, the foreskin of your heart, and do not be stubborn any longer." The exhortation followed the statement that explains Israel's election: "Although heaven and heaven of heavens belong to the LORD your God, the earth with all that is in it, yet the LORD set his heart in love on your ancestors alone and chose you, their descendants after them out of all the peoples, as it is today" (Deut 10:14–15). The exhortation comes out of the especial relationship Israel has with God. In Jeremiah 31 also God promised restoration by stating God's familial relationship with Israel: God has "become a Father to Israel," and that Ephraim is God's "firstborn" (31:9). God also promised a new covenant and to put the law within their hearts (31:31–34). These are reflected in *Jubilees* 1:23–25 at the culmination of which God's familial relationship with Israel is stated. This is one example of how the assertion of God's familial relationship with Israel is woven with features that evoke Israel's formative as well as restorative narrative. In so doing, the discourse puts the familial relationship between God and Israel at the center of Israel's formative as well as restorative narrative.

Unlike what we saw in the Hebrew Bible where God's Fatherhood is a condition for restoration, here God's fatherhood will depend on their repentant return to God, in their "cleaving" to all the commandments. Continuing this eschatological aspect, in Jubilees 1:28 God declares that when his "sanctuary is built in their midst . . . and the Lord will appear in the sight of all," that everyone will know that he is the "God of Israel and the father of all the children of Jacob" (1.28). The idea that others will know that God is the Father of Israel and that they are children is a new trend from what we have seen in the Hebrew Bible. The emphasis on this aspect of God's Fatherhood that is given in Jubilees is evident from its repetition. Just three verses above, it was stated that "*they will all be called 'sons of the living God,*" and that "every angel and spirit will know and acknowledge that they are my sons and I am their father in uprightness and righteousness" (Jub 1:25). Here it seems the Fatherhood of God is not only used for internal identification but also as something that distinguishes Israel apart from other nations. God will relate to them as Father and they will relate to God as sons and daughters and this will be known by everyone. Explaining the reference to being recognized by "angel and spirit" Byrne observes, '[h]ere the 'recognition' element has particular reference to the powers of darkness: in his prayer, Moses had pleaded with God not to let the spirit of Beliar rule over the people to accuse them; now God assures Moses that every (potential) accuser (spirit or angel) will know that these are God's children."[28]

28. Byrne, *'Sons of God,'* 31; part of Moses intercession reads, "do not let the spirit

The use of God as Father in Tob 13:4 is also found in the context where restoration is sought.[29] Tobit exhorts "the children of Israel" who were scattered among the nations to "acknowledge . . . [God] before the nations," and to "exalt him in the presence of every living being" (13:3–4). The call to acknowledge is made five times in the chapter (13:3, 6 [twice], 8, 10). Tobit gives the reason for acknowledging God with the following assertion: "he is our Lord and he is our God; he is our Father and he is God for forever" (13:4). The repeated use of the first person plural pronoun in conjunction with God, (God as "our Lord . . . our God . . . our Father"), identifies Tobit and his audience with God, and at the same time it sets them apart from "the nations" in terms of their relation to God. The exhortation reminds that God is the Father of this people and promises future restoration in the form of gathering. Although God afflicts the people for their iniquities, "he will again show mercy" on his people by gathering them "from all the nations" among whom they have been scattered (Tobit 13:5). While in Jubilees it is others who would acknowledge the familial relationship between God and Israel, here Israel is exhorted to acknowledge that feature of kinship even when they are scattered. Neither the situation they were in nor the geographical location could break the familial bond.

Third Maccabees is believed to have been written in the neighborhood of Alexandria in Egypt. Although God is referred to as "the first Father of all" (2:21) what God does as Father clearly limits Fatherhood to the people. The theme of protection, the formative narrative of Israel, and the theme of others acknowledging God as the Father of the people of Israel are associated with the use of God as Father of the people of Israel. In a narrative that describes God's response to the prayer of the high priest Simon against the persecution of Jews by Ptolemy Philopator, God is described as "the first Father of all," who "oversees all things," and who is "holy among the holy ones" (3 Macc 2:21). The problem that God is sought to address is that the people of Israel are "subjected to . . . [their] enemies and overtaken by helplessness" (2:13). The king, who is characterized as an "audacious and profane man", attempts to undertake and "violate the holy place on earth" dedicated to God's "glorious name" (2:14). The prayer looks back to the tradition of the formation of Israel in which God delivered them from Pharaoh (2:6–7) and to God's promise to protect the people of Israel (2:10–12). It identifies God's people as "your people of Israel" (2:6, 16), and "the house of Israel"

of Beliar rule over them to accuse them before you and ensnare them from every path of righteousness so that they might be destroyed from before your face" (Jub 1:20).

29. For the emphasis of kinship in the book of Tobit see Faßbeck, "Tobit's Religious Universe," 173–96.

(2:10). In response to the prayer, God who is "the first Father of all" and "who oversees all things" came to the aid of God's people and "scourged him who had exalted himself in insolence and audacity" (3 Macc 2:21). When the king further planned in order that the "Jews might meet their doom," the Jews prayed again to "the Almighty Lord and Ruler of all power, their merciful God and Father" (5:7). God came to their rescue to the extent that king Ptolemy Philopator in his letter to his generals admits that he has come to realize that "the God of heaven surely defends the Jews, always taking their part as a father does for his children" (7:6). Ptolemy acknowledges God's Fatherhood of the people in their rescue. The protecting aspect of God's Fatherhood is counted on by the Jews, acted up on by God, and also recognized by the enemy.

The use of God as Father of his people in the Wisdom of Solomon is portrayed in terms of the distinction God makes between the godly and the ungodly. God relates to the people as a "Father" and treats them as a parent does. But God relates to the ungodly as a "stern king" does "in condemnation" (Wis 11:10). Here again the way God relates is seen as the mark of his Fatherhood. The old distinction between a tyrant king and a parent king in Greek literature is echoed here.[30] On the other hand, the idea of a "Father" who tests as a parent confirms the theme of discipline and restoration that is observed in the use of God as the Father in the Hebrew Bible.

God is also referred to as the Father in Qumran texts.[31] In 4Q382 104 II, in a prayer that pleads God to uphold the covenant, God is referred to as the Father of his people:

> From your words, and to rely on your covenant, and that their heart may be [. . .] sanctify (?) [. . .] hands, in order that they belong to you, and you to them, and your righteous [. . .] . . . [. . .] for you will give an inheritance . . ., [and] you will rule over them and be for them a father, and not [. . .] you abandon them in the hand of the[ir] kings [and] you will rule over . . . people . . . in your precepts which you gave to them through Moses. (4Q382 104 II, 1–8)

Vocabularies that recall Israel's formative narrative (e.g., covenant, inheritance, precepts from Moses) are used in conjunction with the Fatherhood of God. God's Fatherhood is associated with "ruling over" people instead of abandoning them to their kings, and with giving them "an

30. Stevenson, "The Ideal Benefactor," 421–36; see also the related discussion in chapter 3 of this book.

31. Unless otherwise noted all English translations of Qumran texts are from Martínez and Tigchelaar, *The Dead Sea Scrolls*.

inheritance." Through such kinship relationship God made them God's people, and God became theirs. All of these evoke memories of the formative narrative from Exodus.

In a thanksgiving text where an individual extols God for "upholding" and "establishing" care in the midst of crisis, God is referred to as the "father to all the [son]s of your truth":

> You have delighted me with your holy spirit, and until this very day [. . .] . . . Your just rebuke is with my . . . your wholesome watch has saved my soul, with my steps there is an abundance of forgiveness and multitude of [compas]sion when you judge me, until old age you take care of me. For my father did not know me, and my mother abandoned me to you. Because you are father to all the [son]s of your truth.(1QH XVII, 32–36)

Themes of rebuke, forgiveness, and compassion surround the depiction of God as Father in this text. While the thanksgiving is a thanksgiving of an individual, here God is not referred to as the Father of the individual. Rather God is referred to as the father "to all the [son]s of your truth" of which the author seems to be part. Given the proclivities of the Qumran texts, the "sons of your truth" most likely refers just to the insiders. This use appears to limit God's Fatherhood to those who are referred to as "the sons of your truth" instead of being a Father to all.

God as the Father of an Individual

Unlike the Hebrew Bible, there are texts in ancient Jewish writings where God is *addressed* as Father by an individual (3 Macc 6:3, 8; Sirach 23:1, 4; 51:10; 4Q460 9; 4Q372 I, 16–17, 20–22). This shows one of the new developments in the ancient Jewish writings compared to the use of God as Father in the Hebrew Bible. An individual addresses God as "Father," "our Father," and/or "my Father" mostly in the context of acknowledgement and prayer. As discussed earlier, this was one of the contentious areas in the study of the use of God as Father in relation to Jesus' use of "*Abba*" to refer to God in Mark 14:36. Jeremias argued for the uniqueness of such use mainly based on a perceived absence of a contemporary or earlier text(s) of Palestinian provenance that have a direct vocative address to God in prayer using the first person singular possessive pronoun. The inadequacy of Jeremias' claim has been addressed convincingly by the availability of evidence that stand contrary to his claim. However, as mentioned earlier in chapter 1, a discussion associated with the "no-Fatherhood-of-God-in-early-Judaism" approach unduly limits the study of God as Father to whether or not the early Christians' understanding of God as Father is different from early Judaism. The different function that the use of God as Father in the New Testament possibly plays is left unexamined. In the following texts God is addressed as Father in prayers on behalf of God's people or other individuals, in prayers for oneself, and in thanksgiving.[32]

In 3 Macc 6:3, 8, addressing God as "Father" (twice), the priest Eleazer prays that God would deliver them from the plan of the Egyptian king. The text reads as follows:

> King of great power, Almighty God Most High, governing all creation with mercy, look upon the descendants of Abraham, O Father, upon the children of the sainted Jacob, a people of your consecrated portion who are perishing as foreigners in a foreign land. Pharaoh with the abundance of his chariots, the former rulers of this Egypt, exalted with lawless insolence and boastful tongue, you destroyed together with his arrogant army by drowning them in the sea, manifesting the light of your mercy on the nation of Israel. Senacherib . . .you, O Lord, broke in pieces . . .The three companions in Babylon . . .you rescued unharmed . . . Daniel . . . you brought up to the light unharmed . . . Jonah . . . you, Father, watched over and restored unharmed to all his family. And now . . . reveal yourself quickly to those of the nation of Israel—who are being outrageously treated by the abominable and lawless Gentiles.(6:2–9)

32. There are two texts that do not fit any of the categories used in this study. I will mention them here. In Jubilees, Abraham in his prayer that is part of his blessing to Jacob, although he does not address God as Father, prays that God would relate to Jacob and his descendants as Father and Jacob and his descendants would relate to God as "firstborn son" (Jub. 19:29). The prayer seeks familial relationship between God and the descendants of Abraham. The sought familial relationship with God is put in contrast to "the spirit of Mastema's" ruling over Jacob and his descendants (19:28). The "spirit of Mastema" is portrayed as the spirit that would "remove [people] . . . from following the LORD" (19:28). Segal, *The Book of Jubilees*, 176, explains, "After the Lord acceded to Noah's request to imprison the spirits in the place of judgment, Mastema, 'the leader of the sprits,' appeared, and requested from God that he leave some of the spirits under his control (v.8). Mastema himself is not one of the spirits, but rather, he is accorded a higher status, presumably that of an angel." In page 257, regarding Abraham's blessing, Segal observes that "Abraham's blessing of Jacob was given in the general context of the covenant between God and Abraham's offspring, and in the specific context of the election of Israel (Jacob) as opposed to other nations (Esau)." In the Wisdom of Solomon 14:3, one who trusts for protection from "raging waves" in an idol, which is characterized as "a piece of wood more fragile than the ship" on which one travels, is contrasted with one who acknowledges and relates to God as "Father." God the Father is described as the one who through "providence . . . steers" the course of the sea.

The prayer stresses the identity of God's people, invokes the traditions of God's protection, and puts the present enemy of God's people in parallel with the previous ones. The prayer identifies God's people as "the descendants of Abraham," and "the children of the sainted Jacob," "a people of . . . (God's) consecrated portion" who are "perishing as foreigners in a foreign land." In similar way to the prayer of the priest Simon in 3 Macc 2, here Eleazer relies on God's previous deliverance of his people from Egypt and from Sennacherib of Assyria "manifesting the light" of his mercy on "the nation of Israel" (6:4–5). Evoking God's saving of Jonah, Daniel, and his three companions in Babylon (6:6–9), Eleazer entreats God to reveal himself "quickly to those of the nation Israel" who are "outrageously treated by the abominable and lawless Gentiles." The "abominable and lawless Gentiles" are put on par with traditional enemies such as Pharaoh, Assyria, and Babylon. The prayer concludes with: "Let it be shown to all the Gentiles that you are with us, O Lord, and have not turned your face on us; but just as you have said, 'Not even when they were in the land of their enemies did I neglect them,' so accomplish it, O Lord" (6:15). As seen in the section on God as the Father of his people above, the address to God as Father here is also related to God revealing to the enemy the nature of the relationship between God and the ancient Jewish people, that God is the Father of his people. God's response to the prayer and how God saved his people is also described in terms of revealing himself in the role of protecting his people:

> Then the most glorious, almighty, and true God revealed his holy face and opened the heavenly gates, from which two glorious angels of fearful aspect descended, visible to all but the Jews. They opposed the forces of the enemy and filled them with immovable shackles. Even the king began to shudder bodily, and he forgot his sullen insolence. The animals turned back upon the armed forces following them and began trampling and destroying them.(6:18–21)

Accordingly, the address to God as Father is put in the midst where the existence of God's people was threatened because of who they were. Although God is addressed with only a general term as "Father" (6:6, 8), the prayer makes a distinction between God's people and the Gentiles who are characterized as enemies. The text shows that in response to the prayers God came to the aid of his people, showing that God is with them as requested in the prayer.

In Sirach God is addressed as Father frequently (23:1, 4; 51:10). The first two appear in the same chapter within a gap of two verses. Sirach prays:

> O Lord, Father and Master of my life, do not abandon me to their designs, and do not let me fall because of them! Who will set whips over my thoughts, and the discipline of wisdom over my mind, so as not to spare me in my errors, and not overlook my sins? Otherwise my mistakes may be multiplied, and my sins may abound, and I may fall before my adversaries, and my enemy may rejoice over me. O Lord, Father and God of my life, do not give me haughty eyes, and remove evil desire from me. (23:1–4)

God is addressed as "Father" (v. 1) and "my Father" (v. 4). In both instances the prayer is intensely personal. It is for God to control speech (22:7) and thoughts and remove evil desire from Sirach so that he may not fall before his adversaries. In 51:10 in the context of praising God for deliverance, Sirach reports that he prayed in despair, "Lord, you are my Father; do not forsake me in the days of trouble, when there is no help against the proud." Sirach counted on God as a Father to rescue him from his enemies. Responding to his prayer, God came to his aid as a Father and rescued him from his enemies. In Sirach 51:10 in the context of thanksgiving for the protection received from God, Sirach recalls his prayer: "I cried out, 'Lord, you are my Father; do not forsake me in the days of trouble, when there is no help against the proud.'" As Father, God's people approach God to protect and deliver from adversaries in the face of danger (51:1–7). God's people recall and use as part of the supplication (51:8) God's kindness and mercy that was shown in rescuing people.

In the following Qumran texts, an individual addresses God as "Father" in the context of prayer. Nunnally explains that "the Fatherhood of God is confessed, from memory, in the context of personal and corporate prayer."[33] In 4Q460 9 in a plea to God to judge the wicked for the "unrest in Israel and scandal in Ephraim," God is addressed as "my Father and my Lord."

> [. . .] you, and before you I am in dread, for like the dread of God they plan evil [. . .] for confusion in Israel, and for something horrible in Ephraim. [. . . from the l] and of guilty deeds to the height of the Most High, from generation [to generation . . . f]or you have not forsaken your servant [. . .] my father and my lord. [. . . m]arvels, for he will reprove with rejection, and who [. . . will re]prove because of your leaving your God, Israel.

The text employs "refrains which rebuke and confess and refrains which constitute supplication to God."[34] Nunally explains that "the first person singular possessive pronominal suffix indicates the intimacy of this

33. Nunnally, "The Fatherhood of God," 83.

34. Ibid., 108.

vocative and emphasizes *individual*, as opposed to *corporate* relationship."[35] He further notes, "This passage which contains such a vivid expression of the personal Fatherhood of God and his parental care also speaks of the fear of God . . . servanthood . . . awesome nature and proofs of God . . . responsibility for law keeping . . . the judgment of God . . . and the wrath of God."[36] The reference to God in the form of personal address is similar to Sirach. The theme of restoration which is prevalent in texts in ancient Jewish writings is the focus of the prayer here.

In 4Q372 I, 16–17, 20–22 from exile, in the name of Joseph, the exile cries to God in repentance, seeking rescue:

> My Father, my God, do not abandon me in the hands of gentiles [. . .] do me justice, so that the poor and afflicted do not perish. You have no need of any people or nation for any help. [Your] fing[er] is bigger and stronger than any there are in the world. (4Q372 I, 16–18)[37]
>
> [. . .] they are stronger than me and all my brothers who are associated with me. An enemy people lives in it and [. . .] opens its mouth against all the sons of your beloved Jacob with insults for [. . .] (4Q372 I, 19–21)

God is addressed as "My Father, my God." The individual beseeches God not to abandon him "in the hands of the Gentiles" who are further identified as an "enemy people" who lives in the land and "opens its mouth against all the sons" of God's "beloved Jacob." While God is addressed as "My Father," here also the focus of the prayer is to seek deliverance from the hand of the Gentiles.

Israel as God's Sons/Children

The reference to Israel as God's son(s)/children in ancient Jewish writings partly follows the Hebrew Bible. In similar ways to the Hebrew Bible, there are texts that state Israel as son/children and there are also texts that seek and declare hope based on Israel's status as son/children. In most instances, these two themes are found together. Unlike the Hebrew Bible, however, the theme of measuring Israel in terms of its status as son/children, which is very

35. Ibid., 106. He also writes, "We see once more a passage which fully satisfies all the criteria required by Jeremian methodology: it is early (pre-Christian); it is Palestinian (not deriving from immediate Hellenistic influence); it is a direct vocative address to God in prayer; and it employs the first person singular possessive pronoun *my*."

36. Ibid., 110.

37. Ibid., 68–71; and Schuller, "The Psalm of 4Q372 1," 67–79.

common in prophetic writings, is uncommon here. Both in stating Israel as son/children and in seeking and declaring hope based on Israel's sonship, Israel's unique status against all the other nations is emphasized. As will be seen below, the belongingness of Israel as son/children to God is used to develop a narrative of who they are and what to expect from God because of this identity. Byrne summarizes well the character of the reference to Israel as God's son(s)/children in writing, "Sonship of God is the privilege of Israel alone: it is a status stemming from God's special action in respect of this people: his election, his calling. It features very frequently in contexts where a sharp distinction is made between Israel and other nations."[38]

Israel's relationship with God is a major theme in Jubilees and is contrasted with God's relationship with other nations providing unique identity features.[39] In addition to the references to God as Father that are discussed above, the book of Jubilees identifies Israel as God's "firstborn son" right from the beginning of its account. In chapter 1, which gives the framework to the rest of the book, the Father-children relationship between God and Israel is introduced. In a paragraph which introduces God's eschatological appearance as a Father of the children of Jacob, it is also stated that God's people will be called "sons of the living God" and that this identity will be acknowledged by "every angel and spirit" (1:25).[40] While this identification focuses on the eschatological aspect of Father-children relationship between God and Israel, Jubilees chapter 2 focuses on Israel's formative narrative and in similar way to Exod 4:22 describes that the Father-children relationship that is built into Israel's formation. The text reads:

> Behold I shall separate for myself *a people from among all the nations*. And they will also keep the Sabbath. And I will *sanctify them for myself* and will bless them. Just as I have sanctified and shall sanctify the Sabbath day for myself thus shall I bless them. And *they will be my people and I will be their God*. And *I have chosen the seed of Jacob from among all that I have seen*. And I

38. Byrne, *'Sons of God,'* 62.

39. For instance in Jubilees 15:31–32 we read, "he chose Israel that they might be a people for himself. And he sanctified them and gathered them from all of the sons of man because (there are) many nations and many people, and they all belong to him, but over all of them he caused spirits to rule so that they might lead them astray from following him. But over Israel he did not cause any angel or spirit to rule because he alone is their ruler and he will protect them and he will seek for them at the hand of his angels and at the hand of his spirits and at the hand of all of his authorities so that he might guard them and bless them and they might be his and he might be theirs henceforth and forever."

40. See Byrne, *'Sons of God,'* 31, about being recognized by "angel and spirit."

> have recorded him as *my firstborn son*, and have sanctified him *for myself forever and ever*. (Jub 2:19–20, emphasis added)

It stresses the formation of Israel as a people "from among all the nations."[41] God has chosen "the seed of Jacob from among all" that he has seen and he "recorded him" as his "firstborn son." Israel belongs to God and God to Israel. Segal explains that when "God established the world order from the dawn of creation . . . in the early realm, Israel was chosen from the first week of creation as 'noteworthy people' and as God's 'firstborn-son.'"[42] Ruiten notes that "In Jubilees, Israel is God's first-born son because Israel's existence as a separate people started during the first week of creation. They were the first to come into existence."[43] Segal observes further, "The election of Israel from creation as the Lord's personal possession establishes a certain world order, including the nations, from the beginning of history. The choice of Israel is meaningless without other nations, and therefore God chooses them"[44] from "among all nations." Built into this election is also the promise of inheritance which includes both the land of the forefathers as well as inheritance beyond the land of the forefathers. In Jubilees 17:3 we read that "he [Abraham] rejoiced because the LORD had given him seed upon the earth so that they might inherit the land."[45] On the other hand, in Jubilees 32:19 in Jacob's vision God is portrayed as promising:

> . . . there will be kings from you; they will rule everywhere that the tracks of mankind [humankind] have been trod. And I shall give to your seed all of the land under heaven and they will rule in all nations as they have desired . . . all of the earth will be gathered together and they will inherit it forever.

According to this text, the inheritance of Jacob's descendants goes beyond the promised land to include "all the land under heaven" and to ruling "all nations." This new trend also can be seen in other texts that are shown below.

41. The election of Israel is stressed in Jub. 15:30–31; 19:18; 22:9–10; 33:11. And Ruiten, *Primaeval History Interpreted*, 60, points out that "In all these texts the election of Israel is related to the world of the nations."

42. Segal, *The Book of Jubilees*, 279.

43. Ruiten, *Primaeval History Interpreted*, 61.

44. Segal, *The Book of Jubilees*, 179.

45. See also *Jubilees* 14:8–9. In 1 Macc 15:34 the inheritance is the land itself. Simon, son of Mattathias states, "We have neither taken foreign land nor seized foreign property, but only the inheritance of our ancestors, which at one time had been unjustly taken by our enemies. Now that we have the opportunity, we are firmly holding the inheritance of our ancestors."

In a prayer for God's intervention to rescue his people from the Assyrians, Judith identifies as God's children Israel in general and those who zealously protected that identity as children of God. Recalling the story in Gen 34 where Levi and Simeon avenged the rape of their sister Dinah, Judith portrays her "ancestor Simeon" and his descendants as God's "*beloved children* who burned with zeal and abhorred the pollution of their blood" (Judith 9:4, emphasis added). She depicts God as giving a sword to Simeon "to take revenge on those strangers who had torn off a virgin's clothing" (9:1). This tradition from Israel's formative narrative is recalled and used as the basis for the prayer of rescue at present, "O God, my God, hear me also" (9:4). Then in 9:13 she identifies God's people in general as "your children" (9:13). Based on the status of being children of God, Judith makes a plea to God as follows:

> God of my father, God of the heritage of Israel, Lord of heaven and earth, Creator of the waters, King of all creation, hear my prayer . . . bring wound and bruise on those [Assyrians] who have planned cruel things against your covenant, and against your sacred house, and against Mount Zion, and against the house *your children* possess. Let your whole nation and every tribe know and understand that you are God, the God of all power and might, and there is no other who protects the people of Israel but you alone! (Judith 9:12–14).

She identifies God as "God of my father" referring back to her ancestor Simeon, evoking what was done through him to protect God's people to serve as the basis of the plea at present. In relation to Israel, God is identified as "the heritage of Israel" and protector of the people of Israel. She identifies the land that is in captivity and desolation as "our inheritance" (8:22). She also identifies God with phrases that show sovereignty: "Lord of heaven and earth," "Creator of the waters," "King of all creation," and "the God of all power and might." On the other hand, the Assyrians are depicted as arrogantly planning harm on all that belongs to God: "your covenant . . . your sacred house . . . against Mount Zion, and against the house your children possess." The "us-them" portrayal is sharpened. Based on such characterization she seeks God to deal with the Assyrians showing to his "whole nation and every tribe" that God alone is the protector of Israel. Israel's identity as children of God together with a story from the early formative tradition of Israel are used to invoke God's protection against the enemy from outside.

In similar context in a psalm that pleads national restoration, Sirach identifies Israel as "your firstborn" (36:17). Sirach portrays the nations as "foreign nations" (36:3), "the adversary . . . the enemy" (36:9), "those who harm your people" (36:11), "the unmerciful" (35:22), and "the unrighteous" (35:23). Israel is identified as "his people" (35:25), "your people" (35:22), "the people called by your name" (35:17), and the people "whom you have named your firstborn" (35:17). Based on such characterization of the enemy as well as the people of God, Sirach makes the plea for restoration with a language that looks back to Israel's formation: "Gather all the tribes of Jacob, and give them their inheritance, as at the beginning. Have mercy, O Lord, on the people called by your name, on Israel, whom you have named your firstborn" (Sir 36:13–18). Expressions such as "tribes of Jacob," "their inheritance," "as at the beginning" look to the formative accounts in the book of Exodus. They are used together with Israel's firstborn status to entreat God to act as before in forming Israel as God's people. As in Jubilees, Israel's inheritance is described both in terms of the promised land and in a way that goes beyond the promised land.[46] In Sirach 46 Israel's acquisition of its inheritance through the leadership of Joshua is described. The inheritance is equated with the land (46:8). In 44:21, however, the promise of God to Abraham is described as to give his descendants "an inheritance from sea to sea, and from the Euphrates to the ends of the earth."

God's people are also referred to as children of God in the last section of the Wisdom of Solomon which is commonly referred to as the "Book of History." In this section, it retells the Exodus story to produce a narrative that contrasts the ungodly and the righteous, the people of God and their enemies. It transforms the Exodus tradition of conflict between the Israelites and the Egyptians into a prototypical story of conflict between the Israelites and their oppressors as reflected in the conflict between the evil and the righteous in his day.[47] The comparison begins in the first part of the book. In chapter 2 we find a comparison of the ways and thinking of the ungodly with the ways and thinking of the righteous ones. The righteous are portrayed even by the ungodly ones as children of God and God as their father. On the premise that "if the righteous man [the righteous one] is God's child, he will help him [her], and will deliver him [her] from the hand of his adversaries" (2:18, 20), the ungodly "lie in wait for the righteous man [the righteous one]" (2:12). The wait is to "test what will happen at the end of his life" (2:12, 17) for "he is inconvenient" to them and "opposes" their actions (12:2:12). The righteous is accused for claiming God's sonship and for boasting that "God is his father" (Wis 2:12–13, 16–18).

In the second part of the book (11—19), the contrast sharpens and becomes focused on the status of Israel as God's children and the ungodly as

46. Chen, *God as Father*, 117, 130.

47. Cheon, *The Exodus Story*; Enns, *Exodus Retold*.

God's enemies. From chapters 12—19, God's people are referred to as "your holy ones" (18:1, 2, 5), "the righteous" (16:18, 23; 18:7, 20), "your people" (12:19; 16:2,3,5,20; 18:3, 7, 13; 19:2, 5, 22), and "your children" (12:19, 21; 16:10, 21, 26; 18:4; 19:6). Birge observes that the writer uses these phrases to refer to the Israelites "after telling some portion of their Exodus story in which they have experienced God's saving action."[48] On the other hand, the ungodly are referred to as "oppressors" (16:4), their/our enemies (12:20; 16:8; 18:1, 4, 7, 8), "the ungodly" (16:18; 19:1). God is depicted as differentiating between the ungodly and God's children. While God tests God's people as "a father does in warning," he examines "the ungodly as a stern king does in condemnation" (11:10). In terms of calling, God called and glorified God's people (18:13) and even the ungodly acknowledge God's people "to be God's child" (18:13). While God chastens the children "to whose ancestors" God "gave oaths and covenants full of good promises," God scourges their enemies ten thousand times more" (12:19–22). While the ungodly are killed "by the bites of locusts and flies, and no healing is found for them," God's children "were not conquered even by the fangs of venomous serpents" for God's "mercy came to their help and healed them" (16:9–10, 21). While creation itself "exerts itself to punish the unrighteous," it "in kindness relaxes on behalf of those who trust" in God (chap 16:24).

God teaches and gives hope to God's children (12:19–20). God "supplied them from heaven," so that God's children "might learn that it is not the production of crops that feeds humankind" but that it is the "word [that] sustains those who trust" in God (16:26). The whole creation is made to comply with God's commands with the purpose that God's "children might be kept unharmed" (19:6). The Psalm concludes with joyful assertion, "For in everything, O Lord, you have exalted and glorified your people, and you have not neglected to help them at all times and in all places" (19:22).

In4Q504 3:2–13, in a prayer that celebrates God's election of Israel, Israel is identified as "My son, My firstborn":

> Behold, all the peoples are [like not]hing in front of you; [as] chaos and nothing [they] are reckoned/in your presence. We have [in]voked only your name; for your glory you have created us; you have established us as your sons in the sight of all the peoples. For you called [I]srael 'my son, my first-born' and have corrected us as one corrects his son. You have [created us] raised us over the years of our generations . . . for you chose us [to be your people amongst all] the earth. For that reason you have poured on us your rage [and] your [jealou]sy with all the

48. Birge, *The Language of Belonging*, 85.

> intensity of your anger. And clung to us [. . .] your [pre]cepts which Moses wrote and your servant the prophets who[m] you [s]ent, so that evil would [over]take us in the last days.

While other nations are portrayed with dismissive language as "nothing," Israel's relation with God is extolled as a Father-son relationship. Similar to the language of the Hebrew Bible, Israel's relationship to God as son/children is presented using language that echoes Israel's formation—"created us," "established us," "my son, my first-born," and "raised us over the years of our generations." The Father-son relationship is also depicted as involving both discipline and provision of guidance through precepts. Commenting on this, psalm Byrne writes, "The passage reveals an express consciousness of sonship of God as a privilege marking Israel off from other nations, as something which the latter must recognize in virtue of God's message to Pharaoh in Ex 4:22. Sonship derives from God's 'calling' and 'creation' of Israel; it is a status which Israel has attained by God's direct act."[49]

Finally, in an eschatological context in Enoch 62, God is depicted as judging "the oppressors of his children and the elect ones" (62:12). The text focuses on the division not only between Jews and Gentiles but also between those who align themselves with God and those who trust in kings. While "vengeance shall be executed" on the oppressors of God's "children and his elect ones," the "righteous and elect ones" will be saved and rejoice over the judgment of their oppressors (Enoch 62:11–15). Here the three terms—God's children, elect, and righteous — appear to be used interchangeably. As such, the use appears to narrow the category of "children" to those who are righteous and elect among the Jews. The text highlights that "on that day" the children of God, who are identified as "the righteous and the elect ones" will be saved (62:13), "they shall rise from the earth and shall cease being of downcast face," and they will never "see the faces of the sinners and the oppressors" (62:14–15). Here again the narrative constructs God's children in contrast to the Gentiles.

God's People as Siblings

Another aspect of the use of God as Father in the imaging of Israel as a family in ancient Jewish writings is that God's people are depicted in sibling language.[50] As in the Hebrew Bible, sibling kinship language constructs an orienting framework on how the Jewish people are to relate to each other

49. Byrne, *'Sons of God,'* 27.

50. See Horrell, "From ἀδελφόι to οἶκος θεου," 293–311; von Soden, *TDNT* 1:145.

irrespective of where they are geographically. Although sibling language is not as frequent in ancient Jewish writings as it is in Pauline usage, it is more common compared to the Hebrew Bible and it shows an understanding of Jewish people as a kin-group.

Using sibling language, 1 Esdras constructs a family image with the previous generation, probably with the intention of promoting the same image in the present. Sibling relationship is depicted between the Levites and the rest of Israel (1 Es 1:5, 6), between Zerubbabel and those who were in exile (4:61–62), and between the present and the past generation (8:77). In the beginning of its account that focuses on Josiah's Passover celebration, 1 Esdras stresses the unity between the Levites and the rest of the people with repeated use of sibling language. In Josiah's instruction to the Levites, the people of Israel are referred to as "your brothers the people of Israel" (1 Es 1:5). In 4:61–62, the narrator describes that after acquiring the permission to go and build Jerusalem, Zerubbabel went to Babylon and informed his "brothers" who then praised "the God of their ancestors" for giving them permission to go and build Jerusalem and the temple. In 1 Es 8:77, after hearing that the people and their rulers continued mixed marriage with the result that "the holy race has been mixed with the alien peoples of the land," Ezra acknowledges that it is their corporate sin that was the cause of the captivity that befell them. In this confession he looks back to what led to exile and states that "because of our sins and the sins of our ancestors, we with our brothers . . . were given over to the kings of the earth" (8:77).

In 1 Maccabees, sibling language is used in a way that builds solidarity. The narrator depicts Mattathias and his friends as referring to the Jews who were killed on the Sabbath without fighting as "our brothers," (2:39, 41). Learning a lesson that even when they do not fight the Gentiles would kill them, just as they did to their brothers, Mattathias and his friends "made their decision that day" to fight against anyone who comes to attack them on the Sabbath day (2:39–41). In similar way, when the Israelites who lived in Gilead wrote to Judas seeking rescue from the Gentiles, they referred to those who have been killed as "our brothers who were in the land of Tob (1 Macc 5:11–13). The narrator also indicates that messengers from Galilee came and reported to Judas that "the people of Ptolemais and Tyre and Sidon, and all Galilee of the Gentiles had gathered together against them to annihilate them." In response, Judas and the people sent a group of people to rescue "their brothers who were in distress" (1 Macc 5:14–18). As such, the sibling solidarity is evident in the fight against the oppression of the Gentiles. The narrator creates a discourse that images the people during the Maccabeen period as standing together as one family, with a sibling responsibility, against the Gentiles.

Sibling language is frequent in Tobit. Right at the beginning of the writing, Tobit identifies himself as one who "walked in the ways of truth and righteousness" all the days of his life and who performed many acts of charity for his "brothers" his "people" who had gone with him in exile to Nineveh (Tobit, 1:3). This idea of "brothers," and "my people," permeates the rest of the account in the book. He gives instruction to his son to marry from among his people and refrain from disdaining his "brothers, the sons and daughters" of his people by refusing to take a wife for himself "from among them" (Tobit 4:12–13). In a similar way, Tobias introduced an Israelite to his father Tobit as follows: "I have just found a man who is one of our own Israelite brothers" (Tobit 5:9). In the ensuing conversation with the Israelite, Tobit addresses the Israelite as "brother" five times (5:11, 12, 14). Tobit asks the Israelite, "Brother, of what family are you and from what tribe? Tell me, brother." (Tobit 5:11). When the man introduced his name, Tobit said to him, "Welcome! God save you, brother. Do not feel bitter toward me, brother, because I wanted to be sure about your ancestry" (Tobit 5:14). In Tobit 7:1 Tobias addresses this man, as "brother Azariah" (7:1). When Tobit was about to die, in his farewell advice to his son, he explains that all of their "brothers" whom he identifies as the "inhabitants of the land of Israel," will be "scattered and taken as captives from the good land" (Tobit 14:4). This emphasis on sibling language shows that the image of sibling is central for the writer of Tobit to portray Israel as a family. It promotes charitable action, helps avoid mixed marriage, and provides protection to each other.

In the book of Judith, in the face of the Assyrian advance against the Israelites, the people wanted Uzziah to make peace by surrendering (Judith 7:23–28). In encouraging the people who lost hope in the face of the Assyrian advance, Uzziah addresses the people as "my brothers and sisters" and encourages them to wait for God for five more days (Judith 7:29–31). In chapter 8, encouraging the leaders of the people not to surrender the city to the Assyrians, Judith addressed them as "my brothers" (Judith 8:14, 24). She also refers to her fellow people as "our brothers" (8:22, 24). In doing so, the text portrays that they stood together as siblings to find a way out from the advancing danger from the Assyrians.

Second Maccabees frames its message with a kinship tone. In 1.1 the letter identifies those who are sending the letter as "The Jews in Jerusalem and those in the land of Judea." The recipients of the letter are portrayed as "their Jewish brothers in Egypt."

Finally, in the Qumran community also, although not as frequent as in other writings, the use of sibling language is attested. In the Community Rule that states meeting procedure, the community members are identified as brothers. While explaining how discussion and sharing of ideas should proceed, the community rule states:

> This is the Rule for the session of the Many. Each one by his rank: the priests will sit down first, the elders next and the remainder of all the will sit down in order of rank. And following the same system they shall be questioned with regard to judgment, all counsel and any matter referred to the Community. No-one should talk during the speech of his fellow before his *brother* has finished speaking. And neither should he speak before one whose rank is listed before his own. (1QS VI, 8–10, emphasis added)

The orderliness is promoted not only by using ranks (priests, elders, etc), but also by using a family concept of siblingship. Furthermore, as Birge notes, "[t]he use of the word 'brother' for another member of the group signals that Qumran views membership in the community as establishing a form of relationship among members that resembles the kinship shared between brothers."[51] In the text that gives instruction concerning "anyone from Israel who freely volunteers to enroll in the council of the Community," it is indicated that sibling relationship will be formed upon joining.

> He must not touch the drink of the Many until he completes a second year among the men of the Community. And when this second year is complete he will be examined by command of the many. And if the lot results in him joining the Community, they shall enter him in the order of his rank among his brothers for the law, for the judgment, for purity and for the placing of his possessions. (1QS VI 2b–22)

The gradual testing and proving, and a step-by-step process of training for membership culminates with an acceptance into a familial relationship. It is to be noted that both in the previous text as well as here, rank and sibling relationship do not exclude each other. Rather, in the way the community is organized, they go together. While ranking in the community was based on sibling relationship, there was "a communitarian spirit engendered within the Qumran community." Under that kinship relationship, however, there was a hierarchical relationship based on "a member's relative age in the community . . . and the authority given to the leaders."[52] In other words, just like family

51. Birge, *The Language of Belonging*, 114.

52. Ibid. 115.

structure in its contemporary society, the sibling relationship at Qumran is not egalitarian, but it involves a relationship based on status and rank.[53]

God as Father of the Royal King/Messianic Figure

The period covered by the ancient Jewish writings does not have a Davidic king actually reigning in Israel. The issue is then "of asking whether this language was applied to the ideal Davidic ruler expected to arise in the last days: the Messiah."[54] If so, what familial image does its use construct? The use in the Hebrew Bible is related to establishing a king and kingdom to God's people which involve protection and prosperity. When in the exilic and post-exilic period there was not such a king, the promise was turned into hope. Here in the ancient Jewish writings, that hope is eschatologized. The familial relationship between a Davidic king and God is developed into a familial relationship between God and the coming messianic figure. It is used to generate hope in the coming of deliverance and in receiving God's promises. Michael A. Knibb explains that the expectation of the Davidic messiah "is built up to a great extent from quotations from, and allusions to, passages in the Hebrew Bible, particularly royal psalms and passages concerning the ideal future king."[55] The promise to David in 2 Sam. 7:12–16 that is also reflected in Ps. 89:4–5; 132:11, and Isa 11:1–5 is used in ancient Jewish writings for an appeal to God to raise up a messianic figure who will deliver Israel.[56]

Knibb points out that within the Apocrypha and Pseudepigrapha, messianic beliefs are expressed only in a restricted number of writings.[57] In addition, a number of texts from Qumran contain messianic beliefs. While the link between the tradition of the sonship of Israel's king and the envisioned king from the line of David whom God will send to save his people is implicit in the Hebrew Bible, 4Q174 relates the two directly.[58] In a text that reflect upon the last days, the house of David plays an important role (4Q174 1–3 I):

53. For further use of sibling language in Qumran see The Damascus Document (CD), VI 20–21; VIII 6; XVIII 18–19.

54. Byrne, *'Sons of God,'* 59.

55. Knibb, "Messianism," 165–84.

56. Ibid.

57. Ibid., 166. Knibb mentions *Psalms of Solomon* 17 and 18, 1 *Enoch* 37–71, 4 *Ezra*, 2 *Baruch*, and the Testaments of the Twelve Patriarch as some of the texts that contain messianic belief.

58. Chen, *God as Father*, 132.

> YHWH [de]clares to you that "he will build you a house. I will raise up your seed after you and establish the throne of his kingdom [for ev]er. I will be a father to him and he will be a son to me.' This (refers to the) 'branch of David', who will arise with the Interpreter of the law who [will rise up] in Zi[on in] the [l]ast days, as it is written: 'I will raise up the hut of David which has fallen' This (refers to) 'the hut of David which has fall[en'. W]hich he will raise up to save Israel. (4Q174 1–3 I, 10–13)

Craig Evans rightly states, "In this text we encounter explicit messianic exegesis of 2 Sam. 7:11–14. Nathan's oracle is eschatologized and directly applied to the "branch of David . . . who will stand with the interpreter of Torah, who will sit on the throne in Zion at the end of days."[59] This interpretation merges the Davidic promise with its prophetic interpretation (shoot of David) and then with the eschatological messiah ("the Interpreter of the Laws, and who will arise in Zion in the Last Days") based on the prophecy in Amos 9:11. Thus, Evans concludes, "we have in this instance a messianizing of a "father-son" passage. God will be as father, the Messiah will be as son."[60] In similar vein Chen observes that this text's interpretation of 2 Sam 7:12–14 "basically states that God is the Father of the Davidic Messiah."[61] The purpose is "to save Israel." In other Qumran texts, the royal messiah is identified with "the Prince of the congregation" (4Q285 V, 2–4), and with the "righteous Messiah" (4Q252 V, 1–4).[62] In the former case, the royal messiah represents Israel in its battle with the forces of evil. The latter text (4Q252 V, 1–4) interprets the promise to Judah as fulfilled through a descendant of David:

> The scepter shall [no]t depart from the tribe of Judah. While Israel has dominion, there [will not] be cut off someone who sits on the throne of David. For 'the staff' is the covenant of royalty, [and the thou]sands of Israel are 'the standards'. Until the messiah of righteousness comes, the branch of David. For to him and to his descendants has been given the covenant of the kingship of his people for everlasting generations which he observed . . . (4Q252 V, 1–4)

The "messiah of righteousness" whose coming is awaited is identified as "the branch of David." The text explains that the "covenant of the kingship of his people" is given for the "messiah of righteousness," applying directly

59. Evans, "A Note on the "First-Born Son" of 4Q369," 189.

60. Ibid.

61. Chen, *God as Father*, 132.

62. Ibid.

the promise of David to the messianic king. Furthermore, in 4Q369, we find an eschatological figure referred to as God's "firstborn son":

> [Y]our name, you have distributed his inheritance so that he may establish your name there [. . .] it is the glory of your inhabited world, and at her [you] gaze [. . .] your eye on it, and your glory will appear there to [. . .] for his seed according to their generations an eternal possession, and al[l. . .] and your good judgments you explained to him to [. . .] in eternal light, and you made him for you a first-bo[rn] son [. . .] like him, to (be) a prince and ruler in all/your/ inhabited world [. . .] the c[row]n of the heavens, and glory of the clouds you have placed [on him . . .] and the angel of your peace in his congregation and . . . for him (?) righteous rules, as a father to [his] s[on] . . . (4Q369 1 II, 1–11)

After a comparative study of 4Q369, Evans tentatively concludes, "The 'first-born son' of 4Q369 in all probability is a Davidic and messianic figure. Because this figure is called the 'first-born son,' the text, therefore, does lend a measure of support to the view that 'Son of God' (as in 4Q246) was understood in a messianic sense."[63] In 4Q246 II, I, 1, he is identified as "the son of God," and "son of the Most High":

> He will be called son of God, and they will call him son of the Most High . . . the people of God arises and makes everyone rest from the sword. His kingdom will be an eternal kingdom, and all his paths in truth. He will judge the earth in truth and all will make peace. The sword will cease from the earth and all the provinces will pay him homage. The great God is his strength, he will wage war for him; he will place the peoples in his hand and cast them all away before him. His rule will be an eternal rule. (4Q246 II, I, 1–9)

He will go with the strength of God and bring peace and "all the provinces will pay him homage." His kingdom is identified as an "eternal kingdom," his rule as "eternal rule," and his judgment as well as his ways is "in truth." God as Father "will wage war for him" and "will place the peoples in his hand." Knibb also points out that Psalms of Solomon 17 depicts the son of David as a leader "whose task is to drive the enemy from Jerusalem, and as the righteous ruler of the newly purified city."[64]

63. Evans, "The 'First-Born Son' of 4Q369," 200.

64. "He will gather a holy people whom he will lead in righteousness; and he will judge the tribes of the people that have been made holy by the Lord their God. He will not tolerate unrighteousness (even) to pause among them, and any person who knows

God as Universal Father

In the Hebrew Bible and ancient Jewish writings that are seen above, the Fatherhood of God is limited to God's people, Israel, and the Jewish people. It is, however, not so in the writings of Philo and Josephus. These writings indicate a major shift that broadens God's Fatherhood to all humanity and all creation. While depictions that limit the Fatherhood of God to the Jewish people are not totally absent, Philo's and Josephus' portrayal of God as Father is much more related to all humanity and all creation than to the Jewish people. This broadening of the Fatherhood of God in Philo and Josephus can be seen as part of their attempt to position Judaism within the larger Greco-Roman milieu.

God as Father occurs in Philo quite frequently. Philo's depiction of God as Father stands apart both from the Hebrew Bible and the ancient Jewish literature.[65] It resembles more the Stoics' characterization of Zeus as the father of all.[66] In similar way to the Stoics, in Philo "human beings can claim special kinship with God because their soul and mind are conformed to the one who has begotten them."[67] This can be seen in the *Decal.* 134 where Philo writes,

> [B]ut man [humanity], who is the most excellent of all animals, in respect of that predominant part that is in him, namely, his soul, is also most closely related to the heaven, which is the purest of all things in its essence, and as the common language of the multitude affirms, to the Father of the world, inasmuch as he has received mind, which is of all the things that are upon the earth the closet copy and most faithful representation of the everlasting and blessed idea.[68] (*Decal.* 134)

Humanity's common possession of soul/mind is described as the basis for close relationship with "the Father of the world." In *Cher* 44, Philo describes God as "the Father of the universe," and "the Father of all things" who "sows good seed" in parents. For Philo, God's Fatherhood is related to God's "creative and life giving function" in the sense that he is the "origin

---

wickedness shall not live with them. For he know them that they are all children of their God . . . And he will be a righteous king over them, taught by God. There will be no unrighteousness among them in his days, for all shall be holy, and their king shall be the Lord Messiah" (Psalms of Solomon, 17:26–32).

65. Thompson, *The Promise of the Father*, 52.

66. Byrne, *'Sons of God,'* 57.

67. Chen, *God as Father*, 136–37.

68. See also *Mig.* 194; *Opif.* 72, 74; *Spec.* 3.178.

and first cause" of all creation.[69] This can be seen from the way Philo refers to God: "the primal God and Father of all" (*Abr* 74–75), "the Father of the Universe" (*Abr* 121), "the Father of all" (*Abr* 204; *Spec.* 1.14; *Spec* 3.127), "Father and Maker of all" (*Abr* 9, 58), "Maker and Father and Ruler" (*Spec* 1. 34), "Maker and Father of all," (*Spec* 2.6), and "the supreme Father of gods and men and the Maker of the whole universe" (*Spec* 2.165). He also creates a sibling relationship among the creation based on "shared origin in God."[70] In *Decal* 64, Philo writes, "all created things are brothers to one another, in as much as they are created; since the Father of them all is one, the Creator of the universe."[71] This indicates that, for Philo, God's Fatherhood "encompasses both God's creative and ruling activities over all things" but not just the formation of Israel as the people of God as it is the case in the Hebrew Bible and ancient Jewish writings.[72] Thompson rightly states, "God's Fatherhood therefore pertains to the creation of the world, rather than to the salvation of specific persons, whether that salvation be construed corporately, as the people of Israel, or individually, in terms of a specific righteous individual."[73] Thus, as Chen puts it rightly, "even though the confession of God as the Father of the universe may not directly contradict the confession of God as the Father of Israel, it nonetheless represents a departure from the particularity of Israel's sonship" which is essential to the perception of God as Father both in the Hebrew Bible as well as ancient Jewish literature.[74]

In his writings, Josephus uses both "universal Father"[75] and "the Father of the Jewish people"[76] to refer to God. When he reports the reference to God as Father by the Jews, he shows a tendency to limit God's Fatherhood to the Jewish people. In his report of Joshua's farewell speech encouraging the Transjordan tribes, Josephus has Joshua referring to God as "the Father and Lord of the Hebrew race" who has given them the land and promised "to preserve it for us forever" (*Ant* 5. 93–94). On the other hand, Josephus himself refers to God as "the universal Father and Lord who beholds all things" (*Ant* 1.19–20), "God, who is the Father of all" (Ant 2.151–52), "Father of the whole human race" (Ant 4.262). At times, Josephus combines both the Jewish particularity and God's universal Fatherhood. In reporting

69. Chen, *God as Father*, 137.

70. Birge, *The Language of Belonging*, 98.

71. See also Philo, *Virt* 140.

72. Chen, *God as Father*, 136–37.

73. Thompson, *The Promise of the Father*, 52.

74. Chen, *God as Father*, 137–38.

75. Josephus, *Ant* 1.19–20; 4.262; 2.151–52.

76. Josephus, *Ant* 5.93–94; 7.380.

David's prayer for Solomon, Josephus has David refer to God as "father and source of the universe, creator of things human and divine" who is "the protector and guardian of the Hebrew race and of its posterity and of the kingdom which He had given him" (*Ant* 7.380).

Summary Conclusion

The kinship narrative that images God's people as the family of God continued in the ancient Jewish writings to construct their identity in the ever changing socio-political matrix. The Fatherhood of God and familial language that is associated with it are meshed with formative as well as restorative narratives from Israel's tradition and used to construct an identity in a way that reflects continuity and change.

The family imagery that was constructed in the Hebrew Bible using the Fatherhood of God in conjunction with imaging Israel as sons(s)/children of God, and as siblings with each other, and also the depiction of Israel's king (in this case the messianic figure) continued in similar way in ancient Jewish writings. These writings present God's people, irrespective of where they were, as God's children and siblings who together belong to one Father, the God of Israel. In addition to these categories, we also found in ancient Jewish writing an individual addressing God as "Father," "our Father," and "my Father" in the context of prayer and acknowledgment. As such the familial identification extends to an individual and hence was not limited at a communal level as it was in the Hebrew Bible (with the exception of Israel's king).

Significant differences, however, come in the form of how the family imagery based on the Father-children relationship between God and Israel is constructed and for what purpose it is used. The circumstances in which ancient Jewish people found themselves were largely different from the Hebrew Bible. Due to these differences, the focus and purpose in using the family imagery in ancient Jewish writings became much different compared to the Hebrew Bible. The family image that is constructed in terms of the Father-children relationship between God and Israel in ancient Jewish writings is primarily portrayed against the nations. It focuses on the protection and restoration from Gentiles and on inheritance that goes beyond the promised land. Since in the ancient Jewish writings the focus is on the difference between the children of God and the Gentiles, unlike the Hebrew Bible, the identity of God's people as his children is not assessed in terms of how they measure up to that identity.

Thus, the Father-children relationship between God and Israel is used in ancient Jewish writings in seeking restoration, both eschatological as well as present, and protection from the nations which are depicted as enemies of the people of God. Unlike the Hebrew Bible where the Fatherhood of God is used for internal identification, in ancient Jewish writings it is used in a way that differentiates Israel from other nations. While the themes of restoration and protection are similar, this time the restoration and protection is from Gentile domination. In the midst of seeking protection and restoration is also a request to God to protect and restore in a way that reveals his familial relationship with Israel. While the formation of Israel is at the center of the use of God as Father in the Hebrew Bible, in ancient Jewish writings, mostly the formation is not stated but evoked. There also appears a tendency to limit the Fatherhood of God to "sons of truth," to the elect ones, which is comparable to the Roman Stoic idea that tends to limit kinship with Zeus to those who are able to ascend through reason. While the fatherhood of Zeus is open to all, those who experience it are the ones who are able to ascend through reason.

In addition to this, the universal Fatherhood of God is introduced. This development puts the use of God as Father in Philo and Josephus squarely within a similar use of the Roman Stoics that depicts the fatherhood of Zeus as universal. Such a development can be explained in terms of an attempt by these learned Jewish writers to put Judaism within the Greco-Roman historical, philosophical as well as religious map. While such depiction of God as universal Father gives away the unique familial relationship between God and Israel that is portrayed in the Hebrew Bible and the rest of ancient Jewish writings, Philo and Josephus attempt to retain the Jewish distinction through its unique traditions.

6

God as Father in Paul

Kinship Narrative and Identity Formation

In the preceding chapters, I have examined how the kinship term "father" was used by the Roman Empire and emperor and the Roman Stoic philosophers to construct a sense of familial identity. We have also seen how the authors of the Hebrew Bible and ancient Jewish writings use the term "Father" to refer to God and related familial language (children of God, son of God, and brothers and sisters) to portray the people of God as a family. In this chapter, I will discuss the significance of Paul's use of God as Father and related kinship terms for shaping and expressing the self-understanding of Christ-followers. The chapter has four sections: kinship language and identity formation in Paul, God as Father and identity formation in Paul, Christ-followers as children of God and identity formation in Paul, and Christ-followers as siblings and identity formation in Paul.

Kinship Language and Identity Formation in Paul

The writings of Paul exhibit ongoing efforts to establish a self-understanding for the emerging community. The development of early Christianity from small groups of Jewish communities into larger groups with persons from a great variety of geographical, ethnic, and social backgrounds made it necessary to engage in an ongoing community building process. This community building process involved providing orienting framework(s) that aid in the formation and transformation of existing members and the resocialization of the new. To this end, Paul employs various images and concepts (e.g., "body," "people," "saints," "*ekklesia*") that signify and represent identity.[1]

1. Minear, *Images of the Church*, 22–24; Collins, *Power of Images*; Banks, *Paul's Idea*

Images such as these serve as rhetorical tools to construct impressions, create modes of perception, and advance self-understanding.[2] These identity signifiers and representations tell something about the nature of self-understanding that Paul was promoting.[3]

Among the images Paul uses to advance the self-understanding of the community in the making are kinship images (father, brothers, sisters, household, children, sons and daughters) that coalesce to form a kinship narrative that images the Christ-followers as a family that belongs to God.[4] While these familial vocabularies derive from the natural family/household settings, when applied to a non-natural family/household setting, their role and function are not limited by their use in the natural family/household settings. Transferred to a non-natural household realm of kinship, these are capable of capturing new roles and functions that enrich the familial image that the narrative creates. As such, the term "father" and associated familial terms as used by Paul to refer God and Christ-followers are transferred from natural household to a non-natural household and hence their significance in creating identity is not limited by the corresponding role and function in the natural unit.[5]

Using such a dynamic and versatile nature of kinship, Paul describes the "being and becoming" of the emerging community through the construction of networks of relationships that emphasize a sense of sharing (e.g., Spirit, Christ, baptism) and that apply both to contemporaries and the ancients, to spiritual and corporal connections.[6] The elastic features of kinship that exhibit purging, replacing, adding, and/or supplementing spiritual

of Community; Longenecker, "Paul's Vision of the Church and Community Formation," 73–88; Lewis, "As a Beloved Brother," 10–12.

2. Minear, *Images of the Church*, 22–24.

3. On identity signifiers and representations see Huskinson, "Looking for Culture, Identity and Power,"16–17.

4. On the importance of kinship language in Paul see Banks, *Paul's Idea of Community*, 52–61; Collins, *Power of Images*, 225–27; Lewis, "As a Beloved Brother," 12–16; Hellerman, *The Ancient Church as Family*, 92–126; Birge, *The Language of Belonging*; Burke, *Family Matters*, 2–28; see also Harland, *Dynamics of Identity*, 63 who rightly notes that "early Christians could express their identity in a variety of ways, and this included the use of family language to express belonging."

5. Contra Asagaard, *'My Beloved Brothers and Sisters!'*, 306 who limits the meaning of Paul's use of sibling language to "the domain of family life," to "the family life of his day" rather than the parallel usages in other contexts (e.g., Jewish, Greco-Roman); see the discussion under sibling language below.

6. Jenkins, *Social Identity*, 17; Kelly, *Constructing Inequality*, 522; Shimizu, "On the Notion of Kinship," 377–403; Geertz, *The Interpretation of Cultures*, 363; Beattie, *Other Cultures*, 94; also see the discussion on kinship and identity formation from anthropological perspectives in chapter 2.

and corporal components that enable making a non-kin in one situation into kin in another, or a kin in one situation into non-kin in another situation are at work in the writings of Paul. He utilizes the social and cultural significance of kinship narrative in creating discourse that identifies and sets orienting frameworks to understand self and others, to define relationship categories, and to form and transform self-understanding.[7]

Paul's kinship narrative construction is not unique to him. Rather, it is "implicated in" and interacts with the wider cultural settings.[8] For Paul and his audience, the textual and cultural contexts of the Greco-Roman and ancient Jewish world form "multiple overlapping and . . . competing narratives,"[9] among other things, concerning the use of "father" and related familial languages to construct identity.[10] These kinship terms were used and "partially belong" to others, and have a "socially-charged life" associated with them.[11] Paul takes and utilizes them, charging them with the socio-religious life which his new context demands. While Paul and his audiences share with all the textual and socio-cultural milieus the construction of kinship narrative as a common feature of identity formation,[12] Paul's kinship construction "partake(s), vigorously at times, in [the] dialogical discourse" of that wider society.[13] In other words, Paul's use is not simply "*mediating* a prior narrative"[14] evoked by the kinship terms Father, children, brothers and sisters. Rather, writing to his mixed audiences' "horizon of understanding,"[15] he is "consciously *working* with it—reshaping, amplifying, and advancing" and originating stories in his "*narratological* intentions."[16] He is not engaging them only at the level of theological reflection but also at the level of their narrative thought, sometimes to affirm and sometimes to change their narrative thought. He creates a narrative world in which he intends his readers to find their identity, a discourse that creates a sense

7. Keesing, *Kin Groups and Social Structures*, 121–22 explains the social function of kinship as shaping patterns of relationships, networks, strategies and behavior and its cultural aspect as conceptualizing ideas of symbols, beliefs, rules, roles, and plans.

8. Lieu, *Christian Identity*, 20–21.

9. Wright, *Paul in Fresh Perspective*, 6.

10. Here we see "cultural intertextuality" whereby Paul's texts that use kinship language are part of another sets of texts within the culture. See Carter, *John and Empire*, 235; Kristeva, "The Bounded Text," 36–63.

11. Robbins and Gowler "Introduction," 12.

12. Harland, *Dynamics of Identity*, 61.

13. Robbins and Gowler, "Introduction," 12.

14. Adams, "Paul's Story of God and Creation," 34.

15. Dunn, "Narrative Approach to Paul," 222.

16. Ibid.; Adams, "Paul's Story of God and Creation," 34, emphasis original.

of community. At times it calls for assimilation and accommodation.[17] At other times, it relativizes his audiences' past history and traditions by redefining the value and meaning attached to them.[18] At times, he adds new dimensions to his audiences' past understanding of the term "father" and related familial terms and provides a basis by which the significance of the new and old identities is evaluated by his recipients.[19]

Thus, in anticipation of a fuller discussion below, when we situate Paul's use of God as Father and related kinship language within his contemporary textual and cultural contexts, his use both imitates and contests the prevailing use. He imitates and contests largely by using what Carol A. Newsome calls "non-polemical discourse," which creates "the disposition of affinity and estrangement."[20] In "non-polemical discourse," explains Newsome, "the language of broader linguistic community" is used and gradually transformed "into the distinctive accent" of the community.[21] While what Newsome describes as an identity construction model (i.e., taking the language of the broader community and making one's own) applies accurately to what Paul is doing, her characterization of the model as "non-polemical discourse" needs modification. As I will show below, the effect of what Paul ends up constructing has a polemical edge by gradually constructing the "us" over against "them."[22] On the other hand, it is equally inaccurate to ascribe polemic to Paul's use of any and every language from the broader community. One has to examine such use case by case.

Using kinship language to develop an identity narrative in terms of networks of relationships, Paul imitates not only the strategies of constructing identity but also the intention of creating a family image. The self-understanding constructed in this way provides an orienting framework that promotes a sense of community, belongingness, cohesion, and accountability. At significant points, though, Paul vigorously engages, contests, and redefines the use of the term Father from its surrounding textual and cultural uses. Paul primarily contests the use of the kinship term "father" to refer to the Roman Empire and emperor, and its use by the Roman Stoic philosophers to refer to Zeus. He contests it on two levels: on the applicability of the term "father" and on the nature of the community constructed

17. Korostelina, *Social Identity and Conflict*, 115.

18. Ibid., 113–14; Hogg and Abrams, *Social Identifications*, 55–59; see Jokiranta, "Social Identity," 85–110.

19. Korostelina, *Social Identity and Conflict*, 115.

20. Newsom, "Constructing 'We, You, and the Others,'" 13; for explanation on "affinity and estrangement" see Lincoln, *Discourse*, 9–10.

21. Newsom, "Constructing 'We, You, and the Others,'" 16.

22. Ibid.

and its internal features. He argues that fatherhood is more appropriate to God than to Zeus, the Roman Empire, or the emperor. He also argues that the community thus created through the Fatherhood of God is different on many levels from the Empire as a big household and from the cosmopolitan humanity of the Roman Stoic.

One can also see Paul imitating and contesting the use of "Father" to refer to God and the related familial languages in the Hebrew Bible and ancient Jewish writings. While Paul's use of the term "Father" to refer to God is in line with the Hebrew Bible and ancient Jewish literature, the nature of the community constructed and its internal features are significantly different.

In this chapter, using the kinship-identity approach that applies features from kinship, social identity approach, imperial critical approach, and narrative approach to Paul, I will demonstrate that by using the language of belonging, Paul constructs a self-understanding for the emerging community. By means of kinship language that categorizes and identifies community members through a network of relationships, Paul develops a narrative that images the community of Christ-followers as a family that belongs to God, who, together with "the Lord Jesus Christ," bestows on them "grace and peace" and inheritance. The narrative so constructed forms the foundation for referring to Christ-followers as "children" of God and "brothers and sisters" of one another. The self-understanding ensuing from such a narrative aims at shaping the whole life of the community of the followers of Christ. It forms boundaries and serves as a nexus of transformation and negotiation. To this end, Paul uses kinship language both in stable and in crisis situations, shaping identity not just in opposition to the outside world but also by employing a wide-range of negotiation. He uses God as Father and terms associated with it (children of God and brothers and sisters) consistently, strategically, and purposefully to build self-understanding.

God as Father and Identity Formation in Paul

Paul's use of God as Father is more strategic, consistent, and deliberate, hence more formative compared to any of such uses that we have observed in chapters 3–5. He refers to God by the kinship term "Father" at strategic sections of his letters with a consistency that creates and reinforces a narrative that portrays Christ-followers as having familial relationship with God as Father. He strengthens the family image by adding to the depiction of God as Father the portrayal of Christ-followers as children of God and siblings. The strategic nature of the portion of his letters in which he refers to God as Father, the pattern that emerges from the consistency of his use, and the evocative nature of the vocabulary associated with it are all remarkable. Abraham J. Malherbe correctly observes, "The description of God the Father as progenitor of the church introduces the notion of the church as God's family, which is developed throughout the letter by means of a strong concentration of kinship language."[23] In similar vein, commenting on Paul's use of God as Father at the beginning of his letters, deSilva explains that it shows "the prominence and almost 'givenness' of this new household and its paterfamilias within Christian culture, and thus its availability as a foundational principle from which to derive ethical exhortations and explanations of believers' condition in the world."[24] It serves as a "hegemonic idiom" in terms of which all familial relationships form.[25] It provides an orienting framework for "the content and ideology" of the networks of familial relationships which Paul constructs.[26]

The only use that comes close to its strategic nature is probably Augustus' meticulous planning toward acquiring the title *pater patriae*, packing it with more roles than before, declining to accept it several times only to add more value to it, and then monumentalizing it as an inscription.[27] While there is a pattern that emerges from the use of God as Father in the Hebrew Bible and ancient Jewish literature in terms of defining Israel's identity in relation to God and humanity, apart from Deuteronomy 32, the use does not appear to be positioned as strategically as that which we have in Paul.

The strategic place in which Paul uses God as Father and the consistency with which he uses it even in the letters where believers are not mentioned as children of God (1 Corinthians, 1 & 2 Thessalonians) strongly suggest that Paul's use of God as Father serves as a root/foundation, on which basis he applies the familial terms of children and siblinghood to Christ-followers.[28] Banks rightly points out that Paul's familial language has as its

23. Malherbe, *Thessalonians*, 102; also see idem, "God's Family," 117–28.

24. deSilva, *Honor, Patronage, Kinship and Purity*, 207.

25. Peletz, "Ambivalence in Kinship," 416.

26. Ibid., 416.

27. *Res Gestae*; Suetonius, *Augustus*, 31.5; 58; Güven, "Res Gestae," 3–45; also see the discussion in chapter 3 of this book.

28. See White, "God's Paternity as Root Metaphor," 272, who argues, "Paul's conception of God as Father is the root metaphor on which he grafts his entire system of *communal images*" (emphasis added); Joubert, "Managing the Household," 213–23, also states, "Sociologically the image of God's fatherhood helped to shape the Pauline house-hold group's corporate identity;" also see Burke, *Family Matters*, 9. Regarding the importance of the concept of "family" for the study of early Christian community based on the frequency of familial language that appears in the New Testament, Banks, *Paul's Idea of Community*, 53–54, writes, "the comparison of the Christian community with a 'family' must be regarded as the most significant metaphorical usage of all. For that

basis "the head of the family as being God the Father" and the relationship Christ-followers have with Christ.[29] In a similar vein, writing about siblinghood, Norman R. Petersen explains that being brothers and sisters derives from being children of God, whom Paul depicts as Father.[30]Approaching family language in Paul from a literary aspect, Daniel von Allmen argued for the need to approach the language of family in Paul as a unity rather than as unrelated terms.[31] Combining the fatherhood image with the image of children and sibling, Allmen gives the image of family a fuller portrayal.

Paul refers consistently to God as the Father of Christ-followers in all his letters, primarily in the opening formulas where he lays out the identities of the sender and recipients (Rom 1:7; 1 Cor 1:3; 2 Cor 1:2; Gal 1:3; Phil 1:2; Philm 3), in the thanksgiving, prayer, and benediction sections of his letters (1 Thess 1:3; 3:11, 13; 2 Thess 2:16–17; Gal 1:4; 2 Thess 1:2 and Phil 4:20). He refers to Christ-followers as children of God in four of his letters (Gal 3:26; Rom 8:14–16; Phil 2:14–15; 2 Cor 6:18), and as siblings in all of his letters. In the following section, I will begin with Paul's use of God as Father in the salutation followed by his use of the term in thanksgiving and prayer context and in 1 Corinthians 3.

God as Father in the Pauline Prescripts

In the prescripts of his letters where he establishes the identities of the sender and the receiver, Paul constructs his own and his recipients' identity in terms of relationships. While he describes his identity and his audiences' identity in relation to God and Jesus, he constructs their joint identity in terms of kinship relationship with God. Together with the vocabularies used, the kinship depiction forms dynamics of creating a narrative of networks of relationships that characterize Paul and his recipients as the family of God. In so doing, it serves as a foundation for subsequent uses of God as the Father of Christ-followers and other kinship terms that Paul uses to

reason it has a pride of place in this discussion. More than any of other images utilized by Paul, it reveals the essence of his thinking about community;" Petersen, *Rediscovering Paul*, even goes further in arguing, "Within Paul's symbolic universe, the metaphoric images of God as 'our Father,' and of Christ as 'the' or 'our Lord,' are 'organizing metaphors,' for "they provide images in relation to which the organization of behavior can take place;" for a view that mitigates such argument see that of Barton, "Paul's Sense of Place," 225, who makes a distinction between church and household based on Paul's argument about women speaking and church meal in1 Cor 11:17–34 and 14:33–36.

29. Banks, *Paul's Idea of Community*, 54; Lewis, "As a Beloved Brother," 109.

30. Petersen, *Rediscovering Paul*, 266.

31. Allmen, *La Famille de Dieu*; also see Lewis, "As a Beloved Brother," 108.

depict his audiences' relation to God and to each other. It functions as a "hegemonic idiom" in terms of which subsequent familial description of God and Christ-followers are portrayed.

From Paul's use of God as the Father of Christ-followers in a given section of his letters, the use in the prescript is the largest in proportion (ten, compared to three or less in other sections of his letters). It also is consistent and formulaic in pattern. It serves Paul well to position himself and his recipients rhetorically within the image of family.[32] Philip L. Tite notes that the prescript in Pauline writings plays "a significant role in Paul's discursive engagement with his recipients, constructing the very framework within which the letter was to be received."[33] As such, the identification of God as Father in the prescript, portraying the community as a family that belongs to God, is part of Paul's rhetorical positioning, "discursive engagement," and part of the framework within which he addresses his recipients. In this section of his letters, the strategic role of Paul's use of God as Father for identity formation lies in at least three features: (1) the nature of prescripts—it is a section that establishes the identities of the sender, the receiver, and their relationship. (2) Modified salutation—Paul intentionally modifies the phraseology and wordings of the customary salutation to fit his purpose and consistently applies it in almost all his letters.[34] (3) Evocative vocabulary—he uses consistently the same evocative vocabulary that is associated with his identification of God as Father. (4) Standard formula — while he modifies the identity descriptors for himself as well as his recipients, his greeting formula in which he identifies God as Father remains the standard, unchanging center of his own, as well as his recipients', identity. The discussion below follows each of these points to examine how each enhanced the identity construction function of Paul's identification of God as Father in the prescripts.

The opening formula of the official Greco-Roman letter typically contains prescripts and thanksgiving.[35] The prescript contains a subscription or

32. Tite, "How to Begin, and Why," 59; for similar analysis of the rhetorical function of the prescript in 1 Peter see idem, "Compositional Function," 47–56.

33. Tite, "How to Begin, and Why," 66.

34. The only exception to this is 1 Thessalonians 1:1.

35. The mixed nature of Paul's letter is noted by scholars. While his letters exhibit the general contemporary epistolary structure, several differing features imply that they have mixed character. Adams, "Paul's Letter Opening and Greek Epistolography," writes "Paul's letters are akin to royal correspondence because they are addressed to communities and not just to individuals as well as making use of titles that increase the epistolary presence of the sender. However, at the same time there is a mixture of leadership and equality that is not found within the official royal correspondence, but is similar to that found in personal letters." Also see White, *The Apostle of God*, 62–63; Dahl, "Paul's Letter to the Galatians," 10–11; Richards, *Paul and First Century*

sender, adscription or addressee, and a salutation in the form of "χαίρειν" (greetings).[36] Pauline prescripts exhibit similarity *in form* with official letters as they contain "superscription or sender, adscription or addressee, and salutation."[37] The prescript is a context where sender(s) and receiver(s) are formally/officially identified and greeting is extended. Stirewalt explains,

> of the official conventions appropriated by Paul, the salutation [the prescript] is most distinguishing. It marks the letter as being of the official type. It introduces the writer as one who occupies an authoritative position and identifies the recipients as a corporate body for which the writer is an authority. The recipients would have immediately recognized the nature of the letter, the position of the writer, and their own position in relation to him.[38]

The following two prescripts show the difference and similarity between Pauline and contemporary prescripts. A prescript from a letter by Caesar Augustus reads:

> Emperor Caesar Augustus, son of the deified [Julius], pontifex maximus, consul-designate for the twelfth time, and holding the tribunician power for the eighteenth time, to the magistrates, the Senate, the people of Cnidos, greetings.[39]

The following is a prescript on a letter sent by a Roman strategus to Teos:

> Marcus Valerius, son of Marcus, strategus, [the] tribunes and the senate to the council and people of Teos, greeting.[40]

The first letter identifies the emperor by name (Caesar Augustus) and titles (Emperor, son of the deified, pontifex maximus, consul-designate). The prescript of the letter focuses on identifying the emperor in relation to a god through a kinship connection to Julius Caesar, deified after his assassination in 42 B.C. Augustus, his adopted son, uses "son of the deified" as self-identification, to construct a kinship relationship with a god through sonship to

Letter Writing, 122–40; Adams, "Paul's Letter Opening and Epistolography," 33–56.

36. Aune, *The New Testament in Its Literary Environment*, 184; Adams, "Paul's Letter Opening and Epistolography," 46–48.

37. Aune, *The New Testament in Its Literary Environment*, 184; Adams, "Paul's Letter Opening and Epistolography," 35–38.

38. Stirewalt, *Paul, The Letter Writer*, 33–34.

39. Sherk, *Roman Documents*, no. 67; Stirwalt, *Paul, The Letter Writer*, 35; for collection of ancient letters see also White, *Light from Ancient* Letters.

40. Sherk, *Roman Documents*, no. 34; cf. Stirewalt, *Paul, The Letter Writer*, 35.

Julius Caesar. He also uses his priestly title, "pontifex maximus," and the title, "consul-designate." All of these establish his identity in terms of networks of relationships —to his predecessor, a god, and to the senate, and the Roman people. Then the prescript identifies the recipients as the magistrates, the Senate, and the people of Cnidos. The letter by a Roman strategus identifies the principal sender by his name ("Marcus Valerius"), his family ("son of Marcus"), and his title ("strategus [of the] tribunes"), and the co-senders as "the senate." The recipients are identified as "the council and people of Teos." Both letters end the prescript with the customary word, "greetings."

In terms of form, Paul's prescripts are similar to these examples. Following the convention of the official letter, Paul identifies himself, and his recipients, and then adds the greeting. But in all these he adds his own modifications. As a sender, Paul identifies himself in his letters' prescripts as follows:

Παῦλος (1 Thess 1:1)

Παῦλος (2 Thess 1:1)[41]

Παῦλος ἀπόστολος (Gal 1:1)

κλητὸς ἀπόστολος Χριστοῦ Ἰησοῦ (1 Cor 1:1)

ἀπόστολος Χριστοῦ Ἰησοῦ (2 Cor 1:1)

δοῦλος Χριστοῦ Ἰησοῦ, κλητὸς ἀπόστολος (Rom 1:1)

Παῦλος καὶ Τιμόθεος δοῦλοι Χριστοῦ Ἰησοῦ (Phil 1:1)

Παῦλος δέσμιος Χριστοῦ Ἰησοῦ (Philm 1:1)

While in 1 and 2 Thessalonians he identifies himself simply as Παῦ λος, his identification of himself intensifies in the rest of his letters. Depending on what he is addressing, he emphasizes the aspect of his identity that positions him well to deal with the issue. Accordingly, in Galatians, he adds ἀπόστολος to Παῦλος, highlighting the capacity at which he is addressing the Galatians. He further specifies the source of his apostleship as divine not human with "οὐκ ἀπ' ἀνθρώπων οὐδὲ δι' ἀνθρώπου ἀλλὰ διὰ Ἰησοῦ Χριστοῦ καὶ θεοῦ πατρὸς τοῦ ἐγείραντος αὐτὸν ἐκ νεκρῶν." He denies human origin and claims divine source. He identifies Jesus Christ and God, who raised Jesus from the dead, as the origin of his apostleship. This long statement of denial and claim of the source of his apostolic identity is unique to Galatians. Here Paul is framing his identity in a way that provides him a legitimate authority for the intense rebuke he is going to engage in and anticipates the narrative of chapter 1 in which he underscores God's

41. For the inclusion of 2 Thessalonians among the genuine letters of Paul see note 91 in chapter 1 of this book.

commission.[42] Murphy-O'Connor notes that whereas the earlier Pauline letter (1 Thess 1:1) simply includes the name of the sender(s), the fuller descriptions, such as "not by human persons but by God" (Gal 1:1), mark a new phase reflected in 1 Cor 1:1 and thereafter.[43] This development indicates that Paul continually modified aspects of the official letter for the purpose he desired to accomplish.

His identification of himself as ἀπόστολος continues in 1 and 2 Corinthians and Romans. It is replaced by δοῦλος in Philippians and by δέσμιος in Philemon. Each of these identifications is modified by Χριστοῦ Ἰησοῦ, which indicates the source of his commission as well as his belongingness to Christ (1 Cor 1:1; 2 Cor 1:1; Rom 1:1; Phil 1:1; and Philm 1:1). That he drops ἀπόστολος in Philippians and Philemon but uses it in 1 and 2 Corinthians and Romans, modifying it by κλητὸς (1 Cor 1:1; Rom 1:1) and διὰ θελήματος θεοῦ (1 Cor 1:1; 2 Cor 1:2), both of which again emphasize the origin of his apostleship indicates that in these letters the divine source of his identity is crucial. Each of these uses modifies the description of his vocation and identifies the source of his calling. From these self-identifications he applies κλητὸς to his addressees (Rom 1: 6, 7; 1 Cor 1:2), and δοῦλος to his coworkers (Phil 1:1), indicating shared identity.

J. A. Bühner connects ἀπόστολος to terms such as οικονόμος, διάκονος, and δοῦλος, which correspond "to the customs of the masters who appointed deputies as their representatives in charge of the household."[44] Similarly noting that δοῦλος is a household term, Dale B. Martin explains that Paul's self-identification as δοῦλος depicts a transition from his previous household to the household of Christ.[45] He explains that Paul's portrayal of himself as a "slave of Christ" pictures him as "the slave agent of the founder."[46] Osiek rightly states, "[a] slaves' status did not derive from the legal condition of slavery, but from the status of his or her owner, the slave's own position, and

42. Longenecker, *Galatians*, 4; Stirwalt, *Paul, The Letter Writer*, 37; Aune, *New Testament in Its Literary Environment*, 184, writes, "Galatians and Romans stand out as distinctive, with exceptionally long phrases qualifying Paul's status . . . probably because his status was questioned."

43. Murphy-O'Connor, *Paul the Letter Writer*, 45–48.

44. Bühner, "ἀπόστολος," 142.

45. Martin, *Slavery as Salvation*, 66.

46. Ibid., 58; see also Osiek, *Philippians and Philemon*, 34. Osiek points out that in the Greco-Roman world slavery is "a complex and multilayered institution." Osiek writes further, "In the Greco-Roman world, prisoners of war and condemned criminals in galleys, mines, and public work had a terrible lot, but at the other end of the spectrum, slaves were also trusted and sometimes powerful managers of estates, businesses, and government offices."

its importance."[47] Hence, for Paul to present himself as a δοῦλος identifies him closely "with the highest-status person,"[48] whom he depicts as the originator and founder of the community of Christ-followers. As the agent of the originator and founder of the community in the form of ἀπόστολος, and δοῦλος, Paul participates in God's community-founding task. Paul vividly depicts this participatory aspect of his identity when he describes himself with both a paternal image (1 Cor 4:15) as well as a maternal image (1 Thess 2:7; Gal 4:19) to portray his role in the construction of the community of God as a family.[49]

When Paul's depiction of himself as δοῦλος is put together with his depiction of his co-workers and Christ-followers as slaves, it makes "the entire group a household."[50] A transfer from a previous household to a new household involves new identities and new networks of relationships. John Byron explains that "slavery eradicated family and national ties and replaced them with new relationships created by the individual's position in the institution."[51] Michael J. Brown compares Paul's self-description as δοῦλος Χριστοῦ Ἰησου in Romans with "*servus Caesaris*."[52] In setting his identification in a way that evokes *Familia Caesaris*, the household of Caesar, Paul was communicating "a model by which believers could understand their incorporation into this new community."[53] Paul together with his recipients have become members of "a new household," a household of God.[54]

In a way similar to his self-identification, Paul identifies his recipients by using different identity descriptors that portray their identity in relation to God and Jesus. The identity descriptors emphasize the origin and the nature of the community. The following lists show the expressions Paul uses to identify his audiences in his letters, all of which relate to God and/or Jesus:

τῇ ἐκκλησίᾳ τοῦ θεου (1 Cor 1:2; 2 Cor 1:1)

ταῖς ἐκκλησίαις τῆς Γαλατίας (Gal 1:1)

τῇ ἐκκλησίᾳ Θεσσαλονικέων ἐν θεῷ πατρὶ καὶ κυρίῳ Ἰησοῦ Χριστῷ (1 Thess 1:1; 2 Thess 1:1)

τῇ κατ' οἶκόν σου ἐκκλησίᾳ (Philm 1:2)

47. Osiek, *Philippians and Philemon*, 34.

48. Ibid.

49. For a discussion on maternal imagery see Gaventa, *Our Mother Paul.*

50. Martin, *Slavery as Salvation*, 66.

51. Byron, *Slavery Metaphors*, 39; see also Patterson, *Slavery and Social Death*, 3–5.

52. Brown, "Paul's Use of Δοῦλος Χριστοῦ Ἰησου in Romans 1:1" 723–37.

53. Ibid.,729.

54. Richards, *Paul and First Century Letter Writing*, 129.

While ἐκκλησία is his most common identification of his addressees,[55] Paul further identifies his addressees with expressions such as:

κλητοῖς ἁγίοις (Rom 1:7; 1 Cor 1:2)

ἀγαπητοῖς θεοῦ (Rom 1:7)

ἡγιασμένοις ἐν Χριστῷ Ἰησου (1 Cor 1:2)

τοῖς ἁγίοις ἐν Χριστῷ Ἰησοῦ (Phil 1:1)

Except in Philemon and Galatians, God and/or Christ Jesus are identified as the source of ἐκκλησία and all the other identity makers. As such, each of these identity markers describes the recipients' identity in terms of their relationship to God and Jesus Christ and the resulting communal identity. The most frequent of these, ἐκκλησία, which evokes "the popular political assemblies" of the cities, is grounded in divine origin. Stegemann and Stegemann rightly state, "[I]t goes without saying that the Christ-confessing community understood itself as a special assembly of politically different people who were identified by their relationship to the one God and to Christ."[56] In addition to the idea of assembly, ἐκκλησία also refers to "a group or community" whether "they are gathered or not" (1 Cor 11:16, 22; 15:9; Gal 1:13; Phil 3:6).[57]

Paul further describes the ἐκκλησία, which is depicted as an assembly and also as community, with terms such as ἁγίοις, ἡγιασμένοις, ἀγαπητοῖς, and κλητοῖς. These terms evoke images of God's people in the Hebrew Bible and ancient Jewish writings (Lev 19:1–2; Hos 11:1). Now Paul applies them to the new community of God which is made up of Jewish and Gentile members. They explain the nature of the ἐκκλησία and distinguish it from all the other analogies in terms of source, nature, and purpose.[58] Such identity signifiers depict that the Christ-followers are "a consecrated society established by God."[59]

55. Longenecker, *Community Formation*, 74 observes that ἐκκλησία appears in Paul more frequently than in any other New Testament writings: 63 times, 9 in Romans, 22 times in 1 Corinthians, 9 times in 2 Corinthians, 3 times in Galatians, 2 times in Philippians, 2 in 1 Thessalonians, 2 in 2 Thessalonians and 1 in Philemon.

56. Stegemann and Stegemann, *The Jesus Movement*, 263.

57. Ibid., 264; for a comparison of ἐκκλησία with ancient analogies see Meeks, *The First Urban Christians*, 74–110; Ascough, *What are They Saying about the Formation of Pauline Churches?*

58. See Ascough, *What are They Saying about the Formation of Pauline Churches?*, 11–94.

59. Garland, *1 Corinthians*, 26; Moo, *Romans*, 54; Hays, *First Corinthians*, 16–17.

Thus, in the identification of his recipients, Paul emphasizes the origin (τοῦ θεου and Χριστῷ Ἰησου) and nature of the community (ἐκκλησία, ἁγίοις, ἡγιασμένοις, ἀγαπητοῖς, and κλητοῖς). This emphasis parallels the origin of his vocation (Χριστοῦ Ἰησοῦ, διὰ θελήματος θεοῦ) and the nature of his vocation as the agent of the originator (ἀπόστολος and δοῦλος). Paul's self-identification as the agent of the founder in the form of ἀπόστολος and δοῦλος, and his identification of his recipients as the founder's community, construct a sense of community that he will strengthen further with the use of kinship language that relates them to God and to each other. That Paul changes and modifies his apostolic as well as his recipients' descriptions (see above), and that there is also a difference between his earliest letter (1 Thess) and others in terms of his opening formulas, suggests that he is engaged in an ongoing process of identity construction.[60] On the basis of these identities of himself, of his audience, and of their relationship to God, Paul will urge his readers to take a given course of action.[61]

Following the form of contemporary letters, Pauline prescripts contain greetings, which Paul develops to describe his and his recipients' identities in terms of kinship relationship to God. But the content of the Pauline salutation is remarkably different from the usual content of salutations in official letters. The usual epistolary salutation is "greetings" (χαίρειν) and sometimes includes the health formula, followed by motives for writing.[62] In all undisputed letters, except 1 Thessalonians, the Pauline salutation contains χάρις ὑμῖν καὶ εἰρήνη ἀπὸ θεοῦ πατρὸς ἡμῶν καὶ κυρίου Ἰησοῦ Χριστοῦ (Rom 1:7; 1 Cor 1:3; 2 Cor 1:2; Gal 1:3; Phil 1:2; Philm 3).[63] While Paul changes his identification of himself and also his recipients, depending on the tone of the letter, the greeting part, particularly the salutation formula χάρις ὑμῖν καὶ εἰρήνη ἀπὸ θεοῦ πατρὸς ἡμῶν καὶ κυρίου Ἰησοῦ Χριστοῦ, remains the same. Nine out of ten uses of this construction contain θεοῦ πατρὸς ἡμῶν (Rom 1:7; 1 Cor 1:3; 2 Cor 1:2; Gal 1:3; Phil 1:2; 2 Thess 1:1, 2;[64] Phlm 3). First person plural pronouns consistently modify Paul's use of the term "Father" to refer to God in the salutations. That his earliest letter 1 Thess 1:1 has ἐν θεῷ πατρὶ (without the personal pronoun ἡμῶν), but all

60. Wilson, *Paul's Intercessory Prayers*, 109, writes, "Paul adapts his description of himself and his credentials to the circumstances of each particular letter."

61. Malherbe, *Thessalonians*, 124.

62. Aune, *The New Testament in Its Literary Environment*, 165; Tite, "How to Begin," 57–99.

63. 1 Thessalonians has χάρις ὑμῖν καὶ εἰρήνη (1:1). Even here, there is a reference to God our Father and the Lord Jesus Christ (ἐν θεῷ πατρὶ καὶ κυρίῳ Ἰησοῦ Χριστῷ). It precedes the salutation formula and used to describe the church itself.

64. The use in 2 Thess 1:1 is the dative ἐν θεῷ πατρὶ ἡμῶν.

the rest of his salutations, including 2 Thess 1:1, 2, have ἡμῶν, may suggest a later development and deliberate use of ἡμῶν on Paul's part.[65] "God our Father" is preceded by χάρις ὑμῖν καὶ εἰρήνη in all uses except 1 Thess 1:1[66] and followed by καὶ κυρίου Ἰησοῦ Χριστοῦ in all uses in the salutation.[67] Thus, evocative vocabularies surround the significant modification as Paul wishes his readers χάρις καὶ εἰρήνη, which invariably becomes ἀπὸ θεοῦ πατρὸς ἡμῶν καὶ κυρίου Ἰησοῦ Χριστοῦ.

While the subscription and adscription sections of the prescript describe who Paul is and who his recipients are separately, both in relation to God and Jesus, the Pauline salutation develops a kinship narrative that joins them together and portrays their common identity in terms of kinship to God. Fatherhood applied to God with first person plural pronoun joins Paul and his recipients together as belonging to God. Paul keeps intact the sense of familial equality between himself and his recipients in his salutations by not referring to God as "my Father" or "your Father." When he applies a pronoun to the Fatherhood of God, he always uses the first person plural pronoun that joins him with his recipients.

Moreover, in dialogue with multiple competing narratives of his audience that use the kinship term "father" (Roman Empire, Roman Stoic philosophers, Hebrew Bible, ancient Jewish writings), Paul constructs a self-understanding that shapes how his fellow Christ-followers view each other and the outside world. To begin with, Paul establishes a kinship relationship between the Jewish and Gentile recipients, which he will develop later on in terms of the Fatherhood of God, children of God, and siblinghood whenever it is necessary (e.g., Galatians 3–4). Those who were without kinship ties are brought into kinship relationship through this kinship construction. Under the Fatherhood of God, all his recipients now equally belong to the family of God. This self-understanding calls for a revision in the previous narrative of

65. Malherbe, *Thessalonians*, 99, points out that in 1 Thess 1:1 and 2 Thess 1:1 it is preceded by τῇ ἐκκλησίᾳ Θεσσαλονικέων, that is "in God the Father and the Lord Jesus Christ" is connected to "the church of Thessalonians" rather than to "grace and peace." As such it is unique among the Pauline corpus in the sense that it does not specify "God and Christ as the sources of grace and peace," rather "the formula qualifies the nature of the church." Based on this and on the absence of ἡμῶν, Malherbe argues that instead of a relational aspect that is seen in the passages that use "our father," its absence here "draws attention not to 'our' relationship with God, but to the formulation 'God the Father'" (99). He argues that what Paul intends the Thessalonians to understand from this is similar to 1 Cor 8:6, God as creator. Accordingly, Paul is addressing the church "that owes its existence to the Creator of the universe" (100).

66. Rom 1:7; 1 Cor 1:3; 2 Cor 1:2; Gal 1:3; Phil 1:2; 2 Thess 1:2; Phlm 3.

67. Rom 1:7; 1 Cor 1:3; 2 Cor 1:2; Gal 1:3; Phil 1:2; 2 Thess 1:2; 1 Thess 1:1; 2 Thess 1:1; Phlm 3.

his recipients. The Jewish Christ-followers, whose tradition in the Hebrew Bible and ancient Jewish writings depicts God as the Father of Israel and the Jewish people, now have to broaden that narrative to include the Gentile Christ-followers within the family of God. The Gentile Christ-followers, who were used to the depiction of other gods (e.g., Zeus) as father, now have to abandon that narrative and replace it with the Fatherhood of God. While the purging and replacing aspect of kinship functions in the emerging narrative of the Gentile Christ-followers, it is the adding aspect of kinship that operates in the emerging narrative of the Jewish Christ-followers' self-understanding. Now the Jewish Christ-followers' self-understanding as God's people embraces Gentile Christ-followers as well. Paul recalls and re-explains later on the unity constructed here by using other kinship terms in addition to God as Father.

The words χάρις, εἰρήνη, θεοῦ πατρὸς, and κυρίου are vocabularies of Roman imperial ideology. They are socially charged, and they resonate with the contemporary narrative that Paul and his recipients share from their cultural milieu. Writing to his audiences' horizon of understanding, he contests their prior perceptions. Taking "the language of broader linguistic community," Paul "engages in dialogical discourse" in order to gradually transform such language "into the distinctive accent" of the emerging community.[68]

The Empire and the emperor use these terms to create and sustain identities that define the nature of the relationship that the emperor and the subjects in the Empire should have. These concentrated parallel themes related to imperial ideology inevitably evoke in the receivers' mind the imperial ideology. However, since here these terminologies are used in connection to their relationship to God and Jesus Christ, the fatherhood and lordship of the emperor and the presentation that he is the source of χάρις and εἰρήνη are immediately relativized if not denied. For instance, as we have seen earlier, Augustus presented himself as incomparable source of χάρις, eclipsing all the other competitors, and in return he expected a reciprocation that should be manifested in giving complete allegiance to the emperor and to the cause of the Empire. εἰρήνη is another area in terms of which the imperial ideology memorializes the Roman emperors. A discourse was developed that celebrates the Roman emperors as the source of χάρις and εἰρήνη. According to *Res Gestae*, it was based on such achievement that Augustus was honored with the title of *pater patriae*. As shown earlier, as "a manifesto addressed to the public" and as "a signature of empire, [and] a written contract," the *Res Gestae*, by bestowing the title *pater patriae* on Augustus in recognition of the χάρις and εἰρήνη (sections

68. Newsom, "Constructing 'We, You, and the Others,'" 16.

12, 13) he rendered, establishes the identity of the emperor and defines the expected response from the public. Paul develops an intimately parallel discourse using the same words that the Empire used to represent the emperor.

While the imperial ideology went to a great length to portray the Empire and the emperor with a father language to depict the Empire as a household, Paul applies not only the kinship term 'father' but also significant vocabulary that the Empire used to enhance its image (χάρις and εἰρήνη). While the imperial ideology presents the emperor as bringing χάρις and εἰρήνη, Paul consistently presents God and Jesus Christ as the source of the community's χάρις and εἰρήνη. Furthermore, while the imperial ideology presents the emperor as *Pater Patriae* and as κυρίος, Paul presents God as πατρὸς ἡμῶν and Jesus Christ as κυρίος. The representations the Caesars sought so dearly and put forth scrupulously Paul freely ascribes to God and also to Jesus Christ. He uses these words consistently in the opening formulas, where the identity of senders and receivers is defined according to the modified opening formulas of Paul, where the ultimate source of χάρις and εἰρήνη is declared. When this is performed orally, the discourse not only becomes memorialized by the community, but it also becomes a declaration of faith.

At the surface, it seems that Paul and Rome are simply following common models that do not have much interaction. However, the concentration of exact terminologies, all of which are ascribed to the Roman emperor, consistently at the same place in Pauline writings, a usage that is unique to Pauline letters, strongly suggests that Paul is not merely following a common model. For one, it is not common to use the construction χάρις ὑμῖν καὶ εἰρήνη ἀπὸ θεοῦ πατρὸς ἡμῶν καὶ κυρίου Ἰησοῦ Χριστοῦ in opening formulas. Second, this construction is not in one or two of his letters, but in six of them (Rom 1:7; 1 Cor 1:3; 2 Cor 1:2; Gal 1:3; Phil 1:2; Phlm 3). Thus, without mentioning the empire or the ways of the empire, Paul uses the exact terminologies that the empire uses to define identities and to create a relationship that sustains its ways. Applying them to the relationship between God/Jesus Christ and the new community, Paul creates and shapes an alternative way of self-understanding and relationship. In so doing, Paul again quietly relativizes the fundamental ideology of the empire.

Similarly, his consistent identification of God as the sole source of his vocation and of his recipients as ἐκκλησία, κλητοι/κλητοῖς, ἀγαπητοῖς, ἡγιασμένοις, and ἁγίοις, all of which describe their identity in terms of their relationship to God and Jesus Christ, creates both a different identity and a different discourse for his mixed recipients. In so doing, Paul promotes an alternative way of self-understanding that in effect relativizes all other ways of defining identity. When we take into consideration the oral performance of the opening formulas, we realize that the language of this self-understanding is not simply read, but it is imagined and visualized as it is read, giving it a sense of declaring one's identity.

The kinship narrative Paul constructs at the beginning of each of his letters unfolds with use of further kinship language to give a coherent, rounded picture of a family. As we shall see below, the image of the family constructed in the prescript continues primarily with a sibling narrative, which Paul constructs in each letter, and with a narrative of being children of God that is found in four of his letters. The Fatherhood of God narrative also appears in three of the "children of God" passages, in thanksgiving and prayer contexts and also in a didactic context to establish a boundary as well as unity.

God as Father in Thanksgiving, Prayer/Wish Passages

The kinship narrative of the Fatherhood of God unfolds in the context of thanksgiving and prayer/wish passages primarily in the Thessalonian correspondence (1 Thess 1:3; 3:11, 13; 2 Thess 2:16–17).[69] There are also references to God as Father in Gal 1:4; 2 Thess 1:2 and Phil 4:20 as part of prayers. Wiles observes that Paul mixes different types of prayers together (thanksgiving, report, wish) and some of these have a dialectical relationship with each other, making it difficult to address his prayers from the perspective of a single form.[70] Wiles writes, "within the dynamic activity of prayer there could be no hard and fast line between thanksgivings, intercessions, and representative corporate supplication."[71] Comparing Pauline prayers with ancient letter style, however, Wiles explains that the "conventional usages . . . turned out to be weighted with new meaning."[72] The prayers were "evoked by and adapted to a particular context; the lines of concern flowed together through each threatening occasion" and are reflected in the prayer passages.[73] Placed in a strategic location within a given letter (beginning, ending, transitional points), the prayers "served to focus the letter itself by drawing attention at intervals to its underlying themes."[74]

Accordingly, the repeated use of God as Father in 1 Thessalonians in the context of prayers suggests that one of Paul's underlying concerns is to continue to construct a family image. In the first three chapters of 1

69. This study follows the view that Paul wrote 2 Thessalonians. See chapter 1 of this book.

70. Wiles, *Paul's Intercessory Prayers*, 11–12.

71. Ibid., 293.

72. Ibid.; Artz-Grabner, "Paul's Letter Thanksgiving," 156.

73. Wiles, *Paul's Intercessory Prayers*, 293.

74. Ibid., 293–94.

Thessalonians, which is characterized as "autobiographical thanksgiving,"[75] Paul uses πατρὸς ἡμῶν and its related constructions four times (1 Thess 1:3; 3:11, 13) together with seven occurrences of sibling language (1:4; 2:1, 9, 14, 17; 3:2, 7).[76] Trevor J. Burke rightly states, "from beginning to end 1 Thessalonians breathes" kinship language.[77] Collins further observes a "temporal triad of past, present, and future" in Paul's thanksgiving. Paul reports his prayer on behalf of the Thessalonians (past), expressing it in the present tense, thus implying performative language, which indicates that as Paul "tells about his prayer of thanksgiving," "he is giving thanks."[78] The future is expressed with a prayer that immediately follows the thanksgiving as in 1 Thess 3:11–13.[79] It is in the future aspect of the thanksgiving that unfolds in the form of prayer that Paul further identifies God as ὁ θεὸς καὶ πατὴρ ἡμῶν twice (vv. 11, 13), each time relating it to Jesus as ὁ κύριος ἡμῶν Ἰησοῦς (vv. 11, 13).[80] Sanctified living, which is the concern of 1:2–10 and 2:1—3:10, is brought to a close through a prayer. In his first thanksgiving, Paul began by reminding the Thessalonians of their former self, how they "turned to God from idols, to serve a living and true God, and to wait for his Son from heaven" (1 Thess 1:9–10). Now, as he closes with a climactic prayer, he goes back to sanctified living—"And may he so strengthen your hearts in holiness that you may be blameless before our God and Father at the coming of our Lord Jesus with all his saints" (1 Thess 3:13, NRSV).[81] Paul presents the idea of holiness and blamelessness by which he identifies Christ-followers at the beginning of his letters as part of the accountability of God's community.

The Fatherhood of God that is found in the prayer/wish in 2 Thess 2:16–17 and Phil 4:20 should also be approached from the perspective of the family image with which the letters begin. Just as a prayer/wish related specifically to the purpose of each letter, the kinship language used to create the family image may reflect specific aspects of the family. The prayer in 2 Thess 2:16–17 is to receive comfort (παρακαλέσαι) and strength (στηρίξαι) "in every good work and word" (ἐν παντὶ ἔργῳ καὶ λόγῳ ἀγαθω/). It is based on the love (ὁ ἀγαπήσας ἡμᾶς) and grace (ἐν χάριτι) through which they

75. Malherbe, *Thessalonians*, 104; Lyons, *Pauline Autobiography*, 177–221.

76. More sibling language appears in the remaining sections of the letter: 4:1, 6, 10 (2x), 13; 5:1, 4, 12, 14, 25, 26, 27.

77. Burke, *Family Matters*, 165.

78. Collins, "A Significant Decade," 180.

79. Ibid., 181.

80. In v. 13 we have a genitive construction.

81. Weima, "Sincerely, Paul," 315–16.

have received "eternal comfort and good hope" (δοὺς παράκλησιν αἰωνίαν καὶ ἐλπίδα ἀγαθὴν). These uses of God as Father in 2 Thessalonians and Philippians are also enmeshed with Paul's use of sibling language.[82]

A comparison of one type of these prayers, thanksgiving, with similar types of prayer in the cultural milieu will show how Paul probably was advancing a family image. The first text is from a non-literary personal letter written by a woman, Isias, to her husband Hephaistion around 168 B.C.:

> Isias to Hephaistion greeting. If you are well and your other affairs turn out in a like fashion, it would be as I have been *continually praying to the gods*; I myself am also well and the child and all in the household are continually thinking of you. When I received your letter from Horos, in which you make clear that you are held fast (i.e., in the possession of the god) in the Serapeum in Memphis, *I gave thanks immediately to the gods* that you are well . . .[83]

And a thanksgiving portion of a letter from 2 Maccabees 1:10–12 reads:

> The people of Jerusalem and Judea and the senate and Judas,
> To Aristobulus, who is of the family of the anointed priest, teacher of king Ptolemy, and to the Jews in Egypt, Greetings and good health.
>
> *Having been saved by God* out of grave dangers we *thank him* greatly for taking our side against the king, for he drove out those who fought against the holy city.

In the first letter, prayer is reported in similar way to Paul and then thanks are given in view of receiving what is prayed for. In the second letter, God's rescue is reported and thanks are given. The major difference is that while the first letter refers to "gods" the second refers only to one God. Paul's prayer refers to one God as Father. After comparing the Pauline thanksgiving with such texts, Raymond F. Collins observes as one of the differences the fact that while "the thanksgivings of the papyri letters are addressed to the gods in general (τοῖς θεοῖς), Paul's thanksgiving is addressed to one God (τῷ θεῷ),)" who is also identified as Father at the beginning of the letter.[84] In addition to the above texts, inscriptions that are dedicated to Artemis

82. 2 Thess 1:3; 2:1, 13, 15; 3:1, 6; 13; Phil 1:12; 3:1, 13, 17; 4:1, 8.

83. Letter 34, *Isias to Hephaistion*, (P. Lond I 42 and UPZ I 59), in White, *Ancient Letters*, 65, emphasis added; see also idem, 66.

84. Collins, "A Significant Decade," 180.

and Hestia have public thanksgiving offered to the gods.[85] According to *Res Gestae* 4, thanks is also given to gods on account of Augustus' success.

These examples shed light on the nature of some of the narratives which Paul is engaging by inserting kinship relationship with God in the midst of his thanksgiving. Paul's recipients share the narrative that many gods are "supporting, maintaining and controlling the order of existence of one who is praying."[86] They used to direct their prayers and offer thanksgiving to many gods. By constantly referring to God as "God our Father" in similar literary contexts, Paul contests not only the idea that there are many gods, but also the idea that they are the ones who engage in "supporting, maintaining and controlling the order of existence."[87] With the use of the first person plural pronoun "our" and a kinship term "Father," he builds a family image that portrays the "us" and "them" categories. For his Gentile audiences who came from such a narrative background, he redefines their narrative. The one who supports, maintains, and controls existence and to whom thanks is due is their new God. By including the Gentiles in his reference to this God as "our Father," as he did in the prescript of the letter, he continues to broaden the Jewish Christ-followers' narrative of God's Fatherhood to include the Gentiles. As such, his use reflects both a uniting as well as a boundary setting function.

God as Father in 1 Corinthians 8

In 1 Corinthians, Paul continues the kinship narrative that he began by identifying God as Father at the beginning of the letter (1 Cor 1:3), primarily by depicting the Corinthians as siblings (forty times in the letter).[88] In 1 Cor 8, however, he also enlists the portrayal of God as Father (8:6), together with sibling language (8:11–13) to set a boundary and to promote care among the Corinthian community. He applies the image of God's Fatherhood, introduced at the beginning of his letter, to a situation that demands both caring and boundary setting. Through the use of familial language, he provides orienting framework to the Corinthians regarding how to handle involvement with food associated with idols.

85. Horsley, *New Documents Illustrating Early Christianity*, vol. 4, 127–28; see also idem, *New Documents Illustrating Early Christianity*, vol 1, 57.

86. Malina, "What is a Prayer?" 15.

87. See below the discussion on 1 Cor 8:6.

88. See Aasgaard, *'My Beloved Brothers and Sisters!'*, Appendix 1.

Observing the boundary-making tone of the passage, David E. Garland states, "τὸ εἰδωλόθυτον has a caustic, polemical edge."[89] Margaret M. Mitchell rightly notes that "Paul's overriding concern throughout this proof section 8:1—11:1 is *ecclesiological*."[90] She explains that Paul "agrees with the fundamental principles of both sides, to which he adds a proper reminder of their theological unity" in the form of "one God and one Lord in 8:6."[91] In so doing, "[h]e emphasizes that these theological principles are held by all Christians in common, as opposed to outsiders, and should therefore be a unifying point.[92] In 1 Cor 8:4b–6, 11–13 Paul writes,

> we know that "an idol in this world is nothing," and that "there is no God but one." If after all there are so-called gods, whether in heaven or on earth
> (as there are many gods and many lords),
> yet for us there is one God, the Father,
> from whom are all things and for whom we live,
> and one Lord, Jesus Christ,
> through whom are all things and through whom we live . . .
> So by your knowledge the weak brother or sister, for whom Christ died, is destroyed. If you sin against your brothers or sisters in this way and wound their weak conscience, you sin against Christ. For this reason, if food causes my brother or sister to sin, I will never eat meat again, so that I may not cause one of them to sin. (NET)[93]

In addition to the kinship language of "Father" (8:6) and "brothers and sisters" (vv. 11–13), Paul uses first person plural pronouns "we," and "us" to join himself with the Corinthians. This link sets their relationship to God and Jesus in opposition to a relationship with "many gods and many lords." Paul does not call God, "our Father" nor does he relate God's Fatherhood to "grace and peace." Instead, he relates God's Fatherhood to being the source of "all things" ("from whom all things came") and to the Corinthians' purpose in life ("for whom we live"). In this sense, it appears to be related more to the Stoic idea of Zeus as the creator and father of all than to what Paul was developing at the beginning of his letter. It also resembles the idea

89. Garland, *1 Corinthians*, 364; see also Witherington, "No So Idle Thought," 234–54; Gardner, *The Gifts of God*, 15–16; Collins, *First Corinthians*, 311.

90. Mitchell, *Paul and the Rhetoric of Reconciliation*, 241; see also Willis, *Idol Meat in Corinth*, 280–86.

91. Mitchell, *Paul and the Rhetoric of Reconciliation*, 241.

92. Ibid., 241n314.

93. The NRSV does not maintain the sibling language which is useful in the argument of this study.

of the universal Fatherhood of God found in Philo and Josephus. However, the fact that he qualified it with "yet for us there is . . ." and that he puts Jesus equally on the same ground with God, the Father, as the source of "all things" and as "for whom we live," makes it different from the Stoic concept of the fatherhood of Zeus. The use of "we" and "us" together with the kinship term "father" applied to God continues the kinship identity with which the letter begins.

First person plural pronouns "but for us . . . and we . . . and we" emphasizes the "us-them" contrast. Commenting on the structure of the text, Ciampa and Rosner explain that it "implies both a relationship and a contrast between us and the rest of creation."[94] While as part of creation all are related, the text and its context highlight a contrast between Christ-followers and the outsiders.[95] The contrast is that while for them "there are *many* '*gods*' and *many* '*lords*,'" for "us," "there is only *one God* and *one Lord*."[96] While Paul presents the Fatherhood of God and lordship of Christ as "matters of communal knowledge," he contrasts them with "the popular belief, in the world outside the church, in many 'gods' and many 'lords' (8:5)."[97] Such contrast, together with the Jewish monotheistic claim, οὐδεὶς θεὸς εἰ μὴ εἷς, which echoes the *Shema*, serves to define the boundary from the outside world.[98] To this contrast is added the familial language of God as Father and the identification of the Christ-followers as brothers and sisters both to build a boundary and encourage community building.[99]

In summary, the use of God as Father in the prescripts is part of Paul's self-identification and identification of the community of Christ-followers as the family of God. Just as Paul's self-identification focuses on the origin and nature of his vocation, his identification of his recipients also emphasizes the origin and nature of the community. At the center of these identifications is the portrayal of God as Father, providing a joint familial self-understanding to Paul and his recipients. Paul portrays the nature of his vocation as participation in the construction of the family of God, representing God and Christ, the founders of the community, as their ἀπόστολος and δοῦλος. He identifies God and Christ, the originating founders of the community, as the origin of his vocation, which is continuing the founding task of the

94. Ciampa and Rosner, *The First Letter to the Corinthians*, 385.

95. Ibid.

96. Ibid.

97. Petersen, *Rediscovering Paul*, 207.

98. For the fuller analysis of the relation of this passage to the Shema and the First Commandment see Waaler, *The Shema and the First Commandment*; see also Ciampa and Rosner, *The First Letter to the Corinthians*, 380.

99. Hays, *First Corinthians*, 135.

community that he depicts as the family of God. Paul also indicates that the community of Christ-followers he is addressing originates from God and Christ. He portrays the nature of the community with language that evokes political assembly (ἐκκλησία) as well as God's people in the Hebrew Bible and ancient Jewish literature (ἁγίοις, ἡγιασμένοις, ἀγαπητοῖς, and κλητοῖς). Paul brings his self-identification and the identification of his recipients together by constructing a joint kinship relationship with God that invariably has links to their relationship to Christ as Lord. The language of "Father," "grace," and "peace" that Paul uses to depict his and his recipients' relationship to God, evoke the formative narrative of the Empire, the Roman Stoics, the Hebrew Bible, and ancient Jewish literature. As such, Paul's use imitates the strategy of community formation in these contexts but at the same time presents an alternative community. Paul continues constructing the image of the family of God further by using God as Father in prayer contexts and in the context that demands building boundary and unity (1 Cor 8). Each of these cases evokes and relativizes the competing multiple narratives.

Christ-Followers as Children of God and Identity Formation

As part of the construction of a family image, Paul also depicts the followers of Jesus using kinship terms such as υἱοὶ θεοῦ ("sons of God") in Gal 3:26; 4:6, 7; Rom 8:14, 19; 9:26 and τέκνα θεοῦ ("children of God") in Rom 8:16, 17, 21; 2 Cor 6:18; Phil 2:15.[100] In line with my overall purpose, I will approach the use of "children of God" to refer to Christ-followers from two interrelated concerns. How does Paul's use of this kinship term to refer to God relate to his depiction of God as Father and to the imaging of Christ-followers as the family of God? What does Paul's use of the expression "children of God," as a socially shared language particularly by those who are from a Jewish heritage, involve?

In anticipation of a fuller discussion, I will introduce each of these aspects briefly. Paul bases the connection between his use of God as Father

100. Most commentators do not see any difference in Paul's use of the two terms. Schneider, "τέκνον," 341, writes, "For Paul τέκνα θεοῦ is synonymous with υἱοὶ θεοῦ" (Rom 8:14, 19); Dunn, *Romans 1–8*, 454, explains that Paul uses υἱός (36 times) more frequently than τέκνον (24 times). Dunn observes that "Paul makes no clear distinction between the words at this point, since the variation in the context between the two words in reference to Christians (τέκνον—Rom 8:16, 17, 21; υἱός—Rom 8:14, 19) can only be stylistic. In other words "sons" as well as "children" would in Paul's mind include believers, female as well as male." While Paul also uses υἱός to refer to Jesus frequently (Rom 1:3, 4, 9; 5:10; 8:3, 29, 32; etc.), he never uses τέκνον, see idem, 458.

and Christ-followers as children of God on both kinship logic and textual connection. Concerning the former, the use of one kinship term evokes other related terms. For instance, the use of *pater* to refer to the Roman Empire and *pater patriae* to refer to the Roman emperor is predicated on the assumption that it images the people of the Empire as children. Thus, Paul works on both textual and kinship grounds.

Regarding the latter, as seen in the previous section, in all of these four epistles Paul introduces the Fatherhood of God early on (Gal 1:1, 3, 4; Rom 1:7; Phil 1:2; 2:11; 2 Cor 1:2, 3), establishing a ground for the subsequent depiction of the Christ-followers as "sons/children" and as siblings. Furthermore, in Galatians, Romans, and 2 Corinthians, Paul's use of sons/children language to refer to Christ-followers is attached to the use of God as Father within the immediate context also (Gal 3:26—4:7; Rom 8:14–16; 2 Cor 6:17–18). The kinship narrative that Paul constructs using "children of God" is part of the Fatherhood of God narrative. Furthermore, the "children of God" image is introduced by the sibling language in Galatians and Romans (Gal 3:15; Rom 8:12) that is used in the immediate context in addition to the sibling language that occurs throughout each book. This use of sibling language with the language of "children of God" creates further cohesion in the family image that Paul constructs.

The expression "children of God" is a socially shared expression primarily known to those familiar with the Hebrew Bible and ancient Jewish literature. These two textual traditions reserve the use of the expression to the Israelites and the Jewish people. Thus, Paul's use is not neutral. As I will show below, it involves contesting the previous use and broadening its application (Gal 3–4; Rom 4; 8) both to create unity (Gal 3–4) and to construct boundary (Phil 2: 14–15; 2 Cor 6:14—7:1). Therefore, in Paul's identification of Christ-followers as "Children of God" one can discern two patterns in terms of which Paul intends to shape their self-understanding: a self-understanding that creates unity and a self-understanding that creates boundary. While Paul's use of the "children of God" language in Galatians and Romans deals with internal ethnic conflict, his use of this language in Philippians and 2 Corinthians deals with their lives in relation to the outside world. While the first two uses provide an orienting framework to advance unity, the latter two provide an orienting framework regarding how Christ-followers should live in relation to the outside world. The structure of the discussion below will follow this observation: (1) the use that promotes unity—Galatians and Romans, (2) the use that constructs a boundary—Philippians and 2 Corinthians.

Christ-Followers as Children of God in Galatians and Romans

There is a similarity between what Paul intends to achieve in writing Romans and Galatians in the sense that in both letters he deals with issues that involve the formation of in-group identity.[101] There are thematic similarities between Gal 3–4 and Rom 4 and 8: children of Abraham, children of God, inheritance, receiving the Spirit, and calling God Abba, Father. Comparisons such as slavery/freedom and formerly/now are also common to Galatians and Romans. In these texts, Paul's depiction of Christ-followers as children of God coalesces with God as the Father and Christ-followers as siblings, placing both the Jews and Gentiles within the household of God.

Christ-Followers as Children of God in Galatians

In his book on Galatians, Esler rightly observes that Paul formulates his response to the Galatians problem in terms of answering the question, 'Who are we?"[102] This formulation is partly seen in how Paul describes the community toward the end of his letter. Toward the conclusion of his letter, which provides a summation and "interpretive clues" to his entire argument,[103] Paul depicts the community of Christ-followers he was addressing as the "household of faith," indicating their corporate unity (6:10). He also refers to the community as a "new creation" (6:15) that goes beyond a circumcision-non-circumcision divide. Leading to this portrayal is Paul's fundamental argument in chaps 3–4[104] at the center of which is the depiction of believers as υἱοὶ θεοῦ (Gal 3:26; 4:6, 7). To this depiction is knit the Fatherhood of God that is introduced at the beginning of the chapter (1:1, 3, 4; 4:2, 6).[105]

101. Schnelle, *Apostle Paul*, 270, notes structural and thematic similarity between Galatians and Romans—set apart as apostle (Gal 1:15–16; Rom 1:1–5), righteousness through faith (Gal 2:15–21; Rom 3:19–28), Abraham (Gal 3:6–25, 29; Rom 4:1–25), baptism (Gal 3:26–28; Rom 6:3–5), slavery and freedom (Gal 4:1–7; Rom 8:12–17); law and promise (Gal 4:21–31; Rom 9:6–13), set free to love (Gal 5:13–15; Rom 13:8–10), conflict between willing and doing (Gal 5:17; Rom 7:15–13), and life in the Spirit (Gal 5:16–26; Rom 8:12).

102. Esler, *Galatians*, 37; he notes collective designations such as "brothers" and "sisters" (1:11; 3:15, 4:12, 28, 31; 5:11, 13; 6:1, 18), "my children" (4:19), "those who are rescued by Jesus Christ from the present evil age" (1:4), "believers in Christ Jesus" (2:16), "those seeking to be justified in Christ" (2:17), "sons of God" (3:26), "seed of Abraham" and "promised heirs" (3:29), "people led by the Spirit" (5:18), "a new creation" (6:15), and "the Israel of God" (6:16).

103. Betz, *Galatians*, 313; Longenecker, *Galatians*, 286.

104. Longenecker, *Galatians*, 97.

105. Dunn, *Galatians*, 619.

While Paul's characterization of the followers of Jesus as υἱοὶ Θεου concentrates in Gal 3:26—24:7 (five times), it is a climactic characterization meant to drive his argument home.[106] In chap 3:6–25, he elaborates the new kinship identity the followers of Christ have in Abraham. This is followed by Paul's depiction of Christ-followers as children of God (3:26—24:7), after which he turns to further construct kinship with Abraham and Sarah (4:8–31). Explaining the place of the assertion Πάντες γὰρ υἱοὶ θεοῦ ἐστε διὰ τῆς πίστεως ἐν Χριστῷ Ἰησοῦ, Timothy George writes, "Galatians 3:26 is the fulcrum verse of both chapters. Everything Paul said from 3:6 through 3:25 flows into this verse, just as everything that follows from 3:27 to 4:31 issues from it."[107]

In the context where membership in the family of God is contested, Paul met the challenge through "the explicit use of family language," imaging the Galatian community as a family, a household of God.[108] Paul rejects traditional ways of defining family in terms of circumcision and redefines the nature and boundary of God's family.[109] These two chapters are "joined and elucidated through the use of family language"[110] to establish the identity of the authentic sons and daughters and heirs to the promise of Abraham.[111] Paul takes the contested issue of Abraham and relation to him to construct a kinship narrative that would create cohesion within the Christ-followers in Galatians.[112] Eisenbaum writes, "The figure of Abraham could simultaneously serve as the ultimate symbol of Israel and the point of contact between Israel and the rest of the peoples of the world."[113] As we have seen in ancient Jewish writings, Abraham is used both to describe the unique identity of Jews and to find a place within the larger world. Following a similar trend, Paul enlarges the family of Abraham to include all the

106. Kinship language pervades Galatians: Fatherhood of God (1:1, 3, 4; 4:6), children of God (3:26; 4:1–7); children of Abraham (3:6–29), children of Sarah (4:21–31), language of inheritance, and language of siblingship (1:2, 11; 3:15; 4:12, 28, 31; 5:11, 13; 6:1, 18).

107. George, *Galatians*, 274.

108. Lewis, "As a Beloved Brother," 114.

109. Ibid., 109; To this end, the large proportion of kinship language that is used in Galatians is enlisted in chapters 3 and 4 (3:7, 14, 16, 17, 18, 19, 21, 22, 26, 29; 4:1, 5, 6, 7, 22, 23, 30, 31).

110. Ibid., 119.

111. Asano, *Community-Identity*, 151; Brinsmead, *Galatians*, 83–84; Barclay, *Obeying the Truth*, 86–89.

112. For the discussion of Abraham's place in Jewish as well as early Christian narrative see J. Beker, *Paul the Apostle*, 99; Lincoln, "Abraham Goes to Rome," 176–78; Dunn, *Romans*, 200.

113. Eisenbaum, "Paul as the New Abraham," 145.

Christ-followers in Galatia. He relates them to Abraham on the grounds of *sharing* faith, the promised inheritance (the spirit), and Christ whom he describes as "the singular seed of Abraham" in 3:16.[114] In 3:29, he states, "If you belong to Christ, then you are heirs according to the promise." Lewis explains, "Paul has rearranged the borders of the family of Abraham. Since Christ was the unique "heir" to Abraham, those who are in him receive the promise made to Abraham—the spirit."[115] He points out, "Paul identifies the promised inheritance as the Spirit which is now available to those outside the natural family of Abraham, since the true family of Abraham is determined by faith, not by blood."[116]

Using the dynamic and versatile nature of kinship, he creates "direct connection between Abraham and those who believe (both Gentiles and Jews) through faith in Christ" in 3:6–14.[117] Through such kinship construction, "Abraham and the Gentiles are found to be related," and his inheritance of God's promise is equally shared by Jews and Gentiles.[118] Irrespective of their former identity as Gentiles or Jews, they have become sons and daughters of Abraham and Sarah.

What Paul began by constructing kinship with Abraham (3:6–25) directly leads to kinship with God (Gal 3:26—4:7).[119] Membership in the family of Abraham and membership in the family of God are linked.[120] Paul brings the Galatians together further by describing them as sons and daughters of God (3:26). With the repeated use of πάντες and the reality of the event of Christ, Paul excludes no one from the Christ-followers in Galatians. Through faith in Christ, he transforms all of them into sons and daughters of God, seed of Abraham, and heirs of the promise (3:26, 29). Through Christ (4:4–5), the Galatians, irrespective of their former standing, "received adoption as children," and because they are children they have received the Spirit that enables them to relate to God as "*Abba*, Father" (4:6–7).[121] This reception of adoption and the Spirit advances the narrative

114. Campbell, *Paul and the Creation of Christian Identity*, 62.

115. Lewis, "As a Beloved Brother", 125

116. Ibid., further notes, "Paul defined the content of the promise made to Abraham. He has also particularized the meaning of 'heir' and 'child of Abraham' so that these words enhance the position of the Gentiles who like Abraham were justified apart from the Law through faith."

117. Asano, *Community-Identity*, 152.

118. Ibid., 151.

119. Martyn, *Galatians*, 295.

120. Lewis, "As a Beloved Brother", 126.

121. The Greek word υἱοθεσία that is translated adoption is not found in the LXX and Paul uses it to refer to the sonship of Christ-followers (Gal 4:5; Rom 8:15),

that "in Christ God has abolished the division between Jew and Gentile and adopted them together into one family."[122] The result contrasts their former status with their present (v. 7–9). The unique prerogative that depicts Israel as the household of God Paul applies to all who have faith.[123] In depicting them as children of God, Paul gives to all the Galatians the designation that was a prerogative of Israel (God as Father and Israel as children),[124] which is normally reserved for Jews."[125] Gentiles receive the same title as Jews and this is "exceptional and extraordinary."[126] As the result of this transformation, he re-draws the inherited and existing religious and social map.

The status of Christ-followers as children of God is applied to socio-religious relationships that were manifested in the contemporary society. In a widely studied verse, Paul declares, "There is no longer Jew or Greek, there is no longer slave or free, there is no longer male and female; for all of you are one in Christ Jesus" (NRSV).[127] The large proportion of studies

---

their future resurrection body (8:23), and to Israel's sonship (Rom 9:4–5). Studies on υἱοθεσία focus mainly on the background of the word to explain Paul's use. See Scott, *Adoption as Sons of God*; Burke, *Adopted into God's Family*; Byrne, *'Sons of God'–'Seed of Abraham,'* 79–84.

122. Thompson, *The Promise of the Father*, 129.

123. Amad-Azuogue, *Paul and the Law*, 221–22; Also see Betz, *Galatians*, 190, who rightly comments, "There can be no doubt that Paul's statements have social and political implications of even a revolutionary dimension. The claim is made that very old and decisive ideals and hopes of the ancient world have come true in the Christian community. These ideals include the abolition of the religious and social distinctions between Jews and Greeks, slaves and freemen, men and women. These social changes are claimed as part of the process of redemption and as the result of the ecstatic experiences which the Galatians as well as other Christians had. Being rescued from the present evil aeon (Gal 1:4) and being changed to a 'new creation' implies these radical social and political changes. The Christian's relationship to the social and political structures of 'this world' follows the rule set forth in 6:14: 'through whom [= Christ] the world is crucified to me and I to the world.' The Christian is now 'dead' to the social, religious, and cultural distinctions characteristic of the old world-order . . ."

124. Matera, *Galatians*, 144.

125. Betz, *Galatians*, 186.

126. Ibid.

127. This verse is probably one of the most studied verses in the Bible. Regarding the vastness of studies undertaken on this verse Walden, "Galatians 3:28 Grammar Observations," 45, explains the situation as follows: "Among monographs is Wiley, *Paul and Gentile Women*; and Hove, *Equality in Christ?* For essays and periodical literature, Gal 3:28 competes for the most number of contributions on a single verse. Mills, *Bibliographies for Biblical Research*, 38–45, lists 42 entries published on just the verse, with another 23 on the pericope. Since Mills's (incomplete) listing, another 12 items on the verse and five more on the pericope have appeared . . . Items overlooked by Mills include 11 on the verse and one on the pericope. When contributions doubtlessly overlooked by all are added, the total publications on this verse may well come

on this verse focus on the assertion "there is no longer male or female."[128] Regardless of the focus, however, there is little attention given to the kinship narrative that manifestly surrounds Paul's assertion in v. 28.[129] This assertion is part of Paul's kinship identity construction argument that images Christ-followers as a family that belongs to God irrespective of who they were and who they are. Not only the larger context but also the immediate context links the assertion to the family language both thematically and syntactically. The immediate context (vv. 26–29) reads:

> For in Christ Jesus you are all children of God through faith.
> As many of you as were baptized into Christ have clothed yourselves with Christ.
> There is no longer Jew or Greek,
> there is no longer slave or free,
> there is no longer male and female;
> for all of you are one in Christ Jesus.
> And if you belong to Christ, then you are Abraham's offspring,
> heirs according to the promise (vv. 14–29, NRSV)

Thematically, the section starts with the kinship assertion that the Christ-followers are "children of God" and ends with a related kinship assertion that they are "Abraham's offspring, and heirs according to the promise." The theme of "all" is found in vv. 26 (Πάντες), 27 (ὅσοι), 28 (πάντες). Verse 26 begins with Πάντες γὰρ υἱοὶ θεοῦ ἐστε and verse 28 ends with πάντες γὰρ ὑμεῖς εἶς ἐστε ἐν Χριστῷ Ἰησοῦ. The verses are also interrelated with the emphasis on the centrality of the event of Christ as evidenced by a repeated use of expressions related to Christ—five times in just four verses.[130] Syntactically, the first three verses (vv. 26, 27, 28) are joined with three explanatory γάρ (vv.26, 27, 28b). Longenecker explains that γάρ in v 26a connects 3:26–29 to 3:19–25 "in explanatory and continuative fashion," and that the γάρ in v. 27a is "used to confirm the thesis statement of v. 26."[131] Similarly the γάρ of v. 28b functions "to confirm again that thesis statement

to a hundred items." To this we may add, Hogan, "No Longer Male and Female," who traces the interpretation of Gal 3:28 from post-Pauline writings down to the writings of Ambrose in the late fourth century.

128. Ibid., 1–16.

129. See Hogan, "No Longer Male and Female," 7–13; my purpose here is to suggest that any assessment of this verse's implication should start by giving attention to the familial narrative in which it is found.

130. ἐν Χριστῷ Ἰησοῦ (26) εἰς Χριστὸν (27a) Χριστὸν ἐνεδύσασθε (27b) ἐν Χριστῷ Ἰησοῦ (28) Χριστοῦ (29).

131. Longenecker, *Galatians*, 157.

by paralleling its terms and concepts, and so adding force to its words."[132] Longenecker further explains, "The words πάντες ("all"), ὑμεῖς . . . ἐστε ("you are"), and ἐν Χριστῷ Ἰησοῦ ("in Christ Jesus") are all familiar from the thesis statement of v. 26, as is the concept of oneness implied in "all" being "sons of God."[133] Thus, in 3:26–28, "Paul finds the essence of the Christian proclamation: that "in Christ Jesus" there is a new "oneness" that breaks down all former divisions and heals injustices."[134]

In such a context which constructs the image of Christ-followers as the family of God, Paul states the unity of the followers of Christ with a triple negation followed by an explanatory assertion (v. 28).[135] These are three areas that would cause difficulty for equal membership in the family of God and for the unity in the family. Hence, Paul denies them such potential by promoting the "oneness" of Christ-followers by reminding them that they are all children of God. What sort of equality this "oneness" involves, however, is the major subject of an ongoing debate.[136] It is important to note, however, that one cannot grasp the full implication of what Paul was envisioning by his assertion of "oneness" based on Galatians alone. One of the limiting factors is that among the three couplets denied, only the first one (neither Jew nor gentile) is the subject of what Paul is addressing in Galatians. Furthermore, whatever is said about what Paul intends to do with one couplet is also limited by what one can say about the others. For instance, one would love to argue from Paul's terse assertion here that Paul abolished all divisions between slaves and owners and between male and female. But that is not the case here. Just as it would be implausible to argue that Paul abolished all ethnic divisions between Jew and Gentiles, it is also improbable to argue that he abolished all divisions related to the other couplets.[137]

132. Ibid.

133. Ibid.

134. Ibid., 158.

135. Payne, *Man and Woman One in Christ.*

136. The discussion is manifold and includes such issues as ecclesiological structure (hierarchical vs. egalitarian relationship), ethnic identity, and Paul's teaching on slavery. Literature on this is legion. For recent brief summary see Hogan, "No Longer Male and Female," 7–13.

137. E. P. Sanders and William S. Campbell, among others, are right to see that although Paul does not eradicate the ethnic differences nor did he absolutize ethnic particularities of either the Jews or the Greeks. Sanders points out that the recognition of ethnic peculiarities was true "only so long as ethnic peculiarities did not come into conflict and that when they did, the factors which separated Jews from Greeks had to be given up by the Jews," see E. P. Sanders, *Paul, the Law and the Jewish People*, 178. He argues, "Paul's view of the church, supported by his practice . . . was substantially that it was a third entity, not because it was composed of both Jew and Greek, but also because

The ethnic model (Jew and Gentile) and household models (slave/free, male/female) that Paul mentions conflict with "the model of God's people," which envisions God's people as a family with members from all these models as sons and daughters. When features of identity and social roles that accompany these models conflict with the model of God's people as family, they may deny *equal membership* and *unity*, as is seen in Jewish identity features related to Abraham and the law. In such circumstances, Paul denies functionality to those elements within the household of God. Jew and Gentile, slave and free, and male and female are *equally children of God* and *equally members* of God's family. Therefore, I would suggest that when seen within the family image, Paul's assertion of "oneness" has elements of unity, equality, and diversity within the ecclesial family. As Paul is not abolishing all ethnic distinction between Jews and Gentiles, he is not abolishing all social distinctions within the other two couplets. However, Paul has denounced by his statements of vv. 26–28 and his overall argument in chapters 3–4 whatever element in the nature of Jewishness, Gentileness, and the two other couplets hinders equal membership in God's family.[138]

Christ-Followers as Children of God in Romans

In Romans, as he does in Galatians, Paul portrays the followers of Jesus using family language: as brothers and sisters,[139] as descendants of Abraham (Rom 4), and as children of God (Rom 8:14–16, 21–23). This kinship narrative echoes the kinship portrayal of God as Father not only at the beginning of the letter, which sets the family framework, but also within the immediate context of Romans 8. Together, these images serve a community-building purpose that advances the resocializing process of the followers of Christ with

it was in important ways neither Jewish nor Greek" (178–79). He further explains, "If conceptually Paul . . . had to make the church a third entity, it is all the more the case that it was a third entity in concrete social reality . . ." (176–78). Also see Campbell, *Paul and the Creation of Christian Identity*; idem, *Paul's Gospel in an Intercultural Context*; Esler, *Conflict and Identity*.

138. Hogan, "No Longer Male and Female," 28, explains that the social distinction Paul is rendering ineffective include "any situation where there are interactions between individuals, such as greetings, offers of assistance, serving and eating food, or giving and receiving instructions, that might be affected by perceived differences between two or more persons." She points out, "These differences, whether created by birth or positions of authority or education or legal status and defined by the world outside the Christian community, are apparently meant to affect relationships within the community . . . Paul has in mind abolishing the influence of these statuses . . ."

139. Nineteen times- 1:13; 7:1; 8:12; 10:1; 11:25; 12:1; 14:13, 15 (twice); 15:30; 16:1, 14, 23.

an emphasis on new identity that images them as a family of God. It serves to reimage their self-understanding in a way that indicates their transformation (flesh-Spirit, slavery-freedom), their unity, and their cosmic significance (8:18–25). Irrespective of who they were in the past, Paul has now depicted them as part of the family of God and shown the nature of this identity (what this identity is) by expressing it in terms of realm (flesh/Spirit, slavery/freedom and the mindset related to each of these), and in terms of lineage (descendants of Abraham). The new identity is also expressed in terms of how it is achieved (by faith, through Christ, by sharing the Spirit), in terms of cosmic significance (awaiting), and in terms of what it entails (no fear, relating to God as *Abba,* Father, the testimony and help of the Sprit).

The issue of unity, the need to "welcome one another" (Rom 15:7), is one of the major issues that Paul addresses[140] and the family language serves a significant role in Paul's strategy. The Jewish-Gentile relationship pervades the letter as evidenced by the repeated use of the expression "Jew and Greek" and its variation (1:16; 2:9, 10; 3:9, 29; 9:24; 10:12). Regarding the nature of the relationship, William L. Lane explains that "[t]he persistent focus on the relationship of Jews and Gentiles provides the dominant framework for this letter."[141] He also points out, "In Romans, Paul addresses a church with real tensions and struggles. He stresses the relationship of Jews and Gentiles . . ."[142] While the emphasis in Galatians is on convincing the Jewish believers to accept the Gentile believers as equal members of the family of God, in Romans the emphasis is on persuading the Gentile believers to treat the Jewish believers as equal members of the family of God.[143] In his book, *Conflict and Identity in Romans*, Esler argues that in Romans Paul is writing to "the Christ-movement . . . that is experiencing internal problems, notably those involving tension between Judean and non-Judean members."[144] Paul, Esler argues, is "trying to bring them together by reminding them of the single category they have in common," which Esler identifies as "faith and righteousness in Christ."[145] That is, the way Paul "seeks to reconcile Judeans and Greeks" is "by reminding them of the new common in-group identity

140. While the debate is long and ongoing as to what Paul's purpose was in writing Romans, I read Paul as addressing more than one purpose in Romans such as his own future ministry, resolving tension, and describing the gospel he preached; see Wedderburn, *The Reasons for Romans*; see also Donfried, *The Romans Debate*; Snyder, "Major Motifs in the Interpretation of Paul's Letter to Romans," 42–66.

141. Lane, "Social Perspectives on Roman Christianity," 201.

142. Ibid., 202.

143. Esler, *Conflict and Identity*, 128–34.

144. Ibid., 26.

145. Ibid.

that they share."[146] One aspect of the new common identity that Paul is constructing in Romans is the identity of being a family of God, that embraces all who are in Christ. To this end, Paul constructs two interrelated kinship narratives: kinship with Abraham and kinship with God.

In a similar way to Galatians, in Romans Paul images Abraham as the father of the followers of Jesus. In Romans 4, Paul explains the identity of the descendants of Abraham.[147] Jewett writes, "The passage is designed to appeal to each of the groups in Rome, whether Greco-Roman or Jewish in background, whether 'weak' or 'strong.'"[148] Abraham is identified in two ways: as the Father of the Jewish people according to the flesh[149] and father of all who believe (Jews and Gentiles) according to faith. After introducing Abraham as Αβραὰμ τὸν προπάτορα ἡμῶν κατὰ σάρκα ("our forefather in flesh") referring to Abraham's fatherhood to the Jewish people, Paul identifies him also as πατὴρ πάντων ἡμῶν "the father of us all" (v. 16). The expression "our father Abraham" argues for the new identity of τῷ ἐκ πίστεως 'Αβραάμ "to those from the faith of Abraham" as Abraham's children.

Paul's use of Abraham should be seen in relation to the contemporary and prior narratives of Abraham in Jewish writings. Paul takes the narrative that depicts Abraham as the forefather of the Jewish people, which constitutes one of the sources of their distinctive identity (*Jubilees* 23:10; 44:19–20; *Psalms of Solomon* 9) and widens it to embrace gentile Christ-followers through a kinship construction. Esler notes that "Abraham constituted a collective memory of critical importance, living continually in their consciousness. It constituted a foundational 'reference to the past.'"[150] Paul contests such memory by widening its application to construct a wider kinship relationship. The tradition of Abraham was "capable of interpretation and reinterpretation in a contest to process the past in the present. Abraham represented possible social identities in the past from which contending groups could select a particular version to suit their own immediate needs."[151] Thus, "using the narrative of Abraham, and in locating his communities within that narrative, Paul uses it both to relate gentile Christ-followers to the Jewish symbolic universe, and also to claim that Christ confirmed these promises to Israel as well."[152] Paul

146. Ibid., 133.

147. Jewett, *Romans*, 305.

148. Ibid., 306.

149. Esler, *Conflict and Identity*, 304–6.

150. Ibid., 179.

151. Ibid., 180; see also Watson, *Paul, Judaism and the Gentiles*, 139.

152. Campbell, *Paul and the Creation of Christian Identity*, 63.

depicts Abraham as the father of both gentiles and Jews (4:16), leaving no doubt of "Abraham as linking in a common paternity two groups who differ in their relation to him."[153]

Paul further develops his construction of the family image in Romans 8 by piling up kinship terms (vv. 14–16, 20–23). He identifies the Christ-followers in Rome as υἱοὶ θεοῦ (v. 14), and τέκνα θεοῦ (v. 16), who are κληρονόμοι μὲν θεοῦ, συγκληρονόμοι δὲ Χριστοῦ ("heirs of God" and co-heirs with Christ" v. 17) and who have received πνεῦμα υἱοθεσίας ("Spirit of adoption" v. 15) through which they cry αββα ὁ πατήρ ("cry, Abba, Father", 15). He further gives this kinship identity a cosmic significance by putting it within a cosmic context (vv. 20–23). The creation awaits the revelation of the "children of God" (v. 21) and the children of God await their adoption (υἱοθεσίαν), which is here identified as τὴν ἀπολύτρωσιν τοῦ σώματος ἡμῶν ("the redemption of our body" v. 23). Esler rightly characterizes Romans chapter 8 as "*a crescendo al finale* to Paul's exploration of the foundations of the new identity shared by his Judean and non-Judean audience in Rome that occupies the first half of the letter."[154] In this chapter "Paul draws the most powerful language of relationship in the ancient Mediterranean world to bind together the members of a group—that of kinship."[155] Esler explains, "Paul invokes sonship and heirship of God as a further means of designating the new identity they have achieved in Christ, now using imagery from the realm of kinship and household."[156]

Leading to this assertion of relationship is Paul's emphasis on the new identity of the followers of Jesus "with a series of antithetical statements that differentiate living according to flesh from living according to the Spirit."[157] Being under "the law of the spirit of life" is contrasted with being under "the law of sin and death" (8:2–3); walking according to the flesh is contrasted with walking according to the Spirit (8:4). Thinking according to the flesh is contrasted with thinking according to the Spirit (8:5–6), so also being in flesh with being in the Spirit (8:8–11). They are identified as those who have "the spirit of Christ" (v. 9), who are under obligation to live according to the spirit (vv. 12–13), and who are led by the Spirit of God (v. 14). It is these people that Paul describes as "children of God." The Spirit occupies a central place in this kinship relationship, mentioned five times in vv. 14–17. Paul associates with this status the receiving of the spirit of sonship/adoption,

153. Ibid.

154. Esler, *Conflict and Identity*, 243.

155. Ibid., 247.

156. Ibid., 249.

157. Ibid., 244.

instead of the spirit of slavery (πνεῦμα δουλείας), in which they cry "*Abba*, Father." Jewett comments, "The regulative principle for Christian family members is the Spirit of Christ, which redefines all social obligations."[158] The sharing of the Spirit is portrayed as an identifying element common to those who belong to God. As such, it is central here also to define the identity of the children of God. Following the feature of kinship that emphasizes the sharing of something to form a kinship relationship, the repeated depiction of the Spirit as something that Christ-followers share portrays them as the community characterized by the life of the Spirit (walking, thinking, etc.).

Finally, Paul portrays the self-understanding of the children of God in terms of God's cosmic plan. Esler reads this construction of Paul from what he calls "the diachronic dimensions of group identity."[159] In diachronic dimension, the identity of Christ-followers is depicted not only in terms of how their past is incorporated, and redefined to form their present, but also in terms of how their future shapes their present self-understanding. Esler explains, "[t]he future dimension of group identity provides a fertile ground for . . . 'possible selves,'" in the present.[160] He further notes, "just as leaders of groups process the past, reworking or even inventing collective memories to serve the purposes of the group in the present, they are also able to 'process the future,' meaning to visualize its outcomes."[161] Paul promotes a self-understanding that goes beyond group relationship by placing the identity of the children of God at the center of the longing of creation.

Christ-Followers as Children of God in Philippians and 2 Corinthians

In a similar way to Galatians and Romans, Paul's portrayal of Christ-followers as children of God in Philippians and 2 Corinthians should be seen in relation to the family image he constructs at the beginning of each letter by identifying God as Father (Phil 1:2; 2:11; 4:20; 2 Cor 1:2, 3). While in Galatians and Romans Paul constructs the self-understanding of Christ-followers as the children of God to advance unity, in Philippians and 2 Corinthians he uses the identity of Christ-followers as children of God to define them against the outside world. In Galatians, the primary purpose of this identity is to promote unity between Jewish and gentile believers. In Romans, in addition to promoting unity between Jewish and Gentile believers,

158. Jewett, *Romans*, 493–94.

159. Esler, *Conflict and Identity*, 252.

160. Ibid.

161. Ibid.

Paul uses "children of God" to promote an understanding of a transformed self that has a significant place in the future redemption of creation. In Philippians and 2 Corinthians, however, Paul constructs the image of believers as children directly in contrast with outsiders and with the purpose of promoting a life that reflects this new status. Here we see the role of kinship narrative differentiating a kin from non-kin directly.

In Philippians 2:14–15, Paul instructs the Philippians on how to be "blameless and innocent" and "without blemish" as children of God, and this "in the midst of a crooked and perverse generation." The way to manifest that kind of life, according to Paul, is to "do all things without murmuring and arguing" (2:14). This way of life will enable them to "shine like stars in the world" (2:15). While in Galatians and Romans Paul's use of "children of God" is not directly related to "doing," here he relates it to "doing all things without murmuring and arguing," with becoming "blameless and innocent," and with shining "like stars in the world" (2:14–15). The "murmuring and arguing" which in the Hebrew Bible is generally directed to God but also against Moses, might refer here to relationship within the community (Phil 2:1–4; 4:2).[162] Either way, it focuses on how the community's internal life as children of God should set them apart from the outside world.

Both the vocabularies and the use of the status of being children of God to promote a different living evoke similar usage in the Hebrew Bible. Commenting on Phil 2:14–15, J. M. Scott writes, "The reference here to the 'children' (*tekna*) of God being 'blameless' (*amōma*) alludes to Deuteronomy 32:5, where because they had sinned, the Israelites are characterized as 'blameful' (*mōmēta*) and as 'not his children' (*tekna*) in the context of the Song of Moses."[163] In Deuteronomy 32:5, it is the disobedient Israel that is referred to as "crooked and perverse generation." They behaved as non-children. Here, however, the "crooked and perverse generation" most likely refers to outsiders in whose midst the Philippians, as God's children, are to shine. While the call for blameless living in relation to being the children of God is in line with the Hebrew Bible (e.g., Deut 32: 5; 14:1; Hos 11:1–3; Isa 1:2–4; 30:1, 9), the contrast with the outside world is more similar to the characterization that we have seen in ancient Jewish writings (e.g., *Sirach* 35–36; *Wisdom of Solomon* 11–19). Thus, by combining the strategies in the Hebrew Bible and ancient Jewish literature, Paul is constructing the self-understanding of the Philippians in contrast to the outsiders.

162. O'Brien, *Philippians*, 291writes,"γογγυσμῶν at Phil 2:14 probably refers to those 'grumblings' which promote ill will instead of harmony within the community"; see also Osiek, *Philippians and Philemon*, 71, and suggests that a "rebellion against local leadership may well be part of the problem."

163. Scott, "Adoption, Sonship," 18; also see Hawthorne, *Philippians*, 101–3.

Paul's use of "children and daughters" of God in 2 Cor 6:14—17:1 has an even sharper tone that is set against outsiders.[164] The passage picks the aspect of boundary setting that Paul exercises with the use of kinship language in 1 Cor 8:1–13. Here, while the situation does not appear to involve idol food issues, it does involve idols (v.16) and much more—having "entangling alliances"[165] with the outside world that manifest itself in several ways as indicated by several questions he raises.[166] Murray J. Harris argues that since one of the antitheses refers to idols, Paul may be calling on the Corinthians to withdraw from participation in practices associated with local temples or cults.[167] He also acknowledges that a broader application might also be intended. He writes, "The Corinthians were to avoid any public or private relationship with unbelievers that was incompatible with or would compromise Christian standards."[168] The passage begins with "Do not be mismatched with unbelievers" (NRSV) and ends with "beloved, let us cleanse ourselves from every defilement of body and of spirit, making holiness perfect in the fear of God" (7:1, NRSV). With rhetorical questions Paul drives home that there is no harmony between the Corinthians as God's sons and daughters and the outsiders. The call is that the community cleanses itself "from every defilement of body and of spirit." As such, it has a similar theme with the exhortation in Phil 2:14–15. However, here the cleansing of body and spirit appears to be done by avoiding questionable alliances. Following strings of quotations from the Hebrew Bible in vv. 16–17, and in v. 18, within another quotation, Paul refers to God as Father and to the Corinthians as "sons and daughters" of God. It is depicted as a feature that should set the community apart. With quotations from the Hebrew Bible that strengthen the self-understanding of the Corinthians as God's sons and daughters, Paul constructs "a stronger sense of what the proper moral and social boundaries were for the Christian community in Corinth."[169] It is interesting to note that both in this passage and in Phil 2:14–15 Paul uses the identity of Christ-followers

164. Some argue that chapter 6 is not part of 2 Corinthians as written by Paul. For the history of interpretation of this passage see Webb, *Returning Home*, 16–30. My discussion follows the text as part of 2 Corinthians. For arguments that see 2 Cor 6:14—17:1 as part of the original part of the letter see Fee, "2 Corinthians 6:14—7:1 and Food Offered to Idols," 140–61; Thrall, "The Problem of 2 Cor. 6:14—7:1," 132–48; Murphy-O'Connor, "Relating 2 Corinthians 6:14—7:1 to Its Context," 272–75; Beale, "The OT Background of Reconciliation in 2 Corinthians 5–7," 550–81; Witherington, *Conflict and Community*, 403–4; Garland, *2 Corinthians*, 315–26.

165. Witherington, *Conflict and Community*, 402.

166. Garland, *2 Corinthians*, 331–38.

167. Harris, *The Second Epistle to the Corinthians*, 501.

168. Ibid.

169. Witherington, *Conflict and Community*, 406.

as children of God as a basis to set them apart from the outside world. In both cases, Paul either alludes or quotes directly from the Hebrew Bible. A pattern emerges for Paul's use of Christ-followers as children of God. One pattern is that which we saw above in Galatians and Romans, which is to promote internal unity. The second is what we have in Phil 2:14–15 and 2 Cor 6:14—7:1, which is to set boundaries.

In summary, Paul uses the concept of being children of God to shape the identity of his readers both in terms of building their self-understandings in relation to outsiders and in relation to the issues that are internal to the community. Therefore, it is not only in crisis situations but also in stable situations that Paul uses kinship language (sonship and daughtership) to establish identity. Paul's use is different from the Hebrew Bible and the ancient Jewish writings in the sense that in all the letters in which Paul uses sonship language, he introduces his letters by identifying God as Father. Furthermore, in Paul the kinship expression "children of God" refers to both Jewish and Gentile followers of Christ.

Christ-Followers as Siblings and Identity Formation in Paul

In the previous section, I have discussed how Paul's depiction of Christ-followers as children of God forms part of Paul's imaging of early Christians as a family of God through the use of God as Father. In this section, I will argue that Paul's imaging of Christ-followers as God's family unfolds further through his ubiquitous use of sibling language. Sibling language provides an orienting framework regarding why and how Christ-followers relate to each other. After briefly discussing Paul's use of sibling language, I will focus primarily on critically examining Reidar Aasgaard's rejection of the argument that Paul's use of sibling language works together with Fatherhood and children language to image the Christ-followers as the family of God. Since his work on sibling language in Paul is the most thorough work on the subject to this date, I will engage his approach and his conclusion. I will argue that while Paul's use of sibling language and other familial language is from the category of "fictive kinship,"[170] Aasgaard's rejection of this category as extraneous and his comparison of Paul's use only to what he calls "natural family" hindered him from grasping how Paul's use works to create an image beyond and in a way different from a "natural family." I will suggest that

170. Although I have shown in chapter 2 that anthropologists reject the use of the word "fictive" to describe non-biolcgical kinship as it wrongly implies that somehow it is not as real as biological kinship, I will use it in this section for lack of better word.

Paul's use of kinship language intends to create a sense of peoplehood with the image of family in the manner of the Hebrew Bible, ancient Jewish writings, and the Empire. I will begin with a discussion of Paul's use of sibling language and its relation to Paul's formation of the family of God.

Lloyd Alexander Lewis is one of those scholars who see Paul's use of sibling language as forming part of the image of family that Paul is constructing. Lewis correctly states, "Religious brotherhood . . . presupposes the fatherhood of God and its corollary: that one is adopted as God's child."[171] In this statement he brings together the Fatherhood of God, brotherhood and sisterhood of Christ-followers, and status as children. The family image Paul constructs at the beginning of his letters by identifying God as the Father of Christ-followers unfolds further through the identification of Christ-followers as siblings. These kinship images band together to form the image of the family of God. The narrative of networks of relationships Paul constructs using kinship language deepens as Paul advances the self-understanding of fellow believers as brothers and sisters. While other contemporary groups as well as the Hebrew Bible and ancient Jewish literatures also used sibling language to describe their group members, Paul's use is unprecedented in terms of numbers, intensity, and consistency.

Paul uses sibling language to refer to the insiders but never to outsiders,[172] to refer to Christ-followers in a different location (Gal 1:1–3—brothers and sisters with me, 1 Thess 4:10—brothers and sisters throughout Macedonia), and to refer to Christ-followers in one location.[173] He constructs deviant brothers as pseudo-brothers and sisters (2 Cor 11:26; Gal 2:4). He uses sibling terms as direct address (sixty-four times) and also as a designation (fifty times).[174] The high concentration of the designation of Christ-followers as brothers and sisters is found in passages where Paul deals with tension. Out of fifty occurrences where Paul uses "brothers and sisters" in the form of the designation (not direct address), 1 Corinthians 6–8 has twelve occurrences and Rom 14 has five. From the direct address the highest occurrences are in 1 Corinthians (twenty), 1 Thessalonians (fourteen), Romans (ten), and Galatians (nine), *strongly suggesting that Paul uses sibling language both in stable and in crisis situations to form identity*. Several schol-

171. Lewis, "As a Beloved Brother," 109; since Paul does not put Christ's sonship together with that of believers, I don't consider Jesus' sonship as forming part of Paul's construction of family image.

172. Aasgaard, "Brothers and Sisters in the Faith," 290n12, cites Rom 9:3 as an exception where Paul speaks of the Jewish people as his "siblings" which he specifies as "for the sake of my own people, my kindred according to the flesh."

173. Ibid., 290.

174. Aasgaard, *'My Beloved Brothers and Sisters!'*, Appendix I.

ars note that Paul's use of sibling language constructs self-understandings that advance unity, care, and some sort of equality, although on this matter there is still debate as to what exactly "equality" involves.[175]

Aasgaard argues, "the claims which several scholars have made of a notion of Christians as a 'family of God' in Paul, in which God is father and Christ and the Christians are his children and each other's siblings, are not sufficiently supported."[176] The reason Aasgaard gives is that "unilke other authors who often ground the importance and special character of siblingship biologically and socially (e.g., Plutarch), or religiously and philosophically (the Stoics, the Epicureans), Paul has not offered such a justification."[177] He sees Paul's use as being taken from "the domain of family life" rather than the parallel usages in other contexts (e.g., Jewish as well as Greco-Roman tradition).[178] Even though he admits that the use of sibling language in these contexts represents a "sociological parallel" to Paul's use concerning "self-understanding," "patterns of belonging," and "organization and structure," he limits the meaning of Pauline use to "the family life of his day."[179] He states:

> Christian relations . . . were understood and experienced *in terms of natural family* and siblingship . . . We also find parallel usages of family metaphors in other contexts, particularly within a Jewish tradition, and to some extent Paul may be dependent on such usages. Contrary to the opinion of some scholars, however, *these cannot account for his use of these metaphors* . . . the parallels are only limited, and the frequency, the intensity, the variation, and the conscious ways in which Paul has utilized these metaphors, call for another explanation: *the metaphors have their background in the family life of his day*. It is also likely that the other kinds of metaphorical usage have derived their meaning from the same source domain, namely that of the social family, although their relation to it may be more distant than for Paul.[180]

Aasgaard's otherwise enormously detailed study is marred with an 'either-or' approach to give a one-sided conclusion. While Paul's use of

175. Lewis, "'As a Beloved Brother,'" 108–59; Birge, *The Language of Belonging*, 1–71, 152–80; Burke, *Family Matters*, 163–75; See Hellerman, *The Ancient Church as Family*, 92–126, who adds kinship terminology to studies that highlight Paul's approach to promote concord; also see Mitchell, *Paul and the Rhetoric of Reconciliation*; Martin, *The Corinthian Body*.

176. Aasgaard, *'My Beloved Brothers and Sisters!'* 309.

177. Ibid., 308–9.

178. Ibid., 306.

179. Ibid., 306.

180. Ibid., 306, emphasis added.

kinship is in the category of "fictive kinship," and hence primarily should be seen from that perspective and then also with what he calls "social family," he explains what is "fictive kinship" construction only in terms of a natural family. Contra Aasgaard, Birge is right in stating that "[t]he initial source for Paul's selection of familial and household kinship language and imagery . . . was found in his religious history as a Jew and his cultural setting in first-century C.E. Hellenism."[181] While mentioning the likelihood that the parallel usages have derived their meaning from "the social family," Aasgaard sees their connection to be "more distant" than Paul's use. Had Aasgaard compared Paul's use more to the "fictive kinship" use of his parallel context, he could have allowed "more distance" for Paul's use of sibling language from "the social family." That would have given a wider opportunity to search for meanings and functionality in Paul's use of sibling language.

The difference in frequency is one of the reasons Aasgaard advances not to see a strong parallel between Paul and what he calls "usages of family metaphors in other contexts." However, it should not be the number that is primarily compared but the purpose and strategy involved. The purpose is to construct a family-like image and the strategy is to use familial language. But the meaning and functional role that is given to the familial language used and to the family-like image that is created is not limited solely to the meanings and function given in the natural family. For instance, the Father image is used for God in the Hebrew Bible. But the meaning and functionality of the image is not limited to natural family, as seen in instances where God's Fatherhood is compared to a human Father and portrayed as being superior to any ideal father, going beyond the expectation of natural family (Isa 63:16). The *patria* of the Roman Empire and the *pater patriae* of the emperor do not seem to be limited by the image of a paterfamilias of a household. *It goes beyond that to form a far superior ideal of a state as a household and the emperor as the head of the household to give an irresistible appeal.* Likewise, Paul, using the dynamic and elastic nature of kinship construction, takes familial language and teams it with features called for by the purpose he has at hand. The dynamic and elastic nature of kinship allows him to use it with "the frequency, the intensity, the variation, and the conscious ways" which Aasgaard rightly observed.

Because of an approach that limits his comparison of Pauline use to a "social family" alone disregarding the "fictive family" construction, Aasgaard sees no major development in the meaning and functionality of the sibling terms and also in the image of family created. He writes, "[C]ontrary to the view of several scholars, Paul does not view Christian siblingship as

181. Birge, *The Language of Belonging*, 183.

a new family which makes good the defects of the old."[182] However, the old family with which Paul compares the family he is forming is not limited to a natural family as Aasgaard argues. He has, for instance, as an old family the depiction of God's family in ethnic terms in the manner of the Hebrew Bible and ancient Jewish literature. By applying sibling language to Jews and Gentiles, he is renewing and broadening both the definition as well as the image of the old family. Paul is "reordering relationships" and dissolving boundaries.[183] He has, also the Empire as an old family, which constructs almost entirely a vertical household without much discussion on the horizontal relationship. Read in comparison to this, the Pauline "household of faith" is formed not only vertically with God as Father but also horizontally with a sibling relationship that is based on having God as Father.

Furthermore, with a similar 'either-or' approach, Aasgaard portrays the interaction between Paul's ecclesiology and his use of sibling language as a one way influence. He writes "a central part of Paul's thinking on the church has been informed by his social context, namely by the ideas and ideals generally associated with the sibling role."[184] He continues, "he (Paul) develops his ecclesiology on the basis of it (social context), and to an extent even on the premises given by that context. By this, social dynamics are — in a sense —turned into theology."[185] I argue that Paul is not using a linear relationship but a dialectical interaction between ecclesiology and social context, informing and enriching each other. This dialectical interaction between Paul's use of sibling language and Christology to inform/form an aspect of Pauline ecclesiology (relationship among Christ-followers) is evident for instance, in 1 Cor 8:9–13:

> But be careful that this liberty of your does not become a hindrance to the weak. For if someone weak sees you who possess knowledge dining in an idol's temple, will not his conscience be 'strengthened' to eat food offered to idols? So by your knowledge the weak brother or sister, for whom Christ died, is destroyed. If you sin against your brother or sister in this way and wound their weak conscience, you sin against Christ. For this reason, if food causes my brother or sister to sin, I will never eat meat again, so that I may not cause one of them to sin.[186] (NET)

182. Ibid., 311.

183. Ibid., 184.

184. Ibid., 209–10.

185. Ibid., 310.

186. The NRSV does not maintain the sibling language which is useful in the argument of this study.

Here Paul is arguing for thoughtful consideration of others in using one's knowledge. But he did not simply ground this thoughtful consideration on how brothers and sisters behave in a "social family," although the use of sibling terms evokes that aspect also. Rather he grounded it on Christology by stating, "brother or sister, for whom Christ died." He equates sinning against "brothers and sisters" to sinning "against Christ." While brotherhood and sisterhood evoke the family image and associated behavior of consideration, the caring consideration is given a theological foundation by grounding it on Christology.

Thus, while Aasgaard's work is very detailed and has all the parallel texts, his approach that limits studying Pauline sibling language to a natural family prohibited him immensely from incorporating important dimensions that would have enriched his findings. Among other reasons, kinship logic that creates networks of relationships and Paul's further use of kinship terms such as children in relation to the Fatherhood of God (Gal 3:25—24:7; Rom 8:12–16; 2 Cor 6:14—7:1) strongly suggest that Paul's use of sibling language is part of his use of Father to refer to God at the beginning of his letters. Regarding the first use, one can see that kinship is a process of being and becoming through networks of relationships. And networks of relationships are created through a notion of some sort of sharing. Paul's depiction at the beginning of each of his letters that he and his audience together share God as Father constructs their "being" in the image of family. The use of one kinship term evokes other associated kinship terms and relationships to create networks of relationships. For instance, when Rome is referred to as *patria*, and Augustus as *pater patriae*, it evokes the idea that those who belong to the Empire are its children. When Zeus is referred to as "the father of men and gods,"[187] it evokes that those who share with him "reason" are his children. When in Exodus 4:22, God refers to Israel as "My first born son," it would suggest that he is the Father. Referring to God as Father with rhetorical questions such as Deuteronomy 32:5 and later on in the prophets suggests a looking back not only to prior use of the Fatherhood language but also to the use of kinship terms in formative texts such as Exodus 4:22. Likewise, when Paul refers to God as "our Father" at the beginning of his letters, he suggests not only that the recipients relate to God as children, but also that they are siblings as they share a Father. The kinship term "father" forms a "hegemonic idiom" in terms of which the rest of the relationships are cast.[188]

Since Paul is writing to his recipients' "horizon of understanding" of how kinship works to create "hegemonic idioms," he did not need to

187. Epictetus, *Discourses*, 1.3; 1.13; 3.11; 3.22.

188. Peletz, "Ambivalence in Kinship," 416.

provide a philosophical argument like that of the Stoics, which Aasgaard was expecting to see. He carefully chose a place in which to establish identity and he followed that in all his letters. While Paul did not need to use other familial language as part of his use of the term "father" to refer to God in order to image Christ-followers as a family of God, he did use other familial language to strengthen the family image. He goes beyond leaving the construction of networks of kinship relationships to kinship logic alone after referring to God as Father at the beginning of his letters. He uses other specific familial language such as children, brothers, and sisters that would unambiguously formulate the nature of the network of relationships between God and the Christ-followers and among the Christ-followers. Furthermore, out of four texts where he refers to Christ-followers as children of God (Gal 3:26—4:7; Rom 8:14–23; Phil 2:14–15; 2 Cor 6:14—7:1), in three of them (Gal 3:26—4:7; Rom 8:14–23; 2 Cor 6:14—7:1) Paul also refers to God as Father, forming a close link between God's Fatherhood and Christ-followers' sonship and daughtership.

Summary Conclusion

Using kinship language, Paul develops a narrative of networks of familial relationships that coalesce to image the emerging community of Christ-followers as the family that belongs to God. At the center of this familial narrative that forms the relationship between God and Christ-followers and among Christ-followers is his use of God as Father at strategic parts of his letters with evocative language. His use of God as Father unfolds in his letters with the further use of the term "father" and with the use of other familial language such as children of God and sibling language.

These kinship terminologies are socially shared terminologies both with the outside world as well as with the prior narrative of the Christ-followers. As Paul uses this socially shared language, he engages the multiple and overlapping narratives of his recipients at times to affirm and at times to redefine and change. His use of kinship language to image the community as a family that belongs to God both imitates and contests similar uses in his cultural milieu. He primarily imitates the strategy of using such language to construct a family image. He contests his recipients' prior narrative of relationships on several levels depending on the issue at hand. Paul utilizes very well the dynamic and versatile nature of kinship that makes non-kin in one situation kin in another situation. He uses it both in stable and crisis situations to construct boundaries and also to create unity.

7

Conclusion

THE PURPOSE OF THIS study was to examine the use of God as Father in Paul in relation to the role kinship language plays in the identity formation of early Christianity. With this purpose in view, the study explored the importance of Paul's use of God as Father and related familial language to establish the self-understanding of the early Christians.

Paul uses the kinship term "father" to refer to God in conjunction with the kinship terms "children" and "brothers and sisters" to refer to Christ-followers. The former serves as a foundation, a "hegemonic idiom," out of which the latter two are derived. Paul uses these kinship terms together to construct the being and becoming of early Christ-followers through networks of relationships with God and Jesus, with ancients as well as contemporaries, with Paul and his co-workers, and with one another. He constructs a narrative of networks of relationships in which he intends his audiences to find their identity in relation to God, to each other, and to establish their relationship with the outside world. He provides a multidimensional mapping of their world in terms of their familial relationships to God and to each other.

These kinship representations coalesce to image the followers of Christ as a family, a household, which belongs to God. The image so constructed shapes and expresses the self-understanding(s) of early Christ-followers, providing an orienting framework to understand who they are, how they came into existence as a community, and how they need to relate to God, to one another, and to the outside world. The kinship language also forms the very framework within which Paul typically organizes his conversations with his recipients.

As the Father, together with the "Lord Jesus Christ," God is the originator, sustainer, and the head of the community of Christ-followers which is depicted as a family. Paul, as ἀπόστολος and δοῦλος of God and Christ, as father (1 Cor 4:15) and nursing mother (1 Thess 2:7) for the community of Christ-followers, is an agent, a partaker in the founding and shaping task of God's family. The community of Christ-followers, as the family of God, owed its being and becoming to God as Father and to Jesus Christ as Lord. God, together with Christ, is the source of the identity of the community of Christ-followers as ἐκκλησία, ἁγίοις, ἡγιασμένοις, ἀγαπητοῖς, and κλητοῖς. God, together with Christ, is the common source of grace and peace to the community.

While this portrayal of God, Christ, Paul, and Christ-followers occurs primarily in the prescripts, the idea so established in the prescripts unfolds in the contexts where Paul uses God as Father—prayer/thanksgiving contexts, didactic context, and in contexts where Christ-followers are depicted as children of God and as siblings. The construction forms the basis to depict Christ-followers as equal but diverse members of the household, united to form a community of the family of God. They relate to one another as children of one Father and as brothers and sisters who belong to one family, the household of God.

Paul's use of "Father" to refer to God and "children" and "brothers and sisters" to refer to Christ-followers is part of constructed kinship instead of natural family. While the kinship vocabularies are taken from the realm of the natural family/household setting, when they are applied to non-natural family/household setting, they are capable of taking different and/or additional roles and functions. Their meaning and function are not limited to their meaning and function in the household. Rather, transferred from natural *oikos* into the dynamic, versatile, and elastic realm of "fictive kinship," they capture additional meaning and function. In other words, the meaning and function of the term "father" as applied to God, and the meaning and function of "children" and "brothers and sisters" as applied to Christ-followers are not limited by their meaning and function within the context of a household.

Neither the use of these kinship terms nor the mode of identity construction using such kinship terms is unique to Paul. Rather, Paul shares the kinship terms and the mode of identity constructions with the Roman Empire, the Roman Stoic philosophers, the Hebrew Bible, and ancient Jewish literature. By taking terms that are "socially-charged" in their previous multiple and competing contexts and by applying them to God and to Christ-followers, Paul "partakes, vigorously at times" in dialogical discourse both with these contexts and his audiences' previous horizons of understanding that were shaped by these contexts. Paul engages his audiences' prior narrative of relationships, sometimes to affirm and sometimes to change.

The kinship language and associated vocabularies that are used to depict the relationship of Paul and his recipients to God and to each other evoke the formative narrative of the Empire, the Roman Stoics, the Hebrew Bible, and ancient Jewish literature. Paul imitates both the strategies of constructing identity and the intention of creating a family image that promotes a sense of community, belongingness, cohesion, and accountability. However, at significant points, Paul vigorously engages, contests, and redefines the use of the term "father" in his multiple and competing textual and cultural surroundings. Paul primarily contests the use of the kinship term "father" to refer to the Roman Empire and emperor and its use by the Roman Stoic philosophers to refer to Zeus. He also contests the use of God as Father in the Hebrew Bible as well as in ancient Jewish writings that limits God's Fatherhood to the people of Israel and the ancient Jewish people alone.

He contests these competing narratives on two levels: on the applicability of the term "father" and on the nature of the community constructed and its internal features. He argues that fatherhood is more appropriate to God than to Zeus. It is more fitting to God than the Roman Empire or emperor. He also argues that the community thus created through the Fatherhood of God is different on many levels from the Empire as a big household and from the cosmopolitan humanity of the Roman Stoic. It is the ἐκκλησία of God, ἀγαπητοῖς, and κλητοῖς by him to be ἁγίοις and ἡγιασμένοις. While the household of the Empire is primarily formed and depicted vertically, God's household is formed and depicted both vertically and horizontally.

While the Roman Stoics teach that all humanity belongs to the cosmopolitan universalism, they limit sharing in this universalism to those who could ascend through reason. In the community of Christ-followers, however, there is equal access of membership and equal status as children of God irrespective of one's capacity to reason or one's ethnic and social backgrounds, or gender. Anyone who comes by faith is equally a member of this family of God.

One can also see Paul imitating as well as contesting the use of "Father" to refer to God and the related familial languages in the Hebrew Bible and ancient Jewish writings. While Paul's use of the term "Father" to refer to God is in line with the Hebrew Bible and ancient Jewish literature, the nature of the community constructed and its internal features are significantly different. To begin with, Paul widens the scope of God's Fatherhood from being the Father of the people of Israel and the Jewish people to all kinds of people who become Christ-followers by faith and share the transformative power of the Spirit. Vocabularies such as ἀγαπητοῖς, and κλητοῖς, ἁγίοις and ἡγιασμένοις, which were previously associated with the formation of Israel and the identity of the Jewish people, are now applied to Christ-followers who belong to different contexts.

Thus, Paul's use of kinship language to construct self-understanding through networks of relationships has multiple features. At times, it calls for assimilation and accommodation. At other times, he relativizes his audiences' past history and traditions by redefining the value and meaning attached to these traditions. At times, he adds new dimensions to his audiences' past understanding of the term "father" and related familial terms and provides a basis by which the significance of the new and old identities is evaluated.

This study has also shown the importance of not limiting the inquiry into the formation of early Christians to a crisis and oppositional situation. Previous studies on God as Father, with the assumption that there is "no-Fatherhood-of-God-in-early-Judaism," approached the use of God as Father in the New Testament in opposition to such use in ancient Judaism. The use of God as Father was not compared even with Jewish writings that are deemed to have non-Palestinian origin, let alone to similar use in the Hellenistic context. The previous chapters have shown that early Christianity shared both the need to construct identity as well as the features of identity construction with its multiple and competing milieu. It is not one or the other but all these contexts in varying degree that contribute to the understanding of Paul's use of God as Father. Instead of pitting one context against another, this study has shown that these milieus overlap Paul's use of "Father" to refer to God.

Finally, this study has also shown further the benefit of the use of kinship insights from anthropology together with the concept of identity as analytical category for the study of the formation of early Christianity. Such an approach opens up multiple venues from which one can examine textual constructions.

Bibliography

Aasgaard, Reidar. "Brothers and Sisters in the Faith: Christian Siblingship as an Ecclesiological Mirror in the First Two Centuries." In *The Formation of the Early Church*, edited by Jostein Ådna, 285–316. WUNT 183. Tübingen: Mohr, 2005.

———. *'My Beloved Brothers and Sisters!': Christian Siblingship in Paul*. London: T. & T. Clark, 2004.

Achtemeier, Elizabeth. *The Community and Message of Isaiah 56–66: A Theological Commentary*. Minneapolis: Augsburg, 1982.

Adams, Edward. "Paul's Story of God and Creation: The Story of How God Fulfills His Purpose in Creation." In *Narrative Dynamics in Paul: A Critical Assessment*, edited by Bruce W. Longenecker, 19–43. Louisville: Westminster John Knox, 2002.

Adams, Sean A. "Paul's Letter Opening and Greek Epistolography: A Matter of Relationship." In *Paul and the Ancient Letter Form*, edited by Stanley E. Porter, et al., 33–56. Leiden: Brill, 2010.

Alexander, Philip. "Hellenism and Hellenization as Problematic Historical Category." In *Paul Beyond the Judaism/Hellenism Divide*, edited by Troels Engberg-Pedersen, 63–80. Louisville: Westminster John Knox, 2001.

Alföldi, A. *Der Vater des Vaterlandes im römischen Denken*. Darmstadt: Wissenschaftliche Buchgesellschaft, 1971.

Alföldy, Géza. *The Social History of Rome*. Translated by David Braund and Frank Pollock. Totawa, NJ: Barnes & Noble Books, 1985.

Algra, Keimpe, et al., eds. *The Cambridge History of Hellenistic Philosophy*. Cambridge: Cambridge University Press, 1999.

Allen, David Mark. "Deuteronomic Re-presentation in a Word of Exhortation: An Assessment of the Paraenetic Function of Deuteronomy in the letter to the Hebrews." PhD diss., University of Edinburgh, 2007.

Allmen, Daniel von. *La famille de Dieu: La symbolique familiale dans le paulinisme*. Fribourg: Editions Universitaires. Göttingen: Vandenhoeck & Ruprecht, 1981.

Amad-Azuogue, Chinedu Adolphus. *Paul and the Law in the Arguments of Galatians: A Rhetorical and Exegetical Analysis of Galatians 2:14—6:2*. Weinheim: Beltz Athenäum, 1996.

Andersen, F. I. "Israelite Kinship Structure Terminology and Social Structure." *BT* 20 (1969) 29–39.

Anderson, A. A. *2 Samuel*. WBC. Dallas: Word, 2002.

Anderson, B. *Imagined Communities: Reflections on the Origin and Spread of Nationalism*. 2nd ed. London: Verso, 1991.

Bibliography

Anderson, Paul N. "The Having-Sent-Me Father: Aspects of Agency, Encounter, and Irony in the Johannine Father-Son Relationship." *Semeia* 85 (1999) 33–57.

Ando, Clifford. *Imperial Ideology and Provincial Loyalty in the Roman Empire*. Berkeley: University of California Press, 2000.

Appian. *Roman History*. Translated by Horace White. Vol. 2. LCL. Cambridge: Harvard University Press, 1912–1913.

Argyle, A. W. *God in the New Testament*. Philadelphia: J. B. Lippincott, 1966.

Artz-Grabner, Peter. "Paul's Letter Thanksgiving." In *Paul and the Ancient Letter Form*, edited by Stanley E. Porter, et al., 129–58. Leiden: Brill, 2010.

Asano, Atsuhiro. *Community-Identity: Exegetical, Social-Anthropological and Socio-Historical Studies*. JSNTS. London: T. & T. Clark, 2005.

Ascough, Richard S. "The Thessalonian Christian Community as a Professional Voluntary Association." *JBL* 119 (2000) 311–28.

———. "Voluntary Association and Community Formation: Paul's Macedonian Christian Communities in Context." PhD diss., Toronto School of Theology, 1997.

———. *What Are They Saying about the Formation of Pauline Churches?* New York: Paulist, 1998.

Audi, Robert, editor. *The Cambridge Dictionary of Philosophy*. Cambridge: Cambridge University Press, 1995, 319–21.

Auerbach, Erich. *Mimesis: The Representation of Reality in Western Literature*. Translated by Willard R. Trask. Princeton: Princeton University Press, 1953.

Aune, D. E. *The New Testament in Its Literary Environment*. Cambridge: Clarke, 1987.

Baker, Coleman A. *Identity, Memory, and Narrative in Early Christianity: Peter, Paul, and Recategorization in the Book of Acts*. Eugene, OR: Pickwick, 2011.

Balch, David L. "Hellenization/Acculturation in 1 Peter." In *Perspectives on First John*, 79–101. Macon, GA: Mercer University Press, 1986.

Balch, David L. and Osiek, Carolyn. *Families in the New Testament World: Households and House Churches*. Louisville: Westminster John Knox, 1997.

Baldry, H. C. *The Unity of Mankind in Greek Thought*. Cambridge: Cambridge University Press, 1965.

Balla, Peter. *The Child-Parent Relationship in the New Testament and Its Environment*. WUNT 55. Tübingen: Mohr, 2002.

Banks, Robert. *Paul's Idea of Community: The Early House Churches in their Historical Setting*. Grand Rapids: Eerdmans, 1980.

Barclay, John M. G. *Obeying the Truth: A Study of Paul's Ethics in Galatians*. Edinburgh: T. & T. Clark, 1988.

———. "Paul's Story: Theology as Testimony." In *Narrative Dynamics in Paul: A Critical Assessment*, edited by Bruce W. Longenecker, 133–56. Louisville: Westminster John Knox, 2002.

Barr, James. "Abba and the Familiarity of Jesus' Speech." *Theology* 91 (1988) 173–79.

———. "Abba Isn't Daddy." *JTS* 39 (1988) 28–77.

Barrett, C. K. "'The Father is Greater than I' (John 14:28) Subordinationist Christology in the New Testament." In *Essays on John*, 19–36. Philadelphia: Westminster, 1982.

Barrett, John C. "Chronologies of Remembrance: The Interpretation of Some Roman Inscriptions." *World Archaeology* 25 (1993) 236–47.

Bartchy, S. Scott. "Undermining Ancient Patriarchy: The Apostle Paul's Vision of a Society of Siblings." *BTB* 29.2 (1999) 68–78.

Barton, S. C., and G. H. R. Horsley. "A Hellenistic Cult Group and the New Testament Churches." *Jahrbuch für Antike und Christentum* 24 (1981) 7–41.

Bassler, Jouette M. "The Problem of Self-Definition: What Self and Whose Definition." In *Redefining First-Century Jewish and Christian Identities: Essays in Honor of Ed Parish Sanders*, edited by Fabine E. Udoh, 42-68. Notre Dame: University of Notre Dame, 2008.

Bauer, Walter. *Orthodoxy and Heresy in Earliest Christianity*. Translated by a team from the Philadelphia Seminar on Christian Origins, edited by R. A. Kraft and Gerhard Krodel. Philadelphia: Fortress, 1971.

Baur, F. C. "Die Christuspartei in Der Korinthischen Gemeinde." *Theologie Zeitschrift* 4 (1831) 61-206. Repr. in *Ausgewählte Werke in Einzelausgaben*, edited by Klaus Scholder, 1–146. Stuttgart: Frommann, 1963.

Beale, G. K. "The OT Background of Reconciliation in 2 Corinthians 5–7 and its Bearing on the Literary Problem of 2 Corinthians 6:14–7:1." *NTS* 35 (1987) 550–81.

Beardslee, William. "Narrative Form in the NT and Process Theology." *Encounter* 36 (1975) 301–15.

Beattie, J. *Other Cultures: Aims, Methods and Achievements in Social Anthropology*. London: Cohen and West, 1964.

Beecher, W. J. *The Prophets and the Promise*. Grand Rapids: Baker, 1977.

Beker, J. C. *Paul the Apostle: The Triumph of God in Life and Thought*. Philadelphia: Fortress, 1980.

Blasi, Anthony J., et al. *Hand Book of Early Christianity: Social Science Approaches*. Lanham: Altamira, 2002.

Belliotti, Raymond Angelo. *Roman Philosophy and the Good Life*. Lanham, MD: Lexington Books, 2009.

Bennett, H. William. "The Sons of the Father: The Fatherhood of God in the Synoptic Gospels." *Interpretation* 4 (1950) 12–23.

Bergey, Ronald. "The Song of Moses (Deuteronomy 32.1–43) and Isaianic Prophecies: A Case of Early Intertextuality?" *JSOT* 28. 1 (2003) 33–54.

Betsy, Halpern-Amaru. *Rewriting the Bible: Land and Covenant in Postbiblical Jewish Literature*. Valley Forge, PA: Trinity, 1994.

Bettini, Maurizio. *Anthropology and Roman Culture: Kinship, Time, and Images of the Soul*. Translated by Jon van Sickle. Baltimore: Johns Hopkins University, 1991.

Betz, Hans Dieter. *Galatians: A Commentary on Paul's Letter to the Churches in Galatia*. Philadelphia: Fortress, 1979.

Birge, Mary Katherine. *The Language of Belonging: A Rhetorical Analysis of Kinship Language in First Corinthians*. Leuven: Peters, 2002.

Blasi, Anthony J., et al. *Hand Book of Early Christianity: Social Science Approaches*. Lanham: Altamira, 2002.

Blenkinsopp, J. "Memory, Tradition, and the Construction of Past in Ancient Israel." *BTB* 27 (1997) 76–82.

Block, Daniel. "Israel's House: Reflections on the Use of BYT Y'SR'L in the Old Testament in the Light of Its Ancient Near Eastern Environment." *JETS* 28.3 (1985) 257–75.

———. "'Israel'—'Sons of Israel': A Study in Hebrew Eponymic Usage." *Sciences Religieuses/Studies in Religion* 13.3 (1984) 301–26.

Borgen, Peder. *Early Christianity and Hellenistic Judaism*. Edinburgh: T. & T. Clark, 1998.

Bossman, David M. "Paul's Fictive Kinship Movement." BTB 26.4 (1996) 163–71.

Boston, James R. "The Wisdom Influence upon the Song of Moses." *JBL* 87 (1968) 198–202.

Boucher, Madeline. "Scriptural Readings: God-Language and Nonsexist Translation." In *Language and the Church: Articles and Designs for Workshop*, edited by Barbara A. Withers, 28–32. New York: Division of Publication Services, National Council of the Churches of Christ in the U.S.A., 1984.

Bousset, Wilhelm. *Jesu Predigt, in ihrem Gegensatz zum Judentum:ein religionsgeschichtlicher Vergleich*. Göttingen: Vandenhoeck & Ruprecht, 1892.

———. *Kyrios Christos: Geschichte des Christusglaubens von den Anfängen des Christentums bis Irenaeus*. Göttingen: Vandenhoeck & Ruprecht, 1965.

———. *Kyrios Christos: A History of the Belief in Christ from the Beginnings of Christianity to Irenaeus*. Translated by John E. Steely. Nashville: Abingdon, 1970.

Bovon, Francois. "Studies in Luke-Acts: Retrospect and Prospect." *HTR* 85 (1992) 175–96.

Brady, C. J. "Brotherly Love: A Study of the Word Philadelphia and its Contribution to the Biblical Theology of Brotherly Love." PhD diss., University of Fribourg, 1961.

Brettler, M. Z. "Memory in Ancient Israel." In *Memory and History in Christianity and Judaism*, edited by M. A. Signer, 1–17. Notre Dame: University of Notre Dame Press, 2001.

Brichto, Hanan. "Kin, Cult, Land, and Afterlife–A Biblical Complex." *HUCA* 44 (1973) 1–54.

Brinsmead, Bernard H. *Galatians: Dialogical Response Opponents*. SBLDS 65. Chico, CA: Scholars Press, 1982.

Britt, Brian. "Deuteronomy 31–32 as a Textual Memorial." *BibInt* 8.4 (2000) 358–74.

Brown, Michael J. "Paul's Use of Δοῦλος Χριστοῦ 'Iησου in Romans 1:1." *JBL* 120.4 (2001) 723–37.

Brown, Rupert. *Group Processes*. 2nd ed. Oxford: Blackwell, 2000.

Brueggemann, Walter. "The Covenanted Family: A Zone for Humanness." *JCSI* 14 (1977) 18–23.

———. *Deuteronomy*. Nashville: Abingdon, 2001.

———. *To Pluck Up, To Tear Down: Jeremiah 1–25*. Grand Rapids: Eerdmans, 1988.

Bühner, J. –A. "ἀπόστολος." In *Exegetical Dictionary of the New Testament*, edited by H. Balz, G. Schneider, 1:143–46. Grand Rapids: Eerdmans, 1990–1993.

Bultmann, Rudolf K. *Theology of the New Testament*. Translated by Kendrick Grobel. New York: Scribner, 1951–1955.

Burer, Michael H., et al., eds. *New English Translation. Novum Testamentum Graece. New Testament*. Dallas: NET Bible Press, 2004.

Burke, Trevor J. *Adopted into God's Family: Exploring a Pauline Metaphor*. New Studies in Biblical Theology 22. Downers Grove, IL: InterVarsity, 2006.

———. "Adopted as Sons: The Missing Piece in Pauline Soteriolgy." In *Paul as Jew, Greek, and Roman*, edited by Stanley E. Porter, 259–88. Pauline Studies 5. Leiden: Brill, 2008.

———. *Family Matters: A Socio-historical Study of Kinship Metaphors in 1 Thessalonians*. London: T. & T. Clark, 2003

———. "Paul's Role as 'Father' to his Corinthian 'Children' in Socio-Historical Context (1 Cor. 4:14–21)." In *Paul and the Corinthians: Studies on a Community*

in Conflict. Essays in Honour of Margaret Thrall, edited by Trevor J. Burke, et al., 95–114. Leiden: Brill, 2003.
Burkert, Walter. *Ancient Mystery Cults.* Cambridge: Harvard University Press, 1985.
Burnett, F. W. "Exposing the Anti-Jewish Ideology of Matthew's Implied Author: The Characterization of God as Father." *Semeia* 59 (1992) 155–91.
Byrne, Brendan. "Sons of God." In *ABD* 6:156–58. New York: Doubleday, 1992.
———. *'Sons of God'–'Seed of Abraham': A Study of the Idea of the Sonship of God of all Christians in Paul against the Jewish Background.* Rome: Biblical Institute Press, 1979.
Byron, John. *Slavery Metaphors in Early Judaism and Pauline Christianity.* WUNT 162. Tübingen: Mohr, 2003.
Caird, G. B. *New Testament Theology.* Edited by L. D. Hurst. Oxford: Clarendon, 1994.
Cameron, Averil. *Christianity and the Rhetoric of Empire: The Development of Christian Discourse.* Sather Classical Lectures 45. Berkeley: University of California Press, 1991.
Campbell, William S. *Paul and the Creation of Christian Identity.* London: T. & T. Clark, 2008.
———. *Paul's Gospel in an Intercultural Context: Jew and Gentile in the Letter to Romans.* Frankfurt am Main: Peter Lang, 1991.
Carlson, R. A. *David, The Chosen King: A Traditio-Historical Approach to the Second Book of Samuel.* Upsala: Almqvist & Wiksell, 1964.
Carsten, Janet, editor. *Culture of Relatedness: New Approaches to the Study of Kinship.* Cambridge: Cambridge University Press, 2000.
Carter, Warren. "God as 'Father' in Matthew: Imperial Intersections." In *"Finding a Women's Place": Essays in Honor of Carolyn Osiek*, edited by David L. Balch, et al., 81–102. Eugene, OR: Pickwick, 2010.
———. *John and Empire: Initial Exploration.* New York, T. & T. Clark, 2008.
———. "Lecture Imperialiste." In *Guide des Nouvelles Lectures de la Bible*, edited by A. Lacocque, 273–305. Paris: Bayard, 2005.
———. *Matthew and Empire: Initial Exploration.* Harrisburg, PA: Trinity, 2001.
———. "Proclaiming (in/against) Empire Then and Now." *World and Word* 25 (2005) 149–58.
———. *The Roman Empire and the New Testament: An Essential Guide.* Nashville: Abingdon, 2006.
———. Review of Seyoon Kim, *Christ and Caesar: The Gospel and the Roman Empire in the Writings of Paul and Luke. RBL.* No pages. Online: http://www.bookreviews.org (2009).
Cazelles, Henri. "Jeremiah and Deuteronomy." In *A Prophet to the Nations: Essays in Jeremiah Studies*, 89–112. Winona Lake, IN: Eisenbrauns, 1984.
Chaplin, Jane D. *Livy's Exemplary History.* Oxford: Oxford University Press, 2000.
Charles, R. H., editor. *The Apocrypha and Pseudepigrapha of the Old Testament in English.* 2 Vols. Oxford: Oxford University Press, 1913.
Charlesworth, James H. "Christian and Jewish Self-Definition in Light of the Christian Additions to the Appocryphal Writings." In *Jewish and Christian Self-Definition: Aspects of Judaism in the Graeco-Roman Period*, 186–200. Philadelphia: Fortress, 1980.
———, editor. *The Old Testament Pseudepigrapha.* Vol. 1, *Apocalyptic Literature and Testaments.* Garden City, NY: Doubleday, 1983.

———. *The Old Testament Pseudepigrapha*. Vol. 2. *Expansions of the "Old Testament" and Legends, Wisdom and Philosophical Literature, Prayers, Psalms, and Odes, Fragments of Lost Judeo-Hellenistic Works*. Garden City, NY: Doubleday, 1985.

Chen, Diane G. *God as Father in Luke-Acts*. New York: Peter Lang, 2006.

Cheon, Samuel. *The Exodus Story in the Wisdom of Solomon: A Study in Biblical Interpretation*. JSPSup 23. Sheffield: Sheffield Academic, 1997.

Childs, Brevard S. *Introduction to the Old Testament as Scripture*. London: SCM, 1979.

Christensen, Duane L. *Deuteronomy 1–21:9*. WBC. Dallas: Word, 2002.

———. *Deuteronomy 21:10–34:12*. WBC. Dallas: Word, 2002.

Ciampa, Roy E. and Brian S. Rosner. *The First Letter to the Corinthians*. Grand Rapids: Eerdmans, 2010.

Cicero. *De Republica. De Legibus*. Translated by Clinton Walker Keyes. LCL. Cambridge: Harvard University Press, 1928.

Clifford, Richard J. "Psalm 89: A Lament over the Davidic Ruler's Continued Failure." *HTR* 73 (1980) 35–47.

Cohen, Shaye J. D. *From the Maccabees to the Mishnah*. Philadelphia: Westminster, 1987.

Colish, Marcia L. *The Stoic Tradition from Antiquity to the Early Middle Ages: Stoicism in Classical Latin Literature*. Vol. 1. Leiden: Brill, 1985.

Collins, R. F. *First Corinthians*. Sacra Pagina 7. Collegeville, MN: Liturgical, 1999.

———. "A Significant Decade" The Trajectory of the Hellenistic Epistolary Thanksgiving." In *Paul and the Ancient Letter Form*, Pauline Studies 6, edited by Stanley E. Porter, et al., 159–84. Leiden: Brill, 2010.

Connolly, Joy. "Being Greek/Being Roman: Hellenism and Assimilation in the Roman Empire." *Millennium* (2007) 21–42.

Conzelmann, Hans. "Luke's Place in the Development of Early Christianity." In *Studies in Luke-Acts: Essays Presented in Honor of Paul Schubert*, edited by Leander E. Keck et al., 298–316. Nashville: Abingdon, 1966.

———. "Paulus und die Weisheit." *NTS* 12.3 (1966) 231–44.

Cooke, Gerald. "The Israelite King as Son of God." *Zeitschrift für die alttestamentliche Wissenschaft* 73 (1961) 202–25.

Crawford, Sidnie White. *Rewriting Scripture in Second Temple Times*. Grand Rapids: Eerdmans, 2008.

Crites, Stephen. "Angels We Have Heard," In *Religion as Story*, edited by J. B. Wiggins, 23–63. New York: Harper and Row, 1975.

———. "The Narrative Quality of Experience." *JAAR* 39 (1971) 291–311.

Cromhout, Markus. "A Clash of Symbolic Universes: Judeanism Vs Hellenism." *HTS* 63.3 (2007) 1089–1117.

Cross, F. M. *From Epic to Canon: History and Literature in Ancient Israel*. Baltimore: John Hopkins University Press, 1998.

———. "Kinship and Covenant in Ancient Israel." In *From Epic to Canon: History and Literature in Ancient Israel*, 3–22. Baltimore: Johns Hopkins University Press, 1998.

Crossan, John Dominic, and Johnathan L. Reed. *In Search of Paul: How Jesus' Apostle Opposed Rome's Empire with God's Kingdom: A New Vision of Paul's Words and World*. New York: HarperCollins, 2004.

Crüsemann, Frank."Human Solidarity and Ethnic Identity: Israel's Self-Definition in the Genealogical System of Genesis." In *Ethnicity and the Bible*, 57–76. Leiden: Brill, 1996.

Cullman, Oscar. *Christ and Time: The Primitive Christian Conception of Time and History.* Translated by Floyd V. Filson. Philadelphia: Westminster, 1964.

———. *Salvation in History.* Translated by Sidney G. Sowers, et. al. New York: Harper & Row, 1967.

Dahl, Nils A. "Paul's Letter to the Galatians: Epistolary Genre, Content, Structure." Paper Presented at the Annual Meeting of the SBL, Chicago. 1983.

Daly, Mary. *Beyond the Father: Towards a Philosophy of Women's Liberation.* Boston: Beacon, 1985.

D'Angelo, Mary Rose. "Abba and 'Father': Imperial Theology and the Jesus Traditions." *JBL* 3/4 623 (1992) 611–30.

———. "Theology in Mark and Q: Abba and Father in Context." *HTR* 85.2 (1992) 149–74.

De Boer, P. A. H. *Fatherhood and Motherhood in Israelite and Judean Piety.* Leiden: Brill, 1974.

De Geus, C. H. J. *The Tribes of Israel.* Assen: Van Gorum, 1976.

Deissmann, Adolf. *Light from the Ancient East: The New Testament Illustrated by Recently Discovered Texts of the Graeco-Roman World.* Translated by Lionel R. M. Strachan. New York: Harper and Brothers, 1927.

deSilva, David A. *Honor, Patronage, Kinship and Purity: Unlocking New Testament Culture.* Downers Grove, IL: InterVarsity, 2000.

———. *Introducing the Apocrypha: Message, Context, and Significance.* Grand Rapids: Baker Academic, 2002.

———. "Paul and the Stoa: A Comparison." *JETS* 38 (1995) 549–64.

Dilke, Oswald A. W. *Greek and Roman Maps.* New York: Cornell University Press, 1985.

Dio Cassius. *Dio's Roman History.* Translated by Earnest Cary. LCL. Cambridge: Harvard University Press, 1914–1927.

Diogenes Laertius. *Lives of Eminent Philosophers.* Edited by G. P. Goold. Translated by R. D. Hicks. 2 vols. LCL. Cambridge: Harvard University Press, 1925.

Dionysius Halicarnassus. *The Roman Antiquities.* Translated by Earnest Cary. Cambridge, MA: LCL. Cambridge: Harvard University Press, 1974.

Dixon, Suzanne. "Conflict in the Roman Family." In *The Roman Family in Italy: Status, Sentiment, Space*, edited by Beryl Rawson and Paul Weaver, 149–67. Oxford: Clarendon, 1997.

———. *The Roman Family.* Baltimore: John Hopkins University, 1992.

Dobbin, Robert F. *Epictetus: Discourses Book I.* Oxford: Clarendon, 1998.

Dodd, C. H. *According to the Scriptures: The Sub-Structure of New Testament Theology.* London: Nisbet, 1952.

———. *The Apostolic Preaching and Its Development.* New York: Harper & Brothers, 1936.

———. "The Framework of the Gospel Narrative." *ExpTim* 43 (1931–32) 396–400.

Donaldson, M. E. "Kinship Theory in the Patriarchal Narratives." *JAAR* 49 (1981) 77–87.

Donfried, Karl P. *Paul, Thessalonica, and Early Christianity.* Grand Rapids: Eerdmans, 2002.

———, editor. *The Romans Debate.* Rev. and exp. ed. Peabody: Hendrickson, 1991.

Doohan, Leonard. "Images of God in Luke-Acts." *Milltown Studies* 13 (1984) 17–35.

Douglas, Ress Conrad. "Family, Power, Religion: A Discussion of the Background and Functions of References to God as Father in the Gospel of Matthew." PhD diss., Claremont Graduate School, 1990.

Driver, S. R. *Critical and Exegetical Commentary on Deuteronomy*. International Critical Commentary. Edinburgh: T. & T. Clark, 1901.

———. *Deuteronomy*. International Critical Commentary. New York: Scribner, 1916.

Dunn, J. D. G. *A Commentary on the Epistle to the Galatians*. BNTC. London: A. & C. Black. 1993.

———. *The Evidence for Jesus*. Philadelphia: Westminster, 1985.

———. "The Narrative Approach to Paul: Whose Story?" In *Narrative Dynamics in Paul: A Critical Assessment*, edited by Bruce W. Longenecker, 217–32. Louisville: Westminster John Knox, 2002.

———. *The Partings of the Ways: Between Christianity and Judaism and Their Significance for the Character of Christianity*. London: SCM, 2006.

———. *The Theology of Paul the Apostle*. Edinburgh: T. & T. Clark, 1998.

———. *Unity and Diversity in the New Testament: An Inquiry into the Character of Earliest Christianity*. 3rd ed. London: SCM, 2006.

Durham, John. *Exodus*, WBC. Dallas: Word, 2002.

Eder, Walter. "Augustus and the Power of Tradition." In *The Age of Augustus*, edited by Karl Galinsky, 13–32. Cambridge: Cambridge University Press, 2005.

———. "Augustus and the Power of Tradition: The Augustan Principate as Binding Link between Republic and Empire." In *Between Republic and Empire: Interpretations of Augustus and His Principate*, edited by Kurt A. Raaflaub et al., 71–122. Berkeley: University of California Press, 1990.

Eggan, Fred. "Kinship: Introduction." In *International Encyclopedia of the Social Sciences*, edited by David L. Sills, 387–95. New York: Macmillan, 1968.

Eisenbaum, Pamela. "Paul as the New Abraham." In *Paul and Politics: Ekklesia, Israel, Imperium, Interpretation*, edited by Richard A. Horsley, 130–45. Harrisburg, PA: Trinity, 2000.

Eisenstadt S. N., and L. Roniger, *Patrons, Clients and Friends: Interpersonal Relations and the Structure of Trust in Society*. Cambridge: Cambridge University Press, 1984.

Eissfeldt, Otto. *The Old Testament: An Introduction*. New York: Harper & Row and Oxford: Blackwell, 1965.

Elliott, John H. *A Home for the Homeless: A Social Scientific Criticism of 1 Peter, Its Situation and Strategy*. 2nd ed. Minneapolis: Fortress, 1990.

———. "1 Peter, Its Situation and Strategy: A Discussion with David Balch." In *Perspectives on First John*, 61–78. Macon, GA: Mercer University Press, 1986.

Elsner, J. "Inventing Imperium: Texts and the Propaganda of Monuments in Augustan Rome." In *Art and Text in Roman Culture*, edited by J. Elsner, 32–35. Cambridge: Cambridge University Press, 1996.

Elwyn, S. "Interstate Kinship and Roman Foreign Policy." *TAPA* 123 (1993) 261–86.

Engberg-Pedersen, Troels, editor. *Paul Beyond the Judaism/Hellenism Divide*. Louisville: Westminster John Knox, 2001.

———. *Paul and the Stoics*. Louisville: Westminster John Knox, 2000.

———, editor. *Paul in His Hellenistic Context*. Edinburgh: Clark, 1994.

Ennius. *Annals of Quintus Ennius*. Edited by Otto Skutch. Oxford: Oxford University Press, 1985.

Enns, Peter. Exodus Retold: Ancient Exegesis of the Departure from Egypt in Wisdom 10:15–21 and 19:1–9. HSM 57. Atlanta: Scholars, 1997.

Epictetus. *Arrian's Discourses of Epictetus*. Edited by T. E. Page. Translated by W. A. Oldfather. Vol. 1. LCL. Cambridge: Harvard University Press, 1925.

Esler, Philip F. *Conflict and Identity in Romans: The Social Setting of Paul's Letter.* Minneapolis: Fortress, 2003.

———. *Galatians.* London: Routledge, 1998.

———. "'Keeping It in the Family': Culture, Kinship and Identity in 1Thessalonians and Galatians." In *Families and Family Relations as Represented in Early Judaisms and Early Christianities: Texts and Fictions*, edited by Jan Willem van Henten et al., 145–84. Leiden: Deo, 2000.

———. *Lazarus, Mary and Martha: Social Scientific Approaches to the Gospel of John.* Minneapolis: Fortress, 2006.

Evans, Craig A. "A Note on the "First-Born Son" of 4Q369." *Dead Sea Discoveries* 2.2 (1995) 185–201.

Faßbeck, Gabriele. "Tobit's Religious Universe between Kinship Loyalty and the Law of Moses." *JSJ* 36.2 (2005) 173–96.

Fasching, Darrell. *Narrative Theology After Auschwitz: From Alienation To Ethics.* Minneapolis: Augsburg Fortress, 1992.

Fitzmyer, Joseph A. "*Abba* and Jesus' Relation to God." In *A Cause de l'Evangile: Études sur les Synoptiques et Actes: Offertes au P. Jacques Dupont O. S. B. à l'occasion de son 70e anniversaire*, 14–38. Lectio Divina 123. Paris: Cerf, 1985.

Fee, G. D. "2 Corinthians 6:14–7:1 and Food Offered to Idols." *NTS* 23 (1976–77) 140–61.

Feldmeier, Reinhard. "The 'Nation' of Strangers: Social Contempt and Its Theological Interpretation in Ancient Judaism and Early Christianity." In *Ethnicity and the Bible*, edited by Mark G. Brett, 241–70. Leiden: Brill, 1996.

Fiorenza, E. Schüssler. *In Memory of Her: A Feminist Theological Reconstruction of Christian Origins.* New York: Crossroad, 1983.

Fishbane, M. *Biblical Interpretation in Ancient Israel.* Oxford: Clarendon, 1985.

Fisk, B. N. Review of Ben Witherington III, *Paul's Narrative Thought World. JBL* 115 (1996) 552–54.

Foley, J. M. *Immanent Art: From Structure to Meaning in Traditional Oral Epic.* Bloomington: Indiana University Press, 1991.

Forshey, Harold O. "The Construct Chain nahalat YHWH / 'elōhîm." *BASOR* 220 (1975) 51–53.

Fowl, Stephen E. *The Story of Christ in the Ethics of Paul: An Analysis of the Function of the Hymnic Material in the Pauline Corpus.* JSNTSup 36. Sheffield: Sheffield Academic, 1990.

Fox, Robin. *Kinship and Marriage: An Anthropological Perspective.* New York: Penguin, 1967.

Fox, Robin Lane. *Pagans and Christians.* San Francisco: Harper and Row, 1987.

Franklin, Sarah, and Susan Mckinnon, editors. *Relative Values: Reconfiguring Kinship Studies.* Durham: Duke University Press, 2001.

Frye, Northrop. *Anatomy of Criticism.* Princeton: Princeton University, 1957.

———. *Fables of Identity: Studies in Poetic Mythology.* New York: Brace & World, 1963.

———. *The Stubborn Structure of: Essays on Criticism and Society.* Ithaca: Cornell University, 1970.

Funk, Robert W. *Language, Hermeneutic, and Word of God: The Problem of Language in the New Testament and Contemporary Theology.* New York: Harper & Row, 1966.

Gardner, P. D. *The Gifts of God and the Authentication of a Christian: An Exegetical Study of 1 Corinthians 8:1—11:1.* Lanham, MD: University Press of America, 1994.

Garland, David E. *1 Corinthians*. BEC. Grand Rapids: Baker Academic, 2003.

———. *2 Corinthians*. NAC 29. Nashville: Broadman and Holman, 1999.

Gaventa, Beverly Roberts. *Our Mother Paul*. Louisville: Westminster John Knox, 2007.

Geertz, Clifford. *The Interpretation of Cultures: Selected Essays*. New York: Basic Books, 1973.

George, Timothy. *Galatians: An Exegetical and Theological Exposition of Holy Scripture*. NAC 30. Nashville: B & H, 1994.

Gerdmar, Anders. *Rethinking the Judaism–Hellenism Dichotomy: A Historiographical Case Study of Second Peter and Jude*. Stockholm: Almqvist and Wiksell, 2001.

Gileadi, Avraham. *The Literary Message of Isaiah*. New York: Hebraeus, 1964.

Gill, Christopher. "The School in the Roman Empire." In *The Cambridge Companion to the Stoics*, edited by Brad Inwood, 33–58. Cambridge: Cambridge University Press, 2003.

Gillis, J. *Commemorations: The Politics of National Identity*. Princeton: Princeton University Press, 1994.

Goldberg, Michael. *Theology and Narrative: A Critical Introduction*. Philadelphia: Trinity, 1991.

Goodenough, Ward. *Property, Kin and Community in Truk*. Yale University Publications in Anthropology, 46. New Haven, CT: Yale University Press, 1951.

Gottwald, Norman. *The Tribes of Yahweh: A Sociology of the Religion of Liberated Israel, 1250–1050 BCE*. Sheffield: Sheffield Academic, 1999.

Grabbe, Lester L. *Judaic Religion in the Second Temple Period: Belief and Practice from the Exile to Yavneh*. London: Routledge, 2000.

———. *Judaism from Cyrus to Hadrian*. Vol. 1: *The Persian and Greek Periods*. Minneapolis: Fortress, 1992.

———. *Judaism from Cyrus to Hadrian*. Vol. 2: *The Roman Period*. Minneapolis: Fortress, 1992.

Greenstein, E. L. "Mixing Memory and Design: Reading Psalm 78." *Prooftexts* 10 (1990) 197–218.

Gross, Claudia. "Kinship." In *Encyclopedia of Religion*, edited by Lindsay Jones, 5182–86. 2nd ed. Detroit: Gale, 2005.

Gruen, Erich S. "Fact and Fiction: Jewish Legends in a Hellenistic Context." In *Hellenistic Constructs: Essays in Culture, History, and Historiography*, edited by Paul Cartledge, et al., 72–88. Berkeley: University of California Press, 1997.

———. *Heritage and Hellenism: The Reinvention of Tradition*. Berkeley: University of California Press, 1998.

———. "The Jewish-Spartan Affiliation." In *Transitions to Empire: Essays in Greco-Roman History 360 B.C. in Honor of E. Badian*, edited by Robert W. Wallace et al., 254–70. Norman: University of Oklahoma Press, 1996.

Gumperz, John J., editor. *Language and Social Identity*. Cambridge: Cambridge University Press, 1982.

Gunilka, J. "Zum Gottesgedanken in der Jesusüberlieferung." In *Monotheismus und Christologie*, edited by H. J. Kaluck, 144–62. Freiburg: Herder, 1992.

Güven, Suna. "The Res Gestae of Augustus: A Monument of Imperial Image for All." *JSAH* 57.1 (1998) 3–45.

Habinek, Thomas N. *The Politics of Latin Literature: Writing, Identity, and Empire in Ancient Rome*. Princeton: Princeton University Press, 1998.

Hahn, Scott. "Covenant in the Old and New Testaments: Some Current Research (1994–2004)." *CBR* 3.2 (2005) 263–92.

———. *Kinship by Covenant: A Canonical Approach to the Fulfillment of God's Saving Promises*. New Haven, CT: Yale University Press, 2009.

Hall, Jonathan M. *Ethnic Identity in Greek Antiquity*. Cambridge: Cambridge University Press, 1997.

———. *Hellenicity: Between Ethnicity and Culture*. Chicago: The University of Chicago Press, 2002.

Hallbwachs, M. *The Collective Memory*. New York: Harper and Row, 1980.

Halpern-Amaru, Betsy. "God the Father in the Bible." In *God as Father?* Edited by Johannes-Baptist Metz and Edward Schillebeeckx. Edinburgh: T. & T. Clark, 1981.

———. *Rewriting the Bible: Land and Covenant in Postbiblical Jewish Literature*. Valley Forge, PA: Trinity, 1994.

Hamerton-Kelly, R. *God the Father: Theology and Patriarchy in the Teaching of Jesus*. Philadelphia: Fortress, 1979.

———. "God the Father in the Bible and in the Experience of Jesus: the State of the Question." In *God as Father?*, edited by Johannes-Baptist Metz and Edward Schillebeeckx, 95–102. New York: Seabury, 1981.

Hannestad, Niels. *Roman Art and Imperial Policy*. Aarhus: Aarhus University Press, 1988.

Hanson, K. C. "The Herodians and Mediterranean kinship. Part I: Genealogy and Descent." *BTB* 19 (1989a) 75–84.

———. "The Herodians and Mediterranean kinship. Part II: Marriage and Divorce." *BTB* 19 (1989b) 142–52.

———. "The Herodians and Mediterranean kinship. Part III: Economics." *BTB* 20 (1990) 10–21.

———. "Kinship." *The Social Sciences and New Testament Interpretation*. Edited by Richard Rohrbaugh. Peabody, MA: Hendrickson, 1996.

Hanson, K. C., and Douglas E. Oakman. *Palestine in the Time of Jesus: Social Structures and Social Conflicts*. Minneapolis: Fortress, 1998.

Hardwick, Lorna. "Concepts of Peace." In *Experiencing Rome: Culture, Identity and Power in the Roman Empire*, edited by Janet Huskinson, 335–68 London: Routledge, 2000.

Harland, Philip A. *Associations, Synagogues, and Congregations: Claiming a Place in Ancient Mediterranean Society*. Minneapolis: Fortress, 2003.

———. *Dynamics of Identity in the World of the Early Christians: Associations, Judeans, and Cultural Minorities*. New York: T. & T. Clark, 2009.

Harris, Murray J. *The Second Epistle to the Corinthians*. NIGTC. Grand Rapids: Eerdmans, 2005.

Hartley, John E. *Leviticus*. WBC. Dallas: Word, 1992.

Hauerwas, Stanley, and L. Gregory Jones, editors. *Why Narrative? Readings in Narrative Theology*. Grand Rapids: Eerdmans, 1989.

Hawthorne, Gerald F. *Philippians*. WBC43. Dallas: Word, 1983.

Hays, Richard. *Echoes of Scripture in the Letters of Paul*. New Haven, CT: Yale University Press, 1989.

———.*The Faith of Jesus Christ: The Narrative Substructure of Galatians 3:1-4:11*. 2nd ed. Grand Rapids: Eerdmans, 2002.

———. *First Corinthians: Interpretation: A Biblical Commentary for Teaching and Preaching*. Louisville: John Knox, 1997.

Hellerman, Joseph H. *The Ancient Church as Family*. Minneapolis: Fortress, 2001.

Hendel, Ronald. *Remembering Abraham: Culture, Memory, and History in the Hebrew Bible*. New York: Oxford University Press, 2005.

Hengel, Martin. *Jews, Greeks, Barbarians*. Philadelphia: Fortress, 1980.

———. *Judaism and Hellenism*. 2 vols. Philadelphia: Fortress, 1974.

———. *Judaism and Hellenism: Studies in their Encounter in Palestine during the Early Hellenistic Period*. Translated by John Bowden. London: SCM, 1974.

Henten, J. W. van, et al., editors. *Families and Family Relations as Represented in Early Judaisms and Early Christianities: Texts and Fictions*. Leiden: Deo, 2000.

Hill, Lisa. "The Two Republicae of the Roman Stoics: Can a Cosmopolite be a Patriot?" *Citizenship Studies* 4.1 (2000) 65–79.

Hinds, Stephen, and Thomas Schmitz. "Constructing Identities in the Roman Empire: Three Studies." *Millennium* (2007) 1–12.

Hodge, Caroline Johnson. *If Sons, Then Heirs: A Study of Kinship and Ethnicity in the Letters of Paul*. Oxoford: Oxford University Press, 2007.

Hofius, O. "Father." In *The New International Dictionary of* New *Testament Theology*, vol. 1, edited by Colin Brown, 614–21. Exeter: Paternoster, 1975.

Hogan, Pauline Nigh. *"No Longer Male and Female": Interpreting Galatians 3:28 in Early Christianity*. Library of New Testament Studies 380. Edited by Mark Goodacre: New York: T. & T. Clark, 2008.

Hogg, Michael A., and Dominic *Abrams. Social Identifications: A Social Psychology of Intergroup Relations and Group Processes*. London: Routledge, 1988.

Holladay, William L. *The Architecture of Jeremiah 1–20*. London: Associated University Presses, 1976.

———. *A Commentary on the Book of the Prophet Jeremiah Chapters 26–32*. Vol. 2. Minneapolis: Fortress, 1989.

Holiday, Peter J. "Roman Triumphal Paintings: Its Functions, Development, and Reception." *Art Bulletin* 79 (1997) 130–47.

Holmberg, Bengt, editor. *Exploring Early Christian Identity*. Tübingen: Mohr Siebeck, 2008.

Holy, Ladislav. *Anthropological Perspectives on Kinship*. London: Pluto, 1996.

Homer. *The Iliad*. Translated by A. T. Murray. Vol. 1. 2nd ed. revised by William F. Waytt. LCL. Cambridge: Harvard University Press, 1999.

———. *The Odyssey*. Translated by A. T. Murray. 2 vols. Revised by George E. Dmiock. LCL. Cambridge: Harvard University Press, 1995.

Horace. *The Odes and Epodes*. Translated by C. E. Bennett. Loeb Classical Library. Cambridge: Harvard University Press, 1927.

Horrell, David G. "Becoming Christian": Solidifying Christian Identity and Content." In *Handbook of Early Christianity: Social Science Approaches*, edited by Anthony J. Blasi, et al., 309–35. Walnut Creek, CA: AltaMira, 2002.

———. "From ἀδελφός to οἶκος θεου: Social Transformation in Pauline Christianity." *JBL* 120.2 (2001) 293–311.

———. *An Introduction to the Study of Paul*. London: Continuum, 2000.

Horsley, Greg H. R. *New Documents Illustrating Early Christianity*. Volume 4. *A Review of the Greek Inscriptions and Papyri Published in 1979*. New South Wales: Macquarie University, 1987.

———. *New Documents Illustrating Early Christianity*. Volume 1. *A Review of the Greek Inscriptions and Papyri Published in 1976*. New South Wales: Macquarie University, 1981.

Horsley, Richard A., editor. *Paul and the Roman Imperial Order*. Harrisburg, PA: Trinity, 2004.

———. *Jesus and Empire: The Kingdom of God and the New World Disorder*. Minneapolis: Fortress, 2003.

———, editor. *Paul and Politics: Ekklesia, Israel, Imperium, Interpretation*. Harrisburg, PA: Trinity, 2000.

———, editor. *Paul and Empire: Religion and Power in Roman Imperial Society*. Harrisburg, PA: Trinity, 1997.

Hove, Richard. *Equality in Christ? Galatians 3:28 and the Gender Dispute*. Wheaton: Crossway, 1999.

Howard, Judith A. "Social Psychology of Identities." *ARS* 26 (2000) 369–91.

Hubbard, David A. "Hope in the Old Testament." *TynBul* 34 (1983) 33–59.

Huskinson, Janet. "Looking for Culture, Identity and Power." In *Experiencing Rome: Culture, Identity and Power in the Roman Empire*, edited by Janet Huskinson, 3–27. London: Routledge, 2000.

Hyatt, J. Philip. "Jeremiah and Deuteronomy." In *A Prophet to the Nations: Essays in Jeremiah Studies*, edited by Leo G. Perdue, et al., 113–28. Winona Lake, IN: Eisenbrauns, 1984.

Inwood, Brad. *The Cambridge Companion to the Stoics*. Cambridge: Cambridge University Press, 2003.

———. "Stoicism." In *From Aristotle to Augustine: Routledge History of Philosophy*, edited by David Furley, 222–51. London: Routledge, 1999.

Iser, Wolfgang. *The Implied Reader: Patterns of Communication in Prose Fiction from Bunyan to Beckett*. Baltimore and London: The Johns Hopkins University Press, 1974.

———. *The Range of Interpretation*. New York: Columbia University Press, 2000.

Jauss, Hans Robert. *Toward an Aesthetic of Reception*. Translated by Timothy Bahti. Minneapolis: University of Minnesota Press, 1982.

Jenkins, Richard. *Social Identity*. 3rd ed. London: Routledge, 2008.

Jeremias, Joachim. *Abba: Studien zur Neutestamentilichen Theologie und Zeitgeschichte*. Göttingen: Vandenhoeck and Ruprecht, 1966.

———. *The Central Message of the New Testament*. London: SCM, 1965.

———. *Jesus and the Message of the New Testament*. Edited by K. C. Hanson. Minneapolis: Fortress, 2002.

———. *The Prayers of Jesus*. Philadelphia: Fortress, 1978.

———. *New Testament Theology: Part One-The Proclamation of Jesus*. London: SCM, 1971.

Jewett, Robert. *Romans: A Commentary, Hermeneia: A Critical and Historical Commentary on the Bible*. Edited by Eldon Jay Epp. Minneapolis: Fortress, 2007.

Johnson, M. D. *The Purpose of the Biblical Genealogies*. New York: Cambridge University, 1969.

Johnstone, William. *1 and 2 Chronicles*. Volume 1. Sheffield: Sheffield Academic, 1997.

Jokiranta, Jutta. "Social Identity Approach: Identity-Constructing Elements in the Psalms Pesher." In *Defining Identities: We, You, and the Other in the Dead Sea*

Scrolls: Proceedings of the Fifth Meeting of the IOQS in Groningen, edited by Florentino García Martínez et al., 85–110. Leiden: Brill, 2008.

Jones, Christopher P. *Kinship Diplomacy in the Ancient World.* Cambridge: Harvard University Press, 1999.

Jones, Douglas Rawlinson. *Jeremiah.* NCBC. Grand Rapids: Eerdmans, 1992.

Josephus. Translated by H. St. J. Thackeray, et. al. 10 vols. LCL. Cambridge: Harvard University Press, 1929–1965.

Joubert, Stephan F. "Managing the Household: Paul as Paterfamilias of the Christian Household Group in Corinth" In *Modeling Early Christianity: Social Scientific Studies of the New Testament in Its Context*, edited by Philip F. Esler, 208–18. London: Routledge, 1995.

Judge, E. *The Social Pattern of the Christian Groups in the First Century: Some Prolegomena to the Study of New Testament Ideas of Social Obligation.* London: Tyndale, 1960.

Kaiser, W. C. "The Blessing of David: The Charter for Humanity." In *The Law and the Prophets.* Edited by J. H. Skilton. Nutley: Presbyterian and Reformed, 1974.

Kalluveettil, P. "Covenant and Community: Insights into the Relational Aspect of Covenant." *Jeevadhara* 11 (1981) 94–104.

———. *Declaration and Covenant.* Rome: Biblical Institute Press, 1982.

Kamudzandu, Israel. "Abraham as a Spiritual Ancestor in Romans 4 in the Context of the Roman Appropriation of Ancestors: Some Implications of Paul's Use of Abraham for Shona Christians in Postcolonial Zimbabwe." PhD diss., Brite Divinity School, 2007.

Katherine, Clark. "Universal Perspective on Historiography." In *The Limits of Historiography: Genre and Narrative in Ancient Historical Texts*, edited by Christina Shuttleworth Kraus, 249–79. Leiden: Köln, 1999.

Keesing, Roger M. *Kin Groups and Social Structures.* New York: Holt, Rinehart and Winston, 1975.

Keiser, Thomas. "The Song of Moses a Basis for Isaiah's Prophecy." *VT* 55 (2005) 486–500.

Kelber, Werner H. "Roman Imperialism and Early Christian Scribality." In *Postcolonial Biblical Reader*, edited by R. S. Sugirtharajah, 96–111. Oxford: Blackwell, 2006.

Kelly, Raymond C. *Constructing Inequality: The Fabrication of a Hierarchy of Virtue among the Etoro.* Michigan: The University of Michigan Press, 1993.

Keown, Gerald L. *Jeremiah 26–52.* WBC. Dallas: Word, 2002.

Kermode, Frank. *The Sense of an Ending: Studies in the Theory of Fiction.* New York: Oxford University Press, 1966.

Kim, Seyoon. *Christ and Caesar: The Gospel and the Roman Empire in the Writings of Paul and Luke.* Grand Rapids: Eerdmans, 2008.

Kirk, Alan K. "Karl Polanyi, Marshall Sahlins, and the Study of Ancient Social Relations." *JBL* 126.1 (2007) 182–91.

———. "Peasant Wisdom, the 'Our Father,' and the Origins of Christianity." *TJT* 15 (1999) 31–50.

Knibb, Michael A. "Messianism in the Pseudepigrapha in the Light of the Scrolls." *Dead Sea Discoveries* 2.2 (1995) 165–84.

Koehler, Ludwig, and Walter Baumgartner. *The Hebrew and Aramaic Lexicon of the Old Testament.* Revised by Walter Baumgartner and Johann Jakob Stamm. Translated and edited under the supervision of M. E. J. Richardson, in collaboration with G. J. Jongeling-Vos and L. J. de Regt. 2 vols. Leiden: Brill, 2001.

Koop, Raymond Carl. "God as Father in the Synoptic Gospels and Pauline Literature: A Comparison and Differentiation." PhD diss., Golden Gate Baptist Theological Seminary, 1989.

Korostelina, Karina V. *Social Identity and Conflict: Structures, Dynamics, and Implications.* New York: Palgrave Macmillan, 2007.

Krasser, Helmut. "Shifting Identities: Knowledge and the Construction of Social Roles in the Roman Empire." *Millennium* (2007) 43–62.

Kristeva, Julia. "The Bounded Text." In *Desire in Language: A Semiotic Approach to Literature and Art*, edited by Leon S. Roudiez, 36–63. New York: Colombia University Press, 1980.

Kruse, Heinz. "David's Covenant." *VT* 35.2 (1985) 139–64.

Kugel, James L. *The Idea of Biblical Poetry: Parallelism and its History.* Baltimore: Johns Hopkins University Press, 1998.

Labuschagne, C. J. "The Song of Moses: Its Framework and Structure." In *De Fructu Oris Sui: Essays in Honour of Adrianus Van Selms*, edited by. I. H. Eybers et al., 85–98. Leiden: Brill, 1971.

Lacey, W. K. "Patria Potestas." In *The Family in Ancient Rome: New Perspectives*, edited by B. Rawson, 121–44. Ithaca: Cornell University Press, 1986.

Lane, William L. "Social Perspectives on Roman Christianity during the Formative Years from Nero to Nerva: Romans, Hebrews, 1 Clement." In *Judaism and Christianity in First-Century Rome*, edited by Karl P. Donfried, et al.,196–244. Grand Rapids: Eerdmans, 1998.

Lee, Dorothy. "Beyond Suspicion? The Fatherhood of God in the Fourth Gospel." *Pacifica* 8 (1985) 140–54.

Lee, Michelle. *Paul, the Stoics, and the Body of Christ.* Cambridge: Cambridge University Press, 2006.

Levenson, Jon D. "The Universal Horizon of Biblical Particularism." In *Ethnicity and the Bible*, edited by Mark G. Brett, 143–70. Leiden: Brill, 1996.

Lewis, Lloyd Alexander. "'As a Beloved Brother,': The Function of Family Language in the Letters of Paul." PhD diss., Yale University, 1985.

Liddell H. G., and R. Scott. "πάτρα." In *Greek-English Lexicon with a Revised Supplement*, rev. ed., 1348. Oxford: Clarendon, 1996.

Lieu, Judith M. *Christian Identity in the Jewish and Graeco-Roman World.* Oxford: Oxford University Press, 2004.

———. "'Impregnable Ramparts and Walls of Iron': Boundary and Identity in Early 'Judaism' and 'Christianity.'" *NTS* 48 (2002) 297–313.

Lincoln, Andrew T. "Abraham Goes to Rome: Paul's Treatment of Abraham in Romans 4." In *Worship, Theology and Ministry in the Early in the Early Church: Essays in Honor of Ralph P. Martin*, edited by Michael J. Wilkins, 163–79. Sheffield: Sheffield Academic, 1992.

Lincoln, B. *Discourse and the Construction of Society: Comparative Studies of Myth, Ritual, and Classification.* New York: Oxford University Press, 1989.

Livy. *Histories: From The Founding of the City.* Edited by T. E. Page. Translated by Evan T. Sage. LCL. Cambridge: Harvard University Press, 1955.

Long, A. A. *Epictetus: A Stoic and Socratic Guide to Life.* Oxford: Clarendon, 2002.

Long, A. A., and D. N. Sedley. *The Hellenistic Philosophers*. Vols. 1 and 2. Cambridge: Cambridge University Press, 1987.

Longenecker, Richard N. *Galatians*. WBC. Dallas: Word, 2002.

———. "Narrative Interest in the Study of Paul: Retrospective and Prospective." In *Narrative Dynamics in Paul: A Critical Assessment*, edited by Richard N. Longenecker 3–16. Louisville: Westminster John Knox, 2002.

Luce, T. J. "Livy, Augustus, and the Forum Augustum." In *Between Republic and Empire: Interpretations of Augustus and His Principate*, edited by Kurt A. Raaflaub et al., 213–38. Berkeley: University of California, 1990.

Lust, Johan, Erik Eynikel, and Kartin Hauspie. *Greek-English Lexicon of the Septuagint*. Rev. ed. Stuttgart: Deutsche Bibelgesellschaft, 1992–1996.

Lutz, Cora E. *Musonius Rufus: "The Roman Socrates."* New Haven, CT: Yale University Press, 1947.

Lyall, F. "Roman Law in the Writings of Paul." *JBL* 87 (1969) 456–68.

———. *Slaves, Citizens and Sons: Legal Metaphors in the Epistles*. Grand Rapids: Zondervan, 1984.

Lyons, George. *Pauline Autobiography: Toward a New Understanding*. Atlanta: Scholars Press, 1985.

Malherbe, Abraham J. "Hellenistic Moralists and the New Testament." In *Aufstieg und Niedergang der Romischen Welt II*. 26.1., edited by Wolfgang Hasse, 267–333. Berlin: De Gruyter, 1992.

———. "Graeco-Roman Religion and Philosophy and the New Testament." In *The New Testament and Its Modern Interpreters*, edited by Eldon Jay Epp et al., 3–26. Atlanta: Scholars Press, 1989.

———. *The Letters of Paul to the Thessalonians: A New Translation with Introduction and Commentary*. AB 32B; New York: Doubleday, 2000.

———. *Paul and the Popular Philosophers*. Minneapolis: Fortress, 1989.

———. *Paul and the Thessalonians: The Philosophic Tradition of Pastoral Care*. Philadelphia: Fortress, 1987.

Malina, Bruce J. *The New Testament World: Insights from Cultural Anthropology*. 3rd ed. Louisville: Westminster John Knox, 2001.

———. "Patron and Client: The Analogy behind Synoptic Theology." *The Social World of Jesus*. London: Routledge, 1996.

———. "What is a Prayer?" *The Bible Today* 18.4 (1980) 214–20.

Malul, M. "Foundlings and their Adoption in the Bible and in Mesopotamian Documents: A Study of Several Legal Metaphors in Ezek 16:1–7." *JSOT* 46 (1990) 97–126.

Marshall, Mac. "The Nature of Nurture." *AE* vol. 4:4 (1977) 643–62.

Martin, Dale B. *The Corinthian Body*. New Haven, CT: Yale University Press, 1995.

———. "Paul and the Judaism/Hellenism Dichotomy: Toward a Social History of the Question." In *Paul Beyond the Judaism/Hellenism Divide*, edited by Troels Engberg-Pedersen 29–62. Louisville: Westminster John Knox, 2001.

———. *Slavery as Salvation: The Metaphor of Slavery in Pauline Christianity*. New Haven, CT: Yale University, 1990.

Martínez, Florentino García, et al., editors. *The Dead Sea Scrolls: Study Edition*. 2 vols. Leiden: Brill, 1997.

Martyn, J. Louis. *Galatians: A New Translation with Introduction and Commentary*. AB. New York: Doubleday, 1997.

Mason, Rex. *Old Testament Pictures of God*. Regent's Study Guides 2. Macon, GA: Smyth and Helwys, 1993.

Matera, J. Frank. *Galatians*. Edited by Daniel J. Harrington. Collegeville, MN: Liturgical, 1992.

Matlock, R. Barry. "The Arrow and the Web." In *Narrative Dynamics in Paul: Critical Assessment*, edited by Bruce W. Longenecker, 44–57. Louisville: Westminster John Knox, 2002.

Mattingly, Harold. *Coins of the Roman Empire in the British Museum*. Vol. 1: *Augustus to Vitellius*. London: British Museum, 1965–66.

———. *Coins of the Roman Empire in the British Museum*. Vol. 2: *Vespasian to Domitian*. London: British Museum, 1965–66.

Mawhinney, Allen. "Huiothesia in the Pauline Epistles: Its Background, Use and Implications." PhD diss., Baylor University, 1982.

———. "God as Father: Two Popular Theories Reconsidered." *JETS* 31 (1988) 181–89.

McCarthy, Dennis J. "Notes on the Love of God in Deuteronomy and the Father-Son Relationship between Yahweh and Israel." *CBQ* 27 (1965) 144–47.

———. *Treaty and Covenant*. 2nd ed. Rome: Biblical Institute Press, 1978.

McConville, J. G. *Deuteronomy*. Edited by David W. Baker and Gordon J. Wenham. Leicester: Apollos, 2002.

———. *Judgment and Promise: An Interpretation of the Book of Jeremiah*. Leicester: Apollos, 1993.

McKenzie, S. L., and H. N. Wallace. "Covenant Themes in Malachi." *CBQ* 45 (1983) 551–52.

Meeks, W. A. *The First Urban Christians: The Social World of the Apostle Paul*. New Haven, CT: Yale University Press, 1983.

———. "Judaism, Hellenism and the Birth of Christianity." *In Paul Beyond the Judaism/Hellenism Divide*, edited by Troels Engberg-Pedersen, 17–27. Louisville: Westminster John Knox, 2001.

———. *The Moral World of the First Christians*. Philadelphia: Westminster Press, 1986.

Mendenhall, George E. "Samuel's Broken Rib: Deuteronomy 32." In *A Song of Power and the Power of Song: Essays on the Book of Deuteronomy*, edited by Duane L. Christensen, 169–80. Winona Lake, IN: Eisenbrauns, 1993.

———. "Social Organization in Early Israel." In *Magnalia Dei: Essays on the Bible and Archeology in Memory of G. Ernest Wright*, edited by F. M. Cross, et al., 132–51. Garden City, NY: Doubleday, 1979.

———. *The Tenth Generation: The Origins of Biblical Tradition*. Baltimore: Johns Hopkins University Press, 1973.

Merrill, Eugene H. *Deuteronomy*. NAC 4. Broadman and Holman, 1994.

Metzger, Bruce M. and Roland E. Murphy, eds. *The New Oxford Annotated Bible with the Apocryphal/Deuterocanonical Books*. NRSV. New York: Oxford University Press, 1991.

Meyer, Ben F. *Christus Faber: The Master Builder and the House of God*. Princeton Theological Monograph Series 29. Allison Park, PA: Pickwick, 1992.

———. *Critical Realism and the New Testament*. Princeton Theological Monograph Series 17. Allison Park, PA: Pickwick, 1989.

———. *The Early Christians: Their World Mission and Self-Discovery*. Wilmington, DE: Michael Glazier, 1986.

Meyers, Carol. "The Family in Early Israel." In *Families in Ancient Israel*, edited by Leo G. Perdue, et al., 1–49. Louisville: Westminster John Knox, 1997.

Miles, Richard. "Communicating Culture, Identity and Power." In *Experiencing Rome: Culture, Identity and Power in the Roman Empire*, edited by Janet Huskinson, 29–62. London: Routledge, 2000.

Miller, J. W. *Biblical Faith and Fathering*. New York: Paulist, 1989.

———. "God as Father in the Bible and the Father Image in Several Contemporary Ancient Near Eastern Myths: A Comparison." *Studies in Religion/Sciences Religieuses* 14. 3 (1985) 347–54.

Miller, Patrick D. *Deuteronomy: Interpretation: A Biblical Commentary for Teaching and Preaching*. Louisville: John Knox, 1999.

Mills, Watson E. "*Galatians*." In *Bibliographies for Biblical Research*, 38–45. Lewiston, NY: Mellen, 1999.

Minear, P. S. *Images of the Church in the New Testament*. Philadelphia: Westminster, 1960.

Mink, Louis O. "History and Fiction as Modes of Comprehension." In *Historical Understanding*, edited by Brain Fay, et al., 42–60. Cornell University Press, 1987.

Mitchell, Margaret M. *Paul and the Rhetoric of Reconciliation: An Exegetical Investigation of the Language and Composition of 1 Corinthians*. HUT 28. Tübingen: Mohr, 1991.

Moo, Douglas. *The Epistle to the Romans*. NICNT. Grand Rapids: Eerdmans, 1996.

Moore, G. F. "Christian Writers on Judaism." *HTR* 14 (1921) 197–254.

Montefiore, H. W. "God as Father in the Synoptic Gospels." *NTS* 3 (1956) 31–46.

Morford, Mark. *The Roman Philosophers: From Cato the Censor to the Death of Marcus Aurelius*. London: Routledge, 2002.

Morgan, Lewis Henry. *Ancient Society*. New York: Holt, 1877.

———. *Systems of Consanguinity and Affinity of the Human Family*. Washington: Smithsonian Institution Press, 1870.

Motyer, Alec J. *Prophecy of Isaiah: An Introduction and Commentary*. Downers Grove, IL: InterVarsity, 1993.

Mowery, Robert L. "The Activity of God in the Gospel of Matthew." *SBLSP* (1989) 400–411.

———. "The Disappearance of the Father: The References to God the Father in Luke-Acts." *Encounter* 55.4 (1994) 353–58.

———. "From Lord to Father in Matthew 1–7." *CBQ* 59.4 (1997) 642–56.

———. "God the Father in Luke-Acts." In *New Views on Luke and Acts*, 124–32. Collegeville, MN: Liturgical, 1990.

———. "God, Lord, and Father: The Theology of the Gospel of Matthew." *BRev* 33 (1988) 24–36.

———. "Lord, God, and Father: Theological Language in Luke-Acts." *SBLSP* 34 (1995) 82–101.

Moxnes, Halvor, editors. *Constructing Early Christian Families: Family as Social Reality and Metaphor*. London: Routledge, 1997.

———. *The Economy of the Kingdom*. Philadelphia: Fortress, 1988.

Muilenburg, James. "Father and Son." In *Hearing and Speaking the Word: Selections from the Works of James Muilenburg*, edited by Thomas F. Best, 177–87. Chico, CA: Scholars Press, 1984.

Murphy-O'Connor, J. *Paul the Letter Writer*. Collegeville, MN: Liturgical, 1995.

———. "Relating 2 Corinthians 6:14–7:1 to Its Context." *NTS* 33 (1987) 272–75.

Musonius Rufus. *Musonius Rufus: The Roman Socrates.* Translated by Cora E. Luz. Vol. 10. Yale Classical Studies. New Haven, CT: Yale University Press, 1947.

Nathan, Geoffrey. *The Family in Late Antiquity: The Rise of Christianity and the Endurance of Tradition.* London: Routledge, 2000.

Nelson, Richard D. *Deuteronomy: A Commentary.* Louisville: John Knox, 2002.

Newsom, Carol A. "Constructing 'We, You, and the Others' through Non-Polemical Discourse." In *Defining Identities: We, You, and the Other in the Dead Sea Scrolls: Proceedings of the Fifth Meeting of the IOQS in Groningen*, edited by Florentino García Martínez, et al., 13–22. Leiden: Brill, 2008.

Neyrey, Jerome H. "God, Benefactor and Patron: The Major Cultural Model for Interpreting the Deity in Greco-Roman Antiquity." *JSNT* 27.4 (2005) 465–92.

———. "Loss of Wealth, Loss of Family and Loss of Honor." In *Modeling Early Christianity: Social Scientific Studies of the New Testament in its Context*, edited by Philip E. Esler, 139–58. London: Routledge, 1995.

Nguyen, V. Henry T. *Christian Identity in Corinth: A Comparative Study of 2 Corinthians, Epictetus and Valerius Maximus.* WUNT, 2 Reihe 243. Tübingen: Mohr Siebeck, 2008.

Nickelsburg, George W. E. *Jewish Literature between the Bible and the Mishnah.* 2nd ed. Minneapolis: Fortress, 2005.

Nock, A. D. *Conversion: The Old and the New in Religion from Alexander the Great to Augustine of Hippo.* Oxford: Oxford University Press, 1933.

———. "The Historical Importance of Cult-Associations." *Classical Review* 38 (1924) 105–109.

Nunnally, Waverly E. "The Fatherhood of God at Qumran." PhD diss., Hebrew Union College–Jewish Institute of Religion, 1992.

Oakes, Peter "Re-mapping the Universe: Paul and the Emperor in 1 Thessalonians and Philippians." *JSNT* 27.3 (2005) 301–22.

O'Brien, Peter T. *The Epistle to the Philippians. New International Greek Testament Commentary.* Grand Rapids: Eerdmans, 1991.

O'Day, Gail R. "John" In *Women's Bible Commentary*, edited by Carol A. Newsom et al., 392–93. Westminster John Knox, 1998.

———. "Show Us the Father, and We Will Be Satisfied." *Semeia* 85: *God the Father in the Gospel of John*, edited by Adele Reinhartz (1999) 11–17.

Oden, R. A. "Jacob as Father, Husband, and Nephew: Kinship Studies and the Patriarchal Narrative." *JBL* 102 (1983) 189–205.

Olson, Dennis T. *Deuteronomy and the Death of Moses: A Theological Reading.* Minneapolis: Augsburg Fortress, 1994.

Osiek, Carolyn. "The Feminist and the Bible: Hermeneutical Alternatives." In *Feminist Perspective on Biblical Scholarship*, edited by Adela Y. Collins, 93–106. Chico, CA: Scholars Press, 1985.

———. *Philippians and Philemon.* Abingdon New Testament Commentaries. Nashville: Abingdon, 2000.

———. "The Politics of Patronage and the Politics of Kinship: The Meeting of the Ways." *BTB*, 39.3 (2009) 143–52.

Ovid. *Fasti.* Translated by Sir James George Frazer. LCL. Cambridge: Harvard University Press, 1931.

———. *Metamorphoses.* Translated by Frank Justus Miller. LCL. London: W. Heinemann, 1934.

———. *Tristia: Ex Ponto*. Translated by Arthur Leslie Wheeler. LCL. Cambridge: Harvard University Press,1924.

Pangle, Thomas L. "Socratic Cosmopolitanism: Cicero's Critique and Transformation of the Stoic Ideal." *CJPS* 31.2 (June 1998) 235–62.

Parkin, Robert, and Linda Stone, editors. *Kinship and Family: An Anthropological Reader*. Malden, MA: Blackwell, 2004.

Patai, Raphael. *Sex and Family in the Bible and the Middle East*. New York: Macmillan, 1959.

Patterson, Orlando. *Slavery and Social Death: A Comparative Study*. Cambridge: Harvard University Press, 1982.

Payne, Philip B. *Man and Woman One in Christ: An Exegetical and Theological Study of Paul's Letters*. Grand Rapids: Zondervan, 2009.

Peletz, Michael G. "Ambivalence in Kinship since the 1940s." In *Relative Values: Reconfiguring Kinship Studies*, edited by Sarah Franklin et al., 413–44. Durham, NC: Duke University Press, 2001.

Perdue, Leo G, et al., editors. *Families in Ancient Israel*. Louisville: Westminster, 1997.

———. "The Household, Old Testament Theology, and Contemporary Hermeneutics." In *Families in Ancient Israel*, edited by Leo G. Perdue, et al., 223–58. Louisville: Westminster John Knox, 1997.

———. "The Israelite and Early Jewish Family." In *Families in Ancient Israel*, edited by Perdue, Leo G, et al., 163–222. Louisville: Westminster John Knox, 1997.

Petersen, N. R. *Rediscovering Paul: Philemon and the Sociology of Paul's Narrative World*. Philadelphia: Fortress, 1985.

Philo. Translated by F. H. Colson and G. H. Whitaker. 10 vols. LCL. Cambridge: Harvard University Press, 1929–1961.

Pitt-Rivers, J. "The Kith and the Kin." In *Character of Kinship*, edited by J. Goody, 89–105. Cambridge: Cambridge University Press, 1973.

Pliny. *Natural History*. Edited by T. E. Page. Translated by H. Rackham. Vol. 2. LCL. Cambridge: Harvard University Press, 1942.

Pliny the Younger. *Letters, and Panegyricus*. Translated by Betty Radice. 2 vols. LCL. Cambridge: Harvard University Press, 1969.

Plutarch. *Moralia*. Edited by Jeffrey Henderson. Translated by Frank Cole Babbitt. Vol. 4. LCL. Cambridge: Harvard University Press, 1936.

Pomykala, Kenneth E. *The Davidic Dynasty Tradition in Early Judaism: Its History and Significance for Messianism*. Society of Biblical Literature Early Judaism and Its Literature 7. Atlanta: Scholars Press, 1995.

Quint, David. *Epic and Empire: Politics and Generic Form from Virgil to Milton*. Princeton: Princeton University Press, 1993.

Quintilian. *The Institutio Oratoria of Quintilian*. Translated by H. E. Butler. Vol. 3. Cambridge, MA: Harvard University Press, 1922.

Rad, Gerhard von. *Deuteronomy. Old Testament Library*. Philadelphia: Westminster, 1966.

Rajak, Tesa. *The Jewish Dialogue with Greece and Rome: Studies in Cultural and Social Interaction*. Leiden: Brill, 2001.

Reinhartz, Adele. "And the Word Was Begotten: Divine Epigenesis in the Gospel of John." *Semeia* 85 (1999) 83–105.

———. "Introduction: 'Father' as Metaphor in the Fourth Gospel." *Semeia* 85: *God the Father in the Gospel of John*, edited by Adele Reinhartz (1999) 1–10.

Renan, E. "What is a Nation?" In *Nation and Narration*, edited by H. Bhabha, 8–22. London: Routledge, 1990.

Res Gestae Divi Augusti. Translated by Frederick W. Shipley. LCL. London: W. Heinemann, 1924.

Richards, Randolph. *Paul and First Century Letter Writing: Secretaries, Composition and Collection*. Downers Grove, IL: InterVarsity, 2004.

Riches, John. *Conflicting Mythologies: Identity Formation in the Gospel of Mark and Matthew*. Edinburgh: T. & T. Clark, 2000.

Ricoeur, Paul. "Biblical Hermeneutics." *Semeia* 4 (1975) 29–148.

———. "The Narrative Function." *Semeia* 13 (1978) 37–56, 183–84.

Robbins, Vernon K., and David B. Gowler. "Introduction." In *Recruitment, Conquest, and Conflict: Strategies in Judaism, Early Christianity, and Greco-Roman World*, edited by Peder Borgen, et al., 1–13. Atlanta: Scholars Press, 1998.

Robert, Parkin, and Linda Stone, editors. *Kinship and Family: An Anthropological Reader*. Malden, MA: Blackwell, 2004.

Rubin, Donald L. *Composing Social Identity in Written Language*. Hillsdale, NJ: Lawrence Erlbaum, 1995.

Rudolph, Kurt. "Early Christianity as a Religious-Historical Phenomenon." In *The Future of Early Christianity: Essays in Honor of Helmut Koester*, edited by Birger A. Pearson, 9–19. Minneapolis: Fortress, 1991.

Rüpke, Jörg. "Kalender und Öffentlichkeit. Die Geschichte der Repräsentation und religiösen Qualification von Zeit in Ro." In *Religionsgeschichtliche Versuche und Vorarbeiten*, 165-188. Berlin, 1995.

Ruether, Rosemary Radford. *Sexism and God-Talk: Toward a Feminist Theology*. Boston: Beacon, 1983.

Ruiten, J. T. van Primaeval History Interpreted: *The Rewriting of Genesis 1–11 in the Book of Jubilees*. Leiden: Brill, 2000.

Sakenfeld, Katerine Doob. "Feminist Uses of Biblical Materials." In *Feminist Interpretation of the Bible*, edited by Letty M. Russell, 55–64. Philadelphia: Westminster, 1985.

Saller, Richard. "Roman Kinship: Structure and Sentiment." In *The Roman Family: Status, Sentiment, Space*, edited by Beryl Rawson and Paul Weaver, 7–34. Oxford: Clarendon, 1997.

Sanders, E. P. *Paul, the Law and the Jewish People*. Minneapolis: Fortress, 1983.

———, editor. *Jewish and Christian Self-Definition: The Shaping of Christianity in the Second and Third Centuries*. Vol. 1. Philadelphia: Fortress, 1980.

Sander, James A. "Torah and Christ." *Interpretation* 29 (1975) 372–90.

Sanders, Paul. *The Provenance of Deuteronomy 32*. Oudtestamentische Studiën 3. Leiden: Brill, 1996.

Sandnes, Karl Olav. "Equality within Patriarchal Structures: Some New Testament Perspectives on the Christian Fellowship as a Brother or Sisterhood and Family." In *Constructing Early Christian Families: Family as Social Reality and Metaphor*, edited by Halvor Moxnes, 150–65. New York: Routledge, 1997.

———. *A New Family: Conversion and Ecclesiology in the Early Church with Cross-Cultural Comparisons*. Studies in the Intercultural History of Christianity 91. Bern: Lang, 1994.

Sarna, Nahum M. "Psalm 89: A Study in Inner Biblical Exegesis." In *Biblical and Other Studies*, 29–46. Cambridge: Harvard University Press, 1963.

Scheffler, H. W. "Kinship, Descent, and Alliance." In *Handbook of Social and Cultural Anthropology*, 749. Chicago: Rand McNally, 1973.

Schilinder, Alfred. "Gott als Vater in Theologie und Liturgie des christlichen Antike." *Das Vaterbild im Abendland.* Edited by Hubertus Tellenbach. Stuttgart: W. Kohlhammer, 1988.

Schmidt, F. *How the Temple Thinks: Identity and Social Cohesion in Ancient Judaism.* Translated by J. E. Crowley. Sheffield: Sheffield Academic, 2001.

Schmitt, John J. "Israel as Son of God in Torah." *BTB* 34 (2004) 69–79.

Schneider, David M. *American Kinship: A Cultural Account.* Englewood Cliffs: Prentice-Hall, 1968.

———. "What is Kinship All About?" In *Kinship and Family: An Anthropological Reader*, edited by Robert Parkin et al., 257–74. Malden, MA: Blackwell, 2004.

Schneider, G. "τέκνον." In *EDNT* 3, edited by Horst Balz and Gerhard Schneider, 341–42. Grand Rapids: Eerdmans, 1990–1993.

Schnelle, Udo. *Apostle Paul: His Life and Theology.* Translated by M. Eugene Boring. Grand Rapids: Baker Academic, 2005.

Schniedewind, William M. *Society and the Promise to David: The Reception History of 2 Samuel 7:1–17.* New York: Oxford University Press, 1999.

Schofield, Malcolm. "Social and Political Thought." In *The Cambridge History of Hellenistic Philosophy*, edited by Algra, Keimpe, et al., 739–70. Cambridge: Cambridge University Press, 1999.

Scholes, Robert, and Robert Kellogg. *The Nature of Narrative.* New York: Oxford University Press, 1966.

Schuller, Eileen. "4Q372 1: A Text about Joseph." *Römische Quartalschrift für christliche Altertumskunde und Kirchengeschichte,* 14/55 (1990) 343–70.

———. "The Psalm of 4Q372 1 Within the Context of Second Temple Prayer." *CBQ* 54 (1992) 67–79.

Schweitzer, Albert. *Mysticism of Paul the Apostle.* Translated by William Montgomery. London: A & C Black, 1931.

Scott, J. M. *Adoption as Sons of God: An Investigation into the Background of HUIOTHESIA*. WUNT 52.48. Tübingen: Mohr, 1992.

Segal, Michael. *The Book of Jubilees: Rewritten Bible, Redaction, Ideology and Theology.* Leiden: Brill, 2007.

Seneca. *De Clementia.* Translated by John W. Basore. LCL. London: W. Heinemann, 1928–1935.

———. *De Otio; De Brevitate Vitae.* Edited by G. D. Williams. Cambridge Greek and Latin Classics. Cambridge: Cambridge University Press, 2003.

———. *Epistles.* Edited by G. P. Goold. Translated by Richard M. Gummere. Cambridge: Harvard University Press, 1920.

———. *On Benefits.* Edited by G. P. Goold. Translated by Richard M. Gummere. Cambridge: Harvard University Press, 1920.

Sevenster, J. N. *Paul and Seneca.* Leiden: Brill, 1961.

Severy, Beth. *Augustus and the Family at The Birth of The Roman Empire.* New York: Routledge, 2003.

Shaw, B. D. "The Divine Economy: Stoicism as Ideology." *Latomus* 64 (1985) 16–54.

Sherk, Robert K., translator and editor. *Roman Documents from the Greek East: Senatus Consulta and Epistulae to the Age of Augustus.* Baltimore: John Hopkins Press, 1969.

———. *The Roman Empire: Augustus to Hadrian*. Cambridge: Cambridge University Press, 1988.

Shimizu, Akitoshi. "On the Notion of Kinship." *Man*. New Series 26:3 (1991) 377–403.

Siebeneck, Robert T. "May Their Bones Return to Life: Sirach's Praise of the Fathers." *CBQ* 21 (1959) 411–28.

Smith, A. D. *Myths and Memories of the Nation*. Oxford: Oxford University Press, 1999.

Smith, Gary. *Isaiah 40–66*. NAC: An Exegetical and Theological Exposition of Holy Scripture. Nashville: Broadman and Holman, 2009.

Smith, M. S. "Remembering God: Collective Memory in Israelite Religion." *CBQ* 64 (2002) 631–51.

Snyder, Graydon F. "Major Motifs in the Interpretation of Paul's Letter to the Romans." In *Celebrating Romans: Template for Pauline Theology*, edited by Sheila E. McGinn, 42–66. Grand Rapids: Eerdmans, 2004.

Soden, Baron H. von. "ἀδελφός." In *TDNT* 1.145.

Soskice, J. M. "Can a Feminist Call God 'Father'?" In *Women's Voices: Essays in Contemporary Feminist Theology*, edited by T. Elwes, 15–29. London: Marshall Pickering, 1992.

Sparks, F. D. "The Doctrine of the Divine Fatherhood in the Gospels." In *Studies in the Gospels*, edited by D. E. Nineham, 241–262. Oxford: Basil Blackwell, 1955.

Stager, Lawrence E. "The Archaeology of the Family in Ancient Israel." *BASOR* 260 (1985) 1–35.

Stark, Rodney. *The Rise of Christianity: A Sociologist Reconsiders History*. Princeton: Princeton University, 1996.

Stegemann, Ekkehard W., and Wolfgang Stegemann, *The Jesus Movement: A Social History of Its First Century*. Translated by O. C. Dean Jr. Minneapolis: Fortress, 1995.

Stegemann, Wolfgang. "The Emergence of God's New People: The Beginning of Christianity Reconsidered." *HTR* 61.1 (2006) 23–40.

Steinmetz, D. *From Father to Son. Kinship, Conflict, Continuity in Genesis*. Louisville: Westminster John Knox, 1991.

Stendahl, Krister. "The Apostle Paul and the Introspective Conscience of the West." *HRV* 56 (1963) 199–215.

Sterling, Gregory E. "Hellenistic Philosophy and the New Testament." In *Handbook to Exegesis of the New Testament*, edited by Stanley E. Porter, 313–58. Leiden: Brill, 1997.

Stevenson, T. R. "The Ideal Benefactor and the Father Analogy in Greek and Roman Thought." *CQ* 42 (1992) 421–36.

———. "*Parens Patriae* and Livy's Camillus." *Ramus: Critical Studies in Greek and Roman Literature* 20 (2000) 27–46.

Still, T. D. *Conflict at Thessalonica: A Pauline Church and its Neighbors*. Sheffield: Sheffield Academic, 1999.

Stirewalt, Luther M. *Paul, The Letter Writer*. Grand Rapids: Eerdmans, 2003.

Stone, Linda. "Kinship." In *International Encyclopedia of the Social Sciences*, 2nd ed., edited by William A. Darity Jr., 271–73. Detroit: Gale, 2008.

Strabo. *Geography*. Translated by Horace L. Jones. Vol. 6. LCL. Cambridge: Harvard University Press, 1929.

Strathern, Andrew. "Kinship, Descent and Locality: Some New Guinea examples." In *The Character of Kinship*, edited by Jack R. Goody, 21–33. Cambridge: Cambridge University Press,1973.

Suetonius. *The Lives of the Twelve Caesars*. Translated by J. C. Rolfe. LCL. Cambridge: Harvard University Press, 1950.

Tacitus. Translated by M. Hutton et al. 5 vols. Leob Calssical Library. Cambridge: Harvard University Press, 1970–1981.

Tajfel, Henri. *Differentiation between Social Groups: Studies in the Social Psychology of Intergroup Relations*. London: Academic Press, 1978.

———. *Social Identity and Intergroup Relations*. Cambridge: Cambridge University Press, 1982.

Talstra, E. "Deuteronomy 31: Confusion or Conclusion? The Story of Moses' Threefold Succession." In *Deuteronomy and Deuteronomic Literature*, edited by M. Vervenne et al., 88–95. Leuven: Leuven University Press, 1997.

Tasker, David. *Ancient Near Eastern Literature and the Hebrew Scriptures about the Fatherhood of God*. New York: Peter Lang, 2004.

Tate, Marving E. *Psalms 51–100*. WBC. Dallas: Word, 2002.

Taylor, Richard A., and E. Ray Clendenen. *Haggai, Malachi*. NAC 21A. Nashville: Broadman and Holman, 2004.

Thiessen, Matthew. "The Form and Function of the Song of Moses (Deuteronomy 32:1–43)." *JBL* 23/3 (2004) 401–24.

Thrall, M. E. "The Problem of 2 Cor. 6:14–7:1 in Some Recent Discussion." *NTS* 24 (1977–78) 132–48.

Thompson, Marianne Meye. *The Promise of the Father: Jesus and God in the New Testament*. Louisville: Westminster John Knox, 2000.

Tigay, Jeffery H. *Deuteronomy: The Jewish Publication Society Torah Commentary*. Philadelphia: Jewish Publication Society, 1996.

Tite, Philip L. "The Compositional Function of the Petrine Prescript: A Look at 1 Pet 1:1–3." *JETS* 39 (1996) 47–56.

———. "How to Begin, and Why? Diverse Functions of the Pauline Prescript within a Greco-Roman Context." In *Paul and the Ancient Letter Form*, edited by Stanley E. Porter et al., 57–99. Leiden: Brill, 2010.

Tolbert, Mary Ann. "Defining the Problem: The Bible and Feminist Hermeneutics." *Semeia* 28 (1983) 113–26.

———. "Protestant Feminist and the Bible: On the Horns of a Dilemma." In *The Pleasure of Her Text: Feminist Readings of Biblical and Historical Texts*, edited by Alice Bach, 5–23. Philadelphia: Trinity, 1990.

Tucker, J. Brian. *You Belong to Christ: Paul and the Formation of Social Identity in 1 Corinthians 1-4*. Eugene, OR: Pickwick, 2010.

Turek, Margaret M. *Towards a Theology of God the Father: Hans Urs von Balthasar's Theodramatic Approach*. New York: Peter Lang, 2001.

Turner, J. C. "Social Categorization and the Self-Concept: A Social-Cognitive Theory of Group Behavior." *Advances in Group Processes: Theory and Research*. Vol. 2. Connecticut: JAI Press, 1985.

———. "Towards a Cognitive Redefinition." In *Social Identity and Intergroup Relations*, edited by Henri Tajfel, 15–40. Cambridge: Cambridge University Press, 1982.

Turner, Mark. *The Literary Mind: The Origins of Thought and Language*. Oxford: Oxford University Press, 1996.

Valerius Maximus. *Memorable Doings and Sayings*. Translated by D. R. Shackleton Baily. Vol. 1. Cambridge: Harvard University Press, 2000.

VanderKam, James C. *The Book of Jubilees. Guides to Apocrypha and Pseudepigrapha*. Sheffield: Sheffield Academic, 2001.

———. "Studies on the Prologue and Jubilees 1." In *For a Later Generation: The Transformation of Tradition in Israel, Early Judaism, and Early Christianity*, edited by R.A. Argall, et al., 266–79. Harrisburg: Trinity, 2000.

Van der Lans, Brigit. "Belonging to Abraham's Kin: Genealogical Appeals to Abraham as a possible Background for Paul's Abrahamic Argument." In *Abraham, the Nations, and the Hagarites: Themes in Biblical Narrative*, edited by George van Kooten, et al., 307–18. Leiden: Brill, 2010.

VanGemeren, Willem A. "*Abba* in the Old Testament?" *JETS* 31 (1988) 385–98.

Vermes, Geza. "Biblical Interpretation at Qumran." *Eretz-Israel* 20 (1989) 184–91.

———. *Scripture and Tradition in Judaism*. Leiden: Brill, 1961.

Virgil. *Aeneid*. Translated by H. Rushton Fairclough. Revised by G. P. Goold. Rev. ed. LCL. Cambridge: Harvard University Press, 1914–1925.

Via, Dan O. Jr. *Kerygma and Comedy in the New Testament: A Scriptural Approach to Hermeneutic*. Philadelphia: Fortress, 1975.

———. "Narrative World and Ethical Response: The Marvelous and Righteousness in Matthew 1–2." *Semeia* 12 (1978) 123–44.

Waaler, Erik. *The Shema and the First Commandment in First Corinthians*. WUNT 2. Tübingen: Mohr, 2008.

Walden, Wayne. "Galatians 3:28 Grammar Observations." *Restoration Quarterly* 51.1 (2009) 45–50.

Wallace-Hadrill, Andrew. *Patronage in Ancient Society*. London: Routledge, 1990.

Wanamaker, C. *Commentary on 1 and 2 Thessalonians*. Grand Rapids: Eerdmans, 1990.

Ward, James M. "The Literary Form and Liturgical Background of Psalm LXXXIX." *VT* 9 (1961) 321–39.

Waschke, Ernst-Joachim. "The Significance of the David Tradition for the Emergence of Messianic Beliefs in the Old Testament." *WW* 23 (2003) 413–20.

Watson, Francis. *Paul, Judaism and the Gentiles: A Sociological Approach*. SNTSMS 56. Cambridge: Cambridge University Press, 1986.

Watson, J. B. Tairora. *Culture: Contingency and Pragmatism*. Seattle: University of Washington Press, 1983.

Watts, J. D. W. *Isaiah 34–66*. WBC 25. Dallas: Word, 2002.

———. *Psalm and Story: Inset Hymns in Hebrew Narrative*. JSOTSup 139. Sheffield: JSOT Press, 1992.

Webb, W. J. *Returning Home: New Covenant and Second Exodus as the Context for 2 Corinthians 6:14–7:1*. JSNTSup 85. Sheffield: JSOT Press, 1993.

Webster, E. C. "The Rhetoric of Isaiah 63–65." *JSOTSup* 47 (1990) 89–102.

Wedderburn, A. J. M. *The Reasons for Romans*. Studies of the New Testament and Its World. Edinburgh: T. & T. Clark, 1988.

Weima, Jeffery A. "Sincerely, Paul: The Significance of the Pauline Letter." In *Paul and the Ancient Letter Form*, edited by Stanley E. Porter et al., 307–46. Leiden: Brill, 2010.

Weinstock, Stefan. *Divus Julius*. Oxford: Clarendon, 1971.

Weitzman, Steven. "Lessons from the Dying: The Role of Deuteronomy 32 in its Narrative Setting." *HTR* 87:4 (1994) 377–93.

White, John L. *The Apostle of God: Paul and the Promise of Abraham*. Peabody: Hendrickson, 1999.

———. "God's Paternity as Root Metaphor in Paul's Conception of Community." *Foundations and Facets Forum* 8.3–4 (1992) 271–95.

———. *Light from Ancient Letters*. Philadelphia: Fortress, 1986.

White, L. Michael, editor. "Social Networks in the Early Christian Environment: Issues of Methods for Social History." *Semeia* 56. Atlanta: Scholars Press, 1992.

White, Michael J. "Stoic Natural Philosophy (Physics and Cosmology)." In *The Cambridge Companion to the Stoics*, edited by Brad Inwood, 124–52. Cambridge: Cambridge University Press, 2003.

Widdicombe, Peter. *The Fatherhood of God from Origen to Athanasius*. New York: Oxford University, 1994.

Wilder, Amos. *Early Christian Rhetoric: The Language of the Gospel*. 2nd ed. Cambridge: Harvard University, 1977.

Wiles, Gordon P. *Paul's Intercessory Prayers: The Significance of the Intercessory Prayer Passages in the Letters of St. Paul*. Cambridge: Cambridge University Press, 1974.

Wiley, Tatha. *Paul and Gentile Women: Reframing Galatians*. New York: Continuum, 2005.

Wilhite, David E. *Tertullian the African: An Anthropological Reading of Tertullian's Context and Identities*. New York: de Gruyter, 2007.

Wilken, Robert L. "Collegia, Philosophical Schools and Theology." *The Catacombs and the Colosseum: The Roman Empire as the Setting of Primitive Christianity*, edited by Stephen Benko et al, 268–91. Valley Forge, PA: Judson, 1971.

Williams, G. D. editor. *De Otio; De Brevitate Vitae*. Cambridge Greek and Latin Classics. Cambridge: Cambridge University Press, 2003.

Willis, W. L. *Idol Meat in Corinth: The Pauline Argument in 1 Corinthians 8 and 10*. SBLDS 68. Chico, CA: Scholars Press, 1985.

Wintermute, O. S. "Jubilees: A New Translation and Introduction." In *The Old Testament Pseudepigrapha*. Vol. 2: *Expansions of the Old Testament and Legends, Wisdom and Philosophical Literature, Prayers, Psalms, and Odes, Fragments of Lost Judeo-Hellenistic works*, edited by James H. Charlesworth, 35–142. New York: Doubleday, 1985.

Wilson, Bryan R. *Religious Sects: A Sociological Study*. London: World University Library, 1970.

Wilson, Robert R. "Between 'Azel' and 'Azel': Interpreting the Biblical Genealogies." *Biblical Archeologist* (1979) 10–22.

———. *Genealogy and History in the Biblical World*. Yale Near Eastern Researchers 7. New Haven, CT: Yale University Press, 1977.

———. "The Mechanisms of Judicial Authority in Early Israel." In *Studies in Honor of George E. Mendenhall*, edited by H.B. Huffmon, et al., 59–75. Winona Lake, IN: Eisenbrauns, 1983.

———. "The Old Testament Genealogies in Recent Research." *JBL* 94 (1975) 169–89.

Wiseman, T. P. "Legendary Genealogies in Late-Republic Rome." *Greece and Rome*, 21 (1974) 153–64.

Witherington III, Ben. *Conflict and Community in Corinth: A Socio-Rhetorical 1 and 2 Corinthians*. Grand Rapids: Eerdmans, 1995.

———. *1 and 2 Thessalonians: A Socio-Rhetorical Commentary*. Grand Rapids: Eerdmans, 2006.

———. "No So Idle Thoughts about Eidolothuton." *TynBul* 4 (1993) 237–54.

———. *Paul's Narrative Thought World: The Tapestry of Tragedy and Triumph.* Louisville: John Knox, 1994.

Witherington III, Ben, and Laura M. Ice. *The Shadow of the Almighty: Father, Son, and Spirit in Biblical Perspective.* Grand Rapids: Eerdmans, 2002.

Woolf, G. "Becoming Roman, Staying Greek: Culture, Identity and the Civilizing Process in the Roman East." *Proceedings of the Cambridge Philological Society* 40 (1994) 116–43.

Woude, A. S. van der. "Malachi's Struggle for a Pure Community: Reflection on Malachi 2:10–16." In *Tradtion and Re-Interpretation in Jewish and Early Christian Literature: Essays in Honour of Jürgen C. H. Lebram*, 65–71. Leiden: Brill, 1986.

Wright, C. J. H. "Family." In *ABD*, edited by D. N. Freedman, 2:761–69. New York: Doubleday, 1992.

———. *God's People in God's Land, and Property in the Old Testament.* Grand Rapids: Eerdmans, 1990.

———. *Knowing God the Father through the Old Testament.* Downers Grove, IL: IVP Academic, 2007.

Wright, G. Ernest. "The Law Suit of God: A Form Critical Study of Deuteronomy 32." In *Israel's Prophetic Heritage: Essays in Honor of James Muilenburg*, edited by Bernhard W Anderson, et al., 26–67. London: SCM, 1962.

———. "Some Remarks on the Song of Moses in Deuteronomy xxxii." *VT* 9 (1959) 339–46.

Wright, N. T. *The New Testament and the People of God.* Minneapolis: Fortress, 1992.

———. *Paul in Fresh Perspective.* Minneapolis: Fortress, 2005.

Yerushalmi, Y. H. *Zakhor: Jewish History and Jewish Memory.* 2nd ed. New York: Schocken, 1989.

Zanker, Paul. *The Power of Images in the Age of Augustus.* Ann Arbor: University of Michigan Press, 1988.

Zehnder, Markus. "A Fresh Look at Malachi 2:13–16." *VT* 53 (2003) 224–59

Zeller, Dieter. "God as Father in the Proclamation and in the Prayer of Jesus." In *Standing Before God: Studies on Prayer in Scriptures and in Tradition with Essays: In Honor of John M. Oesterreicher*, edited by Asher Finkel et al., 117–29. New York: Ktav, 1981.

Index of Authors

Ancient Authors

Modern Authors

www.ingramcontent.com/pod-product-compliance
Lightning Source LLC
Chambersburg PA
CBHW060331100426
42812CB00003B/957
9781498263924